MYTHS
& LEGENDS

MYTHS
& LEGENDS

PHILIP WILKINSON

LONDON, NEW YORK,
MUNICH, MELBOURNE, DELHI

This book is dedicated to John Wilkinson

DK London

Senior Editors Sam Atkinson, Paula Regan
Editors Patrick Newman, Manisha Thakkar

Project Art Editor Anna Hall
Designers Dean Morris, Adam Walker

Managing Editor Debra Wolter
Managing Art Editor Karen Self
Art Director Bryn Walls
Publisher Jonathan Metcalf
Associate Publisher Liz Wheeler

Production Editors Joanna Byrne, Luca Frassinetti
Production Controller Inderjit Bhullar

Picture Researcher Roland Smithies
Illustrations Anshu Bhatnagar and Debajyoti Dutta

DK Delhi

Project Editor Rohan Sinha
Editors Suchismita Banerjee,
Kingshuk Ghoshal

Design Manager Arunesh Talapatra
Project Designer Tannishtha Chakraborty
Designers Mitun Banerjee, Mahua Mandal, Ivy Roy

Illustration co-ordinator Malavika Talukder

DTP co-ordinator Balwant Singh
DTP Jagtar Singh, Preetam Singh

Head of Publishing Aparna Sharma

First published in Great Britain in 2009 by
Dorling Kindersley Limited
80 Strand, London WC2R 0RL
A Penguin Company

A CIP catalogue record for this book
is available from the British Library.

ISBN: 978 1 4053 3552 2

Printed and bound in China
by Leo Paper Products Limited

Discover more at
www.dk.com

CONTENTS

INTRODUCTION

Myths – stories of gods, heroes, and great cosmic events – are told in all of the world's many cultures. They deal with the deepest, most fundamental issues: the creation of the universe and of the human race, the nature of the gods and spirits, what happens to us when we die, and how the world will end. They examine love and jealousy, war and peace, good and evil. Myths explore these crucial issues with intriguing plots, vivid characters, memorable scenes, and concepts that touch our deepest emotions; and so they have become eternally fascinating.

Myths began as tales told around the fire by successive generations, and in some places they are still passed on orally. Later, with the invention of writing, people began to write their myths down and adapt them in new ways – turning them into plays, poems, or novels, for example. Some of the world's greatest literature, from the Greek epics of Homer to the sagas of the early Icelandic writers, are based on much older myths that were originally told orally.

MYRIAD MYTHS

Because of their oral roots, myths are not set in stone. Each one, endlessly retold, has spawned variations. Often, there is no single "correct" version of a myth. The name of a god will change from one tribe to the next; a twist in a tale will be explained in different ways by neighbouring groups. Written versions of a myth multiply the retellings still further.

This book can tell only a fraction of the world's myths, and usually gives only one version of each story. But it does contain a generous selection of myths from around the globe, including many from the cultures of

Europe that, because they have been written down and widely circulated, have had an enormous influence across the world.

COSMOS AND PEOPLE

Among the seemingly endless variety of myths are common themes. Nearly every mythology starts with the question: "How did the universe begin?" Often, a shadowy creator takes the first step; a god, perhaps, who wills himself into being. Frequently, the creator is faced with a cosmic egg. In one variation of the Chinese creation myth, for instance, the god Pan Gu has to break such an egg to form the land and sky. Sometimes the creator has to fetch land from the depths of a primal ocean – like the Earth Diver, a common figure in Native American myths. In other myths the world is the offspring of a male and a female creator.

Often, people come much later. Usually they are moulded from clay or carved from wood. Like human sculptors, the gods often make several false starts. Myths from Mexico to Greece tell of three versions of people, only the last being right. Sometimes the first people are male, and when they begin to die the gods make women so that the people can reproduce.

GODS AND THEIR POWERS

Most cultures have a large number of gods or spirits – sometimes thousands, because there are spirits everywhere. In places as far apart as

FOR EARLY PEOPLES, THE EXISTENCE OF DEITIES EXPLAINED WHY THE SUN SHONE AND WHERE THE RAINS CAME FROM.

Japan and Africa, every rock, stream, lake, and hill may have its own spirit. Many are local deities, worshipped mainly by the people who live nearby and share their sacred space.

Yet even in cultures that have thousands of deities there are core groups of widely known gods with special powers. There are gods of the sun, the rain, the sea, the sky, the mountains, and the rivers. Specific gods look after hunting, farming, love, childbirth, war, and death. The myths involving these gods tend to relate closely to their roles.

Many myths involve mortals with extraordinary superhuman powers. These heroes accomplish apparently impossible tasks, win battles single-handedly, and even visit the Underworld. They may also be culture heroes, who teach people important skills such as fire-making. Their achievements are often so great that they become gods when they die.

MYTHS OF THE ELEMENTS

Among the most prominent gods are those of the elements, notably the sun and the rain. They determine whether crops grow, so the sun and weather gods are often the most widely worshipped of all the gods. From the Inca sun god Inti to the Greek sky god Zeus, they are supremely powerful.

Some of the most familiar mythical themes concern the elements. Many cultures have a myth in which the sun disappears, depriving

the world of food and warmth and explaining night and day. Other cultures, such as China and parts of Africa, have a myth in which there is too much sunlight, which the gods reduce, or counter with night. Worldwide, wrathful gods send great floods, sometimes wiping out all but one human family before normality is restored. Stories like these explain natural disasters and encourage people to honour the gods, so that they will not unleash their anger; they are also gripping tales of adventure and rescue.

THE IMPORTANCE OF MYTHS

Myths reinforce the cultural identity of the people who tell them. For the Aborigines of Australia, the origin myths of each tribe tell not only of the ancestors, but of the routes they took across the land when they brought each natural feature into being: the land, its people, and their myths are united inextricably. Myths were just as important to the ancient Greeks, who named their greatest city, Athens, after its

patron goddess, Athena; to the Incas, who believed their rulers to be descended from the sun god himself; and to the Norse, whose warriors tried to emulate their great god Odin.

The vitality and importance of myths is seen not only in their countless retellings, but in the way their gods, heroes, and creatures have inspired artists. From China to ancient Rome, artists have painted and carved images of the gods, an activity that is sometimes itself an act of worship, sometimes more simply a celebration of the deities and their deeds.

Myths arise from an intimate relationship between people and the natural and spirit worlds – something so many of us have lost. They operate on the borders between reality and fantasy, celebrate oddity and uncertainty, and describe terrifying cosmic forces. But they also deal with great excitement and inspiration. Myths are the most enthralling stories we have, because they touch our hearts and minds and reach to the very core of our being.

EUROPE

Compared with the vast land areas of the continents of Africa and Asia, Europe is relatively small; nevertheless, it does have a long cultural history. Part of the legacy of this heritage is a body of myth that contains many thousands of different legends, split into a number of very distinct traditions across the continent. These range from the stories told by the Slavs of Eastern Europe to the myths related by the Norsemen of Western Europe, and from the complex pantheon of ancient Greece and Rome to the chivalric stories of the Middle Ages. Most of these traditions have become well known all around the world because of Europe's long history of written culture.

But the myths and legends of Europe, like those of all other parts of the world, originated long before the invention of the written word. Some evidence of these prehistoric traditions survives, but it is often minimal. The Romans, for example, wrote about some of the gods and goddesses of the pre-literate Celts whose territories they overran, but their descriptions of Celtic deities and religious practices are patchy. Even when put together with the archaeological evidence of inscriptions, statues, altars, jewellery, and other paraphernalia, they form only a partial picture.

Other aspects of European mythology have come down to us through popular stories from oral traditions – stories that were not recorded by writers and folklorists until much later, some not until the 19th century. Many of the gods and stories from Central and Eastern Europe have survived in this way, and have been given new life when they have inspired writers, painters, and composers to re-imagine them in new works. Stories from Russian mythology, for example, have given rise to paintings by such well-known illustrators and stage designers as Ivan Bilibin, and music by famous composers such as Tchaikovsky and Stravinsky.

MEN CREATE THE GODS IN THEIR OWN IMAGE.

The Greek philosopher Xenophanes (570–480 BCE)

However, the most familiar European myths have come down to us through literature. Myths originating in ancient Greece – of the gods of Mount Olympus, of heroes, and of many semi-divine beings – were given long life by the Greeks' later poets and dramatists. Fascinating in their own right, stories of gods such as Zeus and Apollo, and of heroes such as Heracles and Perseus, have been made still more enduring and popular because they became the subject matter for, among other Greek writers, Homer, Hesiod, Aeschylus, and Euripides. When the Romans adopted the myths of the Greeks, a new generation of writers, such as Ovid and Virgil, developed these stories even further. Another example of a rich literary culture embracing mythology that had roots in a much earlier period is found in the works of the poets and writers of the Middle Ages, who retold stories of King Arthur and his knights, as well as other tales of chivalry.

The literary retellings of European myth remind us of the sophistication of the societies that produced them, from ancient Greece to medieval Christendom. Yet this sophistication is only one side of the myths, because the world of European mythology is often very far from sophisticated. Extraordinarily bloody battles, bodies torn limb from limb, gods who behave with little or no concern at all for morality – all of these are regular features of Classical Greek and Roman myth, for example. And the witches, ogres, water sprites, werewolves, and other dark beings that loom large in many of the stories from Central Europe can be just as violent and fearsome. For all of its great age and apparent sophistication, then, the mythology of Europe remains as ambiguous and edgy as it ever was.

CMANLIO·CF·CENS·PERPET
CLIENTES·PATRONO

▲ **Altar to the goddess Fortuna**
This altar comes from the city of Cerveteri, built by the Etruscans, who were the Italian
forerunners of the Romans. It depicts a sacrifice to Fortuna, a goddess of destiny who
steered the course of people's lives and who was also later worshipped by the Romans.

CLASSICAL EUROPE

The myths of ancient Greece and Rome, with their tales of the great loves, rivalries, and achievements of the Classical deities and heroes, are some of the most familiar stories in all world literature.

The civilization of ancient Greece, which reached its zenith in the 5th century BCE, was founded not by one large nation or empire, but in a series of city-states, each of which had its own traditions, culture, and deities. As a result, many of the gods and goddesses of ancient Greece had local followings. For example, Athena was closely associated with Athens, Zeus with Olympia, and Apollo with Delphi. But ancient Greeks everywhere came to recognize a large group of deities who interacted with one another – and with the world of people – rather in the manner of an extended human family, with its myriad close relatives. Members of this great pantheon of gods and goddesses fell in love and had relationships – even with mere mortals – had immense personal and political rivalries, and frequently went to war.

▲ Sicilian temple
Classical temples such as this one in Agrigento in Sicily were rectangular structures enclosed by rows of columns. Inside was a room with a cult statue of the temple deity, where valuable offerings such as gold and silver were left.

THE GREEKS AND THEIR GODS
The ancient Greeks worshipped their deities by leaving offerings to them in temples, and honoured them by holding regular festivals. Much is known about this worship because many of their temples, together with ritual objects and cult statues, have survived, and ancient Greek writers described religious rituals such as making offerings of food and wine. In return, worshippers hoped that the deities would look kindly on them, since most gods and goddesses were said to take a keen interest in human affairs. In the mythical great war between Greece and Troy, for example, every stage of the conflict, together with the final outcome, was influenced as much by the actions of the deities as by what the men of the two sides actually achieved on the battlefield.

The myths of Greece also show this interaction between deities and humans in the guise of numerous heroes: figures who are mortal but, because they often have one divine parent, have some of the characteristics of the divine. Stories of heroes like Heracles and Jason, involving great adventures and journeys as far as the Underworld, have been endlessly retold.

AN ENDURING INFLUENCE
When Greek civilization declined, the myths lived on in various ways. As the Romans built up their vast empire, they adopted local deities wherever they went. They found the gods and goddesses of Greece especially appealing, and combined their personalities with their own deities to create figures that were closely related but subtly different. The sky god Jupiter, for example, is the Roman equivalent of the Greek god Zeus, but differs from him in several ways: the Romans linked him with justice, with the keeping of oaths, and with their magistrates, who made sacrifices to him when they took up their office.

The art, architecture, and mythological depictions of the Greeks were also preserved and had a longer-term impact, particularly influencing artists and writers in Western Europe during the Renaissance (c.1350–c.1550).

▲ The sacred robe of Athena
This scene is part of a frieze – a series of carved reliefs – that once decorated the Parthenon, the great temple of Athena on the Acropolis in Athens dating from 438–432 BCE. It depicts temple officials holding up the sacred robe of Athena.

ANCIENT GREEK CREATION

Classical mythology contains several accounts of the creation, telling how creator deities gave the universe shape and form before the first races to inhabit the cosmos were born. These creation stories give the background to the birth of the gods and goddesses who dominate much of Classical mythology and who were believed to dwell on Mount Olympus.

THE MYTH

In the beginning there was nothing but a vast, dark void called Chaos. Out of this emptiness the creative force emerged. The various Greek accounts of creation give this force different names. In some, she was a goddess called Eurynome, who coupled with a primal serpent called Orphion to begin the process of creation, while in others, she was Gaia, Mother Earth.

THE PRIMAL EGG

Eurynome took the form of a dove and laid a great egg, around which Orphion coiled. Warmed by the serpent's coils, the egg hatched, and out of it came all things that exist: Uranus, the sky; Ourea, the mountains; Pontus, the sea; and all the stars and planets. Gaia, the Earth, and her mountains and rivers emerged from the egg at the same time. When all these things were born, Eurynome and Orphion travelled to Mount Olympus and made their home there. But Orphion declared himself sole creator of the cosmos, and Eurynome punished him for this by first kicking him and then, when he persisted, by banishing him to the Underworld forever.

MOTHER EARTH

Others say that the primal creator was Gaia. She and Uranus, the sky, made love, and Uranus sent life-giving water onto her surface. From this union were born not just

> **Orphion**
> The serpent Orphion coiled itself around the egg laid by Eurynome, which contained the beginnings of all things that exist.

the lakes and seas, but also the earliest races of creatures that inhabited the Earth. The first of these were the Hundred-Handed Giants, each of whom had 50 heads and 100 arms branching out from their shoulders. Then came the Cyclopes, a race of one-eyed giants who were skilled in metalworking. Some say that later they attacked the god Asclepius, so his father, Apollo, killed them. Their ghosts still haunt the caves beneath the volcano Mount Etna.

Others claim that the power and skill of the Cyclopes frightened Uranus, who thought that they might rob him of his power. So Uranus banished them to the Underworld.

The most important race produced by Gaia and Uranus were a group of giants known as the Titans. They became the first rulers of Earth and started families with their female counterparts, the Titanesses. Their children became some of the most powerful gods and goddesses, such as Helios, the sun god, and Eos, the goddess of dawn, who were the children of Hyperion. Most influential of all were the children of Cronus, the leader of the Titans, who became the deities of Mount Olympus.

▲ **The dove**
The story of the primal goddess Eurynome taking the form of a dove is a very early one that exists mainly in fragments of ancient Greek writings.

KEY CHARACTERS

The ancient Greek cosmos begins with shadowy characters whose main purpose is to get creation started, but who do not have the highly developed personalities or complex myths associated with the later Olympian deities. Eurynome, for example, is described as the goddess of all things, a figure who can dance across the primal chaos, brood on the water, or take the form of the bird that lays the universal egg. Other characters, such as Cronus, originally a harvest god, preside over natural forces. The Titaness Rhea was a primal goddess like Gaia, a maternal figure strongly identified with the Earth. The Titans also ruled the various heavenly bodies. Phoebe and Atlas ruled the moon, while Rhea and Cronus governed the planet Saturn. Theia and Hyperion were the rulers of the sun.

▲ Gaia, the mother goddess
With her consort Uranus, Gaia was said to be mother of such geographical features as seas, rivers, and streams.

► Cronus eating his child
Famous for swallowing the first five of his children (*see p.18*), the Titan Cronus lived with his consort Rhea in a rocky citadel on Mount Othrys.

▲ Uranus
Uranus was castrated by his son, Cronus, who was incited by his mother, Gaia, since Uranus had imprisoned her other children.

◄ Rhea tricking Cronus
To save her sixth child from being swallowed by his father, Rhea handed Cronus a stone wrapped in swaddling clothes (*see p.18*).

THE GIANTS AND CYCLOPES

Among the first creatures in the universe were races of giants, such as the one-eyed Cyclopes and the Hundred-Handed Giants. These races had superhuman strength and because of this (and their disturbing appearance) the Titans banished them to the Underworld. Later myths, however, tell of a number of Cyclopes who found a route back to Earth, where they lived as shepherds. Most of these Earth-dwelling Cyclopes were gentle, but a few liked to eat human flesh.

▲ Cyclopes
The name Cyclopes means "round-eyes", and these creatures were so called because of the single eye in the middle of their forehead.

◄ Hundred-Handed Giants
The Hundred-Handed Giants lived in Tartarus, the deepest part of the Underworld, guarding those who were condemned to dwell there.

THE TRINITIES

The Titans and other primal beings produced a number of children who had the status of lesser deities, but could still have great influence over the lives of others. They often came in groups of three, such as the three Hesperides and the three Fates. The latter were endowed with tremendous power, controlling the lives not only of humans but also of the gods – the Greeks believed that no one could escape the power of fate.

▲ The three Hesperides
The three daughters of the Titan Atlas were called the Hesperides, which means "daughters of the evening". They tended a beautiful garden with a tree bearing golden apples (*see pp.48–49*).

► The three Fates
The three Fates were the daughters of Night. Clotho was believed to spin the thread of life, and Lachesis measured its length. Atropos, the third daughter, cut it at the moment of death.

SEE ALSO European creation stories 90–91, 100–03 • Giants 64–67, 96–97, 104–05

COSMIC WAR

The gods of Mount Olympus, who are the dominant characters in most of the myths of ancient Greece, took control of the universe by fighting a long war with their ancestors and rivals, the Titans. The story of this Cosmic War, which is also known as the Titanomachia, involves many themes – such as oracles, lost children, and revenge – that are prominent in later myths. At the end of the struggle, Zeus emerged as the supreme ruler of the entire cosmos, and the defeated Titans were banished to the Underworld.

THE MYTH

An oracle had told the Titan Cronus that one of his children would kill him. As a result, whenever a child was born to his wife, Rhea, Cronus would swallow it. After Cronus had disposed of five children, Rhea hatched a plan. When their next child, Zeus, was born, she sent him to Crete, where Amalthea, a friendly goat-nymph, brought up the child. Meanwhile, Rhea wrapped a stone in swaddling clothes and gave it to Cronus to swallow.

▲ Bronze shield and sword
The Greeks used to make fine bronze weapons. Myths about metalworkers like the Cyclopes show how vital these skills were to them.

THE RETURN OF ZEUS

After Zeus grew up, one day his foster-mother, Amalthea, revealed his true identity to him and narrated how Cronus had swallowed all his siblings. An enraged Zeus then resolved to take revenge on his father for this crime. When he declared his intention to the Titaness Metis, she told him that he could still rescue his brothers and sisters. She gave him a drug that, when it was administered to Cronus, would make him vomit up all his children. Zeus followed Metis's instructions and rescued his siblings – the gods Poseidon and Hades, and the goddesses Hera, Hestia, and Demeter. Then Zeus freed the Cyclopes, the one-eyed giants whom Uranus had banished to the Underworld. The gods and the Cyclopes led by Zeus declared war on Cronus.

The two sides were equally matched and the conflict seemed destined to last forever. But the Cyclopes were master metalworkers, and they created a number of magical weapons, including a thunderbolt for Zeus, a trident for Poseidon, and a helmet for Hades that made the wearer invisible. These eventually gave the gods the upper hand in the conflict. At the end of the war, the gods controlled the cosmos and the Titans were imprisoned in Tartarus, a region in the Underworld full of fearsome monsters guarded by the Hundred-Handed Giants.

FURTHER BATTLES

Gaia, outraged that her children had been dispatched to Tartarus, began another war against the gods, bringing the Giants, who were also her children, into battle against Zeus and the other gods and goddesses. The gods were finally the victors in this battle, known as the Gigantomachia, and the Giants were buried beneath volcanoes. But even then their rule was not secure. Zeus was challenged one last time by Typhon, yet another of Gaia's offspring. Although Zeus injured Typhon – a huge creature with many heads and countless legs and arms – with his thunderbolt, the monster continued to hurl enormous rocks at him. Zeus retaliated by attacking the rocks with thunderbolts, so that they rebounded on Typhon, knocking the strength out of him. Finally, Zeus hurled him down to Tartarus. His rule was secure at last.

◀ In battle
Hurling heavy rocks was one way in which the gods and giants attacked each other. This painting shows a scene from the Gigantomachia, the battle between the gods and Gaia's children, the giants.

WEAPONS OF THE GODS

The deities of ancient Greece resembled humans in several ways. When the gods fought a war, the Greeks imagined them as beings in human form, fighting with weapons. These weapons were made for them by Hephaestus, the god of metalworking, craftsmanship, and fire, who was a kind of celestial blacksmith. But the weapons of the gods had powers that went far beyond earthly swords and daggers. When Zeus wielded his thunderbolt or Poseidon struck his trident, the entire cosmos shook. Hephaestus sometimes made armour for mortal heroes like Achilles (see pp.60–61), and when a hero showed special prowess in arms, people said his weaponry must have been made by Hephaestus.

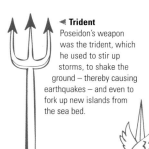

◄ Trident
Poseidon's weapon was the trident, which he used to stir up storms, to shake the ground – thereby causing earthquakes – and even to fork up new islands from the sea bed.

► Thunderbolt
Zeus used a thunderbolt as his weapon. As well as making the whole sky shake with its power, he could aim it with precision, either to kill an opponent or to shatter his opponent's weapon.

▲ Helmet
Hades's helmet made him invisible, so that he could attack his enemies without being detected. Because he ruled the dark realms of the Underworld, Hades was never depicted in ancient Greek art.

ATLAS

Son of the Titan Iapetus and a sea nymph called Clymene, Atlas ruled a large island kingdom called Atlantis. He had many subjects, but they became degenerate, so the gods decided to punish them by destroying the entire race. They sent a great flood that killed all the people and sank the island beneath the sea. Resentful towards the gods at the loss of his kingdom, Atlas led the Titans in the Cosmic War. When the gods won the war, they punished Atlas for his part in it by making him hold the sky on his shoulders forever.

► Bearer of the skies
The celestial globe held by Atlas was sometimes mistaken for the Earth, leading both to the belief that he held the world on his shoulders, and to the use of Atlas's name for books of maps.

DISGUISES OF THE GODS

One enduring theme in Greek mythology is the way in which the gods could disguise themselves. Deities used their shape-changing ability to serve different purposes – from fighting battles to pursuing loved ones. When they were challenged by the monster Typhon, all the deities except the brave Athena fled to Egypt, where they disguised themselves as different creatures and went into hiding. However, Zeus eventually forsook his disguise and came forth to fight the monster.

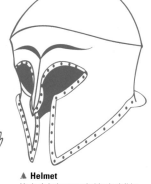

▲ The ram
The normally brave Zeus disguised himself as a ram, a creature that was aggressive and impressively armed with a pair of horns.

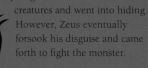

▲ The crow
While hiding, Apollo took the form of a crow, a rather unassuming disguise considering that he was the god of music.

◄ The cat
Artemis, who was a huntress and the goddess of the chase, chose to transform herself into a cat, also a hunting creature.

TYPHON AND THE WINDS

Gaia bore the fire-breathing monster Typhon, who was the god of winds, with the intention of creating a son so powerful that he could defeat the gods. Some accounts say that after Zeus overcame him, he was condemned to the Underworld. Other versions of the story relate how he survived and went to live on Mount Olympus. There he made peace with the gods, occasionally giving birth to mighty storms called typhoons. Certain myths also claim he dwelled in Mount Etna where he spewed out smoke and lava.

► Typhon in hell
In the most widespread retelling of the myth, Typhon was imprisoned in the Underworld after his defeat by Zeus.

19

SEE ALSO Wars 60–61, 98–99, 104–05, 116–17, 118–19, 126–27, 170–71, 176–77, 206–07

THE TWELVE OLYMPIANS

The twelve dominant deities in Greek myth lived on Mount Olympus and controlled life on Earth: they were Zeus (king of the gods), Aphrodite, Apollo, Ares, Artemis, Athena, Demeter, Hephaestus, Hera, Hermes, Hestia, and Poseidon. This family tree shows their relationships to each other, as well as to some of the Titans (*see pp.16–19*), such as Cronus and Rhea, and a number of lesser gods.

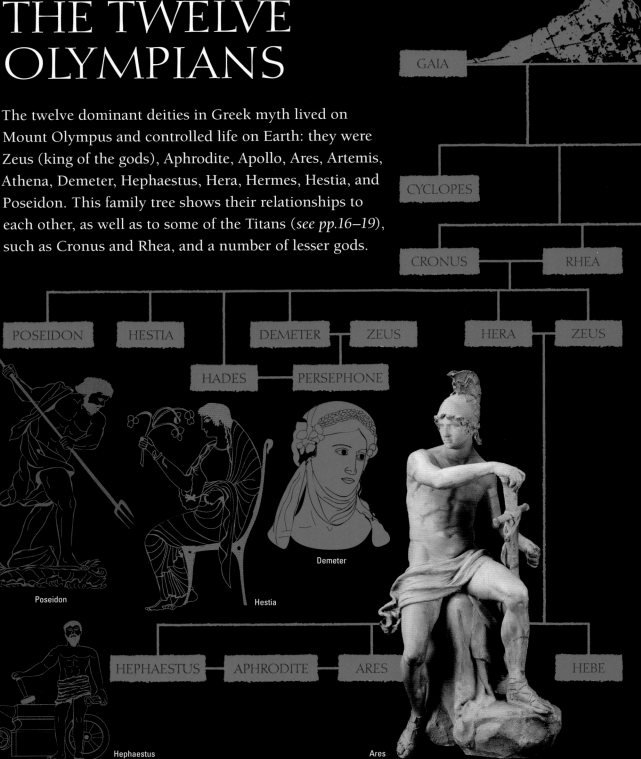

GAIA

CYCLOPES

CRONUS — RHEA

POSEIDON   HESTIA   DEMETER — ZEUS   HERA — ZEUS

HADES — PERSEPHONE

Demeter

Poseidon

Hestia

HEPHAESTUS — APHRODITE — ARES   HEBE

Hephaestus

Ares

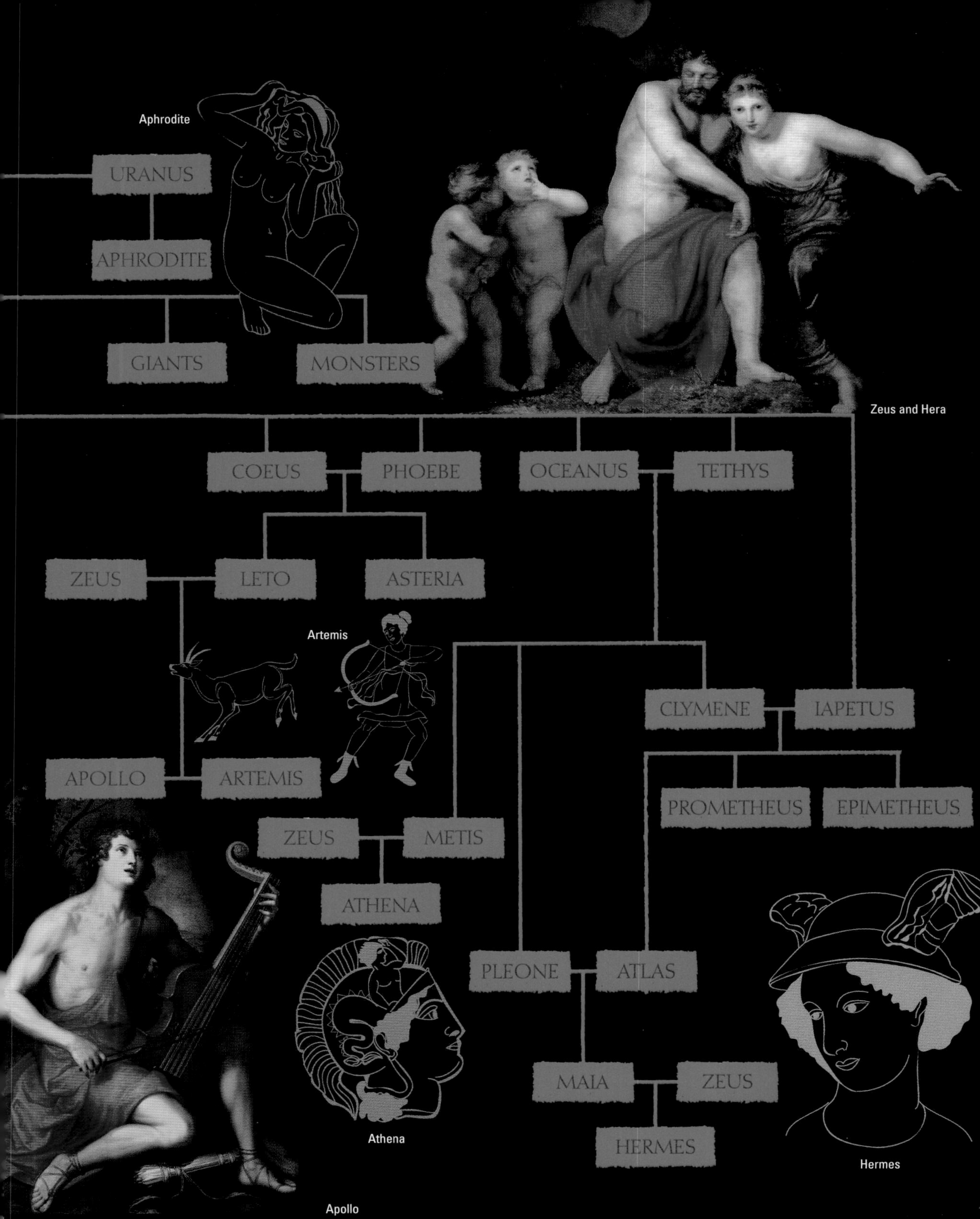

Aphrodite

URANUS

APHRODITE

GIANTS   MONSTERS

Zeus and Hera

COEUS   PHOEBE   OCEANUS   TETHYS

ZEUS   LETO   ASTERIA

Artemis

CLYMENE   IAPETUS

APOLLO   ARTEMIS

PROMETHEUS   EPIMETHEUS

ZEUS   METIS

ATHENA

PLEONE   ATLAS

MAIA   ZEUS

HERMES

Athena

Hermes

Apollo

The gods of Mount Olympus
The ancient Greek gods were said to live on Mount Olympus, the highest peak in Greece, but artists of the Renaissance (c.1350–c.1550) often depicted them living in a heaven of clouds.

ZEUS

Zeus, son of the Titans Cronus and Rhea, was the god of the sky and thunder. His most feared weapon was his thunderbolt, fashioned by the Cyclopes. He became ruler of the gods when he led them in their defeat of the Titans during the Cosmic War (*see pp.18–19*). Though he married the goddess Hera, he was famous for his many other sexual conquests, which included goddesses, nymphs, and mortal women. Some of the numerous children of these liaisons wielded immense power over the people of Earth.

▶ Zeus the ruler
Although he was the king of the gods, Zeus generally left the work of influencing the lives of humans to his many children, using his personal power sparingly.

THE DISGUISES OF ZEUS

Zeus's shining body could terrify mortals and his thunderbolt could burn to death anything that came too near. For these reasons, and because many of his sexual partners were unwilling, Zeus adopted various guises when approaching his loves. He charmed Europa by taking the form of a bull, got through Danaë's prison by turning into a shower of gold, became a satyr to rape Antiope, a princess of Thebes, and approached Leda as a swan. He tricked Alcmene (*see p.46*) by disguising himself as her husband, Amphitryon, and turned into an eagle to carry off Ganymede, a young man he had fallen in love with. Zeus could disguise the objects of his love too, turning Io, a priestess of Hera, into a cow and Callisto, a nymph of Artemis, into a bear to allay the suspicions of his wife.

◀ Europa and the bull
Europa, a Phoenician maiden, saw Zeus in the form of a white bull. Just as she stroked it lovingly and climbed on its back, the bull sped away with her.

◀ Danaë and the shower of gold
Imprisoned by her father because her child was destined to kill him, Danaë fell prey to Zeus in the form of a golden shower.

▶ Leda and the swan
Zeus took the form of a swan to woo the Spartan queen, Leda. Their children included Helen of Troy (*see pp.60–61*) and the Dioscuri (*see p.83*).

ZEUS AND HERA

Zeus took his sister, Hera, the goddess of marriage, as his wife. Hera had been ignored when the great gods Zeus, Poseidon, and Hades divided up the cosmos between them, so marrying Zeus and ruling the sky as his consort gave her the power she had been denied. Most of the stories about Hera recount the jealousy she felt at her husband's affairs and the vendettas she launched against her rivals. When Io was transformed into a cow, Hera sent a fly to sting her perpetually and drive her mad. When the goddess Leto was expecting Zeus's children, Hera banned her from giving birth on the mainland or on any island. She tricked Semele into demanding that Zeus appear to her in all his glory. When he agreed reluctantly, Semele was burned to ashes by his powerful thunderbolt. Hera also persecuted the offspring of Zeus's affairs, including Dionysus (*see pp.34–35*) and the hero Heracles (*see pp.46–47*), whom she drove insane – as a result of which he killed his own wife and children in a fit of madness. However, the effects on Hera's victims were rarely permanent.

▲ The divine couple
Although Hera was famously jealous, her worshippers stressed the importance of marriage, and some artists portrayed her and Zeus as a tender, loving couple.

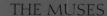

► The three Graces
The three Graces accompanied Aphrodite and Eros. They brought people happiness, especially in love, and their breath helped plants flourish.

THE CHILDREN OF ZEUS

Zeus had dozens of children by his various partners, and some of these offspring had prominent parts in other Greek myths – either as immortals who ruled different aspects of the cosmos, or as heroes whose exploits became famous among mortals. Zeus and his wife, Hera, were the parents of deities such as Ares (the god of war) and Hebe (the handmaiden of the gods). Hermes was the product of his union with Maia, and his affair with Metis resulted in the birth of Athena (*see p.36*). With Leto, Zeus fathered the twin deities Apollo and Artemis, while with Eurynome he produced the three Graces. His liaison with the Titaness named Mnemosyne (memory) produced the Muses, and his affair with Ananke produced the Fates. Among his mortal loves, Europa was the mother of Sarpedon (a hero of the Trojan War), Minos (the King of Crete), and Rhadamanthus (who became a judge of the dead). Danaë gave birth to the hero Perseus, while Alcmene was the mother of the famed Heracles.

THE MUSES

The daughters of Zeus and Mnemosyne were the Muses, who presided over the arts and were associated with Apollo in his role as the god of the arts. There were originally said to be many Muses, who together inspired poetry and other arts, but later writers named nine, giving each a specific art. The nine Muses were Calliope (Muse of poetic inspiration), Clio (history), Erato (lyric poetry), Euterpe (instrumental music), Melpomene (tragedy), Polyhymnia (harmony), Terpsichore (dance and choral song), Thalia (comedy), and Urania (scholarship or astronomy). The Muses were said to dwell on mountains, where their singing and dancing charmed and inspired all those who encountered them.

The Muses with Apollo

SEE ALSO Sky deities 114–15, 142–43, 158–59, 160–61, 162–63, 188–89, 236–39, 252–53, 266–67, 294–97, 318–19, 338–39

THE CREATION OF HUMANKIND

Unlike many cultures, ancient Greece did not have a single story narrating the origins of humanity. Greek myths mention several attempts at creating humans, or mortals as they were known. Three of these attempts failed before the current race of humans finally emerged, although it is not clear who is responsible for their creation. However, the origins of key cultural skills, such as fire-making, are firmly attributed to the Titan Prometheus, who is portrayed as a friend of humanity.

THE MYTH

The first attempt at creating a human race took place when the Titans, led by Cronus, ruled the cosmos (*see pp.16–17*). The result was the Golden Race, a group of people who lived an ideal existence without work or ageing, and for whom life was one long feast. When the people of the Golden Race finally died, their death was like a peaceful sleep. Nevertheless, it left the Earth unpopulated.

Intent on filling up the void, the Olympians (*see pp.20–21*) created the Silver Race, who lived for a long time but grew very slowly to maturity. Their children were brought up carefully by their mothers, and spent one hundred years as babies before reaching adulthood. However, they turned out to be dull and unintelligent people, fighting continuously among themselves, and once they became adults they tended to die quickly. These qualities, together with their refusal to worship or even respect the gods, exasperated Zeus, so he banished them to the Underworld. Zeus then crafted a new race out of clay. The people of this race wore bronze armour and used tools made of the same metal, so they were called the Bronze Race. Like the Silver Race, they were aggressive, and destroyed themselves in ruthless battles.

▲ The forge of Hephaestus
Prometheus found his fire in the workshop of Hephaestus, where the craftsman god (and, some say, the Cyclopes) forged Zeus's thunderbolts and other powerful weapons.

▶ Prometheus steals fire
Prometheus stole a spark from Mount Olympus and wrapped it in a stalk of fennel, where it burned safely as he carried it to humanity.

THE HUMAN RACE

Finally, the current race of humans appeared. Some say that the great Titan craftsman, Prometheus, was its creator. Whether or not he actually created humanity, Prometheus certainly became its protector. He taught humans many important skills, including navigation and medicine, and showed them how to make sacrifices, by keeping some of the meat for themselves and offering the rest to the gods. Once, the people killed a bull but could not agree on which part to offer the gods. Prometheus cleverly wrapped the meat in the bull's skin, and the bones in its fat. Zeus chose the bones covered in fat, and became so angry at the deception that he refused to give fire to the humans.

THE THEFT OF FIRE

Taking the side of humanity, Prometheus stole fire from heaven and carried it to Earth so that the people could cook their food and heat their homes. Zeus punished Prometheus for the theft by having him chained to a rock, where an eagle came to peck at his liver every day.

THE GOLDEN AGE

During the Golden Age, the world was ruled by Cronus (known to the Romans as Saturn). It was a time of peace and tranquillity, as there was no war or injustice, and the Golden Race did not have to work because enough food was readily available from plants and trees. In later eras, the Golden Age became a byword for a time in the distant past when things were much better than the present. The idea of the Golden Age became fashionable in the Renaissance (c.1350–c.1550), when Italian artists and writers rediscovered the culture of ancient Greece, and this Classical era became a favourite subject for painters.

◄ The Golden Race
Renaissance artists saw the Golden Age as a time of such peace that humans could live side by side with wild animals without any fear of attack.

► Cronus
Despite his violence towards his own children (see p.18), Cronus is often seen as a gentle, just, and kind ruler of the Golden Age. He was worshipped as a harvest deity.

PROMETHEUS BOUND

As punishment for stealing fire from the gods, Zeus had Prometheus chained to a rock in a place said to be on the borders of Earth and Chaos. Here, he was condemned to suffer while an eagle pecked at his liver, which constantly repaired itself so that the torture could continue. Zeus decreed that Prometheus should remain bound until another creature offered to be bound in his place. After thousands of years, a wounded centaur called Cheiron offered to take Prometheus's place. When he arrived at the rock, Zeus turned Cheiron into a constellation of stars, while the Greek hero Heracles (see pp.46–47) killed the eagle, ending Prometheus's agony.

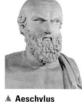

▲ Aeschylus
The Greek dramatist Aeschylus, who lived in the 5th century BCE, wrote several plays about the myth of Prometheus.

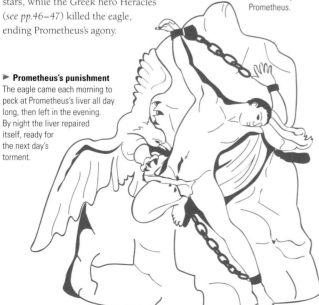

► Prometheus's punishment
The eagle came each morning to peck at Prometheus's liver all day long, then left in the evening. By night the liver repaired itself, ready for the next day's torment.

PANDORA

Zeus wanted to punish the humans after Prometheus stole fire for them, so he (or, some say, Hephaestus) created a beautiful mortal woman called Pandora. She married Prometheus's brother, Epimetheus, who took her to Earth. The gods gave her many gifts, which she kept in a jar. When she opened the jar, it contained plagues and disasters, which condemned humanity to a life marred by misery. The only positive thing in the jar was hope, the sole consolation for the human race.

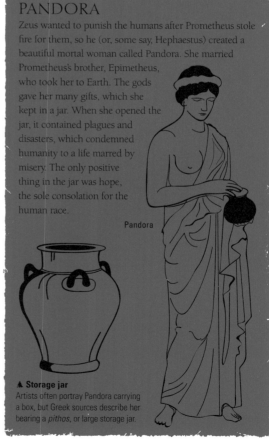

Pandora

▲ Storage jar
Artists often portray Pandora carrying a box, but Greek sources describe her bearing a *pithos*, or large storage jar.

SEE ALSO The first humans 90–91, 162–63, 168–69, 250–51, 282–83, 306–07, 314–15, 328–29, 338–39

APOLLO

Portrayed as a handsome young man, the god Apollo had power over many aspects of life. Patron of archers, his bow brought pain to humans, but he was also a god of healing and father to the mythical physician Asclepius. He was the god of music and the arts, and an accomplished player of the lyre. The son of Zeus and Leto, Apollo was also worshipped as the god of light and the sun.

THE LYRE OF APOLLO

Once when Apollo went on a journey in pursuit of one of his lovers, he left his fine herd of cattle untended. Hermes, who had long admired the creatures, saw that they were left alone and decided to steal them and hide them in a cave. But Apollo, who had the gift of prophecy, knew exactly where the cattle were and went to find Hermes and demand his animals back. When Apollo arrived, Hermes began playing an instrument that he had created from the intestines of one of Apollo's cattle. Apollo was enchanted on hearing the music of the lyre, and agreed to exchange it for the cattle.

◄ **Apollo with his lyre**
The lyre of Apollo (also called the *kithara*) was originally made with the strings stretched across the shell of a tortoise.

◄ **Hermes**
Both a trickster and the messenger of the gods, Hermes wore winged sandals to enable him to fly between Olympus, Earth, and the Underworld.

▼ **Eros**
Eros was the son of Aphrodite, from whom he got his beauty, and Ares, from whom he inherited his love for mischief.

APOLLO AND DAPHNE

When Apollo scorned the archery skills of Eros, the god of love, Eros decided to take revenge. He shot Apollo with a gold-headed arrow, to make him fall in love, but shot the object of his desire, Daphne, with an arrow tipped with lead, so that she would reject him. Apollo chased Daphne, but she would not give in to him and, as she ran, she prayed to Zeus to be transformed into something that would save her from Apollo's pursuit. Zeus responded by turning her into a laurel tree.

► **Daphne**
When Zeus turned the fleeing Daphne into a laurel tree, Apollo made a wreath from her leaves, which he wore as a crown.

APOLLO AND DELPHI

When Zeus's wife, Hera, found out that her husband had had an affair with Leto (see p.25), she decided to take revenge on her and sent a great serpent, known as the Python, to attack her. The snake lurked around the great peak of Mount Parnassus and laid waste the area of Delphi. Apollo killed the serpent with a bow and arrows given by Hephaestus, the divine craftsman (see p.39). Afterwards, Delphi became sacred to Apollo, and his shrine was built there. The Pythian Games were held there every four years to commemorate Apollo's triumph over the Python, and Apollo has been associated with Delphi ever since. The activities at the games included poetry and music competitions, in addition to several athletic events.

▲ **The temple at Delphi**
The Temple of Apollo at Delphi, first built around the 7th century BCE, stands on a hillside and was originally surrounded by statues of mythical Greek heroes.

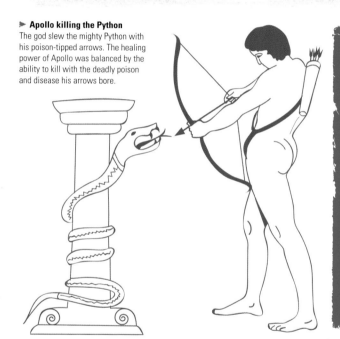

▶ **Apollo killing the Python**
The god slew the mighty Python with his poison-tipped arrows. The healing power of Apollo was balanced by the ability to kill with the deadly poison and disease his arrows bore.

THE ORACLE OF DELPHI

Apollo had the power of prophecy, and at Delphi, his priestess, known as the Pythia, delivered oracles as she sat on her tripod seat holding laurel leaves and a bowl of water from the Kassotis spring. She answered people's questions while in a trance-like state. These questions could be on matters of political and religious policy, as well as enquiries about the questioner's future.

Since the Pythia's words were hard to understand, priests stood by to interpret them for the listeners. However, these interpretations were also puzzling and difficult to understand – but often they came true in the most unpredictable ways.

The Pythia

▲ **Musical duel with Marsyas**
Marsyas was foolish to tangle with Apollo, who tricked him into losing the musical challenge, then punished him for his impudence in one of the cruellest ways imaginable.

THE FLAYING OF MARSYAS

The satyr (see p.32) Marsyas was just as accomplished a performer on the double flute as Apollo was on the lyre. Marsyas thought that he was the better musician and challenged the god to a contest. Apollo agreed on the condition that the winner could punish the loser in any way he chose. No one could decide who was the better player until Apollo suggested they both play their instruments upside-down. This worked with Apollo's lyre, but not with Marsyas's flute, so Apollo was judged the winner. He punished Marsyas by skinning him alive.

APOLLO

29

SEE ALSO Sun deities 114–15, 160–61, 188–89, 218–19, 222–23, 238–39, 290–91, 314–15, 318–19

POSEIDON AND THE FLOOD

Many ancient Greeks lived on islands or in settlements close to the coast, so their lives were dominated by the sea. Consequently, the sea god Poseidon, a bringer of violent storms, who also controlled natural forces such as earthquakes, was one of the most powerful gods of Mount Olympus. But he longed for more power, and became involved in a dispute with Athena for the great honour of being the patron deity of the city of Athens.

THE MYTH
Poseidon and Athena both wanted to be the controlling deity of the city of Athens. Rather than declaring war and fighting a battle, the two gods decided that they would settle their dispute by competing to provide the best gift for the city's people. The sea god climbed the Acropolis (the hill overlooking Athens); when he reached the top, he struck the ground hard with his trident and a saltwater spring began to flow. Then Athena came to the Acropolis and offered her gift: the first olive tree to grow in the city.

THE GODS' JUDGEMENT
Zeus summoned the other gods from Mount Olympus to judge the gifts and decide which of the two was greater. The appearance of the spring was impressive, but salt water was of little use to the people. The olive tree, on the other hand, provided a source of olives, and their oil was useful for both cooking and lighting. Olive oil was valuable not just to the

▶ **Poseidon**
The god of the sea is often shown as a bearded man holding a trident and enthroned in a giant clam shell or aboard a shell-like chariot pulled by dolphins or seahorses.

Athenians but also to those with whom they traded – so the tree could both nourish the people of Athens and make them rich. They would be able to use the olive wood, too, to construct things. King Cecrops, the ruler of Greece, confirmed that such a tree had never been seen on the Acropolis. After hearing all the evidence, Zeus declared Athena to be the winner of the contest. She became the city's patron deity, and the place was named after her.

THE COMING OF THE FLOOD
Poseidon was furious when he heard the result of the competition. He took up his trident and smote the sea many times, causing a great storm. The waters rose and the plain of Eleusis, where Athens stood, was flooded. The waters covered the plain for a long time, but finally they subsided, allowing the Athenians to repair their city. They built a temple to their new goddess, Athena, who would bring them prosperity, but also made offerings to Poseidon, to placate the angry god.

▶ **The dispute with Athena**
Poseidon with his trident and Athena with her spear made formidable opponents, although they decided to settle their dispute peacefully.

POSEIDON AND THE BEASTS

Poseidon was linked closely with the vitality and energy of animals. Two creatures especially associated with him were the bull and the stallion. Both were singled out by the Greeks for their sexual potency and violence. During his sexual exploits, Poseidon sometimes took the form of a horse, as on the occasion when he was pursuing the goddess Demeter, who had turned herself into a mare. The destructive bull that rose from the sea in some myths, such as that of Hippolytus (*see p.70*), is also a manifestation of Poseidon's power.

▲ Stallion
One myth tells how the first horse grew from semen that Poseidon had spilled on a rock.

▲ Pasiphae and the Cretan Bull
After a curse from Poseidon, the queen of Crete, Pasiphae, fell in love with, and mated with, a bull sent by the sea god. The offspring of this union was the Minotaur (*see pp.50–51*).

OTHER CLASSICAL SEA GODS

The Greeks worshipped several other sea gods, although they were not as powerful as Poseidon. Some of them were linked with particular sea creatures. For example, Glaucus was associated with fish, while Proteus was a herder of seals. Others possessed special abilities. Triton, for example, was famous as a musician who played on the conch shell. Proteus was also known for his great wisdom, although he did not like answering people's questions.

▲ Glaucus
Originally a fisherman, Glaucus was made immortal when he ate a herb with magical powers. He became one of the minor gods of the sea.

▶ Proteus
Renowned for his wisdom, Proteus was called the "ancient one of the sea". He often changed his shape to avoid being questioned.

◀ Triton
Half-fish, half-man, Triton was a familiar deity of the sea. Some myths say there were several Tritons.

POSEIDON AND ODYSSEUS

Homer's *Odyssey* (*see pp.64–67*) describes the return of the tragic hero Odysseus from Troy to Ithaca as a series of mishaps at sea. Most of these were due to Poseidon and came about because Odysseus had blinded the Cyclopes Polyphemus, who was the sea god's son. The poem describes vividly how the god stirred up storms and tempests, which wrecked Odysseus's ship and drowned his companions. Many of the perils Odysseus faced, such as the whirlpool Charybdis, were the offspring of Poseidon.

▶ Poseidon stirs the waves
Sometimes Poseidon smote the sea with his trident to create stormy waves, and sometimes he stirred them up with it.

TEMPLES TO POSEIDON

As a powerful deity, Poseidon was widely revered and some of his temples have survived. He was not always worshipped as a sea god – some temples were dedicated to Poseidon Hippios ("Poseidon of horses"), and many people worshipped a form of Poseidon who was a god of plants. At least one of his temples in Greece, though – the temple at Sounion, in Attica – is sited on a spectacular clifftop overlooking the sea, a clear reminder of the deity's sphere of influence. Boat races were held there in honour of the god.

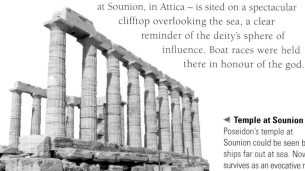

◀ Temple at Sounion
Poseidon's temple at Sounion could be seen by ships far out at sea. Now it survives as an evocative ruin, with two rows of columns set on a stone platform.

31

SEE ALSO Sea deities 158–59, 160–61, 290–91, 294–97, 338–39 • Flood stories 196–97, 212–13, 214–15, 288–89, 314–15, 328–29

MYTHICAL BEINGS

Bizarre beings sharing human and animal features, violent giants, and tiny fairies are among the most common kinds of mythical creatures that can be found across world mythologies. These varied creatures often intervene in human affairs and are frequently described as "ancient", because they precede the creation of the gods and goddesses or occupy a time frame different from humanity.

HYBRID RACES

Mythologies often include beings with the attributes of two different species, as a way of combining contrasting psychological qualities in one creature. Greek mythology contains several such examples, while hybrid beings such as mermaids, water nymphs, and water fairies appear in many different cultures.

◁ Centaurs
Part human, part horse, the centaurs of Classical mythology were said to be the offspring of Ixion, King of the Lapiths (see p.68), and a cloud moulded by Zeus into the form of the goddess Hera. They are a combination of the wild nature of the horse and human wisdom.

▷ Satyrs
In Greek mythology, a satyr had the upper body of a man but the lower parts, and sometimes the ears and horns, of a goat. Satyrs were the noisy and lustful followers of Dionysus (see pp.34–35).

▷ Mermaids
Many mythologies feature creatures, usually female, which are half fish and half human. Fatally attractive, they lure men to their underwater homes.

CONTROLLERS OF DESTINY

The unpredictable twists and turns of life are frequently explained in myths and legends as the results of the activities of mythical beings. These creatures, such as the Greek Furies and Fates, or the Norns – female beings, often depicted as giantesses, who control fate in Norse mythology – have little regard for the emotions of their human victims.

▲ Furies
The Furies, usually appearing as a trio of old women, punished anyone whose actions violated the natural order. They were also known as the Eumenides, an ironic title meaning "kindly ones".

▷ Fates
The Fates controlled human destiny. At first they were three deities – Lachesis, who set life in motion; Clotho, who spun the thread of life; and Atropos, who cut the thread – but later they were seen as a larger race of females.

DEMONS AND MALIGN BEINGS

Races of malign beings exist in many cultures, wreaking havoc, threatening the innocent, and challenging humans and gods alike. Many are giants, creatures of superhuman strength who can be defeated only by heroes or those armed with magical weapons or impenetrable armour. Others, like the vampires and werewolves, are humans with bizarre powers or evil personalities. Their stories may have helped early peoples to explain crimes or deformities that otherwise seemed to have no obvious cause.

▶ Werewolves
Much feared in Northern European legends, werewolves are born of human mothers with mainly human characteristics, but turn into howling wolves at full moon.

◀ Vampires
In Slavic myths, vampires are humans who are dead, but cling on to their bodily existence by drinking fresh blood, which they suck from sleeping humans.

▲ Trolls
Trolls are giant-like creatures in Norse mythology. They often appear in parent-child combinations to harass or attack humans and can be fearsomely violent.

▼ Ogres
There are several races of ogres in European legends; they are usually large, ugly, muscular, and slow-witted. Some are cannibals, others corpse-eaters. In the Christian world, the Devil is sometimes said to take the form of an ogre.

◀ Demons
Hindu mythology has many demons or *rakshasas*, who are active at night and are said to attack women and children. Sometimes, they unleash formidable strength in hard-fought battles with the gods. In some texts, *vanaras*, monkey-like forest-dwellers, are also seen as demons.

HIDDEN RACES
Members of the hidden races are usually concealed from human view. Some, like the dwarfs, dwell far away from people, while others, such as the fairies or the Irish "little people", can make themselves invisible or can be seen only by those with special vision. Often, these creatures take two forms, one well disposed towards humans, the other meddling or malign – the latter perhaps originating as a means of explaining unpleasant phenomena.

▶ Dwarfs
In Norse mythology, dwarfs are wise and highly skilled in crafts such as metalworking. They dwell in dark, rocky places. The ancient texts say little about their small size.

▲ Elves
Northern European myths feature many kinds of elves – some malign, shadow-dwelling, and ugly, others beautiful and helpful to humans.

▲ Fairies
Fairies, creatures who can intervene in human life in all kinds of ways from bountiful to mischievous, occur in the legends of many different cultures. They usually have the power of flight.

DIONYSUS

The god of wine, Dionysus was an anarchic figure who presided over drunkenness and other irrational or altered states, such as religious ecstasy. A shape-changer, he could take the form of an animal but also appeared as a human, when he was often accompanied by revellers or animals. These qualities made him a patron of actors, and plays were regularly performed at the Athenian festivals held in his name.

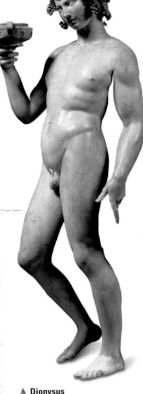

▲ Dionysus
The god of wine in all its aspects, Dionysus has often been portrayed as a handsome young man carrying a cup, with vine leaves in his hair.

THE RESCUE OF DIONYSUS

When Zeus, disguised as a mortal, began an affair with Semele, the daughter of King Cadmus and Queen Harmonia of Thebes, his wife, Hera, grew jealous and plotted her revenge. She took the form of an old woman and persuaded Semele to ask the god to appear before her in all his splendour. When he did so, the heat from his thunderbolt killed Semele, who was a mortal. One of the gods – some say Hermes, others the river goddess Dirce – rescued her unborn child, Dionysius, and took him to Zeus, who cut an opening in his thigh and placed the child safely inside until it was ready to be born. When Dionysus emerged from Zeus's thigh, Hera was so angry that she incited the Titans (see pp.16-19) to tear the baby into pieces. His grandmother, Rhea, took pity on Dionysus, put his body back together, and carried him to foster parents. Again, Hera discovered what had happened, so to protect him Rhea disguised the child as a ram.

▲ Hera
In the story of Dionysus, Hera plays her usual role as jealous wife. She defeats her rival Semele, but not Semele's child.

► Semele
Flames from Zeus's thunderbolt killed Semele. Her story became a popular subject for painters and for the composer Handel, who wrote an opera about her.

THE JOURNEY OF DIONYSUS

As he grew up, Dionysus became restless and went on a series of long journeys. Wherever he travelled, he became famous for his drunken excesses, which ended in a kind of insane frenzy. Many said that this frenzy was caused by Hera, who was still resentful that the son of Semele had survived. Dionysus was accompanied on his travels by satyrs, led by their king, Silenus. Also among his companions were a group of female followers called the "Maenads". The Maenads were possessed with a kind of madness, in which they worked themselves into an ecstatic frenzy. As they did this, they danced a wild dance, eventually getting so out of control that they would rip apart any creature they came across. The Maenads drew their strength from Dionysus, so that nothing – neither fire nor the sword – could stop their dance or bring them to harm.

► Satyrs
The offspring of a mountain nymph and a goat, a satyr was half-man, half-goat. Satyrs were famous for getting drunk and for being lewd.

◄ Maenads
The Maenads wore sheer dresses and danced to the music of the double flute and tambourine. They had power over wild beasts and were sometimes shown riding panthers.

► Silenus
A wise old satyr, Silenus led Dionysus's followers. Some myths say he was one of those who brought up the god when he was a child.

THE WINE-DARK SEA

As he travelled around the Mediterranean, Dionysus told those who met and followed him how to harvest the grapes, press them, and turn their juice into wine. When people tasted the results, he became very popular. Once the god was on his travels when he was captured by pirates, who thought he was a wealthy young man. When the pirates tried to tie him up, however, the knots kept untying of their own accord. Dionysus then made the mast and rigging turn into grape vines, and transformed the sea around the ship into wine. The pirates were so frightened by the sight of this that they jumped into the sea.

► Pirate porpoises
When the terrified pirates jumped into the sea, Dionysus turned them all into porpoises, as depicted in this painting on the inside of a cup from around 530 BCE.

THE TRAGEDY OF PENTHEUS

The dancing journey of Dionysus and the Maenads brought them to Thebes, which was ruled by Pentheus. The young king's mother, Agave, was attracted to Dionysus and became a Maenad, getting drunk and joining the frenzied dance. Pentheus was horrified to see his mother's behaviour and decided to try to stop the dance. He turned for advice to Dionysus, who told the king to hide and watch secretly before doing anything. However, the Maenads discovered Pentheus and tore him to pieces.

◄ Death of Pentheus
Among the Maenads who attacked Pentheus was his own mother, Agave. In her frenzy, she at first thought she was killing a lion, before realizing it was her son.

DIONYSUS

35

SEE ALSO Journeys 44–45, 64–67, 78–79, 120–21, 220–21

ATHENA

A powerful war goddess, Athena was usually depicted with her shield or protective cloak, known as the aegis. She was also a patron of crafts, especially pottery, weaving, and shipbuilding, and the goddess of the city of Athens. She inherited the wisdom of her mother, Metis, an attribute that made her favour Odysseus, the wisest and most cunning of the Greek heroes. In all these roles she was especially valued because she was always accessible, unlike many gods who kept their distance from humans.

THE BIRTH OF ATHENA

One of the first loves of the god Zeus was Metis, daughter of the Titans Oceanus and Tethys. Metis was known not only for her beauty but also for her brains – her name means "cunning intelligence". She was especially dear to Zeus, but when she became pregnant, Gaia and Uranus told Zeus that after she had given birth to a daughter, Metis would then have a son, also by Zeus, who would take away all his power. They advised Zeus to act at once to prevent this. Gaia told Zeus that the best way to stop this chain of events was to swallow Metis whole before she gave birth. Zeus did this, but when it was time for Metis's daughter to be born, Hephaestus intervened, splitting open Zeus's head with an axe and enabling the child to step forth. Miraculously, Athena emerged from Zeus's skull fully armed, uttering a war cry. According to several accounts, Athena was her father's favourite child, and the only one allowed to use his aegis.

➤ Athena armed for war
Athena's favoured weapon was her spear, which she held upright when at rest, and brandished aloft when in battle. She also wore a helmet to protect her head.

GODDESS OF ATHENS

Athena won the right to be venerated as the goddess of Athens when, in a competition with Poseidon, she gave the citizens of Athens the valuable gift of the olive tree (*see p.30*). The people acknowledged her importance by putting images of her and her sacred bird, the owl, on their coins. To worship her, they built the Parthenon on the Acropolis above the city, where the contest between Athena and Poseidon was depicted in a sculpture. This temple also housed a massive ivory and gold statue of Athena, created by the noted sculptor Phidias. Unfortunately, the statue no longer exists, though many miniature reproductions of it have been found. The temple's name comes from the title Parthenos (virgin), given to the goddess because she guarded her chastity so carefully.

The Parthenon   Athenian coin

◄ Athena's birth
Early depictions of the birth of Athena, such as this vase painting, show the goddess emerging from her father's head, already equipped with arms and armour.

▼ Arachne turning into a spider
Athena took pity on Arachne and turned her into a spider, so that she could go on spinning and weaving forever while hanging by a thread.

THE WEAVING CONTEST

One of Athena's roles was as the goddess of weavers and embroiderers. When someone was good at weaving, people said their gift came from Athena. But Arachne, a mortal girl and a fine weaver, insisted that her gift was her own, and had nothing to do with the goddess. This angered Athena, so she challenged Arachne to a weaving and embroidery contest. Athena saw that Arachne's weaving was at least as good as her own work, which showed the gods victorious over the mortals. However, she was offended by the subject of Arachne's tapestry, which depicted the various infidelities of her father, Zeus. In her jealousy and rage she tore up Arachne's work. A humiliated Arachne resolved to hang herself. But Athena decided that this was too harsh a punishment and transformed Arachne into a spider instead, so that she could continue weaving.

▼ Arachne weaving
Athena was spellbound by the beauty and quality of Arachne's work. Some say she was so jealous that in a fit of anger she struck the girl with her own weaving shuttle.

TO THE GODDESS YIELD, AND HUMBLY MEEK A PARDON FOR YOUR BOLD PRESUMPTION SEEK.

Ovid, *Metamorphoses*

ATHENA AND HEPHAESTUS

The craftsman god Hephaestus, who rescued Athena from her father's skull, had a lasting interest in the goddess. As she grew up, Hephaestus fell in love with her and asked Zeus for permission to marry her. Zeus agreed, provided that his daughter was willing. But Athena valued her virginity and did not want to marry, so she turned Hephaestus down. Hephaestus then tried to rape Athena, but the powerful goddess pushed him away and Hephaestus spilled his seed onto the ground. The seed fertilized Gaia (Mother Earth) and Erichthonius was created. Athena agreed to rear the child, and he grew up to later become the ruler of Athens.

► Athena the foster mother
Gaia hands over her newborn son Erichthonius to the waiting Athena while Hephaestus looks on.

THE BATHING OF ATHENA

Athena, who was a modest goddess, did not like others to watch when she bathed at the sacred spring called Hippocrene on Mount Helicon. But Tiresias, a man from Thebes, was so entranced by the beauty of the goddess that he followed her and her attendant nymphs, and spied on the goddess as she took off her clothes and bathed. When Athena realized she was being watched, she climbed out and in her anger hit Tiresias across the eyes, making him go blind. One of the nymphs was sorry for Tiresias and begged Athena to give him something in compensation for the loss of his sight. So Athena gave Tiresias the gift of prophecy.

► Tiresias
The seer Tiresias predicted many events, using his gift of prophecy to intervene in numerous myths, including those about Oedipus and the city of Thebes (*see pp.58–59*).

SEE ALSO War deities 38–39, 40–41, 142–43, 174–75, 244–45 • Virgin goddesses 40–41, 82–83, 86–87

THE LOVES OF APHRODITE

The name of Aphrodite, the goddess of love, means "born from the foam". She was born in the frothing sea and was famous both for her exquisite beauty and for her many lovers, who included both gods and mortals. Her partners found it impossible to resist her charms, and this magnetic attraction made her one of the most powerful of all the deities. Yet some accounts describe her as vain, ill-tempered, and easily offended. Her children included the Trojan prince, Aeneas (*see pp.78–79*), and Priapus, the god of fertility.

THE MYTH

Aphrodite was married to Hephaestus, the divine blacksmith. He adored her and crafted beautiful gifts for her. Among them was a golden chariot drawn by doves, which were sacred to her. However, she was frequently unfaithful to him. Of her many affairs, the most famous of all was with Ares, the god of war. This affair produced four children, the first two of whom took after their father, while the second two inherited their mother's character. They were Deimos (Terror), Phobos (Fear), Harmonia (Harmony), and, according to some accounts of the story, Eros (Sexual Love).

THE LOVERS TRAPPED

It was some time before Hephaestus found out about his wife's liaison with his brother, Ares, but when he did, he decided to take revenge by ridiculing the couple. He used his skill in metalworking to make a large net out of bronze wire, and secretly suspended this above the lovers' bed. When the pair were in bed together, Hephaestus tugged the net so that it fell on to the couple, trapping them. Then he called the gods to witness the ludicrous sight.

MORTAL LOVES

Another of Aphrodite's loves was a mortal called Adonis. Unfortunately, Persephone, wife of Hades, the god of the Underworld, also fell in love with him. Of the two, Adonis preferred Aphrodite, and a jealous Persephone told Ares about the affair. Enraged, Ares unleashed a wild boar, which attacked Adonis and killed him. When he died, Adonis arrived in the Underworld, where he was immediately pursued by Persephone. Aphrodite appealed to Zeus, and the king of the gods decided on a compromise. Adonis would spend half the year in the Underworld with Persephone, and the other half with Aphrodite.

The death of Adonis shows how dangerous it was for a mere mortal to fall in love with Aphrodite. Another mortal who fell for her charms, Anchises, also paid dearly. Anchises was a shepherd, whose liaison with Aphrodite produced the hero Aeneas, ancestor of the Romans. Aphrodite disguised herself as a mortal to sleep with Anchises, but he glimpsed her in her true form. Aphrodite made him promise not to reveal the affair – an alliance with a mere shepherd would damage her reputation. But once, when Anchises was drunk, he revealed the secret and was blinded (or, some say, lamed) by Zeus as punishment.

Dove, symbol of Aphrodite

◄ **The goddess of love**
Usually depicted as a beautiful young woman, Aphrodite is often shown naked. Because she represented physical perfection, she was a favourite subject for sculptors.

APHRODITE'S BIRTH

Aphrodite is said to be the daughter of the Titan Uranus. Gaia and Uranus had many children, including the Cyclopes and the Hundred-Handed Giants. Aghast at their monstrous appearance, Uranus decided to imprison all of them in Tartarus. Gaia did not want any more children and pleaded with her offspring to protect her from Uranus's advances. Finally, Cronus borrowed a sickle from his mother and cut off his father's genitals, which he threw into the sea. Their seed fertilized the water, and Aphrodite rose fully grown from the foaming waves.

▶ Aphrodite
The birth of Aphrodite is often depicted in paintings where the goddess is shown rising from the waves on a shell.

HEPHAESTUS

The god of fire and metalworking, Hephaestus was also the deity who controlled volcanoes, which were said to be his workshops. He was lame, as the result of an injury that came about when he had an argument with Zeus, who then threw him off Mount Olympus. This infirmity gave Hephaestus a comic quality for the Greeks, who revered physical perfection. In spite of this, he was admired for his ingenuity and skill in making things, from the net that captured Aphrodite and Ares, to a magical throne on which he could imprison his enemies.

▼ Hephaestus's net
The gods looked down from Mount Olympus and laughed at the sight of the adulterous couple ensnared in Hephaestus's net.

APHRODITE'S LOVERS

Aphrodite's power to make others fall in love with her came from her great physical beauty. She also had an aphrodisiac girdle, ironically gifted to her by Hephaestus, which she wore next to her breasts. This girdle was the envy of other goddesses who wanted Aphrodite's allure. Homer's *Iliad*, for example, tells how the goddess Hera borrowed it to distract Zeus with her charms during the Trojan War so that the Greeks could win. Although Aphrodite was married to Hephaestus and was in love with Ares, she also used her charms to attract many other lovers.

◀ Adonis
The mortal Adonis was a passionate hunter. He disregarded Aphrodite's warning about hunting an animal that knows no fear, and paid the price when he was killed by a wild boar sent by Ares.

▲ Hermes
The messenger of the gods was attracted to Aphrodite when he saw her under the net with Ares. His affair with her produced the child Hermaphroditus.

◀ Ares and Aphrodite
The sun god Helios, from whom nothing was hidden, spied Ares and Aphrodite together and informed Hephaestus, who then planned his revenge.

PYGMALION

Pygmalion was a remarkable sculptor who poured all his energy into his work. He was so skilled that once he carved a statue of a beautiful woman that was incredibly lifelike. He fell in love with it and prayed to Aphrodite to let him make love to his creation. Aphrodite took pity on him and transformed the statue into a real woman named Galatea, whom Pygmalion later married.

Pygmalion and Galatea

THE LOVES OF APHRODITE

39

SEE ALSO Love deities 138–39, 154–55, 180–81, 244–45, 310–11 • Jealousy 24–25, 200–03

THE GREEK GODDESSES

The Greeks had many goddesses who played a variety of roles in their mythology. Some were primal, shadowy figures, such as Gaia (Mother Earth), who existed before most other deities, and Rhea, often seen as a Titaness, who was the mother of many of the Olympians. Others ruled over different aspects of the daily life of the people. Like most ancient cultures, the Greeks sought to explain natural phenomena by attributing them to the activities of the gods. Greek myths typically ascribe human emotions to their deities, hence there are numerous stories featuring the loves and rivalries of the Greek goddesses.

DEMETER AND PERSEPHONE

Persephone was the only daughter of Demeter, the goddess of the Earth, grain, and fertility. Hades, the ruler of the Underworld, fell in love with Persephone, but knew that Demeter would not part with her because she helped her mother in making the plants grow and the crops ripen. So, one day, when Demeter's attention was elsewhere, Hades snatched Persephone while she was playing with her companions, and dragged her down with him to the Underworld. Demeter was enraged and distraught. She went on a long search for her daughter, during which time all the crops withered and died. Zeus realized that if this state was allowed to continue, life on Earth would perish, since Demeter was also responsible for the cycle of the seasons. Finally, he persuaded Hades to agree to a compromise, whereby Persephone would be allowed to live on Earth with Demeter in spring and summer, but would have to spend the rest of the year with Hades. Accordingly, the land prospers whenever Persephone visits her mother, but becomes infertile when she goes back to the Underworld during autumn and winter.

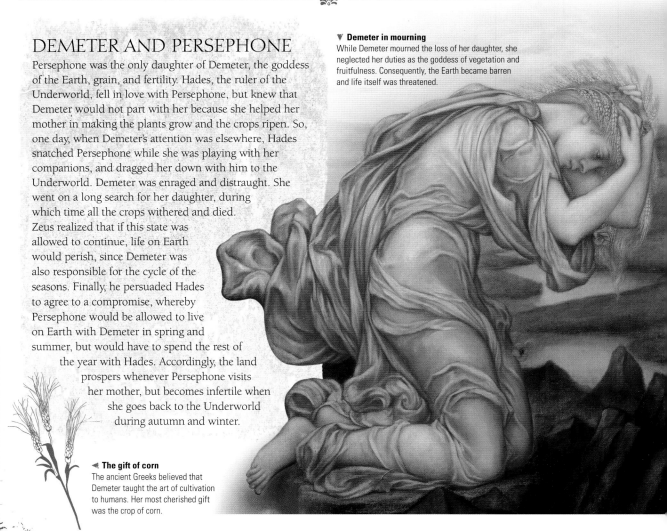

▼ Demeter in mourning
While Demeter mourned the loss of her daughter, she neglected her duties as the goddess of vegetation and fruitfulness. Consequently, the Earth became barren and life itself was threatened.

◄ The gift of corn
The ancient Greeks believed that Demeter taught the art of cultivation to humans. Her most cherished gift was the crop of corn.

◄ Artemis the huntress
The Greeks portrayed Artemis as a young woman carrying a bow and arrows. She is often shown with a stag to symbolize her role as the patroness of hunting.

ARTEMIS

The goddess Artemis was the twin sister of Apollo (*see pp.28–29*) and the daughter of Leto and Zeus. She was the patroness of hunting, and the protector of the weak. The deer and the cypress tree were sacred to her. Artemis was a virgin and devoted to the hunt, but she also used her weapons against her enemies. When the hunter Orion tried to rape one of her followers, Artemis killed him. When another hunter, Actaeon, spied on her while she was bathing, she turned him into a stag and he was killed by his own hounds.

◄ Artemis with her family
Zeus and Leto had two children – Apollo, who became the god of music, and Artemis (far left), the goddess of the hunt.

HESTIA

The daughter of Cronus and Rhea, Hestia was the goddess of the hearth and domesticity. Unusually for an Olympian goddess, Hestia remained a virgin – in spite of the fact that both Poseidon and Apollo were in love with her. She had sworn an oath upon the head of Zeus that she would always be chaste and never marry. Another way in which she differed from the other Greek deities was that she did not travel. Instead, she lived her life on Mount Olympus, becoming the symbol of home and family. She had no throne, but was responsible for tending the sacred fire at Mount Olympus. Hestia represented domestic stability and the hearth was her altar. In every sacrifice, the first offering was made to Hestia.

▲ Mount Olympus
Hestia tended the fire on Mount Olympus. Since it was shrouded in clouds, the Greeks believed it to be the home of the gods.

▲ Hestia and the hearth
The Greeks made their domestic hearths into shrines where the goddess Hestia was worshipped.

HECATE

The goddess Hecate is a shadowy figure – some say her parents were Titans, some that she was a daughter of Zeus. Hecate had many different aspects. As the moon goddess, she travelled across the night sky in her chariot, casting her cold light across the whole cosmos. She was also worshipped as a goddess of the Underworld. In addition, as she was the goddess of childbirth, she was often invoked to ease the pain of labour. Crossroads were sacred to Hecate, and offerings of meat were often left by the ancient Greeks at places where three roads met.

◄ Triple Hecate
Hecate was sometimes portrayed as a triple goddess carrying a torch (symbolizing lunar fire), a serpent (representing immortality), and a knife (symbolic of midwifery).

► Selene
The Greek moon goddess Selene was often confused with Hecate. She was usually depicted with a windblown veil resembling the arched canopy of the sky, and a half-moon on her head.

THE GREEK GODDESSES

41

SEE ALSO Fertility deities 84–85, 114–15, 158–59, 214–15, 244–45, 308–09, 310–11 • Virgin goddesses 36–37, 82–83, 86–87

THE UNDERWORLD

The Underworld is usually seen as a parallel world to our own, with its own deities. In most cultures it is populated by the souls of the dead, and fenced off by rivers, walls, or flames, making it impossible for living mortals to enter. Souls pass through on their way to a new life – or spend an eternity among the demons of this dark realm.

RULERS OF THE UNDERWORLD

The ruler of the Underworld has supreme power there, acting with all the authority of an earthly ruler, and as such is one of the most feared beings in the cosmos. He or she is also often a judge, hearing each newly arrived soul's account of its life in the world of the living before passing sentence. Underworld rulers vary greatly in their appearance – some look like decaying corpses, while others are so dark that they are barely visible.

▲ **Mictlantecuhtli**
The Aztec Underworld has nine layers, the deepest of which is Mictlan, ruled over by the terrifying Mictlantecuhtli.

▶ **Yama**
In Tibetan and Chinese Buddhism, Yama is the king of hell and judge of the dead. He is said to be directly answerable to the supreme ruler of heaven.

▲ **Hades**
The ruler of the gloomy Greek Underworld bears the same name as his kingdom and is usually invisible in his dark domain.

▲ **Hel**
The Norse ruler of the dead, Hel (*see p.99*) is said to recline on a bed called Disease, where her lower body rots while her face remains beautiful.

CHTHONIC CREATURES

The Underworld would be frightening enough if it was populated solely by a ruler and the souls of the dead. But mythologies add to its terrors by imagining all kinds of hellish demons and monsters – creatures that exist either to terrify the souls or inflict agony on them. In addition, the gates of the Underworld are usually guarded, to prevent mortals intruding and souls attempting to escape. Cerberus, the guard dog of Hades, is one of the most famous of these chthonic, or Underworld, creatures. Some accounts give him three heads, others 50.

Cerberus

GUIDING THE DEAD

A dark and remote place, the Underworld is not easy to reach or find, so some cultures tell of figures called psychopomps, who lead the souls of the dead on their way. Images of these guides are often found on coffins or on the walls of tombs, to ensure that the dead person's soul has a safe passage. Psychopomps can take many different forms, although a number of them have wings or inhabit the bodies of birds, for swift flight to and from the Underworld.

Hermes
The Greek god Hermes escorted souls to Hades. Some sources say that as he was a trickster deity, he could not be fooled into neglecting this task.

Baron Samedi
The spirit Baron Samedi (*see p.311*) is a key figure in Haitian voodoo. He is said to wait at crossroads, where dead souls will pass, ready to guide them to the Underworld.

Ankou
In the folklore of the Breton people of Western Europe, Ankou gathered up the souls of the dead in an old cart.

Xolotl
In some stories this dog-shaped Aztec god created the human race, but so hated his handiwork that he took on the job of leading the dead to the Underworld.

Charon
The Classical Underworld Hades was surrounded by the dark waters of the River Styx. For the fee of a single coin placed on the dead person's tongue, the ferryman Charon took his or her soul across in his boat.

UNDERWORLD GODDESSES

Many goddesses of darkness are associated with the Underworld. Some act as queens there, alongside male rulers; others have a less clear, but equally terrifying, role – some even visiting Earth. Because of the contrast between the light Earth and the dark Underworld, many are also linked with the sun, rain, and fertility.

Hecate
A Greek moon goddess and queen of the ghosts of Hades, Hecate (*see p.41*) led her troop of howling, dancing spirits on terrifying visits to Earth.

Izanami
This Japanese creator goddess (*see pp.222–23*) was so badly burned when she gave birth to the fire spirit Kagutsuchi that she went down to rule Yomi, the Underworld.

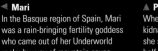

Mari
In the Basque region of Spain, Mari was a rain-bringing fertility goddess who came out of her Underworld realm by way of mountain caves.

Persephone
When this beautiful Greek goddess of fertility was kidnapped by Hades (*see p.40*), Zeus decreed that she should spend half the year in his world, and half on Earth, where she could make crops grow.

THE UNDERWORLD

ORPHEUS IN THE UNDERWORLD

The hero Orpheus was famed for two major qualities. The first was his remarkable musicianship, which, according to some, he had learned from Apollo. With his music, he was able to charm gods and mortals alike. Orpheus was also very brave, and had accompanied Jason on his quest for the Golden Fleece (*see pp.72–73*). But his most daring adventure was his legendary journey to the Underworld.

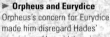

THE MYTH

The power of Orpheus's music was mirrored in his very mysterious origins, because it was not known for certain where he came from or who his parents were. Although it was rumoured that he was a son of Apollo (*see pp.28–29*), his real father was purportedly a man from Thrace – an area that many southern Greeks considered uncivilized. His mother was believed to be one of the nine Muses.

ORPHEUS AND HADES

When Orpheus's beloved wife, the nymph Eurydice, died from a snakebite, he decided to go to the Underworld to get her back. It was a journey from which virtually no mortal had ever returned. The great hero Heracles (*see pp.46–47*) had made the journey and survived, but his strength was superhuman. Orpheus was not as strong, but he had his incredible musical skill. He sang and played the lyre so well that people believed he could move even inanimate objects.

After arriving in the Underworld, Orpheus played his lyre to Hades, the king of the dark realm, and

▶ **Orpheus and Eurydice**
Orpheus's concern for Eurydice made him disregard Hades' warning, and he paid the price as Eurydice was snatched from him.

his queen, Persephone. Hades was generally not moved by appeals from mere mortals, but Orpheus's eloquent music softened his heart and he listened to the musician's request. Hades decreed that Eurydice could accompany Orpheus back to Earth, but forbade him from looking at his wife on the way.

THE RETURN JOURNEY

Orpheus and his wife began their journey and it went well initially, with the musician playing his lyre and the beautiful chords guiding Eurydice back through the darkness of the Underworld towards the light of the Earth. But Orpheus was concerned about his wife, and worried that Hades had not allowed her to follow him. Unable to resist himself, he took one fleeting glance at her. As soon as he looked back, Hades pounced on Eurydice and pulled her back into the Underworld. Orpheus had to continue homewards on his own, and was condemned to wander the Earth, lamenting his lost wife, and moving those who heard him to tears.

▶ **Orpheus in the Underworld**
According to some versions of the myth, it was Persephone who was so moved by Orpheus's music that she asked Hades to let Eurydice leave with Orpheus.

ORPHEUS AND HIS MUSIC

The beguiling beauty of Orpheus's music was famous. It was said that when he played his lyre or sang, rivers changed their courses and trees uprooted themselves to move closer so that they could hear the beautiful sounds more clearly. For the culture-loving Greeks, this musical ability gave Orpheus a special place in their mythology. But the beauty of his music was not always art for its own sake. For example, when Orpheus accompanied the Argonauts on their journey (see pp.72–73), his music saved his fellow adventurers by distracting them from the entrancing song of the Sirens.

▲ **Greek lyre**
Musicians like Orpheus may have played a seven-stringed lyre (also called a *kithara*) with a wooden sounding board.

▲ **The head of Orpheus**
After Orpheus's death, his head floated down the River Hebros in Thrace and out to sea. When it reached Lesbos, still singing, it gave its musical and poetic gifts to the people of that island.

ORPHEUS'S DEATH

Later in his life, Orpheus retired to a cave and gave up the company of women. He attracted many male followers, who were worshippers of Apollo like him. He taught them musical skills and the hidden mysteries that he had learned as a result of his trip to the Underworld. Eurydice's fellow nymphs, worshippers of Dionysus, were already angry with Orpheus because of the way he had looked back in the Underworld and lost his wife. They were further enraged over his decision to forsake women and because of his devotion to Apollo. When they came upon Orpheus teaching his male followers, the nymphs attacked him and tore his body apart.

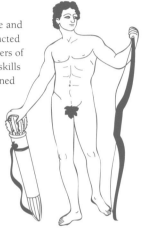

▲ **Apollo**
Orpheus was devoted to Apollo, who was the god of music, poetry, and the arts, and the rival and polar opposite of Dionysus.

THE CULT OF ORPHEUS

The wisdom and songs of Orpheus lived on after his death. He became the object of a cult that began on Lesbos, where a shrine was built at a place called Antissa for people to consult an oracle that supposedly relayed Orpheus's wisdom. The followers of the cult believed that they could cheat death by freely passing in and out of the Underworld. Orpheus's spirit was said to have inspired many famous poets who lived in Lesbos, notably Alcaeus and Sappho, who both flourished in the late 7th century BCE.

➤ **Sappho**
The lyric poet Sappho was the greatest female writer in antiquity. Her love poems, addressed to other women, have inspired poets and are still read today.

▼ **The death of Orpheus**
The nymphs who killed Orpheus were Maenads (see p.35), worshippers of Dionysus, acting in a frenzy of drunken violence.

LATER INTERPRETATIONS

Orpheus's story is a popular Classical myth that has been retold many times, inspiring musicians, poets, and writers. Its musical content has also made it popular with composers of opera – Jacopo Peri's *Euridice* (1600), Monteverdi's *Orfeo* (1607), and Gluck's *Orfeo Ed Euridice* (1762) were all based on the story. Offenbach's comic opera, *Orphée aux Enfers* (1858), was also inspired by the myth, and was followed by a stage version and the film adaptation, *Orphée* (1949), by Jean Cocteau.

Poster of *Orphée aux Enfers*

45

SEE ALSO Love stories 78–79, 100–03, 108–09, 116–17, 124–25, 126–27, 140–41, 176–77

THE LABOURS OF HERACLES

The hero Heracles, renowned for his great strength, was the son of Zeus and the mortal woman Alcmene. Zeus's wife, Hera, was jealous of the affair and resentful towards Heracles, and she persecuted him throughout his life. The hero married Megara, daughter of King Creon of Thebes, but Hera made him go mad and kill his wife and children. To punish Heracles, King Eurystheus of Mycenae set him twelve apparently impossible tasks to accomplish.

THE MYTH

The labours imposed on Heracles by King Eurystheus involved slaying horrific monsters, bringing back trophies for the king, and other tasks, each of which was more difficult and sent the hero on a longer journey than the preceding one. The first labour was to kill the lion of Nemaea, not far from Mycenae. Heracles throttled the beast and skinned it, taking the creature's pelt as his cloak. The second labour was to slay the Hydra, a water monster with many heads that lived at Lerna. Heracles found that each time he cut off one of the creature's heads, two new ones grew. So he asked his helper, Iolaos, to cauterize the stumps, to stop the new heads growing. The third labour was to capture and bring back the Keryneian hind, a golden-horned deer consecrated to the goddess Artemis. This involved the hero in a long chase, but eventually he succeeded. The fourth task was to sieze the Erymanthian boar, a fierce creature that posed little problem for Heracles.

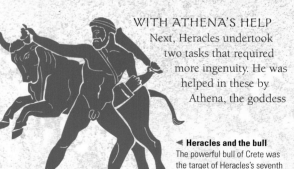

WITH ATHENA'S HELP
Next, Heracles undertook two tasks that required more ingenuity. He was helped in these by Athena, the goddess

◄ **Heracles and the bull**
The powerful bull of Crete was the target of Heracles's seventh labour. The hero needed all his strength to subdue the beast.

► **The Stymphalian birds**
This vase shows Heracles shooting the Stymphalian birds with a sling, a more effective weapon than his club or bow.

of wisdom. For the fifth labour, he was told to go to Elis and clean the stables of King Augeas, which were fouled with great heaps of horse dung. Heracles ingeniously cleared out the stables by diverting two rivers so that they washed the mess away. Then, for his sixth labour, Heracles had to visit Lake Stymphalis, northwest of Mycenae, to rid it of a plague of birds. He frightened the birds with castanets that Athena had lent him, then shot them as they flew into the air.

FARTHER AFIELD
For his subsequent labours, Heracles had to travel farther, leaving mainland Greece. His seventh labour was to capture a monstrous bull belonging to King Minos of Crete. After that he was sent north to Thrace, where he caught some man-eating mares that belonged to King Diomedes. The ninth, tenth, and eleventh labours required Heracles to steal items of great value. First he took the belt of Hippolyta, queen of the Amazons, who lived to the south of the Black Sea. Next he led away the cattle of the giant Geryon, who dwelled in the far west. After this, he managed to obtain the golden apples of the Hesperides (*see pp.48–49*). But even these labours were straightforward compared with the twelfth: to go to the Underworld and bring back its guard dog, Cerberus. To the amazement of Eurystheus, Heracles succeeded in this seemingly impossible feat too.

THE MONSTERS OF GREECE

Like other Greek heroes, such as Perseus (*see pp.54–55*), Heracles was tested during confrontations with numerous creatures, many of whom were monsters that would terrify most people. These creatures ranged from the Nemaean lion, an animal of supreme strength, to monstrous creatures – such as the three-headed dog, Cerberus – which seemed to come from the world of horror and nightmare. By overcoming them, Heracles was able to demonstrate both his superhuman strength and his exceptional bravery. He also gained from some of these combats by adopting the attributes of his adversaries – for example, he took the lion's skin as his cloak and the Hydra's gall to poison his arrowheads.

◀ The Nemaean lion
Wrestling the Nemaean lion brought Heracles into danger from the animal's claws and jaws, but he finally prevailed.

▼ The Hydra
Heracles dispatched the multi-headed Hydra with the help of Iolaos. As Heracles cut off each head, Iolaos cauterized the stumps.

▼ The Erymanthian boar
When Heracles brought the vicious boar to Eurystheus, the frightened king hid from the beast by climbing into a large storage jar.

▼ Cerberus
After showing the terrifying guard dog of the Underworld to Eurystheus, Heracles returned the creature to Hades, its master.

THE HERO'S CLUB

King Thespius, ruler of a kingdom called Thespiae, was troubled by a lion that attacked his cattle. Thespius's men had failed in killing the lion, so Heracles volunteered to try. He made himself an enormous club by tearing up an olive tree. He clubbed the lion to death and was allowed to sleep with all but one of Thespius's fifty daughters as a reward.

➤ A formidable weapon
The legendary club of Heracles, with which he overcame many opponents, was so heavy that only he could pick it up and wield it with ease.

HERACLES AND NESSUS

Heracles was travelling with his third wife, Deianira, when they met a centaur, called Nessus, who offered to carry Deianira across a river. When they were across the water and a safe distance from Heracles, Nessus raped Deianira, but Heracles saw what was happening and shot the centaur with one of his deadly arrows. As he died, Nessus told Deianira that if she wove Heracles a shirt from the hairs on his back, the wearer would never leave her for another woman. Some time later, Deianira suspected her husband's fidelity, and gave him the shirt to wear. But when Heracles put the shirt on, he discovered it was an evil trick. Its hairs made his skin blister and burn as if attacked by flames. In agony and begging for death, the hero asked to be put on his funeral pyre.

▲ Heracles fighting the centaur
The centaur Nessus had once been defeated in a fight with Heracles, and longed for revenge.

➤ On his funeral pyre
As the smoke from Heracles's pyre reached the heavens, Zeus saw his agony. He drew him up to Olympus and made him a god.

THE CHARACTER OF HERACLES

First and foremost, Heracles is a hero, a figure of incredible strength and outstanding bravery. But ancient Greek writers treat his character in different ways according to the parts of his story they are narrating. For example, in *The Children of Heracles*, Euripides portrays him as the tragic figure who kills his own children, but in another play, *Alcestis*, he gets comically drunk. Sophocles deals with the hero's relationship with his wife, Deianira, and other writers concentrate on his heroic adventures.

The dramatists Aeschylus, Sophocles, and Euripides

47

SEE ALSO Quests & challenges 44–45, 50–51, 52–53, 54–55, 64–67, 72–73, 100–03, 126–29, 294–97

THE GARDEN OF THE HESPERIDES

For the eleventh of his twelve labours (*see pp.46–47*), Heracles was told by his master, King Eurystheus, to go to the garden of the Hesperides – the daughters of Hesperis and Atlas (*see p.19*) – and steal the precious golden apples that grew on a tree there. The apples belonged to the goddess Hera and were a wedding gift from her grandmother, Gaia. To accomplish his task, Heracles first had to find the garden, which was at the far western edge of the Earth, then somehow slay the ever-watchful serpent that guarded the tree. In some versions of the myth, the wily hero persuaded Atlas to carry out the task on his behalf. This depiction by the British painter Frederic Leighton (1830–96) dwells on the beauty of the garden and its inhabitants, together forming a scene of peace and repose.

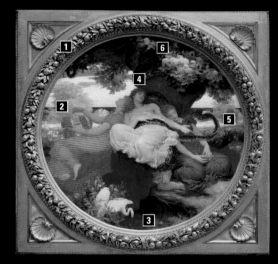

3. Symbols of vigilance
In the foreground of the picture are two cranes, one of which bends to take a drink from a spring issuing from beneath a rock. The Hesperides often gathered to sing near one of the springs in their garden – springs that spurted forth not water, but ambrosia, the nectar-like food of the gods that made whoever drank it immortal. In Christian art, cranes symbolize vigilance, so their prominent presence in Leighton's painting is an ironic reminder to the viewer that the sleepy Hesperides are meant to be alert and standing guard over the apples.

4. Daughters of the evening
Leighton's picture shows three Hesperides, although some accounts say there were four. The most commonly named three were Aegle (Brightness), Erythia (Scarlet), and Hesperarethusa (Sunset Glow) – the last name is sometimes said to be a conflation of the names of two nymphs, Hesperia and Arethusa. When the Hesperides lost the apples, their life of leisure turned into one of sadness and despair, until they were transformed into willow, elm, and poplar trees.

5. Serpent in the garden
The creature that helped the Hesperides guard the apples was called Ladon. Some versions of the myth say that he was a dragon with 100 heads, each of which spoke a different language, although here he is depicted as an enormous serpent entwined around both the tree and one of the Hesperides. Never sleeping, he kept constant guard of the tree and its fruit. Ladon's parentage was uncertain. Some say he was the offspring of the monsters Typhon and Echidna, others that he was a child of Gaia, and so a relative of Hera, owner of the apples. After Heracles slew Ladon, Hera, in her grief, turned the creature's body into the constellation Draco, the dragon.

6. The golden apples
Hera, the wife of Zeus, was the most powerful of all the goddesses of Mount Olympus. Eurystheus was confident that stealing such precious possessions as the golden apples from such a powerful deity would be beyond Heracles. When the hero succeeded, Eurystheus feared Hera's notorious anger, so he decided to give the apples back to her with the aid of the goddess Athena, who returned them to the garden.

1. The garden in the west
The garden was a place of great beauty, surrounded by a high wall. Accounts of its location varied – some put it in the north, but the name Hesperides means "daughters of the evening", so most people said it was in the west, where the sun sets. Heracles had to travel far to reach it, and had many adventures on the way, including freeing Prometheus from torment by killing the eagle that pecked at his liver (*see pp.26–27*), and killing the cruel Egyptian ruler Bousiris, who practised human sacrifice.

2. Music and song
The Hesperides lived a life of ease. They spent a lot of their time making music, and in Leighton's picture one of them plays a lyre to accompany her song. Her instrument has seven strings, and is the version of the lyre most commonly shown in depictions of ancient Greek musicians.

Frederic Leighton,
The Garden of the Hesperides, c.1892

SEE ALSO Gardens 216–17, 220–21 • Snakes & serpents 28–29, 92–93, 98–99, 100–03, 160–61, 238–39, 298–99, 328–29, 330–31

THESEUS AND THE MINOTAUR

The Minotaur was a monstrous flesh-eating creature, half man, half bull. Minos, the King of Crete, kept it imprisoned in a labyrinth near his palace. According to a treaty between Minos and Aegeus, the King of Athens, 14 young people had to be sent every year from Athens to be devoured by it. But the Greek hero Theseus resolved to kill the creature and put an end to the carnage.

THE MYTH

The sea god Poseidon once gifted a white bull, known as the Cretan Bull, to King Minos. However, when the king decided to keep the beast rather than sacrificing it, Poseidon was angered. He asked Aphrodite, the goddess of love, to make Minos's wife, Pasiphae, fall in love with the bull as punishment. This union produced a beast called the Minotaur, which had a monstrous appetite for human flesh.

King Minos wanted to avenge the death of his son at the hands of the Athenians. He waged a war on King Aegeus of Athens and won. As compensation, he demanded that 14 young people be sent from Athens each year to feed the Minotaur. Aegeus's son, Theseus, decided to go to Crete as one of the ill-fated people, and kill the beast. The ship carrying Theseus and the other victims set sail from Athens with black sails, and the hero promised his father that he would return with white sails hoisted on his ship if he succeeded in killing the Minotaur.

THESEUS ON CRETE

When the Athenians arrived at Crete, Minos's daughter, Ariadne, saw Theseus and fell in love with him. She knew that Theseus would need help in finding his way out of the impenetrable labyrinth, once he had slain the creature. So Ariadne gave him a spindle wound with woollen thread. As Theseus made his way into the labyrinth, he unwound the thread behind him, so that it would mark his winding path and show him how to exit the labyrinth.

▲ Leaving the labyrinth
The central portion of this vessel from Greece shows Theseus dragging his dead victim out of its prison as he retraces his steps through the labyrinth using Ariadne's thread.

► Theseus kills the Minotaur
The Minotaur almost managed to defeat Theseus in battle, but the hero fought courageously and stabbed the monster with his sword.

In the middle of the labyrinth, Theseus confronted the beast and killed it with a blow from his father's golden sword. He then retraced his steps with the body of the Minotaur by following Ariadne's thread, until he finally emerged from the entrance to the maze. His fellow Athenians rejoiced when they saw that Theseus had been victorious and quickly ran to their ship to set sail for home, Theseus taking Ariadne with him. In the excitement, they forgot to hoist the white sails to signal Theseus's success.

TRAGIC ENDINGS

On the way home, they called at the island of Naxos for water. When they returned to the ship, Theseus abandoned Ariadne on the island, sailing away without her. Some say that he did this since he already had a wife at home; others that Dionysus spotted Ariadne on the island, fell in love with her, and put a spell on Theseus, making him forget her. After marrying Ariadne, Dionysus gave her a crown made of seven stars.

As the ship approached Athens, Aegeus was watching anxiously for his son from a cliff-top. He saw the black sails from afar and assumed that Theseus had been killed. Overcome with grief, he flung himself into the sea, never to know of his son's success.

THE LABYRINTH

King Minos ordered the building of the labyrinth as a prison for the Minotaur. He entrusted the design of the labyrinth to the master-craftsman Daedalus, who was famous as an inventor – he was said to have invented sailing boats and sharp underwater rams that made the Cretan ships unbeatable in battle. His labyrinth became a byword in the ancient world for complexity and impenetrability. The story of the labyrinth seems to combine two ideas – the real palace at Knossos, Crete, which has hundreds of rooms and appears impenetrable; and drawings of mazes found on ancient carvings and coins.

▲ Ancient labyrinth
Unlike the puzzle-mazes seen in European gardens, which have many alternative routes, most ancient labyrinths had only one route, which led to the centre.

IN THE MIDDLE OF THE LABYRINTH, THESEUS KILLED THE BEAST WITH A BLOW OF HIS GOLDEN SWORD.

THE CRETAN BULL CULT

The bull plays a central part in the myths surrounding Crete – the creature that fathered the Minotaur had been sent to Minos by the sea god Poseidon as a confirmation of the king's right to rule on the island. Many ancient images of bulls have been found on Crete, so the animals seem to have been important in the customs and beliefs of the real islanders, too.

▼ Bull head
This Cretan Bronze-Age vessel in the form of a bull's head is carved from black stone.

➤ Double-headed axe
Two-headed axes are a common feature in Cretan art. Experts believe they are based on weapons used for sacrificing animals, a ritual of the bull cult.

▼ Bull-leaping
A fresco from Knossos shows a young man turning a somersault over a bull's back. This feat was perhaps performed as a sport or had some ritual significance.

KEY CHARACTERS

The myth of Theseus and the Minotaur contains a varied cast of characters, most of whom are people who mean well but meet tragic ends. Ariadne's abandonment and Aegeus's suicide come about because they play minor roles in a larger drama – the career of the hero Theseus. The lives of the characters are driven more by destiny than by personal choices or their individual traits.

➤ Ariadne
Ariadne had begged Daedalus to help her ensure Theseus's safe return from the labyrinth. He gave her a magical ball of thread, which she handed over to Theseus to find his way back after killing the Minotaur.

◄ Aegeus
When Aegeus saw the black sails of the returning ship, he was convinced that his son was dead. In despair, he threw himself off the cliff. The sea in which he drowned has been known as the Aegean Sea ever since.

THESEUS

After becoming the King of Athens following the death of his father, Theseus embarked on a long trip to the Underworld with his friend Pirithous. On his return, Theseus's throne was taken away from him, and he spent his last years as a beggar. His life ended at the behest of the goddess Artemis, who had Theseus murdered in revenge for his killing Antiope, her follower.

Theseus

51

SEE ALSO Bulls 116–17, 156–57, 194–95 • Tragedies 58–59, 70–71, 104–05, 170–71

BELLEROPHON AND PEGASUS

Like most Greek heroes, Bellerophon was given a seemingly impossible task – killing a monster called the Chimaera. With divine assistance and the aid of the fabulous flying horse, Pegasus, Bellerophon succeeded, but his triumph gave him an inflated view of his own status. He overreached himself when he used the horse's flying ability to try to visit the gods at Mount Olympus. The gods saw this act as supremely presumptuous. Although Bellerophon was a hero, he did not have the rank of a god, and so was punished.

THE MYTH

Bellerophon was a young hero who had unintentionally killed a man in his home city of Corinth and was banished. He was accepted at Tiryns, which was ruled by Proetus, but the king's wife, Stheneboia, fell in love with him. When Bellerophon rejected her advances, the queen vengefully accused the young man of trying to seduce her. Proetus believed his wife's false words, and so Bellerophon found himself banished again. This time, Proetus sent him to Lycia, the kingdom of Stheneboia's father, Iobates. Proetus asked Iobates to kill Bellerophon, but Iobates did not want to murder a guest. Instead, he sent Bellerophon on an apparently vain quest to kill the monstrous Chimaera, a creature that was part serpent, part goat, and part lion.

HUNTING THE CHIMAERA

Athena helped the young hero by giving him the magical winged horse, Pegasus. With his assistance, Bellerophon was able to swoop down on the monster and dispatch it with his sword, freeing Iobates's kingdom of the deadly menace. Athena allowed Bellerophon to retain the horse and, riding on this remarkable mount, he fulfilled many other quests. He defeated the Chimaera's father, killed some giants who threatened Iobates's kingdom, and repelled a force of Amazons – female warriors who were famous for fighting like men.

Iobates was impressed with Bellerophon and the two became friends – the king even offered the hero his daughter in marriage. Soon the spiteful Stheneboia died. Some myths claim she committed suicide in despair when Bellerophon married, others say Bellerophon killed her in fury when he discovered that she had accused him of trying to seduce her. After her death, the family was able to live in peace.

BELLEROPHON'S DEMISE

The series of triumphs on Pegasus made Bellerophon ambitious. He decided that the horse made him as powerful as a god, so he planned to fly to Mount Olympus. Zeus became angry at Bellerophon's presumption, since no mortal could be allowed to come to Mount Olympus uninvited. The king of the gods sent a fly to sting the horse midway in his flight. Pegasus reared on his hindlegs in pain, sending Bellerophon tumbling all the way to Earth, where he met his death.

◄ **Bellerophon and Pegasus**
Some say that when Athena brought Pegasus to Bellerophon, the horse was already broken in and ready to ride, others that Bellerophon found the wild winged horse and had to tame him first.

OVERREACHERS

In Classical mythology there is a clear hierarchy, with gods at the top, mortals below, and animals lower still. Heroes, however, occupied an ambiguous place in this framework – they were mortals, but often had one divine parent. This sometimes made them into overreachers – beings who aspired to a higher status than their allotted position. Their ambition drove them to great heights but finally brought them to grief. Bellerophon, Icarus, and Phaeton were all heroes who flew too high and paid the price.

► Phaeton
Phaeton was killed when he insisted on driving the chariot of his father Helios, the sun god. He lost control of the horses and fell to Earth.

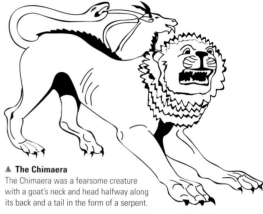

▲ Bellerophon
Although he looked invincible on Pegasus, Bellerophon incurred the wrath of Zeus with his arrogance and fell to Earth when he tried to fly too high.

▲ Daedalus and Icarus
The great craftsman Daedalus made wings so he and his son, Icarus, could fly. But Icarus flew too close to the sun and his waxen wings melted.

PEGASUS

The name Pegasus is related to the Greek word for "spring", and one myth of his birth says that he was born in the far west at the springs of the Ocean. After his adventures with Bellerophon he flew back to Mount Olympus, where he caused another spring, Hippocrene ("horse spring") to flow from Mount Helicon during a singing contest involving the Muses (see p.25).

Pegasus

◄ The Muses
Mount Helicon swelled in pleasure when the Muses sang. Pegasus kicked the mountain to make it shrink again; the spring called Hippocrene gushed from the spot where he had kicked the ground.

THE CHIMAERA

The child of two monsters, the man-dragon Typhon and the woman-serpent Echidna, the Chimaera was one of the most bizarre hybrids of Classical mythology. It was terrifying both because of its strange compound form, and because it breathed fire from its mouth. When it raided Iobates's kingdom, the king sent his men after it, but they were all burned by the creature's scorching breath.

▲ The Chimaera
The Chimaera was a fearsome creature with a goat's neck and head halfway along its back and a tail in the form of a serpent.

TIRYNS
Proetus's kingdom, Tiryns, is a real place on mainland Greece. It is the site of a ruined citadel dating to the 2nd millennium BCE and, therefore, was already in existence when the Greek myths reached their mature form about 1,000 years later. The ancient buildings of Tiryns are constructed with stones so large that in ancient times people thought they had been built by giants or Cyclopes.

A Cyclopean tunnel at Tiryns

53

SEE ALSO Monsters 46–47, 54–55, 64–67, 72–73, 98–99, 106–07, 156–57, 228–29, 274–75

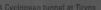

THE EXPLOITS OF PERSEUS

Perseus – one of the greatest Greek heroes – was the son of Zeus and Danaë, the daughter of Acrisius, the King of Argos. An oracle had once predicted that Acrisius would be killed by his daughter's son. To prevent the oracle's warning from coming true, he imprisoned his daughter and grandson, Perseus, in a wooden chest and threw it into the sea. The chest reached the island of Seriphos, where Perseus and his mother were rescued by the king, Polydectes, who brought him up. Many years later, Polydectes would be the one to send Perseus on his most perilous journey – to retrieve the head of the Gorgon Medusa.

THE SLAYING OF MEDUSA

Perseus rashly boasted to Polydectes that he would behead one of the three monstrous Gorgons. When Polydectes held him to his boast, Perseus decided to slay Medusa, a Gorgon who could turn men to stone with her gaze. Divine assistance was needed for Perseus to complete his task, so the deities of Mount Olympus lent Perseus several objects that helped him succeed. He used Hermes's winged sandals to fly to the place where Medusa lived, and Hades's helmet of invisibility to gain access to her dwelling. With Athena's shield, polished like a mirror, he approached the Gorgon, avoiding her direct gaze. And with Hephaestus's diamond sword, he chopped off Medusa's head, thus making good his boast.

▼ Head of Medusa
Like the other Gorgons, Medusa was a female monster with snakes for hair. However, she was the only mortal among the Gorgons.

► Medusa meets her death
Medusa's deadly glance only worked when she looked at her victims directly, so Athena helped Perseus use her shield as a mirror as he took aim with his sword.

► The three Graeae
Wearing Hades's helmet, Perseus crept past the Graeae, three sisters with one eye and one tooth between them, who guarded the cave of the Gorgons.

THE RESCUE OF ANDROMEDA

Some say the winged horse Pegasus (*see pp.52–53*) grew from Medusa's blood after Perseus had slain the Gorgon, and he left for home on this magical steed. As he flew, he saw a woman chained to some rocks on the Phoenician coast. She was Andromeda, the daughter of Cepheus, the King of Ethiopia. His wife, Cassiopeia, had boasted that Andromeda was more beautiful than the sea nymphs. Furious at this insult, the god Poseidon had sent a sea monster to terrorize Ethiopia; the beast would only be satisfied with the sacrifice of Cassiopeia's daughter. Perseus swooped down and killed the monster, rescuing Andromeda. He asked for her hand in marriage but when her parents refused, Perseus showed them Medusa's head, turning them to stone, and left with Andromeda.

▲ **Perseus and Andromeda**
This painting of the rescue of Andromeda by Perseus shows the hero still flying on the winged sandals of Hermes. Some versions of the story have him riding across the sky on the winged steed, Pegasus.

▲ **Turned to stone**
Perseus confronted Polydectes with Medusa's head just as the king was about to force Danaë to submit to his demands. The Gorgon's gaze was enough to petrify Polydectes and his men instantly where they stood.

THE PETRIFICATION OF POLYDECTES

After his adventures with the Gorgon and the sea monster, Perseus finally returned home to the island of Seriphos. King Polydectes had fallen in love with Perseus's mother, Danaë, and had been trying to persuade her to marry him. He had sent Perseus away in the first place for this very purpose. Danaë hid herself in the temple of Athena and Polydectes laid siege to the building. Enraged by what he saw on his arrival, Perseus revealed Medusa's head to the king and his soldiers, turning them to stone. Perseus then returned the gifts that the gods had loaned to him, and gave Medusa's head to Athena, who attached it to the front of her shield.

THE DEATH OF ACRISIUS

Perseus was going to return to his homeland of Argos, but he heard about the oracle that had predicted that Danaë's son would kill his own grandfather, and so he decided to stay away. He travelled instead to Pelasgiotis (or according to some accounts, Larissa) in Thessaly, where the local king, Teutamides, was holding funeral games for his recently deceased father. Perseus was keen to compete in the games, especially in the discus, which was his favourite event. But when he took his throw, the discus went astray, hitting and killing one of the men watching. Unfortunately, the victim turned out to be Perseus's grandfather, Acrisius.

▲ **Abandonment of Danaë and Perseus**
Acrisius's death had been foretold in a prophecy, which led him to put his daughter and grandson in a chest and throw it in the sea.

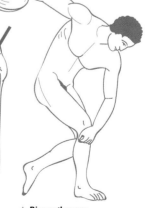

▲ **Discus thrower**
Perseus was fond of discus throwing, which became a very popular sport in the ancient Greek Olympic games.

SEE ALSO Quests & challenges 44–45, 46–49, 50–51, 52–53, 64–67, 72–73, 100–03, 126–29, 294–97

THE EXPLOITS OF PERSEUS

55

ABANDONED CHILDREN

The lives of mythical heroes often begin in difficulty. A number of them are abandoned by their parents as infants, for such reasons as the shame of a birth out of wedlock or – as in the famous case of the Greek tragic hero Oedipus (*see pp.58–59*) – a futile attempt to avoid the fulfilment of a prophecy.

CHILDREN OF THE GODS

When a deity fathers a child with a mortal woman, it is often a problem for the mother, because of the shame of illegitimacy or because her family do not want the child. Worldwide, myths tell how children fathered by gods are abandoned, then found by kind passers-by, who bring them up, often as their own.

▼ Amphion and Zethus
The abandoned twin sons of Zeus and the Boeotian princess, Antiope, grew up to be the founders of Thebes. Amphion's music charmed the city's stones into place.

▲ Karna
The Indian hero Karna (*see p.206*) was the son of the god Surya and the unmarried Kunti. Ashamed, Kunti left him by the Ganges, where the charioteer Adhiratha found him.

▲ Perseus, son of Zeus
The hero Perseus's grandfather threw him and his mother into the sea in a chest (*see pp.54–55*), but shepherds saved them both.

BROUGHT UP BY ANIMALS

Some mythical children are raised by animals. Their stories are tales of survival against the odds, with creatures normally feared as predators, such as wolves, caring for human outcasts. Heroes such as Romulus and Remus seem to gain strength from their encounters with the animals, and sometimes a supernatural element is added when it is a mythical beast – such as the phoenix-like Simurgh – that brings up the child.

▲ Zal of Persia
Abandoned for having white hair, the father of the great hero Rustum (*see pp.170–71*) was raised by a mythical bird called the Simurgh.

◄ The Greek huntress Atalanta
When Atalanta was born her father abandoned her on a hillside because she was not a boy, so the goddess Artemis sent a bear to suckle her.

► Romulus and Remus
Rome's famous ancestors (*see p.79*) were the twin sons of a woman raped by the god Mars. After she abandoned them, a wolf raised the boys.

ABANDONED CHILDREN

EUROPEAN FOLK TALES

European folklore is rich with tales of abandoned children. Often these stories involve an evil stepmother who resents the offspring of her husband's dead wife. Once abandoned, the children usually survive on their wits – Hansel and Gretel meet a witch who intends to eat them, but they outwit her and trap her in her own oven.

▲ Hansel and Gretel
In this traditional German tale, a stepmother persuades her husband, a poor woodcutter, to abandon his two children in a forest. Here they encounter a wicked witch, but survive.

▼ Le Petit Poucet
In this story from France, the youngest of seven abandoned children uses his wits to help them all survive by stealing magical "seven league boots" from a sleeping giant.

▲ Father Frost
In this Russian tale, a stepmother makes her spouse abandon his daughter, but Father Frost rescues the girl. When the woman's daughter goes to see Father Frost, she is frozen to death.

OMENS OF ILL FORTUNE

Often children in myths are abandoned by their parents following a fateful prophecy, either to save the child or to prevent the prediction from coming to pass. Typically, the abandoned child is then raised under a different identity by kind people of much humbler means than their natural parents – until the day inevitably arrives when the child is full-grown and the prophecy can be fulfilled.

▼ Paris of Troy
Paris's mother dreamed she gave birth to a torch that set her home city of Troy ablaze. His father ordered Paris killed, but she abandoned him instead. He grew up to play a key role in the fall of Troy (*see pp.60–61*).

▷ Lord Krishna
Before he was born, it was foretold that Krishna (*see pp.196–97*) would kill Kamsa, his evil uncle. Kamsa therefore ordered Krishna to be killed, but Krishna's father saved the baby boy.

▲ Cyrus the Great
Legend has it that a herdsman saved the Persian ruler, Cyrus, as a baby when he was ordered to be killed after his destiny was foretold.

OEDIPUS

Laius and Jocasta, the King and Queen of the city of Thebes, were told by the oracle at Delphi that their son would kill his father and marry his mother. Terrified by the prophecy, when their son, Oedipus, was born, they abandoned the child on a mountain and left him to die. So began one of the most tragic tales in all Classical mythology. By the end of the story, the entire family was destroyed, victims of fate and the impossibility of avoiding it. Oedipus became the archetypal tragic hero, trying to live well but thwarted by destiny.

THE MYTH

Soon after he was abandoned on the mountainside by Laius and Jocasta, Oedipus was found by a group of shepherds who took him to the city of Corinth, where the king and queen, Polybus and Merope, brought him up as their own son. One day someone told him he was a foundling, so he went to the oracle at Delphi to find out the truth. But rather than enlightening him about his true parentage, the oracle told him he was destined to kill his father and marry his mother. Thinking the oracle had meant Polybus and Merope, Oedipus decided to leave Corinth and set off on a long journey. On the way he came to a crossroads where an old man in a chariot was travelling in the opposite direction. The man ordered Oedipus to get out of his way, offending him with his rudeness. The pair quarrelled and fought, and Oedipus ended up killing the man.

▲ The infant Oedipus
When the shepherds found Oedipus, they took him to their king and queen who were childless and longed for a son.

ANSWERING THE RIDDLE

Oedipus continued his journey and eventually arrived in Thebes, where a monster called the Sphinx was devouring the city's children and the king had mysteriously disappeared. Each day the Sphinx asked a baffling riddle and when nobody could answer it correctly, it grabbed another child and ate it up. Oedipus alone was able to guess the correct answer to the riddle and, when he did so, the Sphinx died, breaking its neck in a fit of rage. A triumphant Oedipus became the most popular man in Thebes, and having caught the attention of Queen Jocasta, a descendant of the founding family of the city, he married her.

THE TRUTH REVEALED

For some years Oedipus and Jocasta enjoyed a happy marriage and had four children – daughters Antigone and Ismene, and sons Eteocles and Polynices. But after this period of contentment, Oedipus discovered the horrifying truth about his life when the prophet Tiresias revealed what had happened. The chariot rider that Oedipus killed at the crossroads was his true father, Laius, and the queen he had married in Thebes was his own mother, Jocasta. The queen killed herself in despair over what had happened, and Oedipus took a pin from her dress to stab his eyes, blinding himself. He left Thebes to spend the rest of his life as a wanderer, comforted only by his daughter Antigone, the one member of his family who had not rejected him for his deeds.

After many years of travelling as a blind beggar, Oedipus reached the city of Colonus, on the edge of Athens, where the oracle had said he would die. Here, the King of Athens, Theseus, welcomed him. However, Oedipus's sons wanted him to return to Thebes, convinced that his return would bring good fortune to the city. Oedipus ignored their demands and walked into the sacred grove at Colonus, disappearing from view and starting his last journey – to the Underworld.

▲ The death of Laius
The fatal meeting of Oedipus and Laius took place at a crossroads not far from Delphi. There, the words of the oracle were partly fulfilled.

THE FAMILY OF OEDIPUS

As a royal dynasty, Oedipus's family were closely involved with the politics of their city, Thebes. When Oedipus blinded himself and left the city, Jocasta's brother, Creon, took over the throne until Oedipus's sons, Eteocles and Polynices, were old enough to rule. But the brothers fought and killed each other, and Creon returned to the throne. He tried to rule for the good of the city but was known for his ruthlessness. He did not even spare Antigone, who was betrothed to his son, Haemon, and confined her in a cave to die for supporting her brother Polynices against his wishes.

▲ **Jocasta**
Queen Jocasta hung herself in anguish on realizing that she had mistakenly married her own son, Oedipus.

▲ **Antigone**
Oedipus's daughter Antigone supported her father and stood up for her brother, Polynices, after his rebellion (*see right*).

▲ **Creon**
Trying to deal firmly with the rows and tragedies in his family, Creon acted violently and became the archetype of the cruel ruler.

THE RIDDLE OF THE SPHINX

The puzzle posed by the Sphinx to the people of Thebes is now a familiar riddle, but it baffled everyone when they first heard it. In its most famous form, the riddle is: "What goes on four legs in the morning, two legs in the daytime, and three legs at night?"

Oedipus rightly guessed that the answer was a man, who crawls on four limbs as a baby, walks upright on two legs as an adult, and uses a stick, or third leg, in old age.

➤ **The sphinx**
Sphinxes take various forms in the ancient world, but the Greek Sphinx had the head of a woman, the body and legs of a lion, and the wings of a bird.

THEBES

Although it is a family tragedy, the story of Oedipus and his sons is intimately bound with the history of their city, Thebes, in Boeotia, whose ruling family traced its ancestry back to a magical event in the life of the hero Cadmus, the founder of Thebes. Much later, when Polynices was ousted by his brother Eteocles, he fled to Argos seeking help from its king, Adrastus. Together, they started a war with five other rebels, collectively known as the "Seven Against Thebes". Their army was slaughtered, both brothers were killed, and the noble line begun by Cadmus came to an end.

➤ **Cadmus slaying the dragon**
Cadmus killed a dragon that lived on the plains of Thebes and planted its teeth in the ground. From the monster's teeth grew an army of men who became the ancestors of the Thebans.

OEDIPUS AT COLONUS

The oracle had told Oedipus that he would die in a place sacred to the Furies (*see p.32*). Colonus was such a place; it was also special because it was the location of one of the entrances to the Underworld. After Oedipus came to Colonus, there was a thunderstorm, which he thought was a sign from Zeus that his life was coming to an end. It was from here that, ignoring the demands of the Thebans, Oedipus passed below the Earth to the next world. The Greek playwright Sophocles (496–406 BCE) was born in the area and described these events in his play *Oedipus at Colonus*.

◀ **Oedipus as a blind beggar**
In his blind wanderings, Oedipus was guided by his daughter Antigone, the only member of his family who remained faithful to him.

FREUD AND OEDIPUS

The pioneering psychoanalyst Sigmund Freud (1856–1939) has been linked with the Oedipus myth ever since he coined the term "Oedipus complex" to describe the sexual obsession of a child (usually male) with the parent of the opposite sex. The phrase is somewhat misleading, as Oedipus did not know that Jocasta was his real mother. It has been widely used in both psychology and literary studies.

Sigmund Freud

OEDIPUS

59

SEE ALSO Tragedies 50–51, 70–71, 104–05, 170–71

THE TROJAN WAR

Homer's great epic poem, the *Iliad*, describes a war between the Greeks and the Trojans that lasted for ten years. The conflict began after Paris, a prince from Troy, eloped with Helen, the wife of the Greek king, Menelaus, and the Greeks mounted an expedition to get her back. On Mount Olympus, the gods and goddesses looked down on the battlefield, taking sides and influencing events as heroes of both sides fell. Finally, the Greeks were victorious and took Helen back home.

THE MYTH

The two sides were well matched. Each had the services of good leaders, like the Trojan prince, Hector, and the Greek general, Agamemnon. Each had other famous soldiers and fighters on their side – Paris for the Trojans and men such as Achilles and the cunning Odysseus for the Greeks. Each side also had the backing of several gods and goddesses – Aphrodite and Poseidon were on the side of Troy; Apollo, Athena, and Hera favoured the Greeks. Therefore the stalemate continued, with many minor battles but no overall victory, for years.

▶ **The Trojan horse**
The Trojans were known as skilled tamers of horses, so the booby-trapped wooden horse was an ironic gift from the Greeks, which had disastrous results.

ACHILLES AND PATROCLUS

The war reached a climax when two of the Greek leaders quarrelled. Agamemnon, who had been forced to give up one of his concubines, took as his mistress one of the many women of Achilles. In disgust, Achilles withdrew his forces from the fighting and the Trojans began to get the upper hand. To win back the initiative, Patroclus, a close friend of Achilles, asked his comrade for permission to lead his troops and disguise himself in the armour of Achilles. When the Trojan soldiers saw the best of the Greek troops back on the battlefield, apparently led by Achilles himself, they began to lose heart. This gave the Greeks more success, but just as they seemed to be winning, Hector killed Patroclus.

THE GREEKS GAIN GROUND

The death of Patroclus roused Achilles, who returned to the fight, killing Hector and dragging his body around Troy's walls. Next, the gods encouraged the Greeks to bring the great archer Philocretes into the battle, and the bowman killed Paris, a huge psychological blow for the Trojans. The Greeks then stole Athena's statue, which was a sign of good fortune for the Trojans, from her shrine in Troy.

Finally, the gods put into the mind of Odysseus the trick of the hollow wooden horse, in which soldiers could hide. The Greeks left the horse in front of the city and feigned a withdrawal. The Trojans dragged the statue into the city. During the night, Greek soldiers emerged from its belly and opened the city gates. The rest of the Greek army poured in and Troy was destroyed.

▲ **Soldiers in combat**
In this engraving created in the style of Greek vase painting, Trojans attack the Greek ships with fire, while the Greeks defend themselves with their spears.

THE JUDGEMENT OF PARIS

The event that started the war occurred on Mount Ida, where the Trojan prince, Paris, was visited by three goddesses: Hera, Athena, and Aphrodite. Eris, goddess of discord, had given them a golden apple, inscribed, "For the fairest". Each of the three claimed the apple. Zeus commanded Hermes to take them to Paris, who would decide which was the most beautiful. The goddesses tried to influence his decision by offering bribes. Athena pledged to grant him success in war, Hera promised power, and Aphrodite offered the hand of the world's most beautiful woman, Helen. Paris chose Aphrodite's offer – but Helen was already married to Menelaus of Sparta. When she eloped with Paris, hostilities between Greece and Troy began.

▲ The three goddesses
After Paris judged Aphrodite to be the fairest among the three goddesses, he earned the wrath of both Athena and Hera.

▶ Helen of Troy
Several reasons have been given for Helen's desertion, including wickedness, forced abduction, and the influence of Aphrodite.

THE HEROES

The story of the Trojan War is full of heroes who are the epic's main characters. They are generally brave in battle, but Homer's depiction of their characters is particularly interesting. Many are motivated by honour – the dispute between Achilles and Agamemnon over their concubines, for example, ignites because when Agamemnon appropriates the woman of Achilles, the latter's honour is affected. Homer shows that intelligence is essential in battle too: the hero Odysseus is renowned for his cunning.

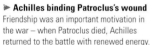

▶ Achilles binding Patroclus's wound
Friendship was an important motivation in the war – when Patroclus died, Achilles returned to the battle with renewed energy.

▲ Agamemnon returning with Cassandra
At the end of the war, Troy was captured and sacked. Agamemnon carried off Cassandra, the daughter of King Priam of Troy, as a prize.

▲ Menelaus pursuing Helen
Seen here pursuing his wife, Helen, Menelaus is portrayed in the *Iliad* as a noble king who fights bravely for his cause.

▲ Hector fighting Achilles
Achilles and Hector's fight was a key moment in the war. With Hector's death, the Trojans were weakened by the loss of one of their greatest fighters.

▲ Ajax committing suicide
A great warrior, Ajax survived the war, but went mad after a dispute with Odysseus, and killed himself.

ATHENE AND HERA THUNDERED, DOING HONOUR TO THE KING OF MYCENAE, RICH IN GOLD.

Homer, *Iliad*, Book XI

THE ANCIENT CITY OF MYCENAE

Although the story of the *Iliad* is a myth, all its characters come from real places in ancient Greece. Mycenae, in the northeastern Peloponnese, was said to be the home of Agamemnon. The city state was a strong military power during the Late Bronze Age. This ancient site was excavated in the 19th century by the German archaeologist Heinrich Schliemann. He discovered stunning jewellery and other artefacts among the ruins, dating back to the 2nd millennium BCE. He claimed these objects belonged to Agamemnon, though there has never been any evidence to support this.

◀ Gold mask
Schliemann called this face of beaten gold unearthed from Mycenae "the mask of Agamemnon", but it could have belonged to any early Mycenaean king.

SEE ALSO Wars 18–19, 98–99, 104–05, 116–17, 118–19, 126–27, 170–71, 176–77, 206–07

The death of Hector
After Achilles killed Hector, he dragged his fallen enemy behind his chariot for the next twelve days. The gods took pity on Hector, and made sure that his body was preserved from injury.

THE ODYSSEY

Homer's second epic, the *Odyssey,* tells the story of the Greek hero Odysseus (Ulysses to the Romans) on his journey home to Ithaca after the Trojan War (*see pp.60–61*). He faces many perils, including monstrous creatures and seductive women. Each encounter stretches his intelligence and cunning. But his greatest challenge comes when he arrives home to find his wife besieged by suitors who believe him to be dead.

THE MYTH

After leaving Troy, Odysseus and his sailors first came to the country of the Lotos Eaters. These inhabitants, who lived a lazy life of ease, tempted them with the lotos fruit, which had the power to make them forget the past. Odysseus had to force his reluctant companions back to their ships. Next they encountered the Cyclopes, a race of one-eyed giants. Odysseus and his followers were caught by one of the Cyclopes, Polyphemus, who kept them captive in a cave and ate some of them. When the Greek hero was asked to identify himself, he cleverly said he was called Outis (meaning "no one"). Odysseus plied Polyphemus with wine and then blinded the giant with a heated stake. When Polyphemus shouted, "Outis [no one] is killing me", the other Cyclopes heard him but did not come to his rescue because they thought he was drunk, and the Greeks managed to escape. Polyphemus complained to his father, the sea god Poseidon, who sent terrible storms to hinder Odysseus's journey.

AT THE MERCY OF THE WINDS

At their next port of call, Aeolus, the god of the winds, gave Odysseus the winds tied up in a bag, allowing him to control his course homewards. But Odysseus's men, filled with curiosity about the contents of the bag, untied it, letting loose all the winds. The ship was blown far off course, first to the land of the giant Laestrygonians, who destroyed most of their ships, and then to an island inhabited by the enchantress Circe, who turned Odysseus's

men into pigs. But Odysseus saved himself by eating a protective herb given to him by the god Hermes. Circe saw that Odysseus was resistant to her magic, and turned his crew back into men again. Circe advised Odysseus to visit the Underworld to find out more about his future. He travelled there, and had a vision in which his homeland was occupied by hostile invaders. The hero decided to hurry home.

But his journey took longer than he had expected. Odysseus first encountered the Sirens, enchanting creatures whose beautiful song lured all passing sailors. He sailed past them by commanding his men to block their ears. After this, Odysseus's ship had to pass between Scylla, a six-headed, man-devouring monster, and Charybdis, a whirlpool. Odysseus was forced to take the painful decision of losing six of his sailors to Scylla, each of whose six heads could only eat one man at a time, rather than have all of them drown in the whirlpool of Charybdis. **»**

> **Greek ship**
> Greek ships had banks of oars but were also equipped with sails, so Odysseus's ships would have been able to take advantage of the wind.

◀ **Odysseus**
Like all Greek heroes, Odysseus was physically strong. But he was also cunning, which helped him overcome the obstacles that beset his voyage.

MONSTERS AND OBSTACLES

Odysseus encountered several obstacles on his journey. The giant Laestrygonians destroyed all the ships in his armada except for his own. When they were trapped in Polyphemus's cave, he and his men tied themselves to the underbellies of the Cyclops's sheep. The next day, Polyphemus let his sheep out to graze, and the Greeks escaped. On Circe's island, Odysseus's men were turned into pigs, thus delaying the voyage.

◄ The Laestrygonians
Antiphates, the king of the Laestrygonians, killed and ate one of Odysseus's men. Then all the giants pelted the Greek ships with huge rocks, sinking all but one.

► The magic of Circe
The enchantress Circe turned men into animals by giving them a potion and striking them with her wand.

◄ Odysseus and Polyphemus
Using a sharpened stake of olive wood, Odysseus put out the single eye of Polyphemus so that he and his men could escape from the Cyclops's cave.

THE WORLD OF THE DEAD

Odysseus visited the Underworld to find out about his future. First he consulted the prophet Tiresias, who warned him not to harm the cattle of Helios. Then he met his mother, Anticleia, who told him how his wife and son were suffering at home. Odysseus also met the ghost of Achilles (*see pp.60–61*). Finally, he grew fearful and left the Underworld in terror.

► Achilles
The ghost of Achilles told Odysseus he would rather live on Earth as a humble labourer than rule among the dead.

PERILS OF THE SEA

The Greeks were a people who lived mainly on islands and in coastal settlements, and hence were accomplished sailors. They knew well that sea voyages, even in the often calm Mediterranean, had their dangers, and that sailors had to watch out for unfavourable winds, dangerous whirlpools or currents, and jagged rocks. Odysseus had to cope with tempests sent by Poseidon, perilous currents, and some more fantastic dangers. Some of these, like the seductive song of the Sirens, could be deceptive – Odysseus was warned by Circe that the song of the Sirens must be resisted.

> NEVER YET HAS ANY MAN ROWED PAST THIS ISLE IN HIS BLACK SHIP UNTIL HE HAS HEARD THE SWEET VOICE FROM OUR LIPS.
> Homer, *Odyssey*, Book IX

▲ Odysseus and the Sirens
While his sailors blocked their ears, Odysseus had himself tied to the mast so that he could not follow the Sirens.

▼ Charybdis
This notorious whirlpool sank all passing ships, but Odysseus steered through the narrow gap between it and Scylla.

THE JOURNEY CONTINUES

Odysseus next stopped at an island where Helios, the sun god, kept his cattle. Although they had been warned not to kill these animals, the sailors slaughtered a few of the cattle. Helios complained to Zeus, who struck their ship with a thunderbolt, killing the crew and shattering the ship. Only Odysseus survived, clinging to the wreckage.

Odysseus was washed up on the island belonging to the goddess Calypso, who wanted him to stay with her. Though he lived there for seven years, Odysseus finally resisted the temptation to stay further, and travelled on. He was then shipwrecked again and washed ashore on the island of Alcinous, the King of the Phaeacians. Here, the goddess Athena contrived to make the king's daughter, Nausicaa, meet Odysseus, and the two were attracted to each other. Odysseus was tempted to stay with her, but finally, longing for his wife and his homeland, Ithaca, he travelled on again.

PENELOPE'S SUITORS

Bruised and greatly aged by his ordeal, Odysseus arrived in Ithaca to find his house full of suitors who, assuming he was dead, were hoping to marry his wife, Penelope, and take over all his

▶ **Nausicaa**
The princess was with her friends at the seashore when a tired and naked Odysseus appeared before them. He was given clothes by Nausicaa.

▶ **Odysseus and Calypso**
Promised agelessness and immortality by Calypso, Odysseus was tempted to remain with her forever, but in the end he constructed a raft and resumed his journey home to Ithaca.

lands and wealth. The suitors were living off Odysseus's food and abusing his wife's hospitality, just like the hostile invaders he had seen in his vision in the Underworld. Penelope did not want to marry any of them, so she said she would declare her choice when she had finished weaving a tapestry on which she was working.

Finally, Penelope had to make up her mind. She said she would marry the man who could string Odysseus's powerful bow. No one recognized Odysseus (he revealed himself only to his son, Telemachus) as he took his place with the others. He was the only one who succeeded in stringing the bow. Then Penelope realized the man was her husband. With the help of Telemachus, he killed all the suitors. But, though he loved Penelope, Odysseus, after wandering for so long, found it hard to settle down in Ithaca. Soon he was planning another journey and looking forward to more adventures.

ITHACA

When Odysseus landed in Ithaca, he disguised himself as a beggar to find out what was going on in his house. He discovered that his wife and his son were alive, but they were beset by trouble. Many suitors were pressing Penelope for her hand in marriage. Because they believed Odysseus to be dead, their requests were legitimate, but still their behaviour was inexcusable. For the Greeks, hospitality was the greatest of virtues, but the suitors abused Penelope's hospitality and showed no respect for her own sentiments. This abuse justified their eventual killing by Odysseus and his son, Telemachus.

▶ **Penelope weaving**
Odysseus's loyal wife unravelled a bit of her tapestry every night, to put off the day when she would have to choose between the many suitors clamouring for her hand.

◀ **Death of the suitors**
Odysseus and Telemachus both launched an attack on the suitors, who quaked behind their shields as they fell one by one.

DIVINE INTERVENTION

The gods of Mount Olympus not only influenced the Trojan War, but also had an impact on the adventures of Odysseus. Whenever the hero offended a deity, his journey home was delayed. Poseidon, Helios, and Zeus himself, all hampered the progress of the voyage. After blinding Polyphemus, Odysseus shouted out his real name to the Cyclops as he sailed away. Polyphemus told Poseidon that Odysseus had blinded him, and the sea god unleashed a series of storms to wreck his ships. When Odysseus's men slew the cattle of Helios, Zeus punished them. Though Hermes saved Odysseus from the magic of Circe, the one deity who consistently protected and advised the cunning hero was Athena.

▲ **Helios on his chariot**
The sun god (referred to as Hyperion by Homer) exerted his power when the Greeks ate the meat of his cattle, making the beef bellow as if it were alive.

▲ **Divine protector**
Athena was Odysseus's benefactor. She persuaded Calypso to release him, set up his meeting with Nausicaa, and advised him to disguise himself before confronting his wife's suitors.

> SOME WORK OF NOBLE NOTE, MAY YET BE DONE, NOT UNBECOMING MEN THAT STROVE WITH GODS.
>
> Alfred, Lord Tennyson, *Ulysses*, 1842

Poseidon

HOMER

Both the *Odyssey* and the *Iliad* are attributed to Homer, a blind poet who probably lived in the 8th century BCE. Little is known about Homer, and some scholars believe the epics were actually the work of earlier poets, who handed down the narratives by word of mouth, adapting and modifying them before they were written down by Homer himself. The two epics combine story, character, and poetic language so effectively that Homer is considered even today as one of the world's greatest writers.

Homer

MODERN ODYSSEYS

The adventures of Odysseus are immensely popular. Because Homer's epic is a powerful tale with an open-ended conclusion, its material has been used in new ways. One of these "modern Odysseys" is *The Odyssey: A Modern Sequel* (1938), a long poem by Nikos Kazantzakis (1883–1957), describing Odysseus's new adventures. *Ulysses* (1922), a novel by James Joyce (1882–1941), also uses the idea of an odyssey in its story about Leopold Bloom, a native of Dublin, who makes a meandering journey around his home city.

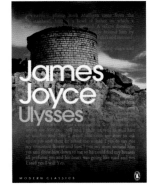

▶ **Joyce's *Ulysses***
Bloom's wanderings take place in the course of a single day. The characters and encounters allude to episodes from the Greek myth.

SEE ALSO Journeys 34–35, 44–45, 120–21, 220–21 • Classical monsters 46–47, 52–53, 54–55, 72–73

CLASSICAL ANTIHEROES

The myths of ancient Greece are full of people – usually mortals but often powerful figures such as kings or princes – who broke the rules of normal conduct. They did this by cheating their fellow mortals, by abusing gifts or hospitality, or by insulting the gods. These antiheroes often ended up with dire punishments, as a warning to others tempted to break the social or cult rules that normally made social or religious life run smoothly.

IXION

The King of the Lapiths of Thessaly, Ixion, was a cheat and a deceiver. He abducted Dia, the daughter of Eioneus, in order to marry her, and agreed to pay the dowry to the girl's father when he came to the wedding. However, he did not want to part with a large sum of money, so on the day of the wedding, the king set a cruel trap for Eioneus. He dug a pit near his palace and filled it with burning coal, and when his unsuspecting father-in-law arrived, Ixion pushed him to his death. Following this outrage, Ixion was ostracized by all mortals for killing a kinsman, but for some reason Zeus took pity on him and invited him to a banquet on Mount Olympus. Even among the gods, he overstepped the bounds of propriety and tried to seduce Hera, Zeus's wife. Zeus punished Ixion for attempting to outrage his wife's modesty by binding him to a burning wheel, which would turn forever in the Underworld.

◄ The killing of Eioneus
By pushing Eioneus to his death, Ixion was violating the ideal of hospitality, one of the most important values of the Greeks.

▼ Ixion's punishment
Some myths describe Ixion's wheel as the disc of the sun; according to others it was a wheel that turned in the Underworld.

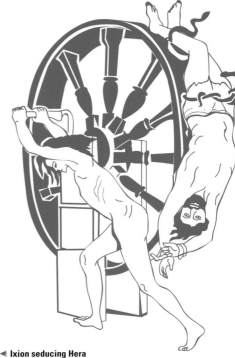

◄ Ixion seducing Hera
When Zeus discovered Ixion's intentions, he tricked him into sleeping with a cloud shaped like Hera. The offspring of this union was Centaurus, the ancestor of the Centaurs.

SISYPHUS

The founder of the city of Corinth, Sisyphus was guilty of several transgressions, including killing guests and seducing his own niece. Banished to the Underworld for his deeds, he tried to cheat death, first by confining Thanatos, the god of mortality, but without success. Then he instructed his wife not to carry out the burial rites for him. When Hades sent him back to Earth to ensure that the rites were performed, Sisyphus refused to return to the Underworld. For his presumption in trying to turn himself into an immortal, Sisyphus was condemned to roll a heavy boulder up a hill. When the rock reached the hilltop, it rolled back down again, so Sisyphus had to keep repeating his task eternally.

▶ Thanatos
The son of Night and Darkness, Thanatos was a much feared but rarely seen god in the myths of Greece.

◀ Sisyphus pushing a rock
For artists and writers in both ancient and modern times, Sisyphus and his terrible punishment became the iconic image of hard, endless, and pointless tasks.

TANTALUS

The King of Sipylus in Lydia, Tantalus was a son of Zeus. As a relative of Zeus he was allowed to dine with the gods, but he abused this privilege. Some myths say he gossiped about the gods' secrets, others that he stole food from them and gave it to mortals. According to an extreme version, he tested the gods by serving the flesh of his own son for them to eat. His punishment for these transgressions was to suffer eternal thirst and hunger. He was made to stand in a pool below a fruit-laden tree. The pool emptied each time Tantalus tried desperately to drink the water, while the overhanging branches blew out of reach whenever he tried to grasp them, hence the word, "tantalize".

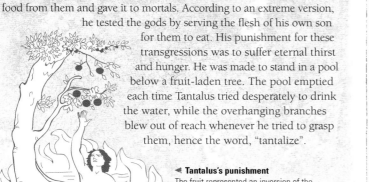

◀ Tantalus's punishment
The fruit represented an inversion of the usual bounty of the gods, a fitting punishment for Tantalus's insults to the Olympians.

MIDAS

King Midas of Phrygia helped Silenus, a follower of Dionysus (*see pp.34–35*), and in return the god granted Midas any favour he wished. The king, who was consumed by greed, asked that everything he touched should change to gold. But when his food and drink were turned to gold, Midas asked Dionysus to take the gift away. One day, he came across Pan and Apollo in the countryside. The two gods were having an argument about who was the better musician. Midas chose Pan over the god of music, and an irate Apollo punished him by giving him the ears of an ass. Midas had to keep his head covered with a turban, but news of his ridiculous ears got out, and he ended his life by drinking hot bull's blood.

◀ Midas wih his daughter
In some versions of Midas's myth, the king touches his daughter and she turns into a golden statue.

▼ Midas with Pan and Apollo
In spite of the fact that other listeners thought Apollo to be the better musician, Midas chose his rival Pan, rousing the anger of the other deity.

SEE ALSO Punishments 26–27, 50–51, 54–55, 70–71, 154–55, 218–19, 288–89

CLASSICAL ANTIHEROINES

Greek mythology has many antiheroines who were embroiled in complex plots, mostly involving revenge. A number of them, such as Ino and Clytemnestra, chose to do so out of jealousy, or because they lacked the moral and social virtues considered necessary in noble women. But the actions of others were guided more by the interference of gods in human affairs. These antiheroines were often responsible, directly or indirectly, for the deaths of others, and their stories frequently ended with their own deaths, often by suicide.

PHAEDRA

The daughter of King Minos of Crete and his wife, Pasiphae, Phaedra married Theseus (*see pp.50–51*) after he had become the ruler of Athens. But she fell in love with Hippolytus, Theseus's son by Antiope, an Amazon queen who had been Theseus's mistress. In some versions of the myth, her passion was caused by the gods as a way of punishing Theseus for killing Antiope. When Hippolytus rebuffed Phaedra's amorous advances, she told Theseus that Hippolytus had tried to rape her. The enraged king turned against his son and called on the gods to punish the young man. Hearing Theseus's cry, Poseidon blew up a storm that knocked Hippolytus off his chariot to his death. Grief-stricken, Phaedra hanged herself on hearing about her stepson's death.

▲ **Phaedra and Theseus**
The death of Hippolytus was the result of the doomed marriage between Phaedra and the Athenian king. Her brother, Deucalion, gave her in marriage to Theseus, despite knowing about his liaison with Antiope.

▲ **The death of Hippolytus**
When Poseidon raised a storm, a monster in the form of a bull rose from the sea, terrifying Hippolytus's horses. Theseus's son was thrown off his chariot and dragged to his death.

JEAN RACINE

The great French dramatist Jean Racine (1639–99) wrote several tragedies on Classical themes, including *Phèdre*. He believed that tragedy was inherent in the human condition and that unfortunate events were not necessary to bring people into tragic situations. In Racine's plays, action is kept to a minimum and the characters analyse their passions in language of great poetic beauty. In *Phèdre*, he affirms the nobility of his heroine by altering the story, so that she falls in love with her stepson only when she believes Theseus to be dead.

Jean Racine

CLASSICAL EUROPE

70

CLYTEMNESTRA

The wife of Agamemnon, the King of Mycenae, Clytemnestra had four children by her husband: Iphigenia, Electra, Chrysothemis, and Orestes. Agamemnon sacrificed Iphigenia to the gods in order to ensure a fair wind for the Greek fleet sailing for the Trojan War (*see pp.60–61*). When Clytemnestra discovered her daughter's death, she vowed revenge. She took a lover, Aegisthus, and placed him on the Mycenaean throne in Agamemnon's absence. When the king returned from the war, Clytemnestra and Aegisthus trapped and killed him and many of his supporters. Her son, Orestes, escaped the carnage and went into exile. He later slew his mother to avenge his father's murder. After her death, Clytemnestra's ghost, with the support of the Furies, tried to punish Orestes, but the gods (or in some versions of the story, a human court) eventually decided that what he had done was justified.

▲ The punishment of Orestes
The Furies, seen here holding Clytemnestra's corpse, attacked Orestes with thunderbolts. Later, Orestes's faithful sister, Electra, nursed him and helped him recover from his wounds.

◀ The murder of Agamemnon
Clytemnestra and Aegisthus trapped Agamemnon in a net and brutally killed him with an axe. Some accounts of his death say that Agamemnon was defenceless, in his bath, cleaning away the dirt of his long journey home, when the murder took place.

INO

King Athamas of Boeotia was married to Nephele, but left her for Ino, the daughter of Cadmus (*see p.59*). Ino resented her stepchildren, Phrixus and Helle, and devised a plot to dispose of them. She lit a fire beneath the granary and dried up all the seeds so that they would not germinate, thereby causing a famine. When Athamas sent a messenger to the oracle at Delphi to ask for a solution, Ino bribed the messenger to say that Athamas should sacrifice Phrixus. The king was about to kill his son when Hera sent a golden ram to carry off his children. Although Phrixus survived, Helle fell from the ram's back and drowned in the sea, which was named the Hellespont (now called the Dardanelles) after her. Nephele wanted Athamas punished, so according to some versions of the story, Hera sent one of the Furies to drive him and Ino mad. Later, Athamas made Ino jump off a cliff into the sea, where she drowned.

▶ Divine justice
Hera was enraged at Athamas and Ino, and Nephele persisted in demanding they should be punished, so the goddess sent one of the Furies, Tisiphone, to torment the guilty couple.

THE DAUGHTERS OF DANAUS

Danaus, a grandson of Poseidon, had 50 daughters, while his brother, Aegyptus, had 50 sons. The two brothers quarrelled over their father's lands after his death, until Aegyptus offered to marry his sons to Danaus's daughters to unite the family. But an oracle had once told Danaus that Aegyptus planned to kill him and his daughters, so he ran away with his family. Aegyptus gave chase, besieging them in the city of Argos until they ran out of food and were forced to agree to the marriages. Danaus gave each of his daughters a hairpin and asked them to kill their husbands with it. All the daughters except one carried out their father's instructions, for which they were severely punished after their death.

▶ Eternal punishment
When the guilty daughters died, they went to the Underworld, where they were forced to pour water into a large vessel that perpetually leaked, so their task was never-ending.

CLASSICAL ANTIHEROINES

71

SEE ALSO Punishments 26–27, 50–51, 54–55, 68–69, 154–55, 218–19, 288–89

THE ARGONAUTS

The myth of Jason and the Argonauts is one of the greatest quest stories in all mythology. It concerns Jason, heir to the throne of Iolcus in northeastern Greece. When Jason was a child, his uncle, Pelias, usurped the kingdom and imprisoned Jason's father, King Aeson. Jason's mother, Alcimede, smuggled him away and entrusted his care to Cheiron the Centaur, who raised him. After Jason grew to manhood, he went to Pelias and demanded the kingdom that was rightfully his own. Pelias said that Jason could only be king if he stole and brought back the precious Golden Fleece from King Aeëtes of Colchis.

THE MYTH

For his journey to Colchis, Jason had a special ship built, named the *Argo*. The ship's timbers included planks taken from a sacred oak tree at the oracle of Zeus at Dodona, making the vessel especially strong. Jason persuaded many of Greece's greatest heroes, including Heracles, Polydeuces, Peleus, and Orpheus, to join him on the *Argo*. This group of heroes became known as the Argonauts.

DANGERS AND OBSTACLES

The heroes faced all kinds of obstacles on their journey, from encounters with attractive women who delayed their quest, to confrontations with the deadly perils of the sea. First, they were seduced by the all-female population of the island of Lemnos, delaying their progress for several months. Then one of their number, Hylas, left the quest when water nymphs pulled him into a well, and his friend, Heracles, distressed at his loss, left the *Argo* to save him. The remaining Argonauts had still more dangerous challenges ahead. They got involved in a boxing match with King Amycus, a formidable fighter who usually killed his opponents. They were saved by the prowess of Polydeuces, who is said to have invented the sport of boxing. In another encounter they met a blind prophet called Phineus who was tortured by the Harpies, bird-like creatures with women's heads, also known as the hounds of Zeus. These frightful beings continually snatched away Phineus's food and pecked at his eyes. Two of the Argonauts chased the Harpies away and in return a grateful Phineus helped them sail through the Clashing Rocks, one of several other perils that they had to negotiate before reaching Colchis.

▲ Harpies
With their hardened beaks and talons and their poisonous droppings, the Harpies were formidable monsters.

CHALLENGES IN COLCHIS

In Colchis, King Aeëtes did not want to lose the Golden Fleece, so he set Jason a challenge – to tame a pair of fire-breathing bulls and use them to pull a plough, dropping the teeth of serpents into the soil as he went. From the teeth, armed warriors would spring up to attack Jason. The hero only succeeded because the daughter of Aeëtes, the sorceress Medea, had fallen in love with him and helped him accomplish the task. Her father, however, still would not let Jason take the fleece. Then she suggested that Orpheus's music would charm the poisonous serpent guarding it and put it to sleep. With the fleece finally in his hands, Jason sailed for home, negotiating hazards such as Scylla and Charybdis, the Sirens, and the giant Talos, who threw huge rocks at the ship until Medea killed him with a deadly glance. At last Jason reached Iolcus and claimed his kingship.

▼ The Argo sets off
Jason wisely decided to take with him some of the strongest heroes in Greece. The crew set off on their perilous quest, cheered by the people of Iolcus.

KEY CHARACTERS

Ancient writings contain several different lists of the Argonauts, but they all agree in including many of the most prominent ancient Greek heroes, such as Heracles, Patroclus, and Peleus, as well as the twins Castor and Polydeuces. Some accounts list the huntress Atalanta as the only woman warrior among the crew. Most of these characters embodied great strength and skill in arms, but such qualities would have been useless without others such as the sorcery of Medea or the music of Orpheus.

◄ Jason
After his successful quest, some accounts state that Jason ruled happily in Iolcus. Others allege that his life was ruined by Medea's scheming.

▲ Medea
As she was a priestess of Hecate, the Underworld goddess, Medea could use her sorcery to help Jason.

◄ Orpheus
Orpheus's entrancing music helped the Argonauts on many occasions throughout their arduous journey.

THE HEROES SHONE LIKE GLEAMING STARS AMONG THE CLOUDS.

Apollonius of Rhodes, *Argonautica I*

THE GOLDEN FLEECE

Athamas, king of Thebes, had a legitimate son, Phrixus, as well as children by Ino, his mistress. Ino tried to cause the death of Phrixus, so that one of her own children could inherit the throne. Nephele, the mother of Phrixus, arranged for him to fly out of danger to Colchis on the back of a golden ram. Aeëtes, ruler of Colchis, welcomed him, hoping that Phrixus would give him the ram, but he sacrificed the beast to Ares and the priests of Ares displayed the fleece in a garden. It was guarded by a serpent that never slept. Pelias, who sent Jason on his quest, was the cousin of Phrixus.

▲ The flying ram
The ram was such a tireless flyer that it carried Phrixus all the way from Thebes to Colchis, which was said to be at the very edge of the world.

DANGERS AT SEA

Jason and the Argonauts had to pass several of the perilous obstacles that had also been faced by Odysseus on his journey home from Troy (*see pp.64–67*) – both heroes faced the Sirens, with their alluring music, and Scylla and Charybdis. In addition, Jason had to pass between the Clashing Rocks. The challenges of weather, navigation, and the perils of the sea took the Argonauts on a much longer route than Odysseus's, however. Their journey encompassed the Black Sea, the Danube, the Adriatic, and the Mediterranean.

▲ The Clashing Rocks
This pair of living rocks, said to be at the entrance to the Black Sea, slammed together when a ship tried to pass between them.

▲ The Sirens
The Sirens lured sailors with their seductive song. When the Argonauts sailed by them, Orpheus played his lyre continuously to drown out their voices.

▲ Scylla
The sea nymph Thetis helped the *Argo* to sail past Scylla, the monster who devoured sailors passing through the Strait of Messina.

THE ARGO

Made by the shipbuilder Argus, the *Argo* had a prow with the gift of prophecy given by Athena. The vessel was thus able to take Jason and his companions through a series of deadly perils. The craft had more than one bank of oars so it could be rowed at speed.

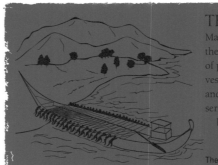

The ship with the magical prow

THE ARGONAUTS

73

SEE ALSO Quests & challenges 44–45, 46–49, 50–51, 52–53, 54–55, 64–67, 100–03, 126–29, 294–97

Medea
When Jason and Medea fled, King Aeëtes gave chase. Medea ordered her brother, Apsyrtus, to be cut up and thrown into the sea, so that Aeëtes would have to stop to pick up the pieces.

ROMAN GODS AND GODDESSES

The Romans adopted many of the gods of the Etruscans, the people who lived in northern Italy before them, and adapted them to Roman ideas and beliefs. These deities were eventually combined with aspects of gods from lands conquered by the Romans, particularly Greece. Many Roman deities are very similar to those of the ancient Greeks, but they usually have different names and sometimes different myths.

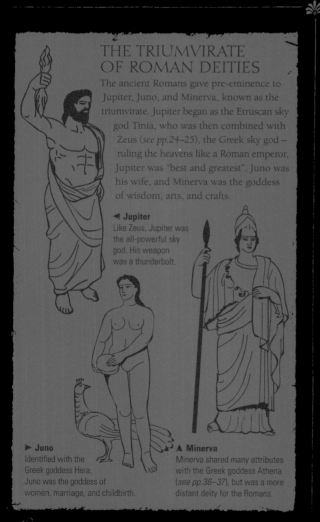

THE TRIUMVIRATE OF ROMAN DEITIES

The ancient Romans gave pre-eminence to Jupiter, Juno, and Minerva, known as the triumvirate. Jupiter began as the Etruscan sky god Tinia, who was then combined with Zeus (see pp.24–25), the Greek sky god – ruling the heavens like a Roman emperor, Jupiter was "best and greatest". Juno was his wife, and Minerva was the goddess of wisdom, arts, and crafts.

◄ **Jupiter**
Like Zeus, Jupiter was the all-powerful sky god. His weapon was a thunderbolt.

▶ **Juno**
Identified with the Greek goddess Hera, Juno was the goddess of women, marriage, and childbirth.

▲ **Minerva**
Minerva shared many attributes with the Greek goddess Athena (see pp.36–37), but was a more distant deity for the Romans.

ROMAN GODDESSES

The goddesses of the Roman pantheon differed greatly in their roles. The most widely worshipped was Vesta, goddess of the hearth, but all the goddesses had festivals and popular shrines. They were also all originally Italian goddesses to whom the Romans added attributes of Greek goddesses (see pp.40–41). Vesta was the counterpart of Hestia, Ceres was an old Earth goddess who became equated with Demeter, Diana was a goddess of light and the moon who became identified with Artemis, and Venus was linked with Aphrodite (see pp.38–39) as goddess of love.

▲ **Diana**
Much worshipped by women, Diana was a goddess of savage and wild places as well as children and childbirth.

▲ **Venus**
Worshipped mainly in the spring, Venus was, perhaps surprisingly, most dear to ordinary Roman soldiers who were about to set off on a military campaign.

▲ **Vesta**
The hearth goddess was revered by all Romans. By keeping their fireplaces clean and decorated at all times, they hoped that she would bring their home and family good fortune.

▲ **Ceres**
Associated with the Earth, growth, and the Underworld, Ceres was worshipped by some in Greek, stressing her link to Demeter.

ROMAN GODS

The Romans followed a similar pattern with their gods as with their goddesses, identifying the deities of their Italian predecessors with those of the Greeks. Occasionally, however, they imported a Greek god, such as Apollo (see pp.28–29), who had no Roman parallel. But they tried to make all these deities clearly Roman in character. For example, they portrayed them in Roman clothes or armour, and attributed to most of them a moral rectitude that was very different from the amoral deities of the Greeks.

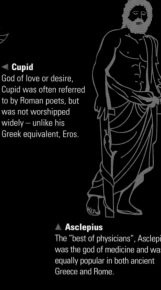

◀ Cupid
God of love or desire, Cupid was often referred to by Roman poets, but was not worshipped widely – unlike his Greek equivalent, Eros.

◀ Apollo
The Romans had no early equivalent to Apollo, and lifted this god of music, prophecy, cattle, and light straight from the Greek pantheon (see pp.28–29).

▲ Asclepius
The "best of physicians", Asclepius was the god of medicine and was equally popular in both ancient Greece and Rome.

▲ Bacchus
Counterpart of the Greek god Dionysus (see pp.34–35), the vine and honey god Bacchus was identified with Liber, the ancient Roman wine and fertility god.

◀ Mars
Long honoured in Italy as a god of war and farming, Mars was the most important Roman god after the triumvirate. He became identified with the Greek god of war Ares.

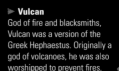

▶ Vulcan
God of fire and blacksmiths, Vulcan was a version of the Greek Hephaestus. Originally a god of volcanoes, he was also worshipped to prevent fires.

▲ Mercury
An ancient god of trade, exchange, and transport, Mercury took on many traits of the Greek heavenly messenger Hermes.

▲ Neptune
The Romans were not great seafarers; Neptune was originally a god of water and rivers that the Romans later linked to the Greek sea god Poseidon (see pp.30–31).

AENEAS AND THE ORIGINS OF ROME

A Trojan prince, Aeneas was the son of a mortal father, Anchises, and Venus, the goddess of love. He was a great hero and leader, whose escape from Troy and arrival in Rome was the result of prophecy, adventure, and divine intervention.

Although Aeneas did not actually found their city, the Romans saw him as the founder of their race. His remarkable life was celebrated in the epic poem, the *Aeneid,* by the great Roman poet Virgil (c.70–19 BCE).

THE MYTH

Aeneas had been told of two prophecies that would shape his life. The first said he would be the founder of a great dynasty, and the second, that he would destroy the city of Carthage in northern Africa. When the Trojan War (*see pp.60–61*) ended, he began a journey to fulfil his destiny. Aeneas took with him his father, Anchises, who had been wounded in battle, but he died on the journey. Crossing the Aegean Sea, Aeneas and his friends visited the land of the Cyclopes – the aggressive one-eyed giants – from whom they escaped and set sail again. The goddess Juno, rival of Venus, did not want Aeneas to reach his goal, so she ordered Aeolus, god of the winds, to raise up a storm and wreck his ship. The waves washed up Aeneas and his men on a shore near Carthage.

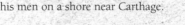
◀ Wounded hero
Aeneas fought bravely during the Trojan War and was wounded by the Greek hero Diomedes. After Hector died, Aeneas played a leading role in the Trojan forces.

the gods, reminded him of his destiny, Aeneas left Carthage and Elissa killed herself in despair.

Landing on the west coast of Italy, Aeneas found himself near Cumae, home of the Cumaean Sibyl, a prophetess who lived near the entrance to the Underworld. Aeneas visited the Underworld to see his father again, but while he was there, the Sibyl showed him a vision of the future of Rome. When he saw the vision, he was convinced that he should continue on his journey to establish the Roman race, so he went to Latium, the region on the banks of the River Tiber.

FROM CARTHAGE TO ITALY

Upon his arrival in Carthage, Aeneas was taken to the court of Queen Elissa and, due to the intervention of the goddess Venus, the two fell in love. But when Mercury, the messenger of

IN LATIUM

After arriving in Latium, Aeneas met the local king, Latinus, and the two agreed on a treaty that allowed Aeneas to marry the king's daughter, Lavinia. However, the princess was already betrothed to Turnus, the King of the Rutilians. An enraged Turnus declared war and the two sides fought for months. In the end, Aeneas killed Turnus and was able to unite the two states. From then on, the people of Latium, the Rutilians, and Aeneas's followers from Troy lived together peacefully and formed the race from which the Romans – including Romulus and Remus, the founders of the city of Rome itself – were descended.

◀ Aeneas and Anchises
Aeneas had to carry his wounded father on their journey, but Anchises died when they reached Sicily, where his son held lavish funeral games.

DIDO OF CARTHAGE

Later known as Dido, Elissa was married to Sichaeus, the King of Tyre. After his death, her brother took over the throne and she left the city. Eventually, she arrived on the North African coast, where she asked the local people for an area of land that could be bounded by a bull's hide. When they agreed, she cut a hide into thin strips, joined them together, and claimed a large area of land. She established the city of Carthage and ruled over it happily until Aeneas left her to go to Latium.

◀ Death of Elissa
When Aeneas left her, Elissa climbed on to a funeral pyre and stabbed herself to death. Her people gave her the name Dido, meaning "brave one".

▲ Aeneas's ship
A storm whipped up by Aeolus, god of the winds, blew Aeneas's ship to Carthage – the hero was under the influence of fate and the gods throughout his journey.

THE DESCENDANTS OF AENEAS

Aeneas played an important role in Roman mythology, not only because the Romans saw him as the founder of their race but also because, as the son of the goddess Venus, he enabled them to trace their lineage back to the gods. This link was immensely significant for the Romans, because it gave their ruler – in both Italy and their wider empire – a kind of legitimacy that put them on a level above the other rulers they had conquered or supplanted. In addition, certain influential Roman families, notably that of Emperor Julius Caesar (c.100–44 BCE), claimed a direct family link with Aeneas and with the gods.

➤ Julius Caesar
The Roman military leader and dictator, Caesar, a member of the family of Julius, claimed to be a descendant of Aeneas's son, Ascanius.

THE CUMAEAN SIBYL

The Sibyls were women who were skilled in prophecy. They often lived at places on the borders of the Earth and the Underworld, or where the worlds of the gods and humans came together. They used their proximity to the gods to predict the future. One of the most famous Sibyls lived at Cumae. She had been a stunningly beautiful young woman, with whom Apollo had fallen in love. He granted her a gift in return for her favours and she asked for immortality. But when she rebuffed Apollo, he condemned her to an eternal old age. When Aeneas came to consult her, she was a pathetic creature said to be about 700 years old.

▲ The Cumaean Sibyl
At the beginning of her prophetic career, the Sibyl of Cumae was a beautiful young woman who entranced both gods and mortals.

◀ Aeneas and the Sibyl
When Aeneas travelled to the Underworld from an entrance near Cumae, the Sibyl acted as his guide.

ROMULUS AND REMUS

The twins Romulus and Remus were the sons of a vestal virgin, the daughter of a usurped king of Alba Longa, who had broken her vows. Condemned to be drowned in the River Tiber, the brothers were found by a wolf that suckled them until a shepherd discovered and adopted them. When the twins grew up, they discovered their parentage and fought to restore Alba Longa to its rightful ruler. Later, they set out to found Rome, a new city on the banks of the Tiber.

She-wolf suckling Romulus and Remus

AENEAS AND THE ORIGINS OF ROME

79

SEE ALSO Journeys 34–35, 44–45, 64–67, 120–21, 220–21

Aeneas becomes a god
When Aeneas died, his mother, the goddess Venus, gained permission from Jupiter to make him a god – Jupiter Indiges – which she did by anointing his head with nectar and ambrosia.

GUARDIAN DEITIES

In addition to the great gods who were related to the Greek Olympians, there were a number of deities who were much closer to the Roman people. Many of these were worshipped at small shrines in people's houses. They were guardian spirits who looked after the members of the household in return for offerings made at the home altars. Some of these deities, such as the goddess Vesta, also had state shrines that the Romans maintained in the hope that they would look after the city and the empire.

THE CHASTE GODDESS

Vesta, the goddess of the domestic hearth and preserver of the flame of immortality, was the daughter of the primal god Saturn and Ops, the goddess of the harvest. Unlike her sisters, Juno and Ceres, Vesta did not want to marry and remained a virgin. Once, when she went to a feast held by the goddess Cybele, she fell asleep. Priapus, the god of fertility, saw her and was filled with desire. But as he approached her, a donkey belonging to the satyr Silenus brayed loudly in her ear. Vesta awoke at once and all the other guests came running to see what had made such a noise. Priapus was foiled and Vesta's honour was preserved. Hence, during the feast held in honour of Vesta, donkeys were crowned with flowers. According to some accounts, the objects sacred to the cult of Vesta were the hearth fire and pure water in a clay vase. Although the goddess Hestia (*see p.41*) is often considered to be the Greek counterpart of Vesta, the Romans accorded far more importance to the hearth goddess in their religion than the Greeks.

▲ **Silenus**
Snub-nosed and thick-lipped, Silenus often got so drunk that he could not even ride his donkey without falling off.

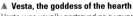

▲ **Vesta, the goddess of the hearth**
Vesta was usually portrayed as a young woman carrying a sceptre. A festival called the Vestalia was celebrated in her honour, during which her temple was opened for offering sacrifices.

THE TEMPLE OF VESTA

Since Vesta was the guardian of both the home and the state, the Roman people worshipped her by making sacrifices to her at home as well as by maintaining her temple. This was a circular building – its round shape may have been an imitation of prehistoric houses, conveying the idea that the temple had been there for many years. Inside, Vesta was represented by a fire, which symbolized both immortality and the well-being of Rome itself. It was never allowed to go out and was always tended by a group of priestesses called the vestal virgins.

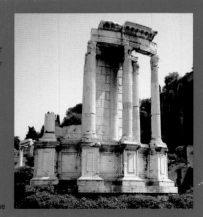

Vesta's temple in Rome

THE GENIUS

The Romans believed that every man was helped all through his life by a Genius, a kind of guardian angel who looked after his interests and took the form of a winged figure or a man holding a cornucopia (horn of plenty). Men made offerings to their Genius on their birthdays, and when they enjoyed good fortune, they offered wine, incense, or flowers. A man's Genius presided over his house and his marriage, ensuring his health and his ability to father children. Men, ancestors, households, specific places, and even the city of Rome itself were all said to possess their own Genius, but women were under the protection of Junones, who served the goddess Juno.

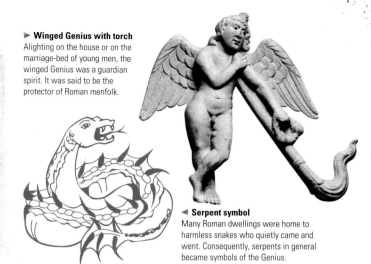

▶ Winged Genius with torch
Alighting on the house or on the marriage-bed of young men, the winged Genius was a guardian spirit. It was said to be the protector of Roman menfolk.

◀ Serpent symbol
Many Roman dwellings were home to harmless snakes who quietly came and went. Consequently, serpents in general became symbols of the Genius.

◀ Household shrine
The Lares were household gods who were worshipped at home shrines and at the hearth. They were often depicted as dancing youths with a horn cup and a bowl, and accompanied by symbolic serpents.

THE PENATES

Like the Lares, the Penates (also known as "the inner ones") were a pair of gods who protected Roman households. They were usually depicted as youths, and their statues were present in every Roman home. The name "Penates" has the same root as the word "penetralia", which means pantry, and hence they became gods of the table and the larder. When a Roman family sat down to a meal, the head of the household offered some of the food to the Penates before the family members themselves were served. It was said that the Penates were originally Trojan deities, and that Aeneas brought them to central Italy when he came to settle there (*see pp.78–79*). Eventually, they became the guardian deities of Rome.

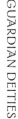

▶ God of the pantry
The Penates were the patron gods of the storeroom and the household. In some Roman homes, it was the custom to move their statues from the home shrine to the dining table when the family were about to eat.

THE LARES

The Romans worshipped several kinds of spirits called Lares on special days and major family occasions. Some of these were malevolent spirits who haunted crossroads and had to be pacified with offerings, while others were kinder rural spirits who brought good crops. Perhaps the most widely worshipped Lares were the benevolent twin gods who protected Roman households. They were the sons of Mania, the goddess of madness, and Mercury, the messenger of the gods, but they also had a close link with Diana, the goddess of the hunt. The Lares were said to borrow Diana's hounds and use them to chase away any thieves or criminals who might threaten any of the households where they were worshipped. Besides having statues of the Lares in the home, Romans also hung an image of Mania at their front doors to ward off evildoers.

◀ The Dioscuri
Pairs of deities were dear to the Romans. The divine twins Castor and Pollux, also known as the Dioscuri, were revered as protectors of soldiers and sailors.

SEE ALSO Virgin goddesses 36–37, 40–41, 86–87, 136–137 • Spirits of place 28–29, 30–31, 320–21

FERTILITY DEITIES

Ensuring a regular food supply for their huge population was of vital importance to the Romans. Hence, many of their deities were patrons of vineyard-keepers, shepherds, farmers, and others who produced food for the people. They included Lupercus, who protected herds and flocks from wolves, Ops, who was the goddess of the harvest, and Liber, who ruled over the vines and fields. Most of these deities had existed in Italy before the Romans built up their empire, and were later included in the Roman pantheon.

◄ Zephyrus and Flora
Although both helped the plants bloom, Flora was the more widely worshipped, and special games, the Floralia, were held in her honour.

► Spring flower
Flora's greatest gift to humankind, remembered especially in the spring, was the seeds of many different species of flowers.

FLORA

The goddess of springtime, flowers, and fertility, Flora is usually portrayed as an attractive young nymph carrying a bunch of flowers. At first she was shy and retiring, but Zephyrus, the west wind (also known as Favonius), caught sight of her and, enchanted by her beauty, blew in her direction. She ran from him in fright, but eventually he caught her and made love to her. The story ended well for Flora, however, because soon Zephyrus made her his wife and the pair lived happily together, combining their abilities to bring fertile soil and favourable weather so that the plants grew and the flowers bloomed.

SATURN

Saturn (the Roman version of the Greek god Cronus) was one of the founding deities of the Roman people. He had been a deity on Mount Olympus, but had quarrelled with Jupiter, who expelled him from the home of the gods. He hid in Italy, and the place where he settled became known as Latium, from the Latin word meaning "to hide". It was said that he built a village by the River Tiber, on the site where Rome was later to stand. Here, during the prosperous time known as the Golden Age (see pp.26–27), he showed the locals how best to cultivate the ground and how to grow vines and produce wine. The Romans worshipped him at a festival called Saturnalia, held in the month of December, when masters became servants and servants masters.

◄ Saturn with a sickle
Because he was a god of cultivation, Saturn was usually depicted carrying a scythe or a sickle. The barrel signifies his role as a grower of grapes for wine.

THE GREAT MOTHER

The Great Mother was also known as Bona Dea ("the good goddess"). She was variously identified with Ops, Fauna, and the nature goddess Cybele. Some say she was the mother of Faunus (*see right*), and was a modest, shy deity who had the gift of prophecy, but would tell her predictions only to women. It is believed that she began life as a mortal. She drank a lot of wine one day and got drunk. When Faunus saw the state she was in, he was enraged and killed her, after which she became an immortal and a special guardian of Rome. But in the form of Cybele she was more a goddess of sexuality.

Pomegranate   Tambourine   Amphora

◄ Cybele's attributes
Since Cybele was also the goddess of fertility, the pomegranate, the horn of plenty (cornucopia), and the amphora were her special attributes. The cymbals and the tambourine were played at the frenzied dances during her festival.

Horn of plenty   Cymbals

◄ Armed dance of the Corybantes
The worshippers of Cybele were known as the Corybantes. They used to dance ecstatically to music in her honour, sometimes slashing one another with their swords.

◄ Cybele
The nature goddess Cybele usually rode a chariot drawn by lions, which were symbolic of her complete dominion over the powerful forces of nature.

FAUNUS

Faunus was worshipped as the patron of agriculture and the protector of shepherds. One day he saw Hercules (the Greek hero Heracles) with his mistress, Omphale. Faunus fell passionately in love with Omphale and decided to follow the couple. When Hercules and Omphale took shelter for the night in a cave, Faunus crept in after them and, when all was still, slid in quietly beside Omphale. When he touched her he was astounded to feel a hairy chest and strong arms – the couple had swapped clothes for the night. Hercules pushed him from the bed and the pair burst out laughing.

◄ Hercules and Omphale
Omphale was a queen from Lydia who was deeply in love with Hercules.

► Faunus
After his encounter with Hercules and Omphale, Faunus preferred his devotees to worship him naked.

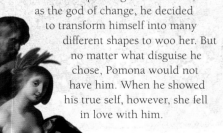

POMONA AND VERTUMNUS

Pomona, a beautiful nymph who was also a skilled gardener, was the goddess of fruit trees. Vertumnus was a deity who presided over all kinds of change, including the turning seasons and the transformation from blossom to fruit. Vertumnus was attracted to Pomona when he saw her pruning her trees and, as the god of change, he decided to transform himself into many different shapes to woo her. But no matter what disguise he chose, Pomona would not have him. When he showed his true self, however, she fell in love with him.

◄ Guardians of the fruit
After their union, Pomona and Vertumnus nurtured the trees together, thus ensuring a bountiful harvest of fruit.

FERTILITY DEITIES

85

SEE ALSO Fertility deities 40–41, 114–15, 158–59, 214–15, 244–45, 308–09, 310–11

PAN AND SYRINX

God of shepherds and their flocks, Pan was best known both for his voracious sexual appetite and for his ability to make people suddenly and bewilderingly afraid – literally, to inspire "panic". He often hid in bushes to spy on groups of nymphs, and sometimes he chased them when they refused to give in to his advances. One object of his desire was the nymph Syrinx. As well as being beautiful, Syrinx was fleet of foot, but Pan pursued her to the banks of a river, where he caught up with her. To escape his clutches, Syrinx called on the goddess of the river to turn her into a clump of reeds. From their hollow stems Pan made the first pan pipes, which became the instrument of shepherds.

1. Lustful god
Pan is usually shown as part human, part animal, with the legs and lower body – and sometimes the horns and ears – of a goat, and the head and upper body of a man. Here, the French painter François Boucher (1703–70) depicts him wearing a wreath of fir. This alludes to one of Pan's lovers, Pitys, who was changed into a fir tree when she fled from him. Although many rejected Pan's rough advances, he claimed to have slept with all of Dionysus's devoted female followers, the Maenads (*see p.35*).

2. God of desire
Eros, the god of desire, is often present in depictions of scenes from ancient Greek mythology, piercing his victims with his arrows of desire. His wings enabled him to fly swiftly, so he was able to keep pace with Pan whenever the god of shepherds chased a nymph. Here, Eros holds an arrow in one hand, while in the other he carries a flaming torch, to symbolize the burning desire that he has inspired in Pan for Syrinx.

3. Arcadian nymph
A nymph who lived in the beautiful land of Arcadia, Syrinx was said to be a follower of the virgin goddess Artemis, and therefore committed to remaining chaste. When Pan pursued her she ran from Mount Lycaeum to the River Ladon. In some accounts, Syrinx is said to be a child of the river, to which she came for protection.

4. River goddess
When she reached the river, Syrinx was terrified both of Pan and of the ire Artemis would show if she gave in to him. She called for help, and the goddess of the river answered. Here, the goddess – reclining on a jar, from which water flows like a river – embraces Syrinx protectively and is on the point of turning her into reeds.

François Boucher, *Pan and Syrinx*, 1759

SEE ALSO River deities 208–09, 244–45, 300–01, 308–09 • Virgin goddesses 36–37, 40–41, 82–83

PAN AND SYRINX

▲ **Thor fighting the serpent Nidhogg**
In Norse mythology, serpents are the enemies of deities and heroes.
Here, one of the most notorious, Nidhogg, rises from the ocean but
is attacked by the great god Thor, who wields his famous hammer.

NORTHERN EUROPE

The early cultures of far Northern Europe produced a fascinating body of myths about the creation of the cosmos and the lives and adventures of their deities. The influence of these great stories eventually spread far and wide.

Between the late 8th and early 11th centuries, the Viking raiders of Denmark, Norway, and Sweden became famous for their ruthless attacks on the coastal communities of Western Europe and for their daring voyages of exploration in ocean-going longships. Although these Norsemen developed writing that used angular symbols called runes, they did not at first produce a great written literature. However, they did have a rich oral tradition, which produced some of the most enthralling stories in all world mythology.

NORSE DEITIES AND HEROES
The great Norse myths deal with the great themes: the creation of the cosmos, the wars and loves of the deities, and the coming of the end of the world. They imagine different races of mythical beings – from giants to dwarfs – who live in different worlds that are parallel to our own home world, which is known as Midgard. The culture of the deities is warlike and heroic, and the real and mythical worlds meet at Valhalla, the great hall of the leading deity Odin, where the souls of deceased human heroes find their heavenly reward.

The stories of the Norse deities were mainly passed on by word of mouth. Some myths were written down by monks in monasteries as early as the 8th century, but most were first recorded in the 13th century. By this time, Norse travellers had even colonized Iceland, and it was

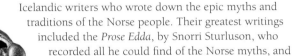
▲ **Early Viking pendant**
This small silver pendant represents the head of either a Viking hero or one of the Norse gods. The figure wears an elaborate crested helmet.

Icelandic writers who wrote down the epic myths and traditions of the Norse people. Their greatest writings included the *Prose Edda*, by Snorri Sturluson, who recorded all he could find of the Norse myths, and the *Poetic Edda*, written by an unknown hand, which adds further tales to the canon. Other Icelandic writers wrote prose sagas – texts that tell the stories of prominent Norse families and are a mixture of mythology and history.

GREAT INFLUENCE
Norse myths and culture proved influential for centuries. The Anglo-Saxons, who came from mainland Europe and settled in England in the 5th century, told stories that were derived from Scandinavia and sometimes even set there. The best-known example is the great Anglo-Saxon poem *Beowulf*, a tale of fantastic heroism and monster slaying set among the Danes and the Geats; the latter were probably the people of Sweden. In the Middle Ages, Norse myths also spread south to Germany, where stories of heroes such as Siegfried, a character who was based on the Norse hero Sigurd, influenced a great many poets and dramatists.

OTHER TRADITIONS
Meanwhile, other parts of Northern Europe had quite separate traditions of myth and legend. One of the richest came from Finland. Here, a large body of complex myths about the creation of the universe and the adventures of the early gods was handed down from generation to generation by word of mouth. Only in the 19th century did the Finnish scholar Elias Lönnrot write the stories down and combine them into a single, vast poetic epic called the *Kalevala*. This masterwork of storytelling became a symbol of Finland's national identity and has since been translated into many different languages, finally bringing the myths and legends of this small country to a worldwide audience.

▶ **Viking longship**
Short of good land to farm at home in Scandinavia, the Vikings travelled widely to find new territory in swift, streamlined longships. These well-built craft were known as "dragon-boats" because of their curving, dragon-like carved prows.

NORSE ORIGINS

Like all creation myths, Norse stories about the origin of the world attempt to explain natural phenomena. The earliest surviving accounts of Norse myths come from Icelandic writers. They set their creation story in a land where ice and fire come together as they do among the glaciers and steaming volcanoes of Iceland. To the north is the land of ice and snow, and to the south is a world of seething fire and flames. Life, in the form of the first giants, emerges from the interaction of these two opposing forces.

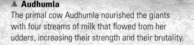

▲ **Audhumla**
The primal cow Audhumla nourished the giants with four streams of milk that flowed from her udders, increasing their strength and their brutality.

THE MYTH

In the beginning there was nothing but a vast void called Ginnungagap. Gradually, two realms appeared on either side of this void. Muspelheim, a region of heat and fire, formed in the south; Niflheim, a place of cold and ice, came into being in the north. In the centre, between these two places, the hot air of Muspelheim met the cold air of Niflheim and the ice started to melt. Slowly the dripping ice formed the shape of a huge and monstrous being, a frost giant called Ymir.

THE GIANTS AND AUDHUMLA

Ymir slept and as the warm air from Muspelheim played across his body, he started to sweat. From his sweat other frost giants emerged – one male and one female from under his left arm, and another six-headed male from his legs. Meanwhile, the ice continued to melt into the shape of a huge cow called Audhumla, and her milk fed the first frost giants. Audhumla licked the ice and drank the water as it melted. As she licked away, a giant's head appeared, followed by his body, and after three days another giant was freed from the ice. So now there was a small group of frost giants who settled down in Niflheim. Buri, the first giant whom Audhumla had freed from the ice, had

▲ **Ash trees**
The first man and woman – Ask and Embla – were said to have been created from an ash and an elm tree.

a son named Bor, who married Bestla, daughter of a giant named Bolthorn. The couple had a trio of children named Odin, Vili, and Ve, who became the first three of the Norse gods, with Odin as their leader.

THE CREATION OF THE WORLD

The three gods were always battling Ymir, who frequently attacked them. Finally they got together and killed him. A flood of blood from Ymir's veins drowned all the frost giants except for Bergelmir (Ymir's grandson) and his wife, who escaped in a boat made from a tree trunk and settled in a place called Jotunheim. The three gods then made the Earth from Ymir's flesh, turning his unbroken bones into mountains. His blood became the rivers, lakes, and sea, and his skull the great dome of the sky. They threw sparks from Muspelheim high into the air to form the sun, the moon, and the stars. The gods then created the first man, called Ask, from an ash tree, and the first woman, called Embla, from an elm tree.

THE CREATORS

Odin, Vili, and Ve, the creator deities of Norse mythology, were the first of the Aesir, or sky gods. They lived in a fortress called Asgard at the highest point in the cosmos. Together they fought a long war with another group of gods, the Earth or fertility deities known as the Vanir, who were led by the sea god Njörd and his two children, Freyr and Freyja. The war was a stalemate, and the two sides agreed to a truce with the exchange of hostages. The Aesir sent two of their gods, the dull Hoenir and the wise Mimir, as hostages from their side. Unhappy with this exchange, the Vanir beheaded Mimir, and sent his head to the Aesir. Odin, who was always in search of wisdom, preserved the head and recited charms over it, and it advised him henceforth.

> ## ODIN WAS THE CLEVEREST OF ALL ALL OTHERS LEARNED FROM HIM.
>
> Snorri Sturluson, *Ynglinga Saga*, c.1225

◄ The Aesir
Of the three leaders of the Aesir, Odin (meaning "frenzy"), a shape-changer who possessed superhuman strength in battle, is the most prominent in myths. By contrast, Vili (meaning "will") and Ve (meaning "sacred enclosure") are more shadowy figures who accompany Odin on his adventures.

▲ Sleipnir
Odin rode a grey, eight-legged horse called Sleipnir. The creature was known as the best and fastest of steeds, giving Odin a great advantage in battle.

▼ Norse spear
The spear was one of the weapons commonly used by Norse warriors. Odin had a spear called Gungnir, which never missed its target.

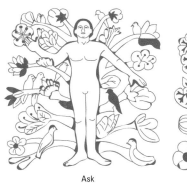

Ask

Embla

ASK AND EMBLA

Most creation myths narrate the origin of a primal couple from whom the human race is descended. According to Norse mythology, Odin, Vili, and Ve were walking along a beach when they came upon two trees. They created Ask from the ash tree and Embla from the elm tree. Then each of the gods gave them a gift. Odin breathed life into them, Vili gave them thoughts and feelings, and Ve provided them with sight and hearing. The pair became the ancestors of all humans. They lived in Midgard (Middle Earth), the home created for them by the gods. It was protected by fortifications constructed from the eyebrows of Ymir.

RUNES

Early Norse writers used letters called runes, made up of vertical and diagonal strokes, to carve inscriptions in stone. Odin is said to have created the runic alphabet. Impaled on his own spear, he hung from Yggdrasil, the world tree, for nine days until the runes appeared before him. Runes were believed to have magical powers. Some of these rune stones combined runic inscriptions with mythological images. The one below shows Odin with the Goth king, Ermaneric, among whose family the god made trouble, leading to the death of Ermaneric's son.

Rune stone

SEE ALSO European creation stories 16–17, 100–03 • Trees 92–93, 124–25, 340–41

THE NORSE COSMOS

The ancient Norse myths imagined the cosmos as a series of separate regions or worlds, each the home of a different race of beings, from giants to dwarfs. These various worlds were supported by the roots and branches of a vast ash tree called Yggdrasil, also known as the world tree. Though the precise details of these worlds differed from one account to another, Yggdrasil remained a constant feature.

THE MYTH

The world tree Yggdrasil supported the entire cosmos, from the deepest regions of the Underworld to the highest heaven. Writers did not agree on precisely how the tree supported the various parts of the Norse cosmos, but all were sure that the tree formed a supporting backbone for the universe.

AT THE ROOTS

There were three enormous roots at the base of Yggdrasil. Some say that one root supported Asgard, the home of the Aesir or principal gods and goddesses. In other versions of the myth, Asgard was seen as a dwelling in the air, held up by some of the tree's branches and linked to the other worlds by a bridge called Bifröst, which took the form of a rainbow. The tree's second root supported Jotunheim, the icy home of the frost giants. Nearby was buried the severed head of the god of wisdom Mimir, and the well of Mimir, with its waters that carried knowledge and wisdom. The third root extended to another cold region called Niflheim, one of the places that existed before the world was formed (*see p.90*). In this region the only source of heat was from a hot spring called Hvergelmir, which bubbled up from

The Norse universe
The branches of Yggdrasil embraced the whole universe. The serpent Nidhogg dwelled at the roots.

the ground. Nearby was the dwelling of Hel, the queen of the Underworld, where evildoers were believed to end their days.

IN THE BRANCHES

At the very heart of Yggdrasil was Midgard, the world of humans. It was held to be at the centre of the cosmos and some accounts said that it was linked to Asgard by the bridge Bifröst. Only the gods and the souls of deceased heroes on their way to Valhalla, Odin's dwelling in Asgard, were allowed to use the bridge, which was guarded by the god Heimdall. Other worlds supported by Yggdrasil's branches included Svartelfheim, the home of the dark elves, and Gimle, the home of the light elves.

VARYING ACCOUNTS

Some accounts of the Norse cosmos give different locations for these worlds. According to one version, Jotunheim lay to the east of Midgard, separated from the human world by rivers and forests. Gimle was seen in some accounts as a shining hall, set high in the sky. When the Norse writers began to be influenced by Christian culture in the Middle Ages, Gimle was seen as a sort of heaven, and the light elves also took on some of the qualities of Christian angels.

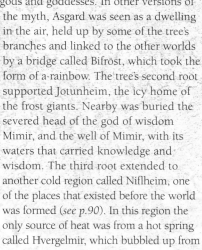

Yggdrasil
Animal imagery lies at the heart of the myth of Yggdrasil. Many creatures lived among the tree's leaves and branches and an eagle perched upon the highest bough.

▲ Ratatosk
The squirrel Ratatosk carried insulting messages from the serpent who lived at the base of the tree to the eagle who dwelled in the upper branches.

THE CREATURES OF YGGDRASIL

The name Yggdrasil means "the horse of Ygg [or Odin]". In the lyrical language of the Norse poets, Odin "rode" the tree when he hung himself from it and acquired the wisdom of the runes (see p.91). The tree was also home to a number of animals. An eagle and a hawk dwelled in its uppermost branches, while at the base lived many snakes, who were led by a large serpent or dragon. In between lived a squirrel and a quartet of stags. The squirrel ran up and down the tree, taking spiteful messages from the serpent below to the eagle at the top, thus continuing the hostility between the two creatures. The stags were natural tree-pruners, eating the shoots and leaves of Yggdrasil.

▼ The stag Dáin
There were four stags living in the tree. Some writers name them as Dáin, Dvalin, Dúneyr, and Durathrór.

▲ Eagle and hawk
The eagle lived at the top of the tree and between his eyes sat a hawk called Vedrfölnir. The eagle's flapping wings made the winds.

➤ The serpent
The dragon or serpent Nidhogg lived among the roots. Some accounts say he was accompanied by many other snakes in this mysterious underground world.

BIFRÖST

The worlds of gods and humans were connected by a rainbow bridge that glimmered in the sky above Midgard. This bridge was given the name of Bifröst by the Icelandic writer Snorri Sturluson. The name is derived from a verb meaning "to shimmer". At the end of the world, the warriors of Muspell, the fiery world of the south, will cross the bridge to wage war on the gods of Asgard while Heimdall blows his horn to summon the gods for the last battle (see pp.98–99).

◀ Heimdall
The watchman of Asgard, Heimdall stood guard at the upper end of Bifröst.

THE REALM OF NIDHOGG

The realm of the serpent or dragon Nidhogg was at the foot of Yggdrasil. This was an ambiguous place, full of both dangers and special gifts. The principal gift among these was wisdom, which flowed from Mimir's well, one of the three wells that lay at the foot of the tree. The other two wells were more dangerous: one was the well of fate, which was guarded by the Norns, who controlled the span of human life; the other was a well of poison, which was the source of the rivers of Hel, the Norse Underworld. Around these dark regions slithered Nidhogg. He feasted on the flesh of human corpses and gnawed at the roots of Yggdrasil.

➤ The world serpent
Nidhogg coiled around the roots of Yggdrasil and continually nibbled away at them, hoping to destroy the tree, but was eternally frustrated in his desire.

THERE NIDHOGG SUCKS THE CORPSES OF THE DEAD, DO YOU STILL SEEK TO KNOW?

Anon, *Völuspá*

93

SEE ALSO Trees 90–91, 124–25, 340–41 • Snakes & serpents 28–29, 48–49, 98–99, 100–03, 160–61, 238–39, 328–29

THE NORSE GODS

The principal Norse gods were descended from the race of giants who were the first inhabitants of the universe (*see pp.90–91*). The oldest and most powerful of the Norse deities was Odin, and many of the other gods – such as the thunder god Thor, and Balder, god of beauty and light – were his descendants. Several other gods and goddesses, including the shape-changing god Loki, descended from the giants, via a separate line. Another branch, not connected to the main tree, included a number of fertility deities, such as the weather god Freyr and his sister, Freyja, goddess of love.

AUDHUMLA

BURI

BOR — BESTLA

VILI   VE   FRIGG   ODIN

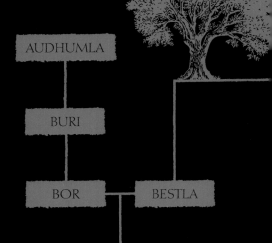

Frigg

Odin

NJORD — SKADI

BALDER — NANNA   HOD

FORSETI

Freyr

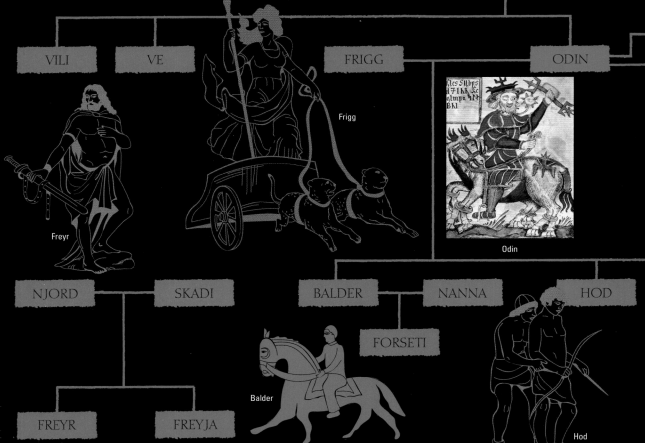

Balder

Hod

FREYR   FREYJA

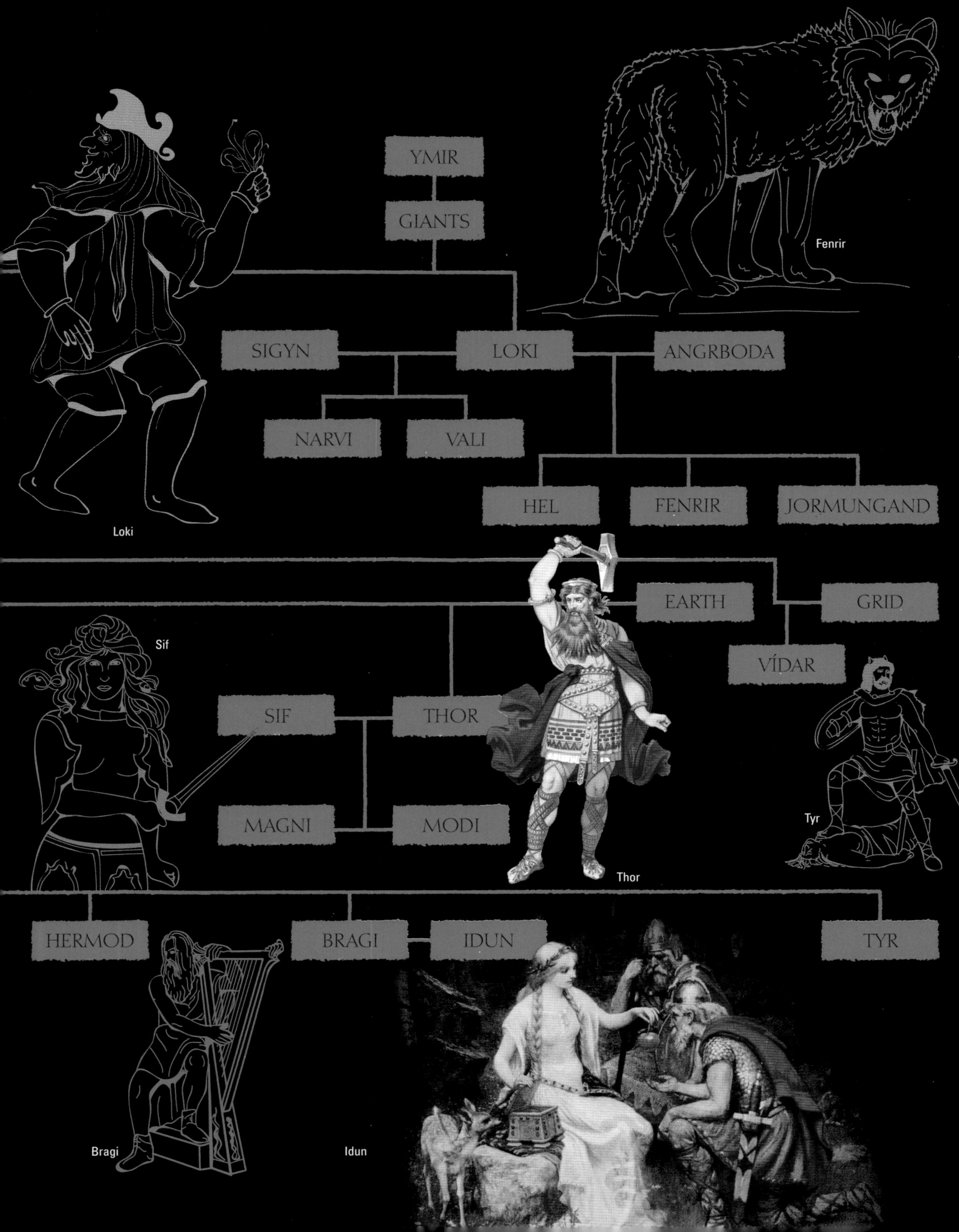

Fenrir

YMIR

GIANTS

Loki

SIGYN — LOKI — ANGRBODA

NARVI — VALI

HEL — FENRIR — JORMUNGAND

EARTH — GRID

VÍDAR

Sif

SIF — THOR

MAGNI — MODI

Thor

Tyr

HERMOD

BRAGI — IDUN

TYR

Bragi

Idun

LOKI

Loki was the trickster of the Norse pantheon and the husband of the goddess Sigyn. He represented disorder, mischief-making, and irrationality, and always stood in the way of those who wanted to bring order and calm to the universe. Some said he interfered in the lives of humans too, and he was often blamed for giving ordinary people the desires and passions that caused problems in their lives. A shape-changer with an insatiable sexual appetite, his tricks ranged from simple pranks to cold-blooded murders.

THE TRICKS OF LOKI

A blood brother of Odin, Loki had three wives who bore him many children, but this was not enough for him. So he used his power of shape-changing to have affairs with goddesses, giants, humans, and animals. Loki also had a rapacious appetite for food, and even killed a dwarf called Otr for the salmon that he had caught. However, he occasionally used his trickery to help the gods. For instance, he hatched a plot to retrieve Thor's hammer, which had been stolen by the giant Thrym. The giant was willing to return the hammer only if the gods let him marry the goddess Freyja. So Loki suggested that Thor disguise himself as Freyja and go to the wedding dressed as a bride. Before the ceremony, Thrym brought out the hammer and Thor snatched it from him.

◀ **The shape-changer**
Although he is usually portrayed in human form, Loki's many disguises included a flea, a fly, a salmon, and a seal. To disguise himself as a bird, he stole Freyja's cloak of feathers.

▲ **Loki and Sif**
When Loki cut off the golden hair of the corn goddess Sif, the crops would not ripen. Sif's husband, Thor, threatened to kill Loki as a result.

▲ **Skilled Norse dwarfs**
Norse dwarfs were skilled craftsmen. When Thor threatened Loki for cutting Sif's hair, the trickster persuaded a dwarf to make new hair for the goddess.

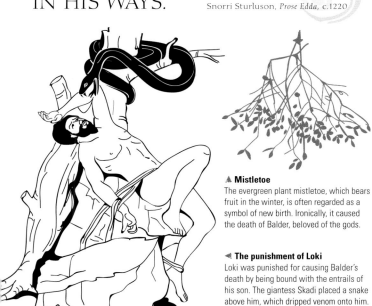

Balder's murder
Höd was pleased when Loki helped him aim the dart made of mistletoe, but devastated when he learned that he had killed Balder, his brother.

THE DEATH OF BALDER

Balder was the son of Odin and Frigg, and the most handsome of all the gods. One night he had a dream that he would die. When Frigg found out about it, she made every living thing – animals, trees, and plants – promise not to harm her son. But while doing this, the goddess forgot to ask one plant, the mistletoe. Assuming that Balder was invincible, the gods often used him as a target for knife-throwing and archery. One day, they were hurling around all kinds of objects, such as rocks and branches. Loki had craftily learned from Frigg the secret that Balder was not immune to the mistletoe. He sharpened a twig of mistletoe to make a dart, placed it in the hand of the blind god Höd and helped Höd aim it at Balder. The dart pierced Balder's heart and killed him.

HANDSOME IN APPEARANCE, WICKED IN CHARACTER, AND VERY CHANGEABLE IN HIS WAYS.

Snorri Sturluson, *Prose Edda*, c.1220

Mistletoe
The evergreen plant mistletoe, which bears fruit in the winter, is often regarded as a symbol of new birth. Ironically, it caused the death of Balder, beloved of the gods.

The punishment of Loki
Loki was punished for causing Balder's death by being bound with the entrails of his son. The giantess Skadi placed a snake above him, which dripped venom onto him.

TRICKSTERS FROM OTHER CULTURES

Most mythologies have a trickster figure, a god who likes to play pranks on other deities or cause widespread chaos. These figures often have a large appetite for sex, food, and mischief. Such tricksters are usually a source of great amusement, but their pranks, like many of Loki's, can also have serious consequences. Some tricksters are also heroes, and carry out brave deeds, like the Hindu god Hanuman (*see p.202*). They may also be culture heroes, figures who bring the skills of civilization – such as fire-making, cooking, and medicine – to the human race.

Enki
The creator god of Mesopotamia was also a trickster with an insatiable sexual appetite that even extended to his own daughter and granddaughter.

Hanuman
The son of the Hindu wind god Vayu, Hanuman once tried to swallow the sun. A trickster in his youth, he later became a staunch devotee of Lord Rama (*see pp.200–03*).

Ananse
This West African spider god (*see pp.252–53*) was credited with teaching humans such skills as fire-making, but he was also an incorrigible trickster.

Coyote
Appearing in many North American myths, Coyote loved making mischief and once blew out the light of the moon.

LOKI

97

SEE ALSO Tricksters 60–61, 100–03, 252–53, 272–73, 286–87, 288–89, 310–11, 340–41

THE LAST BATTLE

The story of the last battle in Norse mythology is different from the other Norse myths because it is a prophecy of an event that has not yet occurred. Known as Ragnarök, or the twilight of the gods, it is a great battle in which almost everything will be destroyed and the world will come to an end. When Ragnarök is over, the few living things that survive will begin a new world, and the cycle of creation will start again.

THE MYTH

The root cause of the last battle is the malevolence of Loki, who was imprisoned after he had brought about the death of the god Balder (*see p.97*). A serpent dripped poison onto his face until Loki's wife, Sigyn, feeling sorry for him, placed a dish below the serpent's mouth to catch the venom. Meanwhile on Earth, everything began to turn to evil because Balder, the great source of good and beauty in the world, was no longer alive. This was the beginning of the end, and the forerunner of Ragnarök.

THE DESTRUCTION OF THE WORLD

One day, Loki will finally break free from his chains. Along with many other deadly beings, he will challenge the gods and fight them. He will be joined by his monster-children, including the wolf Fenrir, the world serpent Jörmungand, and Hel, the goddess of the Underworld. Hel will bring an army of monsters from the Underworld, and frost giants and fire giants will join the assault too. Soon giants, dwarfs,

gods, humans, monsters, and virtually every living being will be drawn into the battle.

The fighting will be vicious and there will be no victor. Both good and evil will be destroyed. Finally, all that will remain of the population of the universe will be a great mountain of corpses. The only creatures that manage to survive will be the fire giant Surt, together with a couple of humans and a few animals who have managed to hide among the branches of the world tree, Yggdrasil. Surt will make a vast bonfire of the dead bodies, ensuring that there are no other survivors among the dead, and ridding the universe for good of monsters and races such as demons and elves. The fire of destruction will blaze for many years and the Earth will sink into the sea.

A NEW BEGINNING

Finally the Earth will rise again, and become lush and green once more. A human couple, a man called Lif (life) and a woman called Lifthrasir (longing for life), will step forward from among the branches of Yggdrasil. The pair will start a new family to begin the work of repopulating the Earth. The beautiful god Balder, who has been languishing in the Underworld, will be resurrected along with his blind brother, Höd (*see p.97*). Balder will become the ruler of the new universe. Life will begin afresh, without the taint of evil.

▶ **Viking warrior**
Also known as the Vikings, the Norse were a warlike race, so it is unsurprising that they envisaged the end of the world as a great battle.

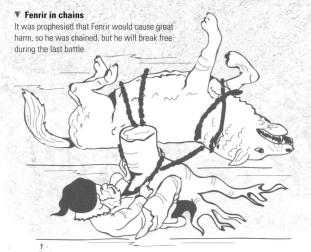

▼ **Fenrir in chains**
It was prophesied that Fenrir would cause great harm, so he was chained, but he will break free during the last battle.

VALHALLA

Meaning the hall of the slain, Valhalla was Odin's great hall. This was where Odin gathered together the Norse warriors who had been killed in battles on Earth, and rewarded them with lavish jewellery and weapons. In this hall, which was lined with armour, the heroes feasted on boar's flesh and drank mead served by the Valkyries. Here, the warriors also trained and prepared for Ragnarök.

Viking brooch

➤ Valkyrie
The Valkyries were female deities who served mead in drinking cups to Odin and his warriors during banquets.

RAGNARÖK AND THE APOCALYPSE

Ragnarök was described by the early Icelandic writers as a battle that will bring about the end of the cosmos. Scholars have seen many parallels with the Apocalypse as portrayed by Christian writers. Ragnarök will be preceded by a three-year winter, when men will kill their relatives, wolves will swallow the moon, forests will be felled, great storms will rage, and the chaos that existed before creation will return. After Ragnarök, life will begin again. Such themes also exist in the Bible and may have influenced Norse writers in their accounts.

▲ Symbol of rebirth
The egg often represents the resurrection that follows total annihilation in many myths.

▲ Horsemen of the Apocalypse
In the Christian Apocalypse, good and evil fight a cosmic battle. The four horsemen who ride into battle are believed to represent pestilence, war, famine, and death.

BRINGERS OF DOOM

There are several figures associated with the terrible events of Ragnarök, including Jörmungand and Hel. Both good and evil characters will perish in this battle. As prophesied, the wolf Fenrir will eat Odin, before being killed in turn by Odin's son, Vida. Some of the gods will also fight to settle old scores. Heimdall, the messenger of the gods, will do battle with Loki. Heimdall had once thwarted Loki's attempt to steal Freyja's necklace. At Ragnarök, the two gods will fight to the death.

➤ Jörmungand
One of the key combats of Ragnarök will be between Thor, the mighty god of thunder, and Jörmungand, the Midgard Serpent. In the end, both will perish.

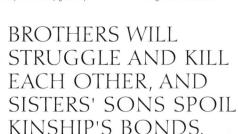

▲ Surt
The fire giant Surt will lead his army from the hot realm of Muspell. They will kill many gods and Surt himself will slay the fertility god Freyr.

▲ The ruler of the Underworld
Another of Loki's monstrous offsprings, Hel is supposed to arrive with an army of monsters to fight the final battle.

> # BROTHERS WILL STRUGGLE AND KILL EACH OTHER, AND SISTERS' SONS SPOIL KINSHIP'S BONDS.
>
> Anon, *Völuspá*

SEE ALSO Wars 18–19, 60–61, 104–05, 116–17, 118–19, 126–27, 170–71, 176–77, 206–07

KALEVALA

The *Kalevala*, an epic poem, is based on the traditional oral poetry of eastern Finland and is the national epic of the country. It tells of the creation of the world, and about rivalries between the country of the Finnish people (Kalevala) and the Northland (Pohjola). It also describes how three Finnish heroes – Väinämöinen, Ilmarinen, and Lemminkäinen – woo the princess of the Northland.

THE MYTH

The story begins with Ilma, the air, who existed before time began. She had a daughter called Luonnotar, who wandered ceaselessly through the clouds made by her mother. After many years she fell, exhausted, into the ocean.

VÄINÄMÖINEN AND THE GIANT

Luonnotar floated in the water for 700 years. Without her knowledge, the lapping water made her pregnant; but her pregnancy was so prolonged that her child, Väinämöinen, had already become an old man while still in her womb. After his birth, Väinämöinen swam across the waters until he reached the land that was to become Finland. He had started to make a home for himself there when he was challenged by a giant named Joukahainen. At first the two quarrelled violently, but Väinämöinen, who was a skilled musician, defeated the giant in a musical contest and won the hand of Aino, Joukahainen's sister, in marriage. However, Aino did not want to marry an old man, and thus chose to drown herself rather than submit to this alliance. So Väinämöinen decided to go to Pohjola, the Northland, to find himself a wife.

▶ **Väinämöinen**
The central character of the *Kalevala* is an unusual hero, an old man who possesses sheer determination and an outstanding musical gift.

IMPOSSIBLE TASKS

The journey to Northland was long and arduous, but finally Väinämöinen reached Pohjola and met its ruler, Louhi. She promised Väinämöinen that he would be allowed to marry her daughter if he could make a sampo, a magical mill that could produce salt, flour, and gold. Väinämöinen agreed to try, in spite of the fact that such a machine had never been made. He returned to Finland to make the sampo, but on the way he met Louhi's daughter, the Maid of the North, and asked her to marry him without the sampo. She agreed – provided that he accomplished a few more apparently impossible tasks, including peeling a stone, knotting an egg, splitting a hair with a blunt knife, and making a boat out of a weaving shuttle.

Väinämöinen was distracted from these tasks by spirits sent by Louhi, and so he asked his brother, Ilmarinen, who was a master craftsman, to make the sampo for him. After a lot of hard work, Ilmarinen managed to forge the sampo. He was then asked to perform some more tasks, including ploughing a field full of vipers. When he succeeded, he was allowed to marry Louhi's daughter. Väinämöinen had forgotten that it was the maker of the sampo who would win the hand of the Maid of the North, so he was disappointed in love once more. ▶▶

▶ **Louhi**
With magical powers, including the ability to fly, Louhi, the ruler of the Northland, made a formidable figure. She would have been even more powerful if she had kept hold of the sampo.

KEY CHARACTERS

The *Kalevala* is a collection of many Finnish legends with several characters. Among these, Väinämöinen is present throughout, and at the end he leaves behind the kantele, his musical instrument, as a symbol of continuing Finnish culture. His brother, Ilmarinen, is a blacksmith-sorcerer. Lemminkäinen is the poem's trickster figure. His many sexual encounters in his quest for a wife are typical of tricksters in myth. But he is also brave enough to visit the Underworld to kill the Swan of Tuonela in a bid to win Louhi's daughter.

▶ Ilmarinen
One of Ilmarinen's tasks is to plough a field of serpents. The Maid of the North helps him in this task by telling him to forge a special plough and use his magic to subdue the serpents.

SLOWLY WAKES THE SON AND HERO, RISES FROM THE DEPTHS OF SLUMBER, SPEAKS AGAIN IN MAGIC ACCENTS.

Elias Lönnrot, *Kalevala*, c.1849

▶ Lemminkäinen
When Lemminkäinen is killed on his perilous visit to the Underworld, his mother is able to reassemble his body, then give him back the breath of life.

THE FINNISH CREATION STORY

While Luonnotar was floating in the ocean, a duck swam by and laid her eggs on Luonnotar's knee, which was sticking out of the water. Then the bird settled down to hatch them. When Luonnotar moved, the duck was frightened and flew off. The eggs rolled away and broke, and from them the world was created. One half of the shells fused together to make up the sky and from the other half the land was created. The yolk was transformed into the sun and the albumen became the moon.

Primal duck

◀ Luonnotar
The myth's creator figure is passive, and the creation from the duck's eggs happens by accident. Some versions claim that it was an eagle that laid its eggs on her knee.

ELIAS LÖNNROT

The compiler of the *Kalevala* was Elias Lönnrot (1802–84), a Finnish doctor who collected the folk poetry, proverbs, and traditional stories of his people. He combined some of these into an epic poem about Väinämöinen and his fellow characters. By promoting the use of Finnish at a time when Finland was still part of Russia, Lönnrot did a great deal to foster a sense of national identity for his country.

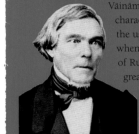

Elias Lönnrot

THE SAMPO

Described as a mill that would produce salt, flour, and gold, the sampo was a strange object made from many bizarre components. It was finally forged by Ilmarinen after his initial attempts produced a crossbow, a boat, a heifer, and a plough, which he threw back into the fire. The sampo has two symbolic qualities: it is the bride price of Louhi's daughter, and it also represents the wealth of the Finnish people.

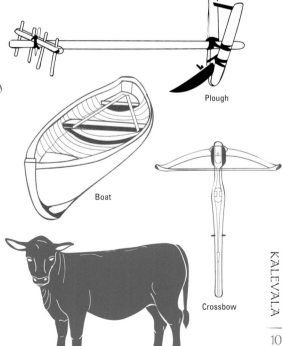

Plough

Boat

Crossbow

Heifer

RECLAIMING THE SAMPO

Ilmarinen and Louhi's daughter did not stay together for long. The Maid of the North was killed soon after the marriage because she had ill-treated a magician called Kullervo (*see opposite*). Ilmarinen wanted to marry Louhi's other daughter, but Louhi refused. So Ilmarinen returned to Finland and the people of Northland kept the sampo.

Väinämöinen and Ilmarinen thought it was unfair that Louhi and her people had kept the sampo and the riches it provided. They decided that if they could not find a wife in Northland, at least they could ensure prosperity for their homeland by stealing the sampo back. So the two brothers set sail for the North, taking with them Lemminkäinen, the adventurer and trickster. Lemminkäinen had once gone to Pohjola to woo one of Louhi's daughters, and there he had been given some tasks to accomplish. One of these was to kill the Swan of Tuonela in the Underworld; Lemminkäinen

The escape
Väinämöinen and his companions had to fight off an infuriated Louhi who pursued them in the form of a gigantic bird.

was killed there, but restored to life by his mother. Now he sought revenge against Louhi. During their voyage the three heroes caught a fish and Väinämöinen made a kantele, a magical harp-like musical instrument, from its backbone. It had the power to charm its listeners and put them to sleep.

When they arrived in the Northland, Väinämöinen played a tune on the kantele and lulled Louhi and her followers into a deep sleep. Then they soon got hold of the sampo and set sail for home. Unfortunately, just then Lemminkäinen began to sing a loud and triumphant song that woke up Louhi and her people. Enraged, Louhi sent storms to wreck their boat and transformed herself into a monstrous bird of prey to pursue them. In the tumult, the sampo was broken into many pieces, some of which sank to the bottom of the sea.

Väinämöinen gathered as many of the pieces of the sampo as he could. Although he and his brother realized that they would never be able to recreate it, they felt that even its magical parts might bring prosperity to their country. Väinämöinen bequeathed these fragments to the Finnish people. By now a very old man, he realized his powers were waning. He sailed away from this life, but it is said that he will return whenever his people need him.

The last journey
The poem suggests that Väinämöinen's last journey in a boat, travelling up the sunbeams, is to a kind of halfway land between the Earth and the sky, from which he will one day return.

FINNISH NATURE SPIRITS

With its deep lakes and dense forests, Finland presents a dramatic and sometimes harsh landscape. Its early poets and storytellers responded to this environment by imagining a host of nature spirits who represented the character of their land. One of the best known spirits is Tapio, the god of forests, who typifies this response to the landscape – some accounts say that his beard was made of trees while his eyes were bottomless lakes. He was so closely identified with Finland that sometimes the country was called Tapiola. Pellervoinen was another such nature spirit, a harvest god who presided over fields and meadows.

Tapio
In the *Kalevala*, Lemminkäinen appeals to Tapio to help him catch the moose of Hisi in the forest, one of the tasks he has to accomplish to marry Louhi's daughter.

Pellervoinen
A spirit of fertility, Pellervoinen appears at the beginning of the *Kalevala*. He sows the seeds in swamps and barren lands from which the trees of Finland grow.

THE TALE OF MARJATTA

At the end of the *Kalevala*, the story of Marjatta is told. Marjatta, a virgin, became pregnant after eating a berry and gave birth to a son. Since the child had been born out of wedlock, Väinämöinen wanted the baby killed. But the sky god Ukko, after hearing certain details of Väinämöinen's own past, declared instead that Marjatta's child should become the king, replacing Väinämöinen as the ruler of Finland.

⚇ Berries
The Finnish word for berry, *marja*, is similar to Marjatta and Maria. In the *Kalevala*, the berry calls to Marjatta, pleading with her to pluck it.

➤ Marjatta with her baby
The birth of Marjatta's child signals the arrival of a new age. The story of Marjatta takes the *Kalevala* into a new direction. It is an allegory that points to the coming of Christianity to Finland.

THE CURSE OF KULLERVO

Kullervo and his sister had been sold into slavery by their stepfather. Kullervo worked for the Maid of the North, who treated him very badly. One day, she baked a stone in his bread. He broke his magic knife trying to slice the bread. Enraged, he cursed his cruel mistress and transformed her cattle into wild animals, which tore her to pieces. Kullervo was heading home when he met and fell in love with a girl. The two made love, but later they discovered that they were brother and sister, and the girl committed suicide. Kullervo then tracked down his mother and stepfather and killed them before taking his own life.

Magic knife

➤ Kullervo
The story of Kullervo is a powerful tragedy in which a hero of great promise is subjected to a cruel fate for no apparent fault of his own.

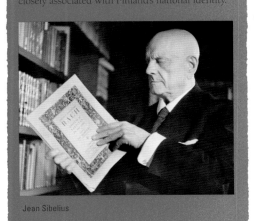

Jean Sibelius

TEAR AND KILL THE WICKED HOSTESS, TEAR HER GUILTY FLESH IN PIECES, WHEN SHE COMES TO VIEW HER CATTLE.

Elias Lönnrot, *Kalevala*, c.1849

TUONELA

The Finnish Underworld, or Tuonela, was the realm of Tuoni and Tuonetar. It was a place of darkness and silence, surrounded by dense thickets, deep forests, and a dark, icy river. These defences made it difficult to escape from Tuonela, and most of those who entered here were eaten by a monster called Surma. Any soul that survived was given the beer of oblivion, which made them forget everything about their life on Earth. The only mortal to visit Tuonela was Lemminkäinen. There, he was killed by a water snake, and torn to pieces by one of Tuoni's children.

◀ The Swan of Tuonela
Lemminkäinen's task was to shoot the swan that swam in the dark river surrounding Tuoni's kingdom.

SEE ALSO European creation stories 16–17, 90–91 • Revenge 18–19, 38–39, 46–47, 70–71, 150–51, 294–97

TALES OF HEROISM AND CHIVALRY

The period that followed the decline of the Roman Empire (from the 5th century onwards) was a rich time for myths and legends in Europe. As new rulers began to expand their territories by conquest, tales of military heroism and chivalry became popular, and sword-wielding heroes – men who were strong, proud, and brave, and who sometimes had to deal with supernatural foes – feature in many of these stories. There were heroines too, who often struggled to make their mark in a world dominated by men.

THE ADVENTURES OF DIETRICH

Dietrich was a figure from a German medieval legend, supposedly based on Theodoric (454–526), the King of the Ostrogoths. He had many adventures in his youth. When a dwarf-king named Laurin abducted the maiden Kunhild, Dietrich decided to rescue her. Fighting valiantly, Dietrich overpowered Laurin, but graciously spared his life. The dwarf rewarded Dietrich by giving him a sword so well forged it was virtually unbeatable. Among Dietrich's other enemies was a giant called Grim, and his wife, Hilde. Dietrich killed the giant, who had robbed many people, but the giantess trapped Dietrich's companion, Hildebrand. Dietrich cut Hilde in two, but she healed magically. This happened many times until Hildebrand suggested that Dietrich force his foot between the two halves. Thus, Hilde was killed and Hildebrand freed.

Dietrich and Laurin
Dwarfs made up for their small size with their fine weapons and excellent skills in battle. Laurin the dwarf was a formidable opponent, even for a man who was as strong and as brave as Dietrich.

Grim the giant
Many legends of Northern Europe speak of giants (*see p.33*), who are usually fearsome, strong, and warlike, but not too intelligent. Dietrich engaged Grim in a long-drawn-out conflict before killing the giant with his sword.

Broadswords
Among the weapons commonly used in Europe from the 5th century onwards were strong broadswords, usually held in two hands to make powerful slashing strokes in battle.

THE DEATH OF HADUBRAND

Dietrich had to fight Odoacer, the ruler of Italy, to win his kingdom. Before the battle, some soldiers from Odoacer's army challenged a few of Dietrich's men to single combat; one such challenge was issued to Dietrich's warrior, Hildebrand, by a young follower of Odoacer. When Hildebrand questioned his challenger, it became clear that the young man was in fact Hildebrand's long-lost son, Hadubrand, whom Hildebrand had not seen since he was a baby. But Hadubrand had been told that his father was dead and refused to believe that he was alive, even when Hildebrand offered his son a gold ring from the family's treasures. Finally, their tempers raised, the two men fought, and Hadubrand was killed.

▲ Gold ring
Hildebrand's offer of his ring reflected the medieval European tradition of fathers handing down their treasure to their sons.

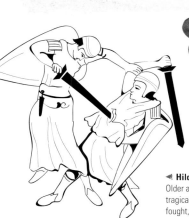

◀ Hildebrand and Hadubrand
Older and more experienced, Hildebrand tragically killed his own son when they fought, as he was more skilled in battle.

▲ The Battle of Roncevaux
After a prolonged and valiant battle at the Roncevaux Pass, the knight Roland finally summoned help. Emperor Charlemagne arrived to defeat the enemy, but was too late to save Roland.

ROLAND AND OLIVER

Emperor Charlemagne ruled over the Frankish kingdoms in Europe in the 8th and early 9th centuries. One of his knights, Roland, was widely known for his bravery in battle. Once, legend has it, he duelled with another knight for five days without knowing his opponent's identity; he finally realized he was fighting his best friend, Oliver, with whom he then made peace. Later, when leading the rearguard of the emperor's army at the Battle of Roncevaux (c.778), Roland did not pay heed to Oliver's advice to blow his horn and summon help if needed, and was thus killed in battle.

Roland the brave

GUDRUN AND HER SUITORS

Gudrun was a Netherlandish princess, daughter of Hetel and sister of Ortwin. She refused two suitors, Siegfried and Hartmut, but a third suitor, the brave knight Herwig, gained her favour. When Siegfried found out about this, he launched an attack on Herwig, and Hetel and Ortwin put on their armour and rode to aid Herwig in battle. Meanwhile, Hartmut, seeing that both his rival suitors were occupied in battle, rode to Hetel's castle and abducted Gudrun. Hartmut and his family then tried to persuade Gudrun to marry him, but the spirited princess staunchly refused, so they forced her to do menial work. When Siegfried came to know of Hartmut's intentions, he made a truce with Herwig, and the three knights – Hetel, Herwig, and Siegfried – banded together to rescue Gudrun.

▼ Gudrun's abduction
An unwilling Gudrun was forcibly taken by Hartmut and his men, and made to work as a servant in his household.

TALES OF HEROISM AND CHIVALRY

105

SEE ALSO Giants 16–17, 64–67, 96–97 • Tragedies 50–51, 58–59, 70–71, 170–71

BEOWULF

The life of the hero Beowulf is depicted in the great Anglo-Saxon poem of the same name, a work that champions the values of honour, valour, and friendship. The poem begins with the story of young Beowulf, a warrior of the Geats, a people from southern Sweden. He is a man with the strength and courage to defeat the most terrible opponents. *Beowulf* goes on to describe how the hero slays the monsters that terrorize the Danes. Later, he becomes the Geatish king and enjoys a long reign before facing his final challenge and a heroic death.

THE MYTH

As a young man, Beowulf travelled to Denmark. For many years, King Hrothgar of Denmark and his people had been terrorized by a monster called Grendel. It would break into Hrothgar's palace hall at night, kill some of the sleeping warriors, and carry them off for food. Beowulf offered to fight the monster, and laid a trap for Grendel, mortally wounding the creature, and eventually killing it. King Hrothgar was overjoyed and bestowed many gifts on Beowulf.

GRENDEL'S MOTHER

Grendel's death infuriated his monstrous mother, and she attacked the people in Heorot, seeking revenge. She lived in a lake, so Beowulf dived into its murky depths to challenge and fight her. It was a long, hard struggle for Beowulf because he could not manage to penetrate the monster's thick, scaly hide with his sword. In the end, he was able to take a weapon from the creature's armoury and stab her with it, killing the monster and ensuring peace for the Danes. After this triumph, Beowulf returned to the land of the Geats, where he was made king and ruled his people for 50 years.

BEOWULF AND THE DRAGON

When Beowulf was an old man, he was faced with the prospect of battling yet another monster, one that was attacking the Geats. A dragon had guarded a hoard of treasure in an ancient burial mound for hundreds of years. When a thief entered the mound and stole a precious cup from the hoard, the enraged dragon went on the rampage. So Beowulf and a group of his bravest warriors set out to confront the beast. Beowulf carried a strong metal shield to protect himself from the dragon's hot breath, but his sword was unable to pierce the beast's scaly skin. His warriors began to desert him one at a time, fleeing in terror, and it seemed that Beowulf would be defeated when the dragon grabbed him by the neck.

A faithful warrior named Wiglaf, who had remained by Beowulf's side, then stabbed at the monster's belly with his sword, while Beowulf attacked the dragon with his knife. The combined effort weakened the dragon and it fell down dead. The monster had been slain, but not before the creature's hot, venomous breath had poisoned Beowulf, and he lay dying. With his death imminent, Beowulf declared Wiglaf as his successor and bequeathed his treasures, weapons, and armour to the young hero who had helped him in ending the menace.

▼ **Beowulf, the monster-slayer**
During his clash with the monster Grendel, Beowulf demonstrated his almost superhuman strength by tearing off one of the creature's arms.

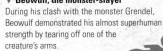

MONSTERS

The monsters in *Beowulf* and in other Northern European myths are creatures whose strength exceeds that of ordinary human warriors. They lurk in dark places, such as the bottom of the lake where Grendel's mother had her lair, and their very appearance is hideous enough to frighten most people. Dragons have a thick, scaly skin, which is invulnerable to most weapons, and they breathe fire, which is poisonous and hot. Their form is often described as serpent-like, but some also have wings. In general, these creatures were conceived to emphasize the heroism of the valiant warriors who defeated them. But in *Beowulf*, there is also a Christian tone to the poem; the monsters are seen as heathen or non-Christian creatures that fight the heroes, who are godly and righteous.

◄ Gruesome Grendel
The monster Grendel is often portrayed as a hideous beast that would carry off its Danish victims to an underwater lair and subsequently feed on them.

WIDE WAS THE DRAGON'S WARRING SEEN, ITS FIENDISH FURY FAR AND NEAR, AS THE GRIM DESTROYER THOSE GEATISH PEOPLE HATED AND HOUNDED.

Beowulf, c.11th century

▲ Slaying the dragon
It took two heroes, Beowulf and Wiglaf, to kill the dragon that attacked the Geats. By staying by his leader's side, Wiglaf showed that he was a true hero, brave and loyal enough to inherit the Geatish throne.

TREASURE

Anglo-Saxon poetry mentions treasures such as rings and jewels, which a king would bestow on his bravest warriors. Also, when great Anglo-Saxon kings died, they were buried with some of their treasures. The largest such collection of precious items was unearthed at a ship burial at Sutton Hoo in eastern England in 1939. This was the grave of an unknown East Anglian king (possibly Redwald, who died c.627), and the collection had both Christian and non-Christian items, showing a mixture of beliefs.

▲ Sutton Hoo treasure
Besides the gilt bronze helmet, coins, and gold buckle (above), the Sutton Hoo burial contained a jewelled sword, a royal sceptre, silver dishes, and drinking vessels.

Anglo-Saxon coins

Anglo-Saxon helmet

THE ANGLO-SAXONS

After the Romans left Britain in the 5th century CE, the southern part of the country was ruled by invaders from northern Germany and Denmark, who came to be called the Anglo-Saxons. Their language, known as Anglo-Saxon or Old English, was a Germanic tongue that later evolved into modern English. Anglo-Saxon monks and scholars used Old English to compose works of prose, riddles, a history book called the *Anglo-Saxon Chronicle*, and poems on heroic and religious subject matter.

***Beowulf* manuscript (10th century)**

107

SEE ALSO Dragons 108–09, 170–71, 216–17, 218–19, 226–27, 260–61

LEGENDS OF THE RING

The stories of the Scandinavian hero Sigurd ("Siegfried" in later German versions) involve adventure, warfare, and love, and characters as diverse as heroes, dwarfs, and shape-changers. Sigurd was a part of the Volsung family, whose members, although related to the god Odin (*see pp.88–89*), were mortals. The rich series of narratives about the heroic deeds of Sigurd and the tales of a magical ring caught the imagination of many later artists, writers, and composers.

THE MYTH

Sigurd was the son of Sigmund, a heroic follower and descendant of Odin. When Sigmund was killed in battle, Odin smashed the dead hero's sword into fragments, but these were saved by Sigmund's wife, Hjordis, for her son. Hjordis remarried, and Sigurd was brought up by Regin, a skilled but devious blacksmith, who was the brother of the dragon Fafnir and of a shape-changer called Otr.

ANDVARI'S TREASURE

One day, Otr took the form of an otter to fish for salmon. Loki, the trickster god (*see pp.96–97*), killed the otter and skinned it because he admired its sleek skin. Otr's father, Hreidmar, was upset and outraged at his son's death, and when Loki, Odin, and Hoenir came to stay with him while travelling, he trapped them in his hall and demanded enough gold to fully cover the otter skin as compensation. Loki went in search of the gold and found it in the hoard of Andvari, a rich dwarf. Andvari's treasure included a ring that had the power to multiply the wealth of its wearer. But the dwarf put a curse on the ring before parting with it. Loki returned with the gold and the gods were freed. Later, Fafnir slew his father, Hreidmar, to obtain the treasure.

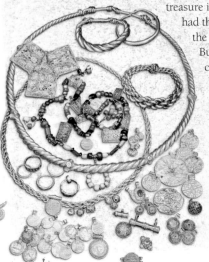

◄ **Hoard of gold**
The hoard guarded by Andvari included gold rings, brooches, torcs, necklaces, and other jewellery, all objects highly prized by the Vikings.

▶ **Sigurd**
Sigurd became all but invulnerable when he bathed in Fafnir's blood. Only one weak spot remained on Sigurd's shoulder, where a leaf had stuck as he bathed.

SIGURD AND THE RING

Regin asked Sigurd to challenge Fafnir for the treasure. The blacksmith used the fragments of Sigmund's weapon and forged them into a new sword, which Sigurd used to kill Fafnir. Regin then instructed Sigurd to bathe in the dragon's blood and cook its heart for him. While doing so, Sigurd burned his finger and put it in his mouth. The moment Fafnir's blood touched his tongue, Sigurd was magically able to understand the language of the birds, who warned him that Regin intended to kill him. Sigurd cut off Regin's head and collected the treasure for himself – this included Andvari's cursed ring, which later brought grief and misery to Sigurd. He fell in love with a Valkyrie (*see p.99*) named Brynhild and gave her the ring. Later, Grimhild, a sorceress, gave Sigurd a potion that made him forget about his betrothal and fall in love with Gudrun, her daughter. Discovering the betrayal, Brynhild had Sigurd killed, but afterwards she repented and threw herself onto Sigurd's funeral pyre.

CHARACTERS

The characters in Sigurd's story were first described in the *Volsunga Saga*, a Norse text from the 13th century. A German poem, the *Nibelungenlied*, which was written at around the same time or soon afterwards, retells the story, changing the names of the characters: the Norse dwarf Andvari becomes Alberich; Regin becomes Mime; Gudrun becomes Kriemhild; and Sigurd becomes Siegfried. But the characters retain their essential traits in both versions of the legend – Sigurd is heroic, Regin is skilled but envious, and Brynhild is beautiful and passionate. The characters also maintain their links with the world of the gods; Sigurd as a member of Odin's family, and Brynhild as one of the Valkyries.

▲ Brynhild
The beautiful Brynhild refused the sexual advances of Odin, who consequently put her to sleep within a ring of fire. Sigurd freed her, but their love was doomed.

▲ Regin
The blacksmith Regin (*left*) made two failed attempts at forging a sword for Sigurd. Here he is shown testing Sigurd's new sword on an anvil.

◀ Fafnir
Like his brothers, Fafnir was a shape-changer. After killing his father, Fafnir turned himself into a dragon to guard the treasure.

OBJECTS OF POWER

Metal objects such as jewellery and weapons were believed to be magical in the ancient cultures of Europe. The skill required to make such objects involved the apparently magical processes of smelting, casting, and forging. The metalworker was perceived to have the ability to make substances change shape at will as miraculously as characters such as Loki and Otr. When a ruler gave a sword or a ring to a follower, it was regarded as a gift of immense significance. The owners of such objects trusted implicitly in their powers, which enhanced their courage, strength, and endurance – qualities that were crucial to ensuring success in warfare.

▲ Gold ring
In ancient Europe, men were just as likely to adorn themselves with jewellery as women. It was a sign of their power and wealth.

◀ Viking sword and shield
It was important for the Vikings to possess weaponry of the highest standard for a good chance of success on raids.

▶ Horned helmet
The horned helmet, unknown to the Vikings, became common in later Germanic retellings of Norse myths and legends.

LATER INTERPRETATIONS

Icelandic sagas like the story of Sigurd and the ring were very popular in the 19th century, being retold by many writers. William Morris (1834–96) wrote an epic poem *Sigurd the Volsung* that came out in 1876. Perhaps the most influential retelling was in the four operas of the *Ring* cycle, *Der Ring des Nibelungen*, by Richard Wagner (1813–83). The first two, *Das Rheingold* and *Die Walküre*, deal with the back story, including the forging of the ring and the laying of Brynhild to sleep. The next two, *Siegfried* and *Götterdämmerung*, cover Siegfried's story and its tragic aftermath.

◀ Wotan
In Wagner's operas, the god Odin is called Wotan, and he appears in the first three operas of the *Ring* cycle. This photograph shows actor Franz Betz as Wotan.

109

SEE ALSO Love stories 44–45, 78–79, 100–03, 116–17, 124–25, 126–27, 140–41, 176–77

EARTH DEITIES

Many gods are concerned with aspects of the Earth and its wellbeing, but some specifically look after it. Such Earth deities are usually universal mother figures, who have a hand in creation and also in nurturing what has been created. They also often look after mortal mothers during pregnancy and childbirth. Earth goddesses were frequently worshipped by women, sometimes in secret rites from which men were rigorously excluded.

EARTH MOTHERS

In many cultures, the Earth is a female figure. As such, often she is fertilized by a male sky god in order to give birth to life or living things. Sometimes the planet itself is said to be made up of her body. As a maternal goddess, she is usually nurturing towards her creation and looks in a kindly way on all humanity. But she can also be wrathful towards her earthly offspring, if they badly misbehave or go against her express wishes.

▷ Mother Earth
With her consort Father Sky, Mother Earth oversees creation in many Native American myths – in some, she gives birth to the first humans.

▷ Bhudevi
The Hindu Earth goddess Bhudevi was rescued from the ocean by the god Vishnu in his avatar of the boar Vahara (*see pp.196–97*).

▽ Gaia
In some stories the Greek Earth goddess Gaia gave birth to the first divine races, most notably the Titans (*see pp.16–17*).

▽ Coatlicue
Some Aztecs said South America was made from their goddess Coatlicue, patron of the Earth.

▲ Prithvi
Sometimes taking the form of a cow, Prithvi was an ancient Indo-European Earth goddess who later became identified with the Hindu goddess Bhudevi.

▷ Mokosha
The Slavic goddess Mokosha was a fertility deity of the land and of women, as well as a goddess of childbirth and a protector of women in general.

Sometimes the Earth is represented by a male deity. Earth gods usually play a slightly different role from Earth goddesses. Although they may be involved in the creation, they are more likely to be authoritarian than nurturing, mirroring on a cosmic scale the role of king or emperor. They can also have a very strong sex drive – the Egyptian Earth god Geb, for example, had to be prised apart from his sister, Nut, so that the Earth and sky could come into being (see *pp.236–37*).

was Geb, a son of Shu, the god of air, and Tefnut, the goddess of moisture. He was the twin of Nut, goddess of the sky.

▼ Earth Diver
In various Native American myths, the Earth Diver in the form of a turtle or other diving animal fetches mud from the ocean floor so the Earth can be made.

► Tu Di Gong
The Chinese Earth god Tu Di Gong is still worshipped today at shrines in fields, under trees, and beside wells. He is said to protect worshippers' gardens and farmland from harm.

◄ Nagaitco
Nagaitco is the creator Earth spirit of the Kato people of California. With his consort and his faithful dog, he forms part of an ancestral trio in myths.

CHANGING SEASONS
Deities associated with the fertility of the planet and its soil – influencing the way crops grow, or governing the eternal pattern of the seasons – occur in most cultures that developed farming. They were afforded particular devotion at such key times as sowing and harvesting, because of their power to ensure a good food supply.

◄ Changing woman
For the Navajo Native Americans, Changing Woman is a creator and controller of the seasons, growing old in winter, and young in spring.

► Persephone
Persephone was a Greek fertility goddess who spent the winter in the Underworld but returned to Earth each spring to make the crops grow.

▲ Cybele
Originally a Turkish mother goddess, Cybele was also known to the Greeks and worshipped by the Romans, who sometimes called her Magna Mater (Great Mother), as a goddess of fertility.

MAGNUS ARTURUS REX POTENTISSIMUS ANGLIAE DOMINUS L UNCELOT DU ! EQUES INVICTUS

▲ **King Arthur as a medieval English monarch**
Although said to be a king of earlier times, Arthur has often been seen as the ideal medieval
English monarch and was frequently portrayed as such in medieval costume, as in this 1862
stained glass representation by the noted Victorian artist William Morris (1834–96).

WESTERN EUROPE

The ancient Celts were an early European people who had an influence on mythology that lasted for hundreds of years. From their shadowy early deities to their later tales of heroes, their myths still fascinate people to this day.

The ancient Celts were a group of tribes, probably originating in Central Europe, who expanded across the whole continent between the 5th century BCE and the growth of Roman power in the 3rd century BCE. Although there was no Celtic empire, there were Celtic settlements in areas as far apart as Spain and Turkey, and at many places in between. But as the Roman Empire expanded, the Celts were pushed out to the edges of Europe, particularly to Ireland, Wales, Scotland, and parts of western France. These areas are the heartlands of the early Celtic mythology that has come down to us through the centuries.

CELTIC MYTHS

The early Celts did not leave written records. Their Roman conquerors described them as being warlike and barbarous, though this was probably a highly biased view. The Romans did, however, record a certain amount of information about early Celtic deities. Archaeological remains from this time – including sites such as burial mounds, around which local legends have grown – have added to our knowledge of these elusive ancient people and their beliefs. Much later, between the 11th and 14th centuries, a few monks in Wales and Ireland wrote down what they knew of the stories of the Celts. These tales – of the Irish gods, of Irish heroes such as Finn and Cúchulain, and of Welsh myths

▲ **Bryn Celli Ddu burial site**
Ancient burial mounds like this one on the Isle of Anglesey (c.2000 BCE) were thought to be magical, and their entrances seen by some as gateways to the Otherworld.

recorded in the books known as the *Mabinogi* – are windows into an enthralling mythical world. They tell of magic and sorcery, of remarkable transformations, of fantastic giants, and of journeys into an Otherworld, where time stands still and people are perpetually youthful. These stories have been much retold over the centuries, and have inspired poetry in many Western European languages.

ARTHURIAN LEGENDS

Another group of myths appeared for the first time in the Middle Ages. These concern King Arthur, a legendary king of Britain who may have been based on a real 5th or 6th-century king or chieftain, although the evidence is scanty. Beginning with Geoffrey of Monmouth (d.1155), a number of writers set down the deeds of King Arthur and his followers. These early versions of the legend vary, but all portray Arthur as a brave and virtuous king who is betrayed by his relative, Mordred. Further elements – the round table and its knights, the search for the Holy Grail, and subplots about the king's various followers – were added to later versions of the Arthurian legends.

During the Middle Ages, poets and prose writers both in Britain and abroad became fascinated with the stories of King Arthur and his associates, or the "Matter of Britain" as these legends became collectively known. Writers from the French poet Chrétien de Troyes to the English prose writer Thomas Malory were famous for recording – and also adding to – the stories of Arthur, as well as other tales of chivalry. In the process, the various knights of the Round Table acquired stories that sometimes became more important than those of King Arthur himself. Sir Gawain, who beheads a mysterious Green Knight, and Sir Lancelot, who becomes the lover of Arthur's queen, Guinevere, are well-known examples. Centuries later, people all over the world are still reading versions of these stories with great fascination.

◄ **Celtic cauldron**
Cauldrons play a key role in several ancient Celtic myths. This is the Gundestrup Cauldron, a 1st-century BCE metal vessel from Denmark, on the edge of the Celtic world. It is covered in images of Cernunnos, Lord of the Beasts.

MYTHS OF THE ANCIENT CELTS

The territory of the ancient Celtic people stretched from Britain, across France and Germany, to Central Europe. Although they were not literate to begin with, these people had a highly developed culture, and excavations of their graves and religious sites show that they worshipped many different gods and goddesses. The Romans, who eventually conquered most of their lands, left descriptions of some of the Celtic deities and religious rituals, and identified many of those deities with their own.

THE GOOD STRIKER

Sucellos, whose name means "the Good Striker", was found in various parts of the Celtic world, especially in Gaul (modern-day France) and Britain. Often said to be a deity of agriculture and forests, his precise significance is still unknown. He is usually depicted as a long-haired, bearded figure, carrying a hammer in his left hand. His main attribute is this hammer, but the symbolism associated with it is unclear; it may have been a weapon, a tool used in one of the crafts, or simply a symbol of the deity's power. Sucellos is generally portrayed as standing with his consort, the goddess Nantosuelta, who carries a dish (perhaps a piece of ritual equipment) and a long pole topped with a house (which may indicate that she was a domestic goddess).

◄ Symbol of Sucellos
Sucellos presided over the grape harvest, sometimes carrying a pot or a barrel to store wine made from the grapes.

▲ Nantosuelta
The goddess Nantosuelta may have been associated with prosperity, wellbeing, and domestic life.

◄ Sucellos's hammer
The hammer or mallet usually carried by Sucellos is the reason for his title, "the Good Striker".

THE HORNED GOD

Cernunnos is known as the horned god because he took the form of a man with the horns (and sometimes the hooves and ears) of a stag. He is usually shown with long hair and a beard, often wearing a neck-ring, or torc, which is the Celtic sign of noble birth. Cernunnos seems to have been widely worshipped in Celtic Europe, and was probably a "wild" god like the Classical Pan (*see pp.86–87*). His horns suggest that he was a deity of fertility, and to emphasize this point, he was associated with symbols such as the cornucopia (horn of plenty), with fruit, and with containers of grain. This function probably encompassed both sexual fertility and the fecundity of the fields.

▲ Cernunnos
The Horned God or Cernunnos was often depicted as the "Lord of the Beasts", surrounded by animals that included a bull, stag, wild boar, and serpent.

Neck-ring or torc

THE THUNDERER

Taranis was a sky god and a major deity in Celtic Britain; he was apparently much worshipped when the Romans invaded the island in the 1st century CE. Latin writers described him as a god of war and likened him to Jupiter; the common attribute between Taranis and Jupiter being the control of thunder. The Celts also had a sky god who was represented by a wheel or disc and who governed the sun. Sometimes, this wheel god is equated with Taranis. The Romans observed that worshippers of Taranis comprised a cruel cult. The Celts made sacrifices to Taranis, with the offerings sometimes including humans who were burned alive in wooden boats or left to drown in bogs. This form of worship may confirm that Taranis, although a sky god, was related to the Romano-Celtic god Dis Pater, an Underworld deity.

▲ Wheel of Taranis
The spoked wheel, representing both the sun's rays as well as its movement, was used in the Celtic world to represent the sun and its deities, possibly including Taranis.

◀ God of the sky
This sky god, with his wheel and lightning bolt, may represent a deity who is a combination of Taranis and Jupiter, the sky god of the invading Romans.

◀ Lightning of the Gods
The Celts considered thunder and lightning to be evidence of the supernatural activity of the gods, and treated places struck by lightning as sacred spots.

GOD OF FIRE AND LIGHT

Belenus, also known as Bel or Belus, was a Celtic god of light and the sun. All his names include an element meaning either "bright" or "shining". A widely worshipped deity across much of Europe, Belenus had shrines that were located as far apart as Britain, Austria, and Italy. Being associated with healing as well as the sun, Belenus is also believed to be the Celtic equivalent of Apollo (*see pp.28–29*). As with Apollo, some of Belenus's shrines were built near springs, where worshippers went to drink water in the hope of a cure. The springtime feast of Beltane in Celtic Britain, during which fires were lit to mark the lengthening of the days and the better weather, may have been linked with the worship of Belenus.

◀ God of the sun
The lines surrounding Belenus's head may depict the warm, glowing rays of light emanating from the sun god.

TRIPLE DEITIES

The Celts were fascinated by things that came in threes. They made images of bulls with three horns and gods with three faces or heads. The Welsh and Irish wrote triads, poems with three lines that described three concepts. And Celtic legends often speak of people with three sons or daughters. Gods and goddesses also came in groups of three. A number of Celtic carvings and reliefs show a trio of female deities standing together. This trio of goddesses or "triple mother" seems to have been considered particularly powerful by the Celts. They represent both human fertility and the bounty of the Earth, and have dominion over human life and wellbeing. They also seem to symbolize the span of human life – many trios of goddesses take the form of women of different ages.

◀ Triple deities
Celtic reliefs often showed the trio of goddesses carrying baskets that probably contained fruits or vegetables, representing the bounty of the Earth.

SEE ALSO Earth deities 16–17, 110–11, 142–43, 196–97, 236–39, 250–51, 308–09, 314–15, 330–31

THE ULSTER CYCLE

One of the most famous and compelling Irish myths involves the deeds of the men of Ulster, in Northern Ireland. The great hero of the Ulster Cycle of myths is Cúchulain, a fearless warrior. He was known for his terrifying battle frenzy, when his eyes glared and his voice roared, and his spear was considered to be almost invincible. His story includes a remarkable childhood, a long period at war with Ulster's rival Irish kingdom Connaught involving dramatic single combats, and a heroic death.

THE MYTH

King Conchobar of Ulster had a retinue of 150 boys who were training to be warriors. His nephew, Cúchulain, wanted to be a part of the band, but the boy's mother insisted that he was too young. Angry at being left out, Cúchulain set off to join the other boys, but they ridiculed him for being too small, and attacked him. Cúchulain went berserk – his head grew so hot that a red glow surrounded it, and he began to snarl fiercely. His attackers ran away, quaking with fear. Conchobar was impressed with his young nephew's power, and he recruited the boy into his service at once.

As a young man, Cúchulain wooed Emer, considered to be the most beautiful woman in Ireland. But Emer's father, Forgall, did not approve of the match; he wanted someone better for his daughter. Forgall persuaded Conchobar to send Cúchulain to Scotland to study the art of war from a famous warrior-woman called

► **Bull of Cooley**
Bulls were a symbol of power or wealth, so Maeve stole the bull of Ulster to get even with her husband.

Sgatha. When Cúchulain returned, Forgall barred him from entering his fortress, but the warrior scaled the walls and carried Emer away.

CÚCHULAIN AT WAR

Queen Maeve of Connaught owned a great white-horned bull, which was one of her most prized possessions. One day, it defected to the herd of her husband, King Ailill, so she stole the Brown Bull of Cooley, one of the finest creatures in Ulster. The men of Ulster wanted to retaliate but they were suffering from an ancient curse that made them ill at times of difficulty. Only Cúchulain remained immune to the curse due to his divine birth; his father was the sun god Lugh. He took on some of Connaught's best warriors in single combat, and they fell one by one. Then he climbed into his chariot and ran amok among the rest of the rival army, killing many others.

Queen Maeve continued to send reinforcements, including Cúchulain's friend, Ferdiad, who was fighting on her side. The hero prepared for battle again, but this time the signs were ominous. His wine turned to blood and he saw a girl weeping and washing bloodstained clothes. Cúchulain knew then that his death was imminent, but he killed many of the enemy, including Ferdiad, until a spear pierced his body. He dragged himself to a standing stone and bound himself to it, so that he would die on his feet. A crow – said to be Morrigan, the death goddess (*see p.175*) – landed on his shoulder, and he died.

◄ **Ferdiad's death**
Beguiled into fighting for Maeve, Ferdiad pushed Cúchulain into a fjord, but was finally slain by him.

ORIGINS OF CÚCHULAIN'S NAME

Originally named Sedanta, Cúchulain was the son of a mortal woman, Deichtine, and the Irish sun god Lugh. While still a boy, Conchobar invited him to a feast held by a blacksmith named Culann. He arrived late, and when Culann's guard dog attacked him, he killed it with his bare hands. To placate the blacksmith, the boy offered to act as a guard until Culann could breed another dog. Thus, he was given the name Cúchulain, "the hound of Culann".

◄ The killing of the hound
Cúchulain came to be associated with dogs, creatures that were seen as both strong and loyal, after killing Culann's hound.

► Lugh, the sun god
Chief of the Irish gods, Cúchulain's father was a great warrior, and skilled in the arts. He gave his great strength and power to his son.

SEDANTA GRABBED THE HOUND BY ITS LEGS AND SMASHED ITS HEAD ON THE STONE COURTYARD.

ULSTER AND CONNAUGHT

Irish myths tell how the land was invaded by legendary races; one of these, known as the Fir Bolg, divided Ireland into five provinces: Ulster, Leinster, Connaught, Munster, and Meath. Much later, Ulster and Connaught became great rivals, and their rivalry was described in a great Irish epic poem, *Táin Bó Cuailgne* (The Cattle Raid of Cooley), written around the 8th century. A source for many stories about Irish heroes, the poem explains how Maeve lost her bull to her husband, leading her to steal the bull of Ulster.

▲ King Conchobar
A man of great power and wisdom, the ruler of Ulster was said to be the son of a druid.

▲ Queen Maeve's warning
Although she was warned about her defeat, Queen Maeve nevertheless stole the Bull of Cooley and forced the men of Connaught to fight against Ulster.

DEIRDRE OF THE SORROWS

A tragic myth associated with Conchobar is that of Deirdre, the daughter of the king's bard. It was predicted that she would be very beautiful, so Conchobar had her brought up in seclusion, intending to marry her later. One day, she saw the king skinning a calf and a raven drinking its blood. She declared that she would marry someone with hair like the raven's feathers, cheeks like the calf's blood, and a body as white as snow. Naoise, one of Conchobar's knights, was such a man. The two fell in love and eloped. The king enticed them back and had Naoise killed. He tried to persuade Deirdre to marry him, but she opted to kill herself instead.

▲ Deirdre and Naoise
To escape King Conchobar, Deirdre and Naoise fled across the sea to Scotland, but even there they were not safe from Conchobar's clutches.

◄ Fergus mac Róich
The great Ulster warrior Fergus mac Róich, who has a role in many Celtic tales, was sent to escort Deirdre and Naoise home. He was later killed in a lake by the jealous ruler of a Connaught district.

117

SEE ALSO Wars 18–19, 60–61, 98–99, 104–05, 118–19, 126–27, 170–71, 176–77, 206–07 • Bulls 50–51, 156–57, 194–95

THE FENIAN CYCLE

There is a large body of Irish myths that deals with the great hero Finn mac Cool and his followers, the Fian. These myths make up the so-called Fenian Cycle of stories. Finn was a warrior, hunter, and, according to many accounts, a prophet who could see into the future. He stood up for Ireland against the country's enemies and such is his power that he is sometimes identified with the ancient Celtic god Lugh.

THE MYTH

Finn acquired his great wisdom in his early youth, when he was called Demhne. He met a poet and druid called Finn the Seer, and studied under him for a while. One day, the poet caught the Salmon of Knowledge after years of trying, and asked Demhne to cook the fish for him, but not to eat any of it himself. Demhne did as he was instructed, but he burned himself while cooking the fish and, in an instinctive action, put his stinging thumb in his mouth. He related to Finn the Seer what had happened, and the poet told him that he was destined to eat the fish and that from then on he would be called Finn. Eating the salmon gave Finn deep knowledge and the power of prophecy. It was said that he was able to conjure the wisdom of the salmon henceforth merely by sucking his thumb.

THE DEFENDER OF IRELAND

Finn grew up to be an outstanding athlete, hunter, and warrior – combined with his gift of knowledge, these abilities gave him unique power. He did much good in the countryside, cutting mountain passes with his powerful sword and slaying serpents. He not only repulsed many people who tried to invade Ireland but also defeated some supernatural opponents, like Aillén mac Midgna, a malevolent fire-breathing musician from the "Otherworld".

◄ Finn's guise
Finn was often associated with deer. He himself could assume the form of a stag, and his wife, Sadbh, came to him in the shape of a doe.

► Finn mac Cool
A well-loved leader, the warrior Finn had only to raise his staff to summon his army, and they would come to stand beside him at once.

Aillén used to come every year to the palace at Tara, put the guards to sleep with his music, and burn the palace down. The beleaguered warriors at Tara appealed to Finn for help. Finn formed a plan to outwit Aillén. He breathed poison from his own spear, which prevented him from falling asleep. Then he lay in wait for Aillén and stabbed him to death.

FINN'S LATER LIFE

Finn was in love with Grainne, a much younger woman, who had been promised to him in marriage. However, Grainne did not want to marry an older man. She was deeply in love with a young man named Diarmaid, one of Finn's followers. She put a spell on Diarmaid to make him love her. The pair eloped and lived together for a while happily until Diarmaid was killed by a boar.

Finn's later adventures either involved his prowess as a warrior, or called on his wisdom and healing powers. There were also tales of his sexual encounters, including one with a young woman who rejected him because he had made love to her already – she was a symbol of passing youth. In the end Finn was murdered by five men, one adversary not being powerful enough to defeat him. Other versions claim he was slain by a warrior called Aichlech mac Dubdrenn.

ASPECTS OF THE MYTH

The stories of Finn and his followers are full of colourful characters and other elements, such as the source of his wisdom that brings magic to the cycle. Finn is followed by a band of heroes, many of whom are outstanding for their bravery or strength. They include Oisín, Finn's son; Goll mac Morna, a great fighter who is also sometimes Finn's rival; Diarmaid, beloved of many women; and Conán, a malicious man who is sometimes a trickster. All these characters live in a wilderness, on the edges of normal society, and are influenced by supernatural powers on the borders of normal existence. Finn and his band of courageous warriors have often been compared to King Arthur and the Knights of the Round Table (*see pp.126–27*).

▲ Wine of the gods
One version of Finn's story says that he acquired his wisdom from sipping the gods' wine when he was given the job of serving them at table.

▲ The Salmon of Knowledge
Finn the Seer waited for seven years to catch the Salmon of Knowledge, which lived in a pool on the Boyne. When he finally caught it, it was the young Finn mac Cool's destiny to eat the fish.

▲ Diarmaid and Grainne
The newly pregnant Grainne craved for a fistful of magic berries from a tree guarded by a giant. Diarmaid killed the giant and plucked the berries for her.

▲ Oisín
Oisín was famous as a bard, and he enthralled his listeners with songs about the Fian. Sadly, he lost his youth, his queen, and his kingdom upon his return from the Land of the Young (*see p.120*).

▲ Manannan mac Lir
The Irish sea god Manannan was, like Finn, seen as a protector of Ireland, which he guarded against invaders with his waves.

TEXTS OF THE CYCLE

The stories of the Fenian Cycle, or Fiannaíocht, are told in a number of early works, in both verse and prose. The stories were compiled in monasteries and castles in Ireland and Scotland between the 9th and 16th centuries. The stories centre on the trials and tribulations of Finn MacCoul and his band of warriors from a coalition of local clans, who are collectively known as the Fianna. Some of the texts in the cycle were originally thought to be about historical characters, but Finn and his compatriots were later understood to be purely mythological. Among the books that deal with his exploits are the 12th-century compilation, *The Colloquy* of Old Men, and *The Book of Lismore*, an Irish vellum manuscript of the early 15th century. Many of the ballads in these early texts were once thought to have been composed by Oisín himself, as he was considered to be one of the greatest legendary poets of Ireland. This is why the Fenian Cycle is also called the Ossianic Cycle. It is the third of the four major cycles of Irish mythology alongside the Mythological Cycle, the Ulster Cycle, and the Historical Cycle, respectively. The cycle also contains stories about other famous Fianna members, including Diarmuid, Cailte, Oisín's son Oscar, and Finn's enemy, Goll mac Morna.

SEE ALSO Heroes 46–49, 60–61, 64–67, 78–79, 104–05, 120–21, 126–29, 206–07, 254–55, 260–61

MAGICAL WORLDS

Ancient Celtic literature abounds with stories of people visiting magical worlds that are separate from but close to our own. The denizens of such Otherworlds do not age, and live a pleasant life, free of pain and despair. Time telescopes in their world so that hundreds of human years pass by quickly, unnoticed by the visiting mortals. But, although life in the Otherworld is tranquil and idyllic, visitors generally feel a fatal longing to return home.

THE LAND OF THE YOUNG

Oisín was the famous son of Finn mac Cool (*see pp.118–19*) and one of the Fian, a group of warriors who fought for Ireland. Once, when hunting, he met a beautiful woman called Niamh Chinn Óir (Niamh of the Golden Hair), riding a white horse. Niamh professed her love to Oisín and asked him to accompany her to Tír na nÓg, the "Land of the Young", of which she was queen. On the way to this magical world, Oisín killed a giant, and having shown his bravery, was given Niamh as his bride. The couple lived happily for centuries, but Oisín eventually grew homesick and decided to visit Ireland. He discovered that much had changed since his departure. Niamh had warned Oisín not to dismount from his horse in Ireland, but he forgot when he saw some men needing help to lift a boulder. As soon as his feet touched the ground, he became old and died.

▲ **Oisín**
Besides being a warrior and a shape-changer, Oisín was the poet of the Fian, and many of the adventures of Finn mac Cool and his people are told from Oisín's point of view.

▶ **Queen of Tír na nÓg**
Niamh Chinn Óir was a young woman of exceptional beauty, who would ride across Ireland on horseback. She ruled a land where nobody aged or fell sick but where the years passed by like minutes.

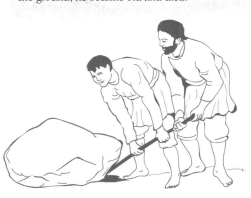

◀ **Oisín and the boulder**
Oisín saw two men struggling to raise a boulder as he passed on his horse. But when he stepped down from his mount to help them, he aged 300 years in a few moments.

THE LAND OF WOMEN

Máel Dúin was an illegitimate child. One day he learned that his father had been slain by raiders and set off to seek the killers. He and his 17 companions visited many islands, each with amazing inhabitants, including enormous birds, fighting horses, and other wonders. Finally, the travellers reached the "Land of Women", where the queen married Máel Dúin and offered her daughters as wives to his crew. After staying there for three months, the men wanted to return home. But every time they set sail, the queen threw a length of twine that stuck to Máel Dúin's hand, and she pulled them back in. Finally, another sailor caught the twine and the others cut off his arm to help them escape.

◀ Isle of the maidens
The land that Máel Dúin and his companions found was populated only by women, all of whom were eager for the visiting men to stay with them.

➤ Celtic ship
Máel Dúin and his crew travelled in a ship that, like Viking ships, was equipped with a sail and oars for use when there was no wind.

▲ Fountain of knowledge
According to legend, there was a fountain in the "Land of Promise" whose waters were said to grant secret knowledge to the drinker.

▲ Voyage of St Brendan
The Irish saint, Brendan, lived in the 6th century and travelled widely. On one voyage he supposedly landed on a whale, believing it to be an island.

THE LAND OF PROMISE

Set far across the sea, Tir Tairngire, or the "Land of Promise", was the place most sought after by explorers. It was a paradise where life was easy and where visitors could acquire magical skills. Some believed that Manannán mac Lir, a sea god and a great warrior, was the ruler of Tir Tairngire, although others thought he merely travelled there, taking with him his young son, Mongán, who stayed here for years and gained much secret knowledge. One of the explorers to reach this land was a Christian saint, Brendan, who journeyed in a boat along with 14 companions. It was one of many marvellous islands that Brendan was said to have visited in a series of travels that may have included expeditions to Iceland.

THE LAND UNDER THE WAVES

There are a number of Celtic tales about the "Land under the Waves", a city or country submerged in the sea. The most famous tale is the story of Ys, off Brittany. This was a prosperous city that was protected from the waves by a strong dyke built by a saintly king called Gradlon Meur. But Gradlon had a wicked daughter called Dahut. Different versions of the story depict her as having opened the sluice gates after either getting drunk or being persuaded by another evil character to do so. Consequently, in all versions of the myth, the sea rushed in from every side and Ys disappeared forever beneath the waves. Some believed that life went on in the strange submarine world of the vanished city.

▲ The submerged city
According to the legend of Ys, people who travelled along the Breton coast could hear the bells of the city's churches ringing below the waves.

MAGICAL WORLDS

121

SEE ALSO Journeys 34–35, 44–45, 64–67, 78–79, 220–21

St Brendan meets Judas Iscariot
Legend has it that the 6th-century Irish ocean voyager St Brendan once encountered Judas Iscariot, who told him that the Lord released him from the torments of hell on holy days.

THE MABINOGI

The four branches, or parts, of the *Mabinogi* (often called the *Mabinogion*) comprise a rich treasury of Welsh myths and legends about early Celtic deities and heroes. These tales were first written down in the 12th century. The four branches deal with: the adventures of Pwyll, prince of Dyfed, especially his visit to the "Otherworld"; the children of the sea god Llyr, Brân and Mananwydan; and other stories, including that of Blodeuwedd. Some of the characters, such as Brân, developed further in the retellings of stories beyond the *Mabinogi*. Christian writers called him "Brân the Blessed" and said that he brought their faith to Wales.

THE WIFE MADE FROM FLOWERS

Lleu Llaw Gyffes (Bright One of the Skilful Hand), the son of Arianrhod, lived under a curse: his mother, Arianrhod, had declared that he would never be able to have a human wife. However, Gwydion, Arianrhod's brother, was a magician, and he decided to help his nephew. He sought the assistance of another magician, Math of Gwynedd. Together they used their powers to create a beautiful woman called Blodeuwedd from the flowers of the meadowsweet, broom, and oak. They wanted Blodeuwedd to be Lleu Llaw Gyffes's wife, but she fell in love with another man, Gronw Pebyr, who killed Lleu. As he died, Lleu turned into an eagle and flew to an oak tree. Gwydion eventually came to his rescue and transformed him back into his human form. Lleu sought out and killed Gronw, and became the Lord of Gwynedd (North Wales).

▼ Blodeuwedd
The name Blodeuwedd means "flower face"; and symbolizes her captivating physical beauty as well as the wild flowers from which she was conjured up.

➤ The magical oak
The Celts considered the oak to be magical. Druids used its wood for their wands and the mistletoe growing on it for their rituals.

◄ Blodeuwedd's punishment
Once Blodeuwedd's treachery was discovered, Gwydion punished her by turning her into an owl.

BRÂN THE BLESSED

Brân, also known as Bendigeidfran, was depicted in many different ways by the ancient writers of England and Wales. To begin with, he was portrayed as a sea god, who was seen striding above the waves. Later, he was described as a mighty British king and leader, who lived at a time when the people of Britain were waging a war against Ireland. His valour and strength helped the British defeat the King of Ireland, even though Brân's forces were outnumbered and he was fatally wounded. After the battle, Brân informed his men about his impending death and instructed them to cut off his head and take it back to Britain, where it would protect them from future invasions. To the astonishment of his companions, Brân's head constantly talked to them all the way back to London, where they buried it, and it continued to act as their guardian.

△ Poisoned spear
Normal weapons could not hurt Brân, but in the battle against the Irish he was mortally wounded by a poison-tipped spear.

△ Brân the giant
As a king, Brân was known to be a giant of superhuman strength. He possessed a magical cauldron that could revive the dead; eventually it passed into the hands of the Irish.

▶ Castell Dinas Bran
These ruins in Llangollen, North Wales, now amounting to just a few stones and earthworks, were believed to be the home of the giant king, Brân.

RHIANNON AND PWYLL

Pwyll, a prince of Dyfed, fell in love with the beautiful Rhiannon, but her family wanted her to marry another man, Gwawl. Pwyll and Rhiannon married without the consent of her parents, who refused to recognize this marriage. Soon the couple had a son, but members of Rhiannon's family stole the baby and accused Rhiannon of murdering her son. As punishment, Pwyll made his wife stand on all fours like a horse and offer rides to whoever passed by. Meanwhile, Pwyll visited a princely neighbour who had been losing foals mysteriously from his stables. Pwyll stood guard outside the stables, caught the monster who had been stealing the foals, and cut off its arm in the ensuing struggle. Upon returning to the stables, Pwyll discovered his son lying in the straw. He took him home to Rhiannon, who named him Pryderi or "care".

▽ Rhiannon
Pwyll was initially attracted to Rhiannon when he saw her on a white horse. Rhiannon was associated with horses because she was a human incarnation of the Celtic horse goddess Epona.

△ Pryderi
Found across stories of the *Mabinogi*, Pryderi was a virtuous character who may have affected the portrayals of Perceval in the Arthurian legends (see pp.126–27).

125

SEE ALSO Trees 90–91, 92–93, 340–41 • Horses 52–53, 172–73

KING ARTHUR
AND HIS KNIGHTS

The legend of King Arthur and the Knights of the Round Table has captured the imagination of writers down the ages. There have been different versions of the story told by British, German, and French authors, but all of them portray Arthur as a wise, just, and brave ruler. The tales extolled the ideals of honour, chivalry, and bravery exemplified by this perfect king and his valiant knights.

THE MYTH

Arthur was the illegitimate son of King Uther Pendragon of Britain and Queen Ygern of Cornwall. Hence he was brought up in secret, away from his parents. However, Uther gave Arthur a chance to become his heir. The king embedded a sword in a block of stone and declared that whomever pulled it out would rightfully become the future King of Britain. Many knights tried to recover the sword but failed, until one day Arthur arrived and removed it easily. Later, when the sword was damaged in a duel, Arthur was given a new sword – the mythical "Excalibur" – by the "Lady of the Lake", a figure shrouded in mystery in the Arthurian legends.

THE KING AND HIS KNIGHTS

Arthur was an honourable king who ruled wisely. He was deeply in love with the beautiful Guinevere, whom he took for his queen. He had many brave knights as his followers, and they discussed matters of state sitting together around the famous Round Table in the castle at Camelot. Many of these knights set out on a quest to find the Holy Grail (*see pp.128–29*), the cup used by Jesus Christ before his death, which is considered one of the most important Christian relics in history. However,

> **King Arthur**
> The mythical ruler is depicted as strong, athletic, and well-versed in the art of warfare. He was the ideal king who presided over a golden age of chivalry.

only Galahad, Perceval, and Bors succeeded in completing the quest. According to some versions of the story, they eventually found the Holy Grail and took it to the city of Jerusalem.

ARTHUR'S DEATH

Meanwhile, problems were brewing at Camelot. One of Arthur's trusted knights, Lancelot, fell in love with Queen Guinevere, and they had a secret affair. When Arthur found out, he banished Lancelot, who was also his dearest friend. Subsequently, Arthur's son, Mordred, decided to challenge his father for control of the kingdom. Many warriors on both sides perished in the fierce battle; those left alive included King Arthur and Mordred, who continued to fight each other relentlessly. Arthur finally killed his treacherous son, but was himself gravely wounded. Knowing that he was nearing death, Arthur sailed to a place called Avalon (the "island of apples"), where he fell into a long, death-like sleep. It was believed that Arthur would return to rule once again when Britain was in dire trouble and in need of a great leader. Thus, he came to be known as the "Once and Future King".

The sword in the stone
Pulling the sword out of the stone was an apparently impossible task. Only a hero could succeed, and when Arthur did so, people were convinced that he was the rightful king.

KEY CHARACTERS

Many characters are involved in the Arthurian legends – some are forces of good, while others bring about the destruction of Arthur's court at Camelot. Besides most of the knights (*see right*), a key figure on the side of good is Merlin – a wizard, prophet, and Arthur's mentor. Flawed characters include Lancelot, a chivalrous knight with one serious moral defect – his love for Queen Guinevere. Lancelot also fails Arthur because he arrives too late to help the king in his battle with Mordred. In some versions of the story, Lancelot becomes a priest upon finding out that Guinevere has repented and become a nun.

▲ Queen Guinevere
The different versions of the story vary in the degree of blame assigned to Guinevere for betraying Arthur by having an affair with Lancelot.

▲ Mordred and Arthur
The battle between the two rivals, son and father, over the throne of Camelot, culminated in a single combat in which Mordred was killed and Arthur received a fatal wound.

PERCEVAL

A young man of noble birth, Perceval became a knight after proving his worth at King Arthur's court. The Grail legends portrayed him as rather naive, a "pure fool". It was this purity, however, that made him worthy of the Grail and helped him resist the seduction of Kundry, a mysterious figure sent to distract him from the Grail quest. His story inspired Richard Wagner's opera, *Parsifal*, where he heals the mortal wounds of Amfortas, the guardian of the Holy Grail.

The Holy Grail

◀ Kundry and Perceval
A female shaman-figure, Kundry was sent to corrupt the Grail knights, but failed to seduce Perceval.

THE KNIGHTS

The Knights of the Round Table were chivalrous men. They were fair in their dealings with others, courteous to women, and helpful to people in need. They were daring and killed monsters and defeated outlaws. There were many tales of their deeds, such as Galahad's quest for the Holy Grail; the adventures of Arthur's nephew, Gawain; the exploits of Pellinore; and the deeds of the naive Perceval. Some stories were about their loves, others about their involvement in political disputes.

➤ Lancelot
The dashing Lancelot was brought up by the "Lady of the Lake", who gave him a shield with three stripes that would magnify his strength in battle.

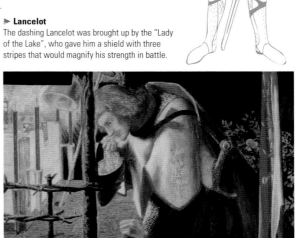

▲ Galahad
The son of Lancelot, Galahad was celibate and pure at heart. He was truly worthy of finding the Grail, although the quest was long and weary, and he died soon afterwards.

THE ROUND TABLE

Descriptions of the circular table in Arthur's castle at Camelot vary – some said it could seat 100 or more knights – but the key principle always remained constant: every knight had equal prominence. One particular seat, known as the "Siege Perilous", or the "Seat of Danger", was traditionally left empty because it was believed that the knight to sit on it would find the Holy Grail, and die, thereby ending the days of the Round Table.

Knights at the Table

SEE ALSO Weapons 18–19, 46–47, 104–05, 124–25, 194–95, 198–99, 258–59, 262–63

THE HOLY GRAIL

The legend of the quest for the Holy Grail is one of the most powerful and enduring of all the tales of the knights of Camelot (*see pp.126–27*). Said to be the cup from which Christ drank at the Last Supper, or alternatively the vessel that caught his dripping blood when he died on the Cross, the Grail was somehow transported to Britain. After a time it became lost, and the land became barren and forlorn. Finding the Holy Grail, and thereby restoring Britain's fortunes, was one of the key quests of Arthur's knights; but only the purest and most virtuous knight would succeed. There are several versions of the story; the one depicted here is taken from a series of tapestries designed by the British artist Sir Edward Burne-Jones (1833–98).

Sir Edward Burne-Jones, *The Quest for the Holy Grail*, 1890–95

1. The Grail

It was said that Joseph of Arimathea, who entombed Christ's body following the Crucifixion, carried the Grail to Britain. There it was kept and cared for by King Pelles, or the Fisher King as he was also known. When the Grail-keeper's father was wounded the land became waste, and the knights of Camelot believed that only by retrieving the relic could they restore the land to its former glory.

2. The chapel

The Grail was housed in a chapel in the Fisher King's castle. It was said to be guarded by angels, and when a virtuous knight found the chapel these attendants would give him food and drink from the sacred vessel. Some accounts of the story even said that Christ himself fed the knights from the Grail when they succeeded in their quest.

3. The open door

The chapel's open door indicates that a knight has reached the end of his journey. To bring the quest to an end, the knight – in this case, Sir Galahad – first has to remove his helmet and put aside his weapons, to show he comes in peace. Then he must ask the correct ritual questions, such as "What is the Grail?" and "Whom does the Grail serve?"

4. Visions of angels

Three angels stand outside the chapel. Their appearance before the approaching knights is a sign that they are about to experience something truly holy and miraculous. The angel on the right holds what seems to be Sir Galahad's set-aside lance. A lance also pierced Christ's side in some accounts of his Crucifixion, and a spear that drips blood into the Grail features in many Grail stories.

5. Sir Galahad

Sir Galahad was the most virtuous of all King Arthur's knights, and in most later versions of the story it is he who finds the Grail. Sir Galahad was the son of Elaine, daughter of the Fisher King, and of Sir Lancelot – a knight who came close to finding the Grail himself but who, as the lover of King Arthur's wife, Queen Guinevere, was not virtuous enough to succeed. Here, tall lilies surround Sir Galahad, signifying his pure character.

6. Sir Bors

One of Sir Galahad's older companions on the Grail quest was his uncle, Sir Bors. When Sir Galahad was a boy, Sir Bors had prayed that his nephew would become as good a knight as Sir Lancelot, and had a vision of the Grail. At the end of the quest Sir Bors was the only knight to return safely to Camelot.

7. Sir Perceval

Those accounts of the legend in which it is Sir Galahad who finds the Grail feature Sir Perceval as his virtuous companion, and say that Sir Perceval dies soon afterwards. But some early versions of the legend make Sir Perceval the true hero. In these accounts, Sir Perceval makes the journey to the chapel twice, but on the first occasion he fails to ask the correct ritual questions, and so is refused entry.

8. The flowering land

Because Sir Galahad has found the Grail, the long-desolate land of Britain flowers once more. The return of fertility to the land links the Grail legend to ancient Celtic tales of similarly magical vessels – including cauldrons and cornucopias, or horns of plenty – that bring nourishment, bounty, and new life to all those who manage to acquire them.

THE HOLY GRAIL

129

SEE ALSO Quests & challenges 44–45, 46–49, 50–51, 52–53, 54–55, 64–67, 72–73, 100–03, 294–97

▲ **The seductive spirits of lakes and streams**
Water sprites, who were said to inhabit streams and lakes in Central Europe, were
famous for playing seductively sweet music in an attempt to lure unwary passers-by,
such as these pretty young peasant girls, into their underwater lair.

CENTRAL AND EASTERN EUROPE

Central and Eastern Europe is home to a fascinating blend of myths and folk tales that reflect both the area's rich natural environment and its diverse heritage of belief systems, from animistic to Christian.

Ranging from the Czech Republic in the west to Russia in the east, Central and Eastern Europe is a region of varied peoples and traditions. Many of the people living in the western part of the area see their roots as Celtic, but the dominant mythology of the region belongs to the Slavs, who between the 5th and 7th centuries spread across Europe from their ancestral homelands in Bulgaria, eastern Slovakia, and neighbouring territories.

▲ Decorated Easter eggs
Decorating eggs at Easter is a traditional custom in the Czech Republic. Today, such eggs symbolize the Resurrection, but they are also pre-Christian symbols of rebirth.

EARLY SLAVIC MYTHOLOGY

The beliefs and myths of the early Slavs centred on notions of good and evil and the role of their ancestors. Human life was understood to be a struggle between light and dark, and the dead were seen as spirits who looked after their family's household. These ancestors lived in the Otherworld, but could be contacted by priests who played a role similar to that performed by shamans in other cultures.

The early Slavs also recognized a group of deities, most of whom presided over the elements and parts of the natural world. Svarog, the most powerful deity, was a sky god and god of light. He had two sons, Dazhbog and Svarozhich, who governed the sun and fire respectively. Perun, the thunder god, and Stribog, god of the winds, were also prominent in the Slav pantheon. A pair of fertility goddesses, the Rozhanitsy, presided over the growing of crops and the harvest.

In addition to the deities, the mythology of Central and Eastern Europe is full of other supernatural beings who act as spirits of places of power. In a countryside of dark, ancient forests, deep lakes, and many rivers, it is not surprising that many of these are spirits of woods and water. Water sprites and similar creatures haunt lakes in numerous myths from the region. They are dangerous to travellers, luring them into the water. Forest spirits work in a similar way, leading people astray so that they become lost among the trees.

MALIGN BEINGS

This part of Europe is also home to a host of powerful and often malign supernatural beings – notably witches, werewolves, and vampires – that have become famous far from their homelands. They are also seen as enemies of the faith that swept through the Slavic world in the 9th and 10th centuries, namely Christianity. Christian missionaries dismissed the ancient deities and spirits, but many Slavs simply combined the old with the new: vampires may be thwarted by a Crucifix, and Easter is celebrated by decorating eggs, pagan symbols of rebirth and renewal.

▲ Sadko on the shores of Lake Ilmen
One Russian folk tale tells of a poor man called Sadko who played his *gusli*, or lyre, by the side of a lake. This so pleased the Sea King that the spirit helped Sadko win a wager that there were fish with golden fins to be caught in the lake, so making Sadko rich.

KOSCHEI THE IMMORTAL

Koschei (Old Bones) is a familiar wicked character in Slavic myth and legend. Like Bába Yagá (*see pp.134–35*), he is regarded as the personification of evil. This skeletal figure is much feared because of his habit of abducting defenceless young girls, and because it is believed he is virtually impossible to kill. One of the best-known stories about Koschei tells how he finally meets his match when he is confronted by a brave warrior-queen who pursues him relentlessly in order to rescue her kidnapped husband.

THE MYTH

Once, a handsome young prince called Ivan was riding through the countryside when he came upon hundreds of corpses strewn on a battlefield. Making inquiries, he learned that these soldiers belonged to the army of Koschei the Immortal, who had been defeated and captured by the warrior-queen Márya Morévna. Soon Ivan came across the queen herself, and the two fell in love. They were married and went to live in Márya Morévna's palace, but after a time the queen had to leave for war once again. Before she departed, she showed Ivan a locked closet in a room in the palace, and told him that he was never to open it.

However, Márya Morévna's shape-changing brothers – the falcon, the raven, and the eagle – sprinkled the water of life over her dismembered body and revived her. In the meantime, Koschei rode away with Ivan on his lightning-fast steed.

RESCUING IVAN

Márya Morévna knew that only one person possessed horses fast enough to catch up with Koschei – the witch Bába Yagá. The queen rushed to the witch, who gave her a sorry-looking colt, which hardly seemed up to the task of pursuing Koschei. But as Márya Morévna rode the creature, it miraculously turned into a swift horse that soon caught up with the kidnapper. Grabbing Ivan, Márya Morévna turned the horse and galloped off, with Koschei in pursuit. They raced on through the forests, until Koschei's horse stumbled on a stone and threw its rider to the ground. Turning quickly, Márya Morévna took her sword and ran it through Koschei before burning his body to be rid of him forever. Then the couple returned to their palace and lived in peace thereafter.

CAPTURED BY KOSCHEI

After Márya Morévna had gone, Ivan could not resist looking in the closet, so he found the key and unlocked it. Inside he saw a wizened old man chained to a post, begging for water. Feeling sorry for the man, Ivan gave him some water. As soon as he had drunk his fill, the old man broke his chains and fled the palace, taking Ivan with him.

When Márya Morévna found out what had happened, she rode out to rescue her husband, but Koschei was waiting for her and cut her up into pieces before she could attack him.

KEY CHARACTERS

Márya Morévna and Ivan are quite straightforward figures, but Koschei is a remarkable character. According to some versions, he was immortal because he had concealed his soul away from his body. It was hidden in a needle, which was placed inside an egg. The egg was inside a duck, which in turn was inside a hare that was kept in an old iron chest. The chest was hidden in an oak tree that grew on an island. These layers of protection ensured Koschei's immortality – for example, if the hare's body was cut open, the duck would fly away. But some said that if the egg was broken by cracking it against Koschei's head, he would die. Other accounts claimed Koschei's body had to be burned to truly kill him.

> I AM KOSCHEI THE DEATHLESS. NO ONE CAN KILL ME. MY SOUL IS CONCEALED IN A FARAWAY LAND.

▲ **Prince Ivan**
Ivan is the typical handsome young prince of legend. In this story, he shows himself to be adventurous, bold, kind-hearted, and loving, but endangered by his own curiosity.

▲ **The warrior-queen**
Márya Morévna was a warrior-queen of great strength, power, and resourcefulness, qualities that helped her to defeat Koschei.

RECURRING FIGURES

Folk tales often have repeating patterns – characters or animals who form links across the story. In another version of the legend, Koschei kidnaps Márya and Ivan sets off to rescue her. Learning that Bába Yagá has a magical horse, he goes to her house. On the way, he shows kindness to a bird, a bee, and a lioness. Bába Yagá promises to reward him if he tends her horses for three days. He is helped in this task by the same creatures he had met earlier. Then he steals Bába Yagá's colt, rescues Márya, and kills Koschei.

▲ **Bird**
The bird begged Ivan to spare her eggs, and he did. Later she helped him guard Bába Yagá's horses.

▲ **Bee**
The bee asked Ivan not to take her honey, and helped him round up the horses in return.

▶ **Lioness**
The lioness helped Ivan lead the horses back to the stables because he spared her cub on her request.

COLLECTING THE STORIES

Russian myths such as those featuring Ivan and Koschei were originally known only to people in particular villages or towns, and many Russians did not realize what a rich tradition of legend existed in their country. In the 19th century, scholars began to visit rural areas, listen to the local storytellers, and write the narratives down. One such collector of folklore was Alexander Afanasiev (1826–71). It is largely because of his work – much of it done despite opposition from the Russian establishment figures, who did not want to popularize what they termed "primitive" culture – that Russian myths and legends have been preserved until today.

◀ **Russian peasants**
Russian peasant farmers of old led a hard life, so their traditional stories often feature dangerous quests and arduous journeys, finally culminating in success, as in the tales about Márya.

KOSCHEI THE IMMORTAL

133

SEE ALSO Immortality 68–69, 156–57, 216–17, 218–19 • Witches 134–35

LEGENDS OF THE WITCH

The folklore of the Slavs often reflects their ancestors' anxieties about evil, the unknown, and the dangers of the forest. There are many tales of witches, who were believed to be sinister women living in these forests, and who preyed on innocent people, or upset family relationships or the social order.

Foremost among such evil characters is Bába Yagá, a witch who appears in Russian legends, and in similar tales found across Central Europe, where her name varies slightly. However, her rapacious appetite for the flesh of young children stays consistent, though many of her victims manage to outwit her.

▲ Bába Yagá
The wicked old witch would use her mortar and pestle to travel in the forest, where she would hide among the trees, waiting to ambush unwary victims that walked past her.

BÁBA YAGÁ

The witch called Bába Yagá was depicted in stories as a wrinkled old woman sitting quietly on a wooden bench or keeping warm by her stove. When travelling, she would step into a large mortar and push herself through the sky with a pestle, starting violent storms as she flew. She specially looked out for young children, whom she liked to capture and eat. Some people believed that the witch could turn people to stone with her gaze, turning them back into flesh at her home to feed on them. Bába Yagá used the bones left over after her feedings to build a gruesome and enchanted house for herself, which terrified people for miles around. Even its fence was decorated with the skulls of the children she had killed, and she would light these skulls up like lanterns.

◄ Horror house
Bába Yagá's house had a pair of hen legs at its base with which it could run around and chase people at the witch's command.

◄ Roses for wishes
Some legends of Bába Yagá say that the witch could grant people their wishes if she were offered roses, although most stories warn that it was still risky to trust the witch.

VASSILISA

Vassilisa was a young girl who lived with her elderly parents in a village. Her mother fell ill and, before dying, gave Vassilisa a magic doll, which would advise her if she offered it good food to eat. Vassilisa's father remarried, but her stepmother and stepsisters did not like Vassilisa and made her do all the hard work at home. One day, when a taper was needed to light the lamps in the house, Vassilisa's stepmother sent her to get some from Bába Yagá, who, instead of giving her some, set the girl some impossible tasks, such as picking out only peas from a mixture of peas and poppy seeds. Vassilisa was able to successfully complete all the tasks with the help of her doll, but Bába Yagá kept devising more for her to do. Seeing no other way of escape, Vassilisa stole away from the house at night while the witch slept, taking with her one of the glowing skulls from Bába Yagá's fence.

▲ Vassilisa and the skull
When Vassilisa returned home with the skull that she had stolen from Bába Yagá's fence, its glowing eyes shone on her stepmother and stepsisters, turning them to ashes.

▲ The powerless crow
Some versions of the story say that after Vassilisa's escape, the witch was turned into a crow and she lost all her powers.

➤ The witch's cat
Bába Yagá's black cat was ill-treated by her, so it helped Vassilisa escape her clutches.

MARIASSA

There was once a young girl called Mariassa, whose stepmother sent her to Bába Yagá to borrow a needle and thread. Luckily, the girl initially called on her aunt, who told Mariassa how to avoid the jaws of Bába Yagá's dog and how to talk to her cat. Mariassa asked the cat for a way out when the witch tried to imprison the girl, and it told her to run away with a towel and a comb. Mariassa escaped, and when she heard the witch approaching, she threw down the towel, which turned into a river, and the comb, which became a forest, thus trapping Bába Yagá.

▲ Bába Yagá chasing Mariassa
The witch became trapped in the swift river and could not row fast enough with her pestle to catch Mariassa.

WITCH BURNING

With the arrival of Christianity in Central and Eastern Europe, witches came to be regarded as evil women who performed the Devil's work. Many women suspected of being witches were burned at the stake, most of whom had nothing to do with witchcraft at all. Making models of witches that are burned on May Day is still a popular custom in Central Europe. Such customs, associated with the many rituals that celebrate the arrival of spring, are also held in remembrance of those who died.

A 16th-century engraving of a witch burning

135

SEE ALSO Witches 132–33 • Forests 136–37, 258–59, 340–41

MYTHS OF WOOD AND WATER

The Slavic lands are full of dense forests and misty lakes, both natural and man-made. From earliest times these places were believed to have their special spirits. Some were threatening beings that embodied the anxiety of travellers, who were fearful of getting lost in the woods or drowning while crossing a lake. Even country people, who knew the forests and lakes of their region well, were wary of these spirits.

RUSALKAS

Rusalkas were alluring water nymphs known for their beautiful song. They probably originated as fertility spirits, associated with particular lakes and with the life-giving power of water. But they were later said to be the souls of children who had died at a young age, or of women who had drowned themselves. Their song lured passers-by into the water. One story told how a Rusalka left the water when she fell in love with a mortal prince. She had to lose her voice to survive in the air, but for a while she was happy. However, her lover left her for a mortal woman and she faded away into the water once more.

▶ **Mythical setting**
As in many other cultures, the people of Central Europe saw dense forests, together with lakes, rivers, and waterfalls, as places of special power and the home of spirits.

▲ **A Rusalka and her victim**
Some mortal men, smitten by the Rusalka's song, dived into the water to be with her and met a sad death by drowning.

◀ **Antonín Dvořák**
The Czech composer Dvořák (1841–1904) wrote a famous opera, *Rusalka*, about the nymph who left her home for a mortal love.

WEREWOLVES

The legends of Central and Eastern Europe often feature werewolves, humans who could change shape to become wolves. Malevolent and bloodthirsty, they appeared when the moon was full and preyed on the unsuspecting. It was said that babies born with a birthmark were likely to become werewolves. Plants such as rye and mistletoe, and a herb called wolfsbane, were believed to ward off werewolf attacks.

The wolf man

WATER SPIRITS

Like the Rusalkas, water spirits and nixes lived in lakes and, especially, mill ponds. A legend from southeastern Europe tells of a nix who helped a mortal. There was a young mill-hand who loved the miller's daughter. But the miller wanted his daughter to marry a rich man from the local castle. One day, the two rivals fought and the mill-hand was pushed into the mill pond, where he was found by a nix. The mill-hand entertained the nix on his violin. The two got on so well that when the mill-hand was about to leave the water, the friendly nix gave him a magical ring, which would grant the wearer three wishes. So the mill-hand's wish to marry the miller's daughter was fulfilled, thanks to the kindly spirit of the pond.

◄ Vodyanoi
The Vodyanoi was the most familiar Russian water spirit. Unlike the kindly nix, he was a dangerous creature who lured passers-by into his watery lair, where they subsequently drowned.

► Carp
Water spirits often sorted the fish in the pond, sending eels on their regular migrations. Fishermen in search of carp placed a pinch of tobacco in the water to please the spirits.

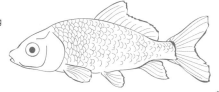

◄ Sadko's lute
Sadko was a minstrel who had fallen on hard times. His most prized possession was the *gusli*, or lute, with which he made his living as a musician.

► The minstrel Sadko
The musical theme of Sadko's story made it attractive to composers. The Russian composer Nikolai Rimsky-Korsakov (1844–1908) wrote an opera based on the tale.

SADKO

A popular Slavic myth tells of the minstrel Sadko who was invited by a water spirit to play in his palace. The spirits danced to Sadko's music till he grew tired and could play no more. A wise water spirit advised Sadko to stop the dance by breaking the strings of his lute. If he did this, the sea god would offer him a wife in return for his playing – but he must choose the last of the women offered to him, and even then he must never touch her. Sadko did as he was told, choosing the last woman the sea god offered, and lying apart from her. But at night, his right foot accidentally touched her. To his amazement, Sadko woke up alone on the river bank, to find he was lame in his right foot.

THE WOOD DOVE

The magic of both woods and water come together in the Slavic legend of the wood dove. There was once an old woodcutter who was poisoned by his wicked wife because she wanted to marry a handsome young man with whom she was in love. Soon after his death, the woman married her lover and they had a lavish wedding feast. At first they lived together happily. Meanwhile, grass grew over the woodcutter's grave and a young oak tree took root there. Whenever the woman passed the grave, a wood dove perched in the tree cooed at her accusingly. Each time she heard the wood dove, she felt it was the voice of her murdered husband. Deeply tormented, she drowned herself in the river.

► Voice of the dove
Birds often speak in folk tales because their song has a vocal quality. To the woodcutter's guilty wife, even the cooing of a dove sounded accusatory.

◄ Woodcutter
Forests were sources of fuel and building material for the Slavic peoples, and woodcutters often figure in their myths of the forest.

MYTHS OF WOOD AND WATER

137

SEE ALSO Spirits of place 28–29, 30–31, 82–83, 320–21 • Forests 134–35, 258–59, 340–41

GODS AND GODDESSES OF LOVE

Most of the world's mythologies have deities responsible for love, some of whom began life as fertility gods or goddesses. Many love deities are sexually promiscuous, pursuing their own love affairs as well as encouraging those of others – sometimes making mischief by causing ill-matched couples to fall in love. Other love deities are more concerned with guiding women through pregnancy and childbirth.

GODS AND GODDESSES OF LOVE

▼ Eros
Son of the war god Ares and the love goddess Aphrodite (*see pp.38–39*), Eros was the Greek god of erotic desire. He shot golden arrows that made people fall in love.

◄ Cupid
The Roman equivalent of Eros, Cupid inspired many love affairs. One of his intended victims, the mortal woman Psyche, was so beautiful that he fell in love with her himself.

► Kama
Son of Vishnu and the goddess Lakshmi, the Hindu love god Kama is a handsome young archer who rides on the back of a parrot. He is married to Rati ("passion").

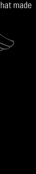

▲ Shiva
The Hindu god Shiva (*see pp.194–95*) is sometimes seen as an ascetic, but is also associated with erotic love and worshipped in the form of a *linga*, or phallus.

▲ Semara
The god of love in Bali, Semara lives in the Floating Sky, one of the six heavens located above the Earth. He turned love into a physical pleasure for people so that they would want to have children.

► Oenghus
The Irish god Oenghus was known as a god who would help those in love. He fell in love himself with a beautiful swan maiden and took the form of a swan to visit her.

Aphrodite

Known for her beauty and her affairs with mortals and gods, the Greek goddess of love Aphrodite (*see pp.38–39*) was often accompanied by her son, Eros.

Venus

The Roman goddess of love, Venus began as a spring fertility figure and a patron of gardeners, then became identified with Aphrodite.

Inanna

The name Inanna belonged to an early Mesopotamian love goddess (*see pp.154–55*) and was also used in many of the Sumerian cities for the goddess known as Ishtar, or Astarte.

Hathor

The Egyptian goddess Hathor (*see p.244*), who often took the form of a cow, was a protector of women, patron of lovers, and goddess of both conception and childbirth.

Bastet

Bastet (*see p.245*) began as a warlike, lion-bodied figure, but in the more sensual form of a domestic cat she was an Egyptian goddess of sexual love. Sometimes she even appeared with her kittens, to symbolize her role as a fertility goddess.

Ishtar

The Babylonian goddess of war and fertility, as well as love, Ishtar was worshipped in Canaan and Egypt as Astarte. Brave as well as beautiful, she was sometimes identified with the planet Venus.

Freyja

With a name meaning simply "lady", the Norse goddess Freyja was especially associated with love. She had many lovers, including mortal kings as well as gods.

Xochiquetzal

Xochiquetzal and her consort Xochipilli were the Aztec goddess and god of flowers. Xochiquetzal had an additional role as goddess of love and childbirth.

THE FIREBIRD

Slavic mythology describes the firebird as a beautiful creature with a long tail and stunning red, yellow, and orange feathers that glow as if on fire. The firebird inspires wonder in all who see it, causing them to desire it. But it is not easy to capture, and those who do manage to catch it often have to face a multitude of problems that come in its wake.

THE MYTH

There was once a king who owned a wonderful apple orchard that he was especially proud of, because one of its trees bore golden apples. But each night, he found that some of the golden apples would disappear. So the king commanded Ivan, a stable boy, to guard the tree at night. The first night that Ivan stood guard in the orchard, a firebird came and stole some apples. Ivan attempted to grab the bird, but the creature was so swift that he could only catch hold of a single feather as it flew away. Ivan delivered the feather to the king who marvelled at it and dispatched Ivan to find and capture the firebird.

CATCHING THE FIREBIRD

After he had travelled a few miles on his quest for the firebird, Ivan came across a grey wolf, who told him how to catch the bird. Ivan would have to soak some cheese in beer and scatter the food on the ground to tempt the firebird. Ivan followed the wolf's instructions

➤ The firebird
Artists usually draw the firebird as a predominantly red and orange creature shaped rather like a peacock, with a long tail adorned with eye-shaped patterns.

and was able to catch his quarry since the firebird became drunk after feeding on the beer-soaked cheese. Then Ivan climbed onto the wolf's back and the wolf took him to the king's palace. The king was very pleased, and locked the firebird in a specially-made golden cage.

IVAN AND YELENA

The king then sent Ivan on another errand – to fetch a beautiful princess named Yelena, who lived far away across the ocean, and whom the king wanted to marry. The grey wolf helped Ivan yet again, taking him to Yelena, and carrying both Ivan and the princess on the return journey.

During their travels, Ivan and Yelena fell in love. But they were faced with a dilemma since the king was waiting to marry Yelena. Once more, the wolf had a plan to aid Ivan. When they reached the palace, the wolf revealed itself to be a shape-changer and transformed into a very beautiful princess, whom Ivan presented to the king. The king proposed marriage, and when the "wolf-princess" accepted, took her straight to church. But as the king was about to kiss his bride, she turned back into the wolf, and the king died instantly of shock.

After the king's death, Ivan became ruler in his place, and married his beloved Yelena. He was very grateful to the firebird, which was the catalyst for the adventures that had culminated in his marriage and coronation. So King Ivan set the creature free, turning a blind eye to the golden apples that would frequently go missing.

◄ Fairytale castle
Mythical figures like the king live in fairytale castles, the grounds of which cannot be entered, except by fantastic creatures such as the firebird.

◄ Ivan and Yelena
The story of the young lovers travelling swiftly through the night on the back of the grey wolf has long been a popular subject for artists.

► The greedy king
The king wanted to keep the firebird because it was said to bring happiness to the owner, although this turned out not to be true for him.

KEY CHARACTERS

There are several versions of the firebird story, but they usually contain the same key characters: the firebird, Ivan, the king, the grey wolf, and Yelena. A common theme is that Yelena's hand has been promised to the king against her wishes, and so Ivan and the wolf kidnap her. In some stories, Yelena's love for Ivan enables her to escape from an unwelcome marriage. In another version, Ivan is one of the king's sons, who has been tasked with catching the firebird as a way of becoming the king's heir. Ivan succeeds and his brothers kill him when he wins the princess, but the wolf's magic revives him.

THE SUPERNATURAL WORLD

In this legend, the world of animals and plants is full of supernatural powers, which have a major influence on the way events turn out. Foremost is the firebird itself, which lets pearls fall from its beak and has feathers that glow like flames. The apples are also said to be special – they bring youth and strength to those who eat them, so by stealing the apples, the bird is symbolically stealing the king's power. Finally, the wolf is not sinister (unlike in other tales), and uses its shape-changing ability to help Ivan.

◄ The magical wolf
The wolf was a complex symbol, with links to both the dead and the world of evil, as well as to good and the overcoming of difficulties.

▲ Apples of eternal youth
The apple tree bore golden apples, which signified not only strength and youth, but also danger and folly.

STRAVINSKY

The composer Igor Stravinsky (1882–1971) was one of the most influential musicians of the 20th century. Starting with writing music for ballets on traditional Slavic themes, he became famous for colourful orchestration and strong rhythms, developing his style in ways that changed the course of music. His

ballet *The Firebird* (1910) was written for the Paris-based company, the Ballets Russes, and brought the traditional Slavic legend before a global audience.

A modern rendition of *The Firebird*

SLAVIC ANIMAL MYTHS

The firebird is one of several mythical creatures in Slavic mythology that have miraculous abilities or that reflect either the dangers of the countryside or the mysterious power of the natural world. Traditional Slavic tales include many locally familiar birds and animals that take on specific characteristics in folklore: proverbially crafty foxes, swift horses, shape-changing wolves, and a golden cockerel that crows to warn a king of invasion.

► The loyal cockerel
The golden cockerel that warned a king about the arrival of his enemies became the centrepiece of an opera by the Russian composer Rimsky-Korsakov (1844–1908).

▲ The unwitting bear
Sometimes slow and easy to deceive, but always strong, bears were once common throughout Europe and appear occasionally in Slavic legends.

> COCKEREL FROM THE TOP OF SPIRE, WATCHES ROUND FOR THE FIRE. IS THE DANGER SEEN BY CHANCE, FAITHFUL SENTRY WAKES AT ONCE.
>
> Alexander Pushkin, *The Tale of the Golden Cockerel*, 1834

SEE ALSO Birds 172–73, 236–37, 258–59, 286–87, 298–99, 306–07

SLAVIC GODS OF POWER

The ancient Slavs, who lived in and around Russia, had numerous deities who ruled with great power over the Earth. Their control extended all the way from the sky, where the thunder god Perun held sway, to deep down into the Earth, the domain of Mati Syra Zemlya. The Slavs worshipped these gods by giving them offerings and assigning special days to them, occasions that combined holiday with devotion. Although their myths were orally transmitted, many of these powerful stories survived the coming of Christianity.

▲ **The sky god**
In addition to his weapons and his eagle, Perun was associated with many other attributes. Among the most important of these were the stone and metal that Slavic people used to make weapons.

PERUN
Perun was the god of thunder and lightning. Although he was primarily a war god and his power was terrifying, he also represented the forces of good. When the sun was threatened by storm clouds that concealed it in their shadows, Perun smashed them with his thunderbolt, allowing the sun to reappear and ensuring that life on Earth could continue. The Slavs believed that humanity was constantly threatened by Veles, the god of the Underworld, who was always stealing cattle, kidnapping people, or otherwise causing mischief. At such times, Perun would strike him with his thunderbolt, sending the evil god hurrying back to his refuge. When Christian missionaries came to the Slavic regions, some of the attributes of Perun were transferred to the prophet called Ilyal, or Elijah.

▲ **The world tree**
In Slavic mythology, the world was represented as a vast oak, with the Underworld in its roots. Perun was symbolized by an eagle that sat in the uppermost branches of the tree.

▲ **Veles the dragon**
The Slavs imagined Veles, the god of the Underworld, as a dragon or serpent, who spent much of his time coiled among the roots of the sacred oak tree.

BYELOBOG AND CHERNOBOG

A benevolent god, Byelobog, and a wicked god, Chernobog, are two of the most ancient deities of Slavic mythology, and some creation stories describe how the pair created the universe together. But the two fell out and were said to be perpetually at war, appearing at regular intervals to fight one another. Because this conflict between good and evil was eternal, they were seen as similar to, and possibly derived from, the Persian deities Ahura Mazda and Ahriman (*see pp.168–69*). Byelobog was held in special regard because he was one of the most prominent companions of the sun god Dazhbog (*see p.285*). People said that he was also a god of sunshine and warmth, and that if worshipped, he would protect their wheat and ensure a good harvest. Sometimes he was depicted as a kindly, white-bearded old man, and sometimes as a powerful light.

▲ The god of light
The ancient Slavs closely associated the life-giving light and warmth of the sun with the benevolent god, Byelobog – especially after enduring a long, cold, dark night.

▶ The god of darkness
As the god of darkness, Chernobog was most powerful during the "waning" phase of the year, when the nights are longer and the days become shorter.

MATI SYRA ZEMLYA

The Slavic Earth goddess was called Mati Syra Zemlya (Damp Mother Earth). Normally, she was not given a specific form, but her spirit was said to be embodied in the fertile earth beneath the feet of her devotees. Even though she usually lacked a shape, she was seen as vibrantly alive and, therefore, helped everything in the soil to come to life. On certain occasions when she did take human form, she was said to appear as a woman with dark, earth-coloured skin, wearing traditional clothes, who would visit people's houses and bless them. On the holy days on which she appeared (notably 1 May and 24 June), no one was allowed to plough the soil. People worshipped her by digging a hole in the ground and putting in offerings of bread and wine.

◀ Ears of wheat
In addition to representing the fertility of the soil, Mati Syra Zemlya was also said to be present in the crops that grew on the ground, especially in the ripe ears of wheat.

▶ The rescue of Kranyatz
When the flood waters continued to rise, Kurent offered Kranyatz his walking stick, actually a vine, and pulled him out of danger.

KURENT

Kurent was the Slavic god of wine. A popular myth tells how the first humans enjoyed an easy life in a valley irrigated by seven rivers that flowed from an egg. They became greedy for more water and broke the egg, causing a great flood. All the people drowned, except for Kranyatz, a watchman, who was saved by Kurent. Later, Kranyatz argued with the god over who should rule the Earth, and after various trials, emerged as the winner. But he got carried away and climbed the mountain where the gods lived. He ate some meat that belonged to them, and got drunk from the wine given to him by Kurent. The gods kicked him down the mountain and he lost his power.

▲ Kurent mask
In Slovenia, sheepskin masks depicting Kurent are worn at the Kurentovanje carnival that is held to celebrate the arrival of spring.

143

SEE ALSO Sky deities 24–25, 114–15, 158–59, 160–61, 162–63, 188–89, 236–39, 252–53, 266–67, 294–97, 318–19, 338–39

WEST AND CENTRAL ASIA

For hundreds of years, the Bible was the main source of our knowledge of ancient Babylon, Ashur, and other great cities of the Middle East. The Old Testament uncompromisingly portrayed all these cities as being dominated by ruthless rulers whose overriding ambitions were to conquer their neighbours and crush all those who did not follow their religion. And that religion, involving belief in a great many deities, was in stark contrast to the Jewish belief in one God. It is perhaps unsurprising that the Bible took a dim view of these societies.

In the 19th century, our understanding of the ancient cultures of West Asia deepened. Archaeologists began to explore the mud-brick remains of cities such as Babylon, Ashur, Ur, and Uruk in earnest. They also got to grips with deciphering the writing on countless clay tablets that were discovered at these sites. What emerged

was a picture of a much more sophisticated society than had previously been imagined, one that had made great advances in mathematics, astrology, medicine, and the law. In addition, archaeologists found out much more about the beliefs of these cities' inhabitants and the stories they told one another. A much fuller, rounder impression of the early culture of ancient Iraq and its neighbours began to emerge.

In some ways, the myths that were revealed confirmed the Biblical prejudices. Some stories were extremely bloodthirsty, and some involved practices – such as temple prostitution – that offended most outsiders. But the myths also included many gripping tales – of the creation, of visits to the Underworld, and of the deeds of great heroes such as Gilgamesh, the mythical king who strove for immortality.

A number of these exciting stories, including accounts of the creation and of wars between the gods, are strikingly similar to stories in other cultures. Perhaps the closest parallel of all is in

WHATEVER A MAN MAY DO, HE IS BUT A REED IN THE WIND.

Mesopotamian proverb

the story of the great flood, a theme that occurs in many mythologies all around the world. The West Asian flood story concerns a patriarchal figure called Utnapishtim who builds a boat to escape a deluge unleashed by a wrathful god. It is remarkably similar to the story of Noah and the Ark in the Old Testament – Utnapishtim even takes animals of each species into his "ark" to ensure their survival. Such powerful stories, most of them written in the Babylonian, or Akkadian, language, are now as well known as the ancient cultures that produced them. Iraq's archaeological sites have recently become highly vulnerable to war damage, so these stories may become the culture's most enduring remains.

But the stories from great cities such as Ur, Uruk, Ashur, and Babylon are not the only mythical traditions of West and Central Asia. At opposite ends of this extensive region, the Hittites of ancient Turkey and the peoples of the Arabian Peninsula added their own rich stores of myths. So too did the ancient Persians, whose prophet Zoroaster described a vision of the cosmos dominated by a constant struggle between the Wise Lord, Ahura Mazda, and his wicked opponent, Ahriman. When the Mongols travelled west from their homelands, they, too, brought with them yet more tales of great heroism and extraordinary adventure.

This rich mix of cultures and their deities, from the weather gods of the Hittites to the Wise Lord of the Persians, makes the region of West and Central Asia one of the most mythologically fascinating of all. There is so much variety in these very different ancient mythologies that there is always something new and exciting for the reader to discover.

   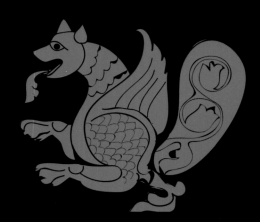

▶ **Assyrian carved relief**
The palaces and temples of the
Assyrian Empire were adorned
with carved stone reliefs. Many
of these reliefs showed mythical
creatures – such as the winged
bull depicted here – which the
Assyrians regarded as guardian
figures who watched over the
building, protecting it from evil.

WEST ASIA

West Asia was the site of some of the world's earliest cities, where riches from agriculture and trade, and the development of writing and organized religion, produced flourishing cultures that recorded their many myths.

The first great cities of West Asia, or the Middle East, sprang up from as early as about 2600 BCE in Mesopotamia, the land between the Tigris and Euphrates rivers in what is now Iraq. Cities such as Ur, Uruk, Babylon, and Ashur all developed powerful political systems, together with a highly organized religion that was based around imposing mud-brick temples known as ziggurats. The development of trade and taxation systems meant that it was necessary to keep records of what people owned, so the Mesopotamians developed a highly sophisticated writing system, too. They wrote by making cuneiform, or wedge-shaped, marks with a reed stylus in small, hand-held tablets of wet clay, which they then baked hard by firing them in a kiln, or simply by drying them in the sun.

▲ Ziggurat at Ur
Mesopotamian ziggurats, like this one from the 14th century BCE in present-day Iraq, were large buildings with external stairs. The steps led to high platforms on which the priests performed rituals in honour of the deities.

PRIESTS AND KINGS

Religious and political institutions overlapped in ancient Mesopotamia. Kingship was seen as a gift from heaven, so priests had a great deal of influence over political power, while rulers were also seen as sacred figures. In addition, the priests were highly literate, and soon they were inscribing religious and literary texts on clay tablets. The durable nature of these tablets has allowed many of them to survive with their inscriptions still intact and legible despite centuries of exposure to the elements, giving us ready access to an impressive group of early myths.

The first Mesopotamian cities were independent city-states, but some, such as Babylon and later Ashur, expanded in power to create great empires. They shared similar myths but with variations in language, so that gods and goddesses had different names in different parts of the region. Inanna, goddess of love, fertility, and warfare, became known in Babylon as Ishtar, while Utu, the sun god, became Shamash, and so on. The clay tablets that have survived from temple archives tell the stories and adventures of these deities, and of great heroes who are semi-divine figures. The texts are often fragmentary because the archives have survived only in part. But those that have been pieced together yield many narratives that grip readers to this day, such as the famous epic of the great hero Gilgamesh.

MAJOR CENTRES

Babylon was the most powerful city of the Sumerian Empire, with two heydays, in the 18th and 6th centuries BCE. Under Nebuchadnezzar (605–562 BCE), Babylon was a flourishing city with a palace and "hanging gardens" that were one of the wonders of the world. Its temples, and the city gate dedicated to the goddess Ishtar, were impressive structures, indicative of the power of the city's religion. Hardly less powerful was the Assyrian Empire (c.880–c.610 BCE), based at Ashur. Assyrian scribes adopted and preserved many of the myths from neighbouring cities.

There were other centres of early civilization and myth in West Asia. One was at Ugarit, in northern Syria, which flourished around 1500–1200 BCE. Another was in Turkey, where the Hittites founded a powerful empire around 1450 BCE. Both of these early cultures had rich collections of myths, which survive in a fragmentary but fascinating form, as well as prominent weather gods: the Ugaritic storm god Baal, and the Hittite weather god Teshub.

▶ Babylonian boundary stone
The Babylonians put up boundary stones to show who owned pieces of land. Carved on them were symbols of the deities protecting the boundaries: here, a crescent moon for the lunar god Sin.

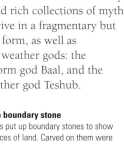

ENUMA ELISH

The Akkadian creation story is called *Enuma Elish*, meaning "When on high", which is the first line of the epic. Inscribed on seven tablets, the myth describes the creation of the first deities from the coming together of the primal waters, and narrates how one god, Marduk, eventually became the ruler of the cosmos, ordering the creation of humans and the foundation of the first city, Babylon.

THE MYTH

In the beginning there were only Apsu, the god of the fresh waters, and Tiamat, the goddess of the salt waters, and everything was silent around them. The pair came together and produced several generations of deities, culminating in Anu, the god of the heavens, and Ea, a cunning and resourceful figure who eventually became the god of both the Earth and the waters.

WAR AMONG THE GODS

The new generation of young and lively deities annoyed Apsu and Tiamat, who longed for the silence that had existed at the beginning of time. Apsu suggested killing the young gods, but Tiamat could not bear the thought of putting to death what they had created. Nevertheless, Apsu decided to kill the other gods on his own. Ea saw what he

▶ Babylonian deity
Gula, the goddess of medicine, was the daughter of Anu. Believed to be the protector of boundaries, she was often depicted on boundary stones.

was about to do and killed him. Then he set himself up as the god of the waters.

MARDUK'S COMING

Ea and his consort, Damkina, produced a son, the mighty god Marduk. When Marduk was given the winds to play with, he caused storms in the waters of Tiamat. She was upset, and decided to avenge the death of her husband, Apsu. So she assembled a force of monsters and ordered the god Kingu to attack Marduk. Several of the gods, fearing a destructive war, tried to stop Tiamat, but she would not listen. Only Marduk was willing to fight her, provided the other gods gave him supreme authority over them all.

THE CREATION

Marduk gathered the four winds, commanded them to blow through Tiamat's mouth so she inflated like a balloon, and then sliced her body open with an arrow. Having defeated Tiamat, Marduk began to rule. He made the heavens from one half of Tiamat's body, creating rain clouds from her saliva. Then he used the other half of her body to create the Earth, so that her breasts became mountains, and the two rivers of Mesopotamia, the Tigris and the Euphrates, flowed from her eyes. He ordered the building of Babylon, and created the first man, Lullu, from the blood of Kingu. Lullu and his descendants dug canals to fertilize the land around Babylon to ensure that the human race could prosper.

▲ The Babylonians
The people of Babylon relied on agriculture for survival, and their creation myth tells how the first man, called Lullu, irrigated his fields so that the people could farm the dry land.

CITIES OF WORSHIP

As in all cultures, religion was crucial to the inhabitants of early Mesopotamian cities such as Babylon, because it offered them a way of understanding the cosmos. Each city was under the protection of a specific god – for example, Marduk in Babylon and the moon god Nanna in Ur – who was worshipped in a temple, usually the most impressive structure in the city. The priests tried to maintain good relations with the gods by making frequent offerings in the hope of good harvests. In addition, each temple owned much land and livestock, so the priests controlled the food supply and the economy of their city.

▲ Making offerings
A priest praying before the symbols of Marduk, the supreme Babylonian god, and Nabi, the god of wisdom.

KEY CHARACTERS

Like many creation myths, *Enuma Elish* begins with a pair of primal deities, Apsu and Tiamat, who create several generations of gods. These gods exist to breed, to fight, and, in the case of Tiamat and Kingu, to provide the raw materials of creation. Kingu becomes Tiamat's consort after Apsu's death, leading her army in the battle against Marduk. Some of the later generations also play many different roles, especially Marduk. He combines the jobs of dragon-slayer, warrior, king, and dispenser of justice – mostly roles that are highly relevant to the people of his city.

▲ Tiamat
The primordial mother, Tiamat, along with her consort, Apsu, symbolize the untamed chaos that existed before there was form and order.

◄ Kingu
A supporter of Tiamat, Kingu held the Tablet of Destiny, which gave him ultimate power over the cosmos. After killing Kingu, Marduk took the tablet from him.

BABYLON

The renowned city of Babylon was one of the most powerful cities in Mesopotamia. It first came to prominence between c.1900–1550 BCE, and later became the centre of a large empire. With its tall ziggurat, the city was always closely identified with the gods, but this link was emphasized by the magnificent city gateway, decorated with glazed bricks depicting beasts associated with the war goddess Ishtar.

Reconstruction of the Ishtar Gate

MARDUK

The Babylonians regarded Marduk as the founder of their city and worshipped him as their supreme god. The creation myth describes how his link with the city began with its construction. When the god had won his battle with Tiamat, he glorified the heavens. He built his own dwelling directly above where Ea had lived and, from the bodies of the monsters that Tiamat had sent to fight him, made statues and placed them by the doorway of Ea's temple. Marduk then told the other gods to build a great city on Earth.

◄ Godly ruler
Often portrayed as a Babylonian warrior king accompanied by a mythical guardian beast, Marduk was said to have invented the idea of kingship.

HE WAS CLOTHED WITH TERROR, WITH OVERPOWERING BRIGHTNESS HIS HEAD WAS CROWNED. THEN HE SET OUT, HE TOOK HIS WAY, AND TOWARDS THE RAGING TIAMAT HE SET HIS FACE.

Enuma Elish

ENUMA ELISH

151

SEE ALSO Asian creation stories 162–63, 168–69, 190–91, 212–13, 222–23

Dragon of the Ishtar Gate
This glazed brick creature decorates the Ishtar Gate of Babylon, which dates from the reign of Nebuchadnezzar (605–562 BCE). The dragon was sacred to the Babylonian god Marduk.

INANNA

The beautiful love goddess Inanna (known in Babylon as Ishtar) controlled many other areas of life; she was also the keeper of the cosmic laws. One myth describes how she stole the tablet of laws from her father, Enki. Her brother was the sun god Utu (also known as Shamash), and she had a twin sister named Ereshkigal. Apart from her amorous encounters with characters such as Gilgamesh (*see pp.156–57*), her best known myths concern her marriage with Dumuzi (also known as Tammuz), the shepherd god, and her visit to the Underworld.

THE MARRIAGE OF INANNA

Inanna, the supremely attractive goddess of sexual love, was desired by many, and was even raped by Shu-kale-tuda, a mortal who was punished with death for his crime. But two suitors in particular vied to be her husband. One was Enkidu, the god of agriculture and patron of those who cultivated crops, while the other was Dumuzi, the shepherd. Inanna's brother, Utu, the sun god, had the power to decide who should be his sister's husband. He declared that Inanna should marry Dumuzi, but the goddess was not happy with this choice. She did not like Dumuzi's cloak made of rough wool, preferring the smooth flax of Enkidu. But the shepherd argued that what he produced – milk, cheese, and wool – was more important to the world than the grain grown by Enkidu. In the end Dumuzi won Inanna round by comparing himself to her brother, Utu. The pair were married, and Inanna gave Dumuzi the kingship of Uruk.

◀ **Utu**
The sun god Utu was known by the bright rays emanating from his body. He used his saw-like knife to cut through mountains and emerge as the dawn.

▶ **Inanna**
Since Inanna was the goddess of fertility and sexual love, she was often depicted as a figure with large thighs or hips and adorned with ornaments.

◀ **Mesopotamian jewellery**
The cities of Mesopotamia had skilled craftsmen who made exquisite jewellery from gold and other precious metals, which were worn on ceremonial occasions like marriages. During her visit to the Underworld (*see opposite*), Inanna had to part with many ornaments.

THE DEATH OF INANNA

Ereshkigal was Inanna's twin sister and counterpart. Whereas Inanna was a goddess of light, Ereshkigal was a goddess of darkness and lived in the Underworld. Inanna grew to miss her sister, and so she decided to go to the Underworld to visit her. She told her maid Ninshubur to ask the gods to help if she did not return from the Underworld in three days. When Inanna entered the realm of the dead, she was made to remove an item of clothing or jewellery as she passed through each of the seven circles of the Underworld. By the time she finally reached her sister, Inanna was naked. She went to embrace Ereshkigal, but the demons of the Underworld thought she was trying to take her sister back to Earth, so they caught her and turned her into a corpse.

▲ The Underworld
Ruled over by Ereshkigal and her husband, Nergal – a hideous and rapacious bull – the Mesopotamian Underworld was a dark place populated by demons who captured Inanna and hung her from a hook.

▲ Rescuing Inanna
The trickster god Enki created two beings from dirt under his fingernails, sending them to rescue Inanna with a cup of the water of immortality.

▼ Mesopotamian demon
When Inanna was finally allowed to leave the Underworld, she was followed by some of Ereshkigal's demons who had been sent to find a replacement for her.

THE REBIRTH OF INANNA

Without Inanna, love perished on the Earth and the world went dark. After three days, her maid Ninshubur appealed to the gods to rescue her from the Underworld. The gods knew that no one who had the spark of life could return from the Underworld, and some wished her to stay there, so they refused. But the trickster god Enki (known as Ea in Babylon) came up with an answer. He created two beings who lacked the attributes of life – they had no inner organs, no sexuality, and no minds. Enki sent them to the Underworld with a cup full of the water of immortality. They revived Inanna with the water, and Ereshkigal helped her sister to return to Earth.

THE DEATH OF DUMUZI

Prior to leaving the Underworld, Inanna promised the judges of the dead that she would send someone to take her place. On her return, Inanna met Ninshubur, but did not want her to die in Inanna's place. Inanna found that her husband Dumuzi had been having an affair with the goddess Geshtinanna in her absence. Enraged, she decided to punish Dumuzi by sending him to the Underworld. Although Utu transformed Dumuzi into a snake to help him hide, the demons of the Underworld eventually found him. It was finally decided that Dumuzi would spend half the year in the Underworld and Geshtinanna the other half, so that they would never be able to meet again.

► Cedar tree
The cedar tree was sacred to the cult of Dumuzi and Inanna. Dumuzi represented the sap dormant in the trees during the dry season.

◄ The shepherd god
Duzumi was released from the Underworld for six months each year because he was useful on Earth as the protector god of shepherds and their flocks.

INANNA

155

SEE ALSO Love deities 38–39, 138–39, 180–81, 244–45, 310–11 • Punishments 26–27, 50–51, 54–55, 68–69, 70–71, 218–19, 288–89

THE EPIC OF GILGAMESH

The story of Gilgamesh, the King of Uruk, is the oldest extended narrative to have come down from the ancient world. It survives in the form of an epic poem written on clay tablets in the 7th century BCE in Assyria, although the story dates back to the 3rd millennium BCE. Its themes of heroism, friendship, and the quest for immortality, together with the poem's exotic cast of characters, have proved fascinating for generations of readers.

THE MYTH

Gilgamesh was a ruthless and cruel ruler of Uruk. He forced the men to be his slaves and the women to be his mistresses. Helpless against the mighty Gilgamesh, the people prayed to the gods for help and they responded by sending a wild man named Enkidu to fight Gilgamesh and subdue him. Gilgamesh attempted to tame Enkidu by sending a temple prostitute to seduce him. The woman took Enkidu to Uruk to civilize him, but when they arrived at a wedding in the city, Enkidu saw Gilgamesh demanding to sleep with the bride, and challenged him to a fight. They were both strong and evenly matched, and realized after a long struggle that there could be no winner. Thus, they embraced and became friends.

THE TWO TYRANTS

Now there were two tyrants terrorizing the people of Uruk. This time the gods sent a creature called Humbaba, who was a fire-breathing monster. But Gilgamesh and Enkidu, who were supported by Shamash, the sun god, fought the monster and killed him. Next the gods tried to trick Gilgamesh by sending the attractive Inanna (known as Ishtar in Babylon)

The Bull of Heaven
Killing supernatural monsters of great strength like the bull was common for the hero and antihero in ancient epic poetry.

> **Gilgamesh**
> The main characteristics of Gilgamesh were his superhuman strength and great willpower – traits symbolized in this statue by the commanding way in which he holds the lion.

to seduce him, but he rejected her. Normally irresistible, she resented this rebuff and complained to the gods, who responded by sending another monster, the Bull of Heaven. But even this creature was killed by Enkidu and Gilgamesh. Now the gods decided that one of them must pay for killing Humbaba and the Bull of Heaven. They decreed that Enkidu would die.

THE SEARCH FOR IMMORTALITY

Enkidu's death forced Gilgamesh to consider his own mortality. He knew of a man named Utnapishtim who was the sole survivor of a great flood and had been granted immortality. So Gilgamesh visited Utnapishtim to find a way of attaining immortality. Utnapishtim told him that the gods had caused the flood because they were angry at the sins of humans. But Enki (Ea in Babylonian myth), the water god, had appeared in a dream to Utnapishtim and instructed him to build a boat.

Utnapishtim advised Gilgamesh to accept his fate as a mortal, but also told him of a plant growing at the bottom of a lake in the Underworld that gave everlasting youth to whomever ate from it. Gilgamesh went to the Underworld and found the plant, but on his way back, a snake stole the plant. Realizing the futility of his quest, Gilgamesh accepted his fate.

KEY CHARACTERS

Although the epic is set in a real place, a city-state called Uruk in the Mesopotamian region, most of its major characters are linked with the supernatural world. The creatures sent to challenge Gilgamesh are gigantic and terrifying because they come from heaven – the wild man Enkidu is created by Ninhursag, the goddess of the Earth, while the Bull of Heaven is sent by Anu, the god of the sky. Gilgamesh himself straddles both worlds. His parents are Ninsun, the goddess of the sky, and Ligulbanda, a semi-divine figure; his mixed parentage is why he is described as part-god and part-human.

◄ The coming of Enkidu
Gilgamesh had a dream about a star falling from heaven, which he and his friends could not lift. This star represented the coming of Enkidu.

▲ Utnapishtim
An old man by the time Gilgamesh met him, Utnapishtim told the king how he had gathered the animals of the world in his boat to save them from the flood.

▲ Humbaba
This forest-dwelling monster was much feared because of the deadly fire he breathed. Even Enkidu was initially reluctant to fight the beast.

DEITIES

The gods and goddesses play a major role in the epic, talking to the earthbound humans and acting directly in the decisive moments of the story. They also influence events in a subtler manner by sending dreams that predict the future – the killing of Humbaba and the death of Enkidu were both foreseen in dreams. Although they are extremely powerful, the deities are fallible – their schemes to defeat Gilgamesh with monsters do not work, and Inanna's plan to seduce Gilgamesh is also a failure.

▲ Shamash
Seen here dictating laws to a king, Shamash, the god of the sun and war, aided Gilgamesh in killing Humbaba.

▲ Enlil
The wind god Enlil (*right*) was widely worshipped. He ordered Enkidu's death after the latter had killed Humbaba, the protector of the forest.

➤ Inanna
The very beautiful Inanna was the goddess of sexuality. She was irresistible to most men, but Gilgamesh spurned her advances, infuriating her in the process.

▲ Uruk
The poem mentions the mud-brick temples and city walls of Uruk, the ruins of which survive near the River Euphrates in West Asia. Some of these date from the 4th millennium BCE.

▲ Clay tablets
Scholars have had to piece together fragments of Akkadian tablets in order to reconstruct epics like *Gilgamesh*.

VERSIONS OF THE MYTH

Several ancient texts tell stories about Gilgamesh, who was probably a real king who later gained mythical status. Most such texts are fragments that together tell Gilgamesh's story – one talks about the Bull of Heaven, another describes Enkidu's journey to the Underworld. At some point, these texts were recorded in Akkadian, a Semitic language that was widely used in Mesopotamia from the 3rd to the 1st millennium BCE. The best surviving copy of the epic – still fragmentary but more complete than the others – was preserved in the library of the Assyrian king, Ashurbanipal II (668–627 BCE), at Nineveh.

157

SEE ALSO Friendship 60–61, 200–03 • Immortality 68–69, 132–33, 216–17, 218–19

MYTHS OF UGARIT

The ancient city of Ugarit flourished near the western coast of modern-day Syria, an area once known as Canaan. Ugarit was a major city in the centuries preceding c.1200 BCE, when it was destroyed by invaders. In the 20th century, thousands of clay tablets were discovered at the ancient site, and some of these described the gods and goddesses of the city's inhabitants. Many myths recorded on these tablets feature the deity Baal, the god of rain and thunder; his sister, the fertility goddess Anat; and their father, the supreme sky god El.

BAAL'S STRUGGLE FOR POWER

Baal was the son of the great god El, and so belonged to the family that stood above all others in Ugarit's pantheon of gods. El's power was eternal, but as he grew older, Baal grew mightier in the sky, becoming the deity in control of the rain, thunder, and lightning. But Baal was challenged for supremacy by one of his brothers, Yamm, the god of the sea, who demanded that El give him all the treasure belonging to Baal. Yamm sent messengers to capture Baal and imprison him, and he made Baal his slave. Baal was saved by a great craftsman, Kothar wa-Hasis, who made two magical clubs for him. Yamm resisted a blow from the first club, but when Baal ordered the second to strike Yamm, the blow brought the sea god down, enabling Baal to tear him up and scatter the pieces. Thus Baal became supreme among the sons of El.

▼ Yamm
The sea god Yamm was believed to be present in the crashing waves and perilous currents of the ocean, and was a figure who represented chaos, disorder, and danger to the human race.

▲ Tablet from Ugarit
Writings from Ugarit survive on clay tablets that were written on when soft by scribes with reed styluses, and baked hard in the sun. Some of the surviving tablets bear small images of Baal.

▶ Baal
The supreme god Baal is shown here wearing a conical headdress. He holds a spear in one hand and raises his club high in the other, ready to attack and strike down his enemies.

BAAL'S PALACE

Even after Baal had defeated his brother, Yamm, and acquired great power, he still had no palace of his own. Baal complained to his sister, Anat, reminding her that his brothers had palaces just like the mortal rulers. Anat went to El to ask for a palatial residence on her brother's behalf, but El stalled her, saying that he could not grant this wish without the consent of his wife, Athirat. El was certain that Athirat would not consent easily because she had always favoured her other sons over Baal. Subsequently, the supreme sky god hatched a plot to persuade her. He called for the craftsman Kothar wa-Hasis and ordered him to make exquisite furniture and ornaments for Baal. On seeing these, Athirat agreed to let Baal have a palace in which to keep the furniture.

▼ Gold ornament
Craft workers in the city-state of Ugarit produced stunning gold jewellery and other artefacts. Objects such as this embossed gold cup, found in the ruins of the temple of Baal, were commonly used items.

◄ Ruins of Ugarit
The royal palace and other structures of Ugarit survive as ruins today. The buildings were primarily made of stone and wood.

THE RETURN OF BAAL

After Baal's palace was constructed, he arrogantly challenged Mot, the god of death. His voice reverberated across the palace's open window and reached Mot, who accepted the challenge. Mot entered through the window and swallowed Baal, taking him away to the Underworld. In Baal's absence, the rains ceased and the Earth was subjected to a terrible drought. The other gods, especially Baal's father, El, and his sister, Anat, were distraught when they heard that the rain god had been taken to the Underworld. So Anat went there and attacked Mot with her knife and winnowing fan. She burned him, ground him into pieces with her millstone, and scattered the pieces far and wide. Baal was able to return and refreshed the Earth with rain.

► The great god El
El, the creator god, who was also called the "Father of Gods and Men", was the ruler of the gods of Ugarit, and a shadowy figure like many other supreme gods.

THE FEARSOME ANAT

The goddess Anat, sister of Baal, was the deity who presided over human sexuality and the fertility of the fields of Canaan. But she also had a sinister side, and was widely known for her violence and love of bloodshed. She held weaponry in such high regard that once she tried to steal the bow and arrows belonging to a mortal warrior named Ahat. Baal was so angry with his sister over this that he withheld the rains for a while. On another occasion, Anat massacred the inhabitants of two cities not far from Ugarit, and then invited an army to eat in her palace before chopping off the heads of the soldiers with her scythe. These attacks seem to be unmotivated, but might have been considered by the people of Canaan as sacrifices to make the fields more fertile.

► Anat
Often depicted as heavily armed for battle, Anat is a goddess who governs both warfare and fertility. In this respect, she is similar to Astarte and Inanna (*see pp.154–55*), deities revered in Mesopotamia.

SEE ALSO Sibling rivalry 240–41 • Battle for kingdom 200–03, 206–07, 260–61

MYTHS OF THE HITTITES

The Hittites settled in Anatolia (modern-day Turkey) about 5,000 years ago, and by the 2nd millennium BCE, ruled over a powerful empire that extended to the Mediterranean Sea. Their mythology featured numerous gods, including many weather deities, because they adopted the myths of the people they had conquered. Some of their most popular stories told of rivalries among the gods and how these deities influenced the lives of mortals.

KUMARBI

The great god Alalu was the ruler of the universe, and the other gods, led by Alalu's chief courtier, bowed down to him. But after having obeyed Alalu for nine years, they revolted and installed his son, Anu, the sky god, in his place. After a further nine years, the gods grew restless once again, and there was another revolt. This time Anu's son, Kumarbi, proved to be the strongest god, and he defeated Anu by biting off his genitals. While doing so, Kumarbi swallowed Anu's sperm, and when he spat it out, a host of other gods were born from it, including Teshub, the powerful storm god. Teshub soon usurped all of his father's power, and in spite of repeated attempts to win it back, Kumarbi could not defeat the mighty storm god.

◀ **Drinking horn**
After Anu was ousted, Kumarbi was made leader of the gods, and the other gods honoured him by filling his rhyton, a drinking cup that was sometimes shaped like an animal.

▲ **A Hittite feast**
The Hittites celebrated spring with feasts; it is said that defeating Illuyanka at a banquet allowed Teshub to bring the spring weather.

TESHUB AND THE SERPENT

Teshub was a powerful deity, but even he was not immune from defeat. One day, he fought an enormous serpent called Illuyanka and lost. Humiliated by this defeat, Teshub asked the other gods for help, and his daughter, Inara, came up with a plan. She and her mortal lover, Hupasiya, threw a great feast for Illuyanka and his children, with scrumptious food and vast quantities of beer and wine. The serpent family fell greedily on the food, becoming drowsy from all the wine and beer, and were so full that none of them could get back inside their hole. Hupasiya cornered Illuyanka and tied him up, and Teshub killed the serpent with his thunder weapons.

◀ **Teshub**
The storm god combined the roles of a war and weather god, keeping the people fed and protecting them from enemies.

▶ **Illuyanka**
The giant serpent was a destructive force, a creature of such power that he could defeat the strongest of the deities.

THE DISAPPEARING GOD

A popular myth tells of the greedy Sea God who decided to kidnap Sun God, as he was hungry for power. He caught Sun God in a net and imprisoned him in a storage jar. With the sun gone, life on Earth came to a standstill – the temperature dropped, the crops would not grow, and all the cattle died. Even the gods shivered with cold. The other deities looked for Sun God, but no one could find him. Teshub's son, Telepinu, came close, but Sea God imprisoned him too.

Finally, the gods made a great sacrifice and persuaded Sea God to allow the sun to return. From that point, the Hittites began to make regular sacrifices to their gods.

Telepinu tablet
This Hittite tablet contains parts of Telepinu's story; in one version, Telepinu frees Sun God and takes Sea God's daughter away.

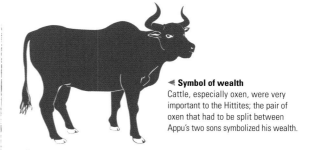

Symbol of wealth
Cattle, especially oxen, were very important to the Hittites; the pair of oxen that had to be split between Appu's two sons symbolized his wealth.

A DIVIDED INHERITANCE

Some early texts of the Hittites mention the story of Appu, a rich man who was very unhappy because he had no children. He prayed to Sun God, and was granted his wish; soon, Appu had not one but two sons, whom he and his wife called Wrong and Right. At first, the two brothers lived together in peace, but gradually Wrong grew independent and wanted to settle apart from his brother. He told Right that since the gods lived separately, so should they. Right agreed to this proposal, and the two brothers decided to divide their inheritance, including a pair of oxen given to them by their father. But Wrong cheated his brother, making sure that he took the stronger ox of the two for himself. When Sun God saw what had happened, he transformed Right's ox so that it became even stronger than Wrong's.

SIXTY CHILDREN

Once, a queen of Kanesh – an ancient city in Turkey – gave birth to 30 sons. She was overwhelmed by such a large number and decided to cast them out. She put all of them in a boat and set it on the river. The gods found the boat and rescued the children, bringing them up, and changing their appearance so that they looked more like gods than humans. Meanwhile, the queen miraculously gave birth to 30 girls, whom she brought up herself. After growing up, the boys wanted to meet their real mother, so they went looking for her. When they reached Kanesh, they stayed at an inn and told the innkeeper about their large family. He informed them about the queen's 30 daughters, and told them that she once had 30 sons too. The young men went to see the queen, but she did not recognize them. She wanted them to marry her daughters, but they refused, fearing incest.

The ruins of Kanesh
The city of Kanesh at Kultepe, Turkey, is now just a cluster of mud-brick ruins, but it was once an important trading centre in the region. For this reason, the ancient city features in several myths of the early Hittite people.

SEE ALSO Snakes & serpents 28–29, 48–49, 92–93, 98–99, 100–03, 238–39 • Abandoned children 56–57, 78–79

THE GREAT SKY GOD

The ancient Mongol and Turkic people were animists who believed in many spirits (*tengri*) that inhabited the natural world. Supreme among these spirits was a sky god called Mongke Tengri (or just Tengri), who was the creator of humanity and the world, and who protected humans from malevolent demons. Tengri also controlled the different elements and influenced the fertility of the land.

THE MYTH

The Mongol account of the Earth's creation involves the high-ranking *tengri* Qormusta, and Sakyamuni – the Buddha – who is also a member of the Mongol pantheon of gods. Qormusta gave Sakyamuni a handful of yellow earth that was composed of precious stones. Sakyamuni threw it into the eternal ocean, causing it to begin to coalesce into a vast continent. At this point, a tortoise emerged from the depths of the ocean and stole the Earth. Sakyamuni realized that only the death of the tortoise would free the Earth and let the ground form. As a monk and a lover of peace, he was hesitant about killing the tortoise, but the *tengri* assured him that it was the right thing to do, because many lives would eventually flourish on the Earth after the loss of one. Thus, Sakyamuni slew the tortoise and subsequently the world was formed.

THE FIRST HUMANS

When the Earth had taken shape, only animals lived on it, so Mongke Tengri created the first man and woman to populate the world. He perfected their physical forms over time, and then covered their bodies with soft hair. Once Tengri was satisfied with his creations, he decided to fetch water from the Spring of Immortality so that the first man and woman could live forever. Worried about their safety, Tengri

Burial stone
The early Turkic people buried their dead in the Earth created by Tengri, and erected burial stones, such as this 6th-century one, to mark the graves.

Mongke Tengri
Tengri is a fierce sky god, and wields his weaponry to fight the demons and evil spirits that threaten human beings.

commanded a cat and a dog to guard the humans. But once he left for the Spring of Immortality, Erlik Khan, the Lord of the Underworld, tempted the cat away with a bowl of milk, and the dog with a piece of meat, and then defiled Tengri's creations by urinating all over them.

THE CAT AND THE DOG

When Tengri returned, he was enraged to find out that Erlik Khan had tainted his creations; he was especially angry with the cat and the dog because they had failed in their task of watching over and protecting the man and woman. Consequently, Tengri punished the animals by making the cat lick off all the body hair from the humans and stick it on the dog's skin. The cat licked off almost all the hair from their bodies, excluding that on their heads, which Erlik Khan had not polluted, and some on the lower parts of their bodies – which the cat avoided because they gave off a foul odour. Once the cat had finished the task, Tengri took the water of eternal life and poured it over his creations in an attempt to immortalize them, but he failed in this venture because the humans had been polluted by Erlik Khan's foul deed.

Primal tortoise

THE TURKIC CREATION STORY

In the Turkic version of the creation story, Tengri flew across the sky as a white goose, over an enormous ocean symbolizing the endless flow of time. He heard a being called the White Mother asking him to create the world. Tengri made another being called Er Kishi, and together they made the Earth and its inhabitants. But Er Kishi was impure, and tried to seduce the people into leading a life of evil. So Tengri sent his sacred animals to Earth to make the shamans, or spirit guides, teach the people about living well and respecting their creator.

◄ The white goose
After creating all things, Tengri flew high enough to reach heaven. He was believed to return to Earth sometimes in the form of a great white goose.

TENGRI AND NATURE

The early Turkic and Mongol people attributed many of the strongest natural phenomena to Tengri and other gods and spirits. Thunder was supposed to symbolize Tengri's voice; lightning was a means of punishment and a display of Tengri's power. Tengri's storms were beneficial as well, because the plants grew and the crops flourished after the rain. These people considered all living beings – birds, animals, plants, and trees – to be inhabited by individual spirits. This meant that everything in nature was sacred.

Maize

▲ Bolts of lightning
Tengri was said to have lit the first fire with one of his lightning bolts. Lightning and fire had long been worshipped in West and Central Asia; they could not only cleanse the world, but ward off demons.

TENGRISM

Tengrism is the modern term for the belief system of the Mongol and Turkic people of ancient times. Based on Mongke Tengri (representing the eternal blue sky), Eje (a female fertility figure and a Mother Earth goddess), and many other benign and malign nature spirits, it involved the practice of shamanism (*see pp.268–69*), or communication with spirits. Tengrism was promoted by later Turkic rulers such as Genghis Khan (reigned 1206–27) and his grandson, Batu Khan (reigned 1227–55). Its followers respected nature spirits and led a life of moral rectitude. If people lost their balance with the natural world due to their actions or the action of malign spirits, the shamans would intervene to restore it.

Turkic ruler Batu Khan

▲ A simple life
The early Turks and Mongols lived in harmony with nature. They settled in fertile areas near rivers, which were conducive not only to agriculture, but also provided suitable pastures for their cattle and horses.

TENGRI IN THE EAST

Linguists have long noticed the similarity between the name Tengri and the Chinese word for sky, *tian*, which also means god. It is not known whether one word led to the other, but the two are related, just like the Chinese and Mongol cultures. The two terms appear together in the names of mountains, which are considered sacred places. In the Tian Shan (Sky Mountain) range on the border of Kazakhstan, the second highest peak is known as Khan Tengri (Lord of the Spirits).

"Tengri" in Orkhon (old Turkic script)

163

SEE ALSO Asian creation stories 150–51, 168–69, 190–91, 212–13, 222–23 • Asian sky deities 158–59, 160–61, 188–89

DEITIES OF FATE AND FORTUNE

Gods and goddesses of fate and fortune appear in many mythologies. They have a particularly strong hold on the imagination because they are said to have the power to shape human lives – and, in some cases, to see into the future and give people a glimpse of what is to happen.

BRINGERS OF GOOD FORTUNE

Many deities are said to have the power to bring good luck. They are usually deities to whom believers appeal when starting a new phase in their lives, such as getting married. Sometimes, as with the Roman goddess Fortuna, their benevolence is a matter of chance, but people still make offerings in the hope that the deity will smile on them.

▷ Benten
This Japanese goddess of learning, music, and wealth is said to have defeated wicked dragons. She is also the most prominent of the Seven Gods of Luck.

◁ Lakshmi
The kind Hindu goddess Lakshmi (*see p.191*) is said to take up her place by the doors of homes and bring good fortune to the families inside.

◁ Seven Gods of Luck
These Japanese deities oversee new ventures. Each has a specific responsibility, bringing such advantages as wealth and good health.

▲ Ganesh
Hindus call the elephant-headed god Ganesh the "Remover of all Obstacles", and often invoke him when they begin a new enterprise.

▷ Fortuna
The Romans believed that Fortuna brought happiness to newly wed women. She was also said to bring fortune to families, cities, and states, and to give good luck without bias or favour.

◁ Three Gods of Happiness
These Chinese gods are Shou Xing, god of long life, Lu Xing, god of rank and wealth, and Fu Xing, god of good fortune.

164

Norns

The three Norns of Norse mythology wove tapestries depicting the course of human destiny. Their work was never finished, meaning human destiny is never fixed.

Brigit

Some Celts saw their sky god's three daughters as aspects of one goddess, Brigit ("exalted"), who had supreme power over human fate.

DEITIES OF DESTINY

Some deities of fate and fortune were so powerful that they controlled destiny itself – dictating the span of human life, and the time and manner of each person's death. Often they operated in groups of three, and even the high gods could not interfere in their work. Such powerful deities were usually rather shadowy figures who commanded respect rather than devout worship.

Fates

The Greek Fates took the form of three old women. While Clotho held the spindle, Lachesis spun the thread of human life and Atropos cut the thread to end a life.

ORACULAR DEITIES

Deities who could see far into the future were especially revered, and their priests, priestesses, and prophets held in high regard. But their prophecies were not always easy to read, and attempts to decipher them often failed. Many mortals in Greek mythology, for example, receive prophecies they misinterpret. In trying to avoid the bad luck prophesied, they stumble on ill fortune in an unexpected way.

Eshu

Eshu was the messenger of the gods in the mythology of the Yoruba people of Nigeria. He tended the smoke from sacrifices as it took messages to the gods, and brought back the replies.

Apollo

One of the main cult centres of the Greek god Apollo (see pp.28–29) was his oracle at Delphi, where he slew the serpent Python. This oracle's prophecies were notoriously ambiguous.

Gefion

A Norse fertility goddess and daughter of the great god Odin, Gefion had the power to see into the future, but was unable to change future events.

Sibyls

In Roman mythology, Sibyls (see p.79) were women who put themselves into a trance and uttered mysterious sounds – said to come from the gods – that priests then tried to interpret.

DEITIES OF FATE AND FORTUNE

165

▲ **The birth of Rustum, from the *Shahnama***
The epic poem the *Shahnama* (Book of Kings) contains a series of legends and
is a key source of Persian mythical history. One central character is Rustum, a
brave hero who overcomes many enemies but tragically kills his own son.

CENTRAL ASIA AND ARABIA

These two regions of Asia, though now identified with Islam, have long been a melting pot of cultures and beliefs, with a number of mythological traditions flourishing through the long history of civilization in both areas.

Persia (modern-day Iran) was one of the most important crossroads of the ancient world, with traders and settlers arriving from almost all points of the compass over the centuries and contributing to the sophisticated culture of the region. One group, the Hittites, whose culture was a blend of Indian and Persian elements, left Persia for Turkey. But other groups – and especially those from the steppes of Central Asia – arrived and settled in Persia, bringing with them a variety of deities.

BULL RITUAL OF MITHRA

One of the most influential gods of the settlers was Mithra, a deity whose name appeared in documents beside early Indian gods such as Indra. Mithra then became popular throughout Persia and was worshipped as an all-knowing protector, a sun god very similar to the Mesopotamian sun god Shamash. Mithra was also a god of agreements and treaties – the very personification, in fact, of the idea of *mitra*, or contract.

The popularity of Mithra spread even further, and when the Romans expanded their empire into Asia, he was one of the deities they adopted. His central ritual was the slaying of a sacrificial bull. This ritual slaughter was the recreation of a rite first performed by Yima, the Persian primal man, and was seen as an act of renewal. By performing the rite, worshippers of Mithra believed they were recreating the ideal conditions that existed when Yima originally ruled the world.

AHURA MAZDA

The other influential deity of Persia was Ahura Mazda, the wise, all-seeing creator sky god. He was originally one of a large pantheon of ancient Persian deities that included, as in many pantheons, a number of gods of the elements, among

whom Tishtrya, god of rain, and Vayu, god of wind, were prominent. Anahita, a goddess of fertility and source of water on Earth, was another key figure; she and Tishtrya were clearly evidence of the precarious water supply in Persia.

▲ Ahura Mazda, the Wise Lord
This gold earring from the 6th to the 4th century BCE depicts Ahura Mazda grasping a pair of antelope by the horns – an image that conveys his rulership over creation.

MONOTHEISTIC BELIEF

In the 7th or 6th century BCE, change came with the work and vision of the prophet Zoroaster, who saw Ahura Mazda as absolute, the one god worthy of worship. With the rise of Zoroastrianism, Ahura Mazda overshadowed the other deities of ancient Persia. In a different way, the rise of Islam in the Arabian peninsula several centuries later eclipsed the "false gods" of the local people denounced by the prophet Muhammad. Yet the mythology of the Arabian peninsula is not so easily forgotten, and its stories of adventure and great heroism still enthral people around the world.

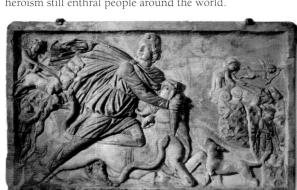

▲ The cult of Mithra
The young god Mithra prepares to slay the sacrificial bull in this dramatic Roman temple relief. Having adopted the Central Asian deity, the Romans made a mystery cult out of Mithra, with secret temples, often concealed underground.

THE FIGHT AGAINST EVIL

At the heart of Zoroastrianism lies a cosmic struggle between the kind god Ahura Mazda and his evil opponent Ahriman. The religion, which flourished in Central Asia until the 7th century, still has followers in Iran and among the Parsis in India. Although Zoroastrians consider Ahura Mazda to be the only god, their religion also features a rich body of traditions about other beings, from benevolent immortals to demons, who influence human life. In the struggle against evil, Zoroastrianism predicts that the forces of good will triumph in the end.

THE MYTH

The first god, Zurvan (Time), lived in the primal void that existed before creation. He longed for a son, but was doubtful of his power of creation. So he conceived two sons: Ahura Mazda (Wise Lord), who was born from his optimism, and Ahriman, who was born out of his uncertainty. Before they came into the world, Zurvan predicted that his first-born would rule the world. Ahriman heard what his father had said and forced himself into the world ahead of his brother, who was rightfully supposed to come first. Ahriman told Zurvan that he was Ahura Mazda, the first-born, but the god saw through his trickery. He knew that Ahura Mazda would be pale and sweet-smelling, whereas Ahriman was dark and foul-smelling.

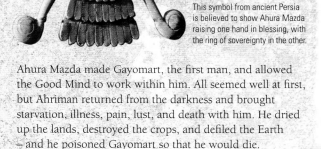

◀ **Ahura Mazda**
This symbol from ancient Persia is believed to show Ahura Mazda raising one hand in blessing, with the ring of sovereignty in the other.

CREATION AND DEATH

After his birth, Ahura Mazda went to work to give the universe its form. He made the sun, moon, and stars, and all that represented good in the world. He also created six immortals, including Vohu Manah (Good Mind), to help govern his creation. Ahriman sent evil demons to attack Ahura Mazda, but the Wise Lord cast his brother out into the darkness. Then

◀ **The dispute over the world**
Ahura Mazda and his wicked brother, Ahriman, fought to control the world, represented by the ring of sovereignty that they both tried to possess.

Ahura Mazda made Gayomart, the first man, and allowed the Good Mind to work within him. All seemed well at first, but Ahriman returned from the darkness and brought starvation, illness, pain, lust, and death with him. He dried up the lands, destroyed the crops, and defiled the Earth – and he poisoned Gayomart so that he would die.

THE HUMAN RACE

When Ahura Mazda saw that Gayomart was going to die, he took the man's seed and made Mashya and Mashyoi, the first human couple. Although they too were destined to die, their children went on to propagate future generations, ensuring the survival of humanity. Ahura Mazda could not defeat Ahriman, so he trapped the evil lord inside creation and gave humans the freedom to choose between good and evil. This struggle between the two forces will be resolved only at the end of time, when a new god called Saoshyant (the Saviour) will come and, together with Ahura Mazda, destroy Ahriman and the evil he represents. The people themselves will become pure and good. The world will be created anew, after which all will be good, and the distinction between body and soul will cease to exist.

SIX IMMORTALS

The Amesha Spentas (Bounteous Immortals) are the children of Ahura Mazda, and second in importance only to that god. On one level, they are abstract entities and aspects of the divine nature of Ahura Mazda. On another level, they are seen as immortals, who sit on golden thrones and look after specific aspects of the natural world, ranging from fire to water. In doing so, they leave Ahura Mazda to concentrate on caring for humankind.

▲ Vohu Manah
The caretaker of domestic animals, Vohu Manah (Good Mind) is also the recorder of the good and bad deeds of humans.

▲ Asha
Meaning "Righteousness" or "Truth", Asha protects the element of fire and fights evil forces, such as disease and sorcery.

▲ Armaiti
Armaiti (Devotion) is the daughter of Ahura Mazda, the protector of the Earth. She is the embodiment of faith and worship.

▲ Khshathra Vairya
Personifying the power of Ahura Mazda, Khshathra (Dominion) protects the sky and metals, and fights Saura, a demon of anarchy.

▲ Haurvatat
Meaning both "Wholeness" and "Integrity", Haurvatat protects water and opposes thirst. She is closely associated with Ameretat.

▲ Ameretat
Ameretat (Immortality) sustains and protects plants, and hence, life and growth. She is the opponent of hunger.

THE FIRST HUMANS

The primal couple, Mashya and Mashyoi, were made from the seed of Gayomart, the first man, whom Ahriman had doomed to die. Initially, the two grew together, entwined as a kind of tree, and the fruit they produced became the ten races of the Earth. They began in goodness, but Ahriman sent demons to corrupt them, and some of their actions became evil. But in spite of their corruption, deep down they kept their "heavenly self", which meant that they still had the power to make good decisions and choose a moral path through life.

➤ Gayomart
When the Wise Lord created the first man, Gayomart, he was perfect in form and radiated his beauty like the sun.

▲ The primal tree
Because the first creation was in an ideal state, the original tree needed no bark to protect its branches and no thorns to defend its fruit.

THE SACRED FLAME

A prominent feature of Zoroastrian worship, the sacred flame burns continuously in the faith temples. The reverence accorded to these flames has led some to wrongly describe the religion as "fire worship". Zoroastrians worship Ahura Mazda, and the fire, which is described as the son of the god, stands for the place where people experience the god's presence. Although all fires are sacred, those set up with the correct ritual in temples are especially symbolic of his presence.

Fire burning in a Zoroastrian temple

ZOROASTER

The prophet of Zoroastrianism, Zoroaster (also known as Zarathustra) was born in Iran or Afghanistan some time in the 2nd millennium BCE. When he was 30 years old, he had a vision of Ahura Mazda, and subsequently began to propagate the worship of the god among his followers. Zoroaster insisted that there was only one true god, who was the source of goodness. He rejected the old religion of his homeland, insisting that some of its gods, who were warlike beings, were agents of Ahriman. Hymns said to be written by Zoroaster are collected in the sacred book of the faith, the *Avesta*.

Zoroaster, prophet of the faith

169

SEE ALSO Asian creation stories 150–51, 162–63, 190–91, 212–13, 222–23 • Prophets 180–181

THE LEGEND OF RUSTUM AND SOHRAB

Rustum was the greatest hero of the early Persians: a brave warrior who defended himself and his people against the most fearsome and powerful foes. Rustum's bravery and skill, not to mention his mastery of the noble stallion Rakhsh, make him an exemplary character, but his life was marred by tragedy when he unwittingly killed his own son, Sohrab. The story of this event is a key episode in the Persian epic *Shahnama* (Book of Kings), and is also the subject of a famous poem by the British poet Matthew Arnold (1822–88).

THE MYTH

Out hunting one day, Rustum decided to take some rest. As he lay asleep, a group of men came across his horse, Rakhsh, and stole it. Rustum awoke to find his mount gone, and set off in search of the animal. When he reached the palace of Afrasiab, the ruler of a Central Asian kingdom, the king entertained Rustum and introduced him to his daughter, Tahmina. Rustum slept with her and, before leaving, gave her a clasp that he wore on his upper arm, asking her to give it to their child. The next day, his horse was found and Rustum went on his way.

YOUNG SOHRAB

Tahmina had a son whom she named Sohrab. He was an accomplished archer by the time he was five years old, and it became apparent that he would grow into a young man of great strength. When he asked about his father, Tahmina told him the truth, swearing him to secrecy.

Eventually, Sohrab became a great warrior and decided to launch an attack against Persia, hoping to meet his famous father in the course of the battle. His ultimate wish was to see Rustum as the Emperor of Persia, while he himself would take over his grandfather's throne. This plan pleased the devious Afrasiab, Sohrab's grandfather. He knew that if father and son came face to face, one would be bound to kill the other. If Rustum were to die, Afrasiab could easily defeat the Emperor of Persia with Sohrab's help; if Sohrab were killed, Rustum would die of grief in any case, and Afrasiab could achieve the same objective.

THE FATAL FIGHT

The war began with Sohrab attacking a Persian castle. Its garrison, however, escaped and sent a message to their emperor that they were being attacked by a powerful leader, a man as mighty as Rustum. The Persian emperor knew that his only hope was to send his greatest warrior to the battlefront.

So Rustum joined the Persian camp. Sohrab proposed a duel and Rustum accepted the challenge, claiming that he was a slave. He did not reveal his identity, thinking that the enemy would be terrified if they found a mere Persian slave to be so strong. The two mighty warriors battled until they were exhausted, fighting with weapons and then with their bare hands. But there was still no victor as the pair was evenly matched. They resumed fighting the next day. This time Rustum, after long preparatory prayers, threw Sohrab and broke his back. As he lay dying, Sohrab showed Rustum the arm jewel and told him that his father would avenge his death. That was when Rustum realized that he had killed his own son. The anguished father built a golden tomb for Sohrab.

◀ **Rustum and Sohrab**
Even though they were exhausted, father and son refused to give up, wrestling one another to the ground and fighting on to the bitter end.

RUSTUM

Son of the legendary warrior Zal (*see p.56*) and a princess called Rudaba, Rustum was destined to be a warrior of great strength. While still in the womb, he grew so large that his mother almost died in childbirth. Both were saved because Zal knew how to perform a surgical operation to ensure a safe birth. Rustum was already very strong when he was born. As he grew up, he became skilled in arms, and his strength increased further. Over time, he became a champion of the early Persians, always ready to defend his people against fearsome enemies.

▲ Rustum the warrior
Rustum's battles not only involved single combats and encounters on the battlefield, but also attacks on mighty castles.

▲ The Simurgh
A mythical bird called the Simurgh taught Zal how to perform the surgical operation that enabled Rustum to be born.

◀ Rakhsh
Rustum picked Rakhsh from a herd of colts because of its size and strength. Famed for both power and loyalty, the horse was the envy of other warriors.

BEHOLD ME! I AM VAST, AND CLAD IN IRON, AND TRIED; AND I HAVE STOOD ON MANY A FIELD OF BLOOD, AND I HAVE FOUGHT WITH MANY A FOE.

Matthew Arnold, *Sohrab and Rustum*, 1853

THE DEEDS OF RUSTUM

Rustum's story was largely one of war and battle. His heroic deeds involved defeating supernatural beasts, such as a dragon and a demon; strong animals, such as a lion; and opponents with the power of sorcery, such as a witch. Many of these encounters were part of a sequence, often called the "Seven Labours", which Rustum undertook in order to save his sovereign, the Emperor of Persia, who had been captured by demons.

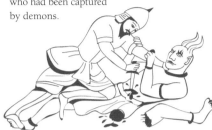

▲ Rustum and the White Demon
One of Rustum's labours involved defeating a creature called the White Demon, together with another demon who was guarding the White Demon's castle.

▲ Rustum and the dragon
Rustum fought hard to kill the dragon – the third of his labours. He was joined by his horse, Rakhsh, who bit and tore at the flesh of the monster.

THE BOOK OF KINGS

Many of the ancient myths and legends of the Persian-speaking world are collected in the *Shahnama* (Book of Kings), an epic poem by the Persian poet Firdausi (c.935–1020). The poem, written in c.1000, consists of nearly 60,000 couplets, and recounts stories of Persia's glorious past from mythical times to the period when the region was conquered by the Arabs and Turks in the 7th century. These stories, which reflect Firdausi's unhappiness at the Islamic conquest, are frequently sad, involving defeats of noble warriors, attacks by demons, incompetent rulers, and people condemned by destiny.

◀ Scene from the Shahnama
A 16th-century manuscript of the *Shahnama* is beautifully illustrated with miniature paintings like this one depicting some of the most dramatic scenes of the Persian epic.

▲ Prince Isfandiyar
Isfandiyar, seen here in bonds and mounted on an elephant, was a legendary hero and heir to the Persian throne. He was destined to be slain by Rustum.

THE LEGEND OF RUSTUM AND SOHRAB

171

SEE ALSO Tragedies 50–51, 58–59, 70–71, 104–05

ANIMAL MYTHS OF MONGOLIA

The Mongol people of Central Asia – especially the group of tribes known as the Khalkha – developed a way of life that was hard but well adapted to the grasslands of their home. Many of their myths feature creatures that the Mongolians found around them, such as the swan, or that explain their specific attributes, such as the buzz of a wasp. Others draw on the animals that were useful in daily life, such as the cow, which was crucial to the Mongols' food supply, and the horse, which played a vital role in everyday life and in warfare.

HORSES AND MEN

Horses, especially white ones, feature in numerous Mongolian myths, with most of the *tengri* (*see pp.162–63*) appearing on horseback. One of the most powerful among them was a sky spirit called the White Lightning Tengri. He was said to ride a white horse because lightning appears to be white when it strikes in the night sky. Shamans (*see pp.268–69*) also rode white horses and believed in "spirit horses", mythical creatures that could take them on journeys through the world of spirits. When a shaman speaks of his spirit horse, he is talking about flying across the sky at high speed and with great power, like White Lightning Tengri.

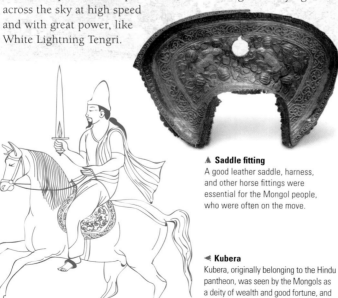

▲ **Saddle fitting**
A good leather saddle, harness, and other horse fittings were essential for the Mongol people, who were often on the move.

◀ **Kubera**
Kubera, originally belonging to the Hindu pantheon, was seen by the Mongols as a deity of wealth and good fortune, and was often portrayed as a horseman.

SACRED COW

The Khalkha people make up a group of tribes that occupy much of Mongolia. They are cattle-herders, moving from one place to the next in search of the best pastures. Their belief system involves nature spirits, and shamanism lies at the heart of Khalkha communities. The importance of both cattle and nature spirits in the lives of the Khalkha is related to their origin myth, which explains how one of the spirits fell in love with a primal cow. The result of their love was the first Khalkha family, which was brought up by the cow. She fed the people with her milk, and was responsible for inspiring them to take up cattle-herding as a way of life.

▶ **Khalkha dress**
The traditional dress has projections that resemble the shoulder blades or horns of cattle. Married women wear their hair parted, combed upwards, and stiffened like horns.

Wasp
The Mongols considered the wasp to be aggressive and well suited to its task of sampling the flesh of other creatures.

Swallow
The myth emphasizes the swallow's playful nature. The bird spends its time in joyful flight, ignoring the fact that it is supposed to be working for the eagle.

THE EAGLE, THE WASP, AND THE SWALLOW

At the beginning of time, the eagle – the king of flying creatures – wondered what to eat. So he asked the wasp and the swallow to taste the meat of all living things and tell him which was the best. The wasp flew quickly to each creature, biting into its flesh at every stop. The swallow, on the other hand, spent all his time flying across the blue sky and forgot about his task. At the end of the day, the two met up and the swallow asked the wasp which meat tasted the best, to which the wasp replied "human flesh". But the swallow thought that eating humans could bring trouble to the eagle. It bit off the wasp's tongue so that all it could do was buzz. Then the swallow told the eagle that snake meat tasted the best, and eagles have loved to eat serpents ever since.

THE TIGER DANCE

A favourite figure in Mongolian mythology is Tsagaan Ebugen (White Old Man), who got his name because of his white robe and hair. Originally a fertility deity, he was also considered to be a god of animals, birds, rivers, and mountains. He carried a staff topped with a dragon's head, which people believed he used to heal animals, or make them ill. He had a special role to play in the welcoming of the new year, so every year a shaman dressed as Tsagaan Ebugen would arrive at the place where people gathered to celebrate. A tiger skin would be displayed, which the old man would beat with his stick, symbolically killing the animal and acquiring its strength. He would then begin to dance and drink large amounts of alcohol, until he was so drunk that he could no longer dance.

Mongolian tiger mask
The tiger, a symbol of vitality and new life, was represented in masks used for many different Mongolian rituals.

THE SWAN WOMAN

One day, a man saw nine swans flying across Lake Baikal in southern Siberia. After landing, the birds removed their feathered dresses to bathe, transforming into beautiful young women. The man hid one of the dresses, so that when they finished bathing, only eight of the swans could fly away. After wooing the remaining swan woman, he made her his wife, and they had 11 sons. One day, she pleaded with him to let her try on the dress and he allowed her to. As she put it on, she flew upwards, but the man was quicker and caught her feet, preventing her from escaping. But he realized that she wanted to leave desperately, so, after their sons had all been named, the man let the swan woman put on her dress once again and fly away.

Mongolian ger
Commonly known as a *ger* or *yurt*, the traditional Mongolian tent has a skylight. It was through this that the swan woman tried to fly to escape from her husband.

At home again
After bidding farewell to her family, the swan woman flew around the tent, blessing it, and then returned to her native home on the lake.

SEE ALSO Birds 140–41, 236–37, 258–59, 286–87, 298–99, 306–07, 328–29 • Horses 52–53, 124–25

GODS OF WAR

Before going into battle, soldiers of old often called on their gods for protection. In most cultures there was a specific war deity they could invoke. This could be a figure who might reward them – such as the Norse god Odin – or else a god who was himself a brave warrior, perhaps having fought in a mythic war between supernatural races.

COSMIC WARRIORS

War gods naturally play a major role in great cosmic battles. They may lead armies of gods in wars for control of the cosmos, or heroically take on supernatural giants and demons that threaten the stability of the universe or the lives of humans. These struggles may involve much bloodshed, but cosmic warriors do the world a great service by ridding it of such monsters.

◀ **Lugh**
The Celtic war god Lugh was skilled in the arts, healing, and prophecy, as well as warfare. He led the Irish gods in battles against a monstrous race called the Formorians.

◀ **Indra**
The chief deity of the early Aryan invaders of India, Indra is the warrior king of the gods in the Vedas (*see pp.188–89*), defeating their demon foes.

◀ **Kali**
The fierce Hindu goddess Kali (*see p.199*) defeated the demon Raktabija, who could reproduce himself from his own blood.

PATRONS OF WARRIORS

One key role of war gods was to protect human warriors. They could do this either by intervening directly in human lives, as Odin liked to do, or by using their divine powers to change the course of a battle, as Greek and Roman war gods sometimes did. Warriors would encourage the support of their patrons by making offerings or sacrifices in their name.

◀ **Mars**
Worshipped more widely than the Greek war god Ares, the Roman god of war was patron not just of the Roman army but of the entire empire of Rome.

◀ **Athena**
Wise Athena (*see pp.36–37*) was the protector of Greek heroes. Bearing the Gorgon's head, her shield turned people who looked at it to stone.

◀ **Odin**
Ruler of the Norse gods of Asgard, Odin was a friend of brave warriors, to whom he gifted weapons. Heroes killed in battle lived with him in his hall, Valhalla.

▶ **Tu**
The magical powers of the Maori war god Tu were so great that he controlled the weather and all the animals.

DEIFIED WARRIORS

Sometimes a hero's career is so remarkable that when he dies, he is allowed to join the ranks of the gods. Deification is reserved for the truly great heroes, usually people who demonstrate great bravery or supernatural strength on a number of occasions. It most often happens in cultures in which the way of the warrior is held in especially high regard – in parts of Africa, for example, and in Japan.

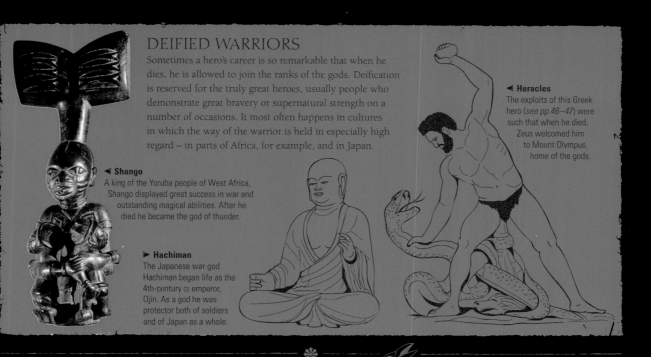

◀ Heracles
The exploits of this Greek hero (*see pp.46–47*) were such that when he died, Zeus welcomed him to Mount Olympus, home of the gods.

◀ Shango
A king of the Yoruba people of West Africa, Shango displayed great success in war and outstanding magical abilities. After he died he became the god of thunder.

➤ Hachiman
The Japanese war god Hachiman began life as the 4th-century CE emperor, Ojin. As a god he was protector both of soldiers and of Japan as a whole.

WAR GODDESSES

Although some female figures actually fight in the battles of myth and legend, they are relatively few. But there are a surprising number of female goddesses of war. Some of these, such as the Egyptian goddess Sekhmet, are formidable fighters who are as aggressive as any male warrior, unleashing terrible violence on their enemies. But others take a less active part in war, influencing the real fighters or predicting that a battle is going to occur.

◀ The Morrigan
Along with her sisters, Badb and Macha, this Celtic goddess took the form of a crow who forecast the coming of war, and afterwards flew down to the battlefield to feast on the flesh of the fallen.

◀ Sekhmet
This lion-headed Egyptian goddess was usually calm, but when angry her power was awesome, with great arrows of fire shooting from her eyes.

◀ Meenakshi
Especially associated with southern India, this Hindu goddess set out to rule the universe, before accepting Shiva (*see pp 194–95*) as her husband and lord.

▲ Nike
After helping the Greek gods in their war with the Titans (*see pp.18–19*), Nike became goddess of victory, bringing good luck to warriors.

THE EPIC OF GESAR KHAN

Told by both the Tibetan and the Mongol peoples, the story of Gesar Khan is set in Ling, Tibet. The myth describes a time when the people were oppressed by warlords, treachery was rife, and famine was endemic. It is based on the life of a brave hero called Gesar, who came to the rescue of his people, battling with traitors and demons until the kingdom was finally made safe.

THE MYTH

Gesar was originally called Joru, and was the son of a dragon princess who had taken the form of a servant girl called Dzeden. When her pregnancy became apparent, the Queen of Ling threw her out of the castle because she believed that her husband, King Singlen, was the father of the unborn child.

When Joru was born, he seemed unremarkable. He was short and ugly, and very mischievous. Some disliked him, especially the king's brother, Todong, a power-hungry man who sensed that Joru was destined for greatness. He tried to have Joru killed but the boy escaped, and Dzeden took him to live in the woods, away from danger. He grew up into a handsome young man, skilled in shape-changing.

THE CONTEST FOR KINGSHIP

Gesar returned to the palace after receiving a message from a Buddhist monk, named Padmasambhava, that he was destined to become a saviour of his people. On arriving, he found out that the king had left on a pilgrimage, and Todong was hoping to rule in his stead. In the guise of a prophetic raven, Gesar told Todong that he could rule Ling if he staged and won a horse race, in which anyone could participate. He could also marry Sechan Dugmo – a beautiful woman who led an unhappy life with her miserly father, but who was destined to become queen. An accomplished horseman, Todong organized the race because he was confident of his victory.

It was decreed that the winner of the race would become king and marry Sechan Dugmo. Gesar defeated Todong easily, and became the King of Ling, with Sechan Dugmo as his queen.

While Tibet prospered under Gesar's rule, Todong plotted to usurp his throne by allying with a monstrous demon called Lutzen. Gesar fought the demon, and chopped off its 12 heads. But Lutzen's wife, a stunning enchantress, seduced Gesar by giving him a cup of wine that made him forget everything but her. He forsook his kingdom, which fell into decline and was taken over by a demon king called Kurkar.

THE RETURN OF GESAR

Six years later, Gesar's brother found him and told him what had happened. Gesar returned to his kingdom disguised as a boy skilled in metalwork. He used his skill to distract and kill Kurkar, while his men destroyed the demon's army. After this, he had to defeat another demon called Shingti, who had a virtuous daughter. Despite his enmity with Todong, Gesar was fond of Todong's son, and arranged his marriage to Shingti's daughter. The couple became heirs to his throne, ending the conflict with Todong.

Padmasambhava
A Buddhist monk named Padmasambhava spread Buddhism in Tibet in the 8th century. Revered by Tibetan Buddhists, he is seen as a second Buddha.

THE BIRTH OF GESAR

Dzeden was a shape-changer, who had transformed into a human girl when she inadvertently wandered far away from her home and took shelter in the kingdom of Ling. One night, she had a prophetic dream, in which a great lord told her that she would give birth to her country's saviour. Nine months later, an egg popped out of her head. She nursed it, and her son hatched from the egg. Dzeden named him Joru, and he grew up to be a strong man.

◄ **Dzeden**
One version of the myth says that Dzeden, in her vision, drank nectar from a golden vase with an image of a lord on the side, and became pregnant.

► **Ladakh**
Home to people of Tibetan descent, Ladakh, a plateau between the Kunlun Mountains and Greater Himalayas in Kashmir, is believed by some to be the birthplace of Gesar Khan.

GESAR'S BATTLES

Tibetan and Mongol life centred on the horse, and warfare generally involved aggressive cavalry charges by armoured warriors, who could be swift and ruthless. But Gesar found out that besides aggression, cleverness was also needed for victory. One of his enemies, Lutzen, had a castle guarded by three defensive rings, comprising gods, human soldiers, and demons. Gesar took over the castle by persuading the gods and humans to fight on his side and help him defeat the demons.

◄ **Horseman's armour**
Suits of plate armour and strong helmets helped protect Gesar's mounted warriors from the slashing sword blows of their enemies.

▼ **Tibetan sword**
Gesar succeeded in distracting Kurkar by posing as a metalworker who could forge fine weapons for the demon.

GESAR RESCUES HIS QUEEN

Gesar Khan rescued his wife, Sechan Dugmo, from a sorry fate on two separate occasions. By marrying her after the horse race, Gesar freed Sechan from a miserable life with her miserly father. He also saved her from the demon Kurkar, who had seized Gesar's kingdom and imprisoned his queen. Gesar's deep affection for his beloved queen equalled his love for his homeland, which he saved twice from tyrannical rule.

▲ **Racing horses**
Gesar, a poor outcast, turned up in tattered rags for the race organized by Todong, but the other riders dressed up in fine clothes, as horse races were grand occasions.

▲ **The Kham region**
From Mount Margyer Pongri in the Kham region of eastern Tibet, Gesar Khan and Sechan Dugmo bid farewell to their faithful and loving subjects, and disappeared forever.

GESAR'S PASSING

Todong's son married the daughter of the demon Shingti, and the pair became the new king and queen of Gesar's kingdom. In spite of their demonic parentage, they were virtuous rulers, and Gesar was convinced that the kingdom would be safe in their hands. So Gesar and Sechan Dugmo decided to retire. They went on a retreat to the side of a mountain in the Kham region, and disappeared the next day. It was believed that they had ascended either to the next world, or to the paradise of Shambala, the mythical home of the spirit kings.

SEE ALSO Demons 170–71, 188–205, 222–23 • Wars 18–19, 60–61, 98–99, 104–05, 116–17, 118–19, 126–27, 170–71, 206–07

Gesar Khan
Legendary Tibetan hero Gesar Khan is typically depicted on horseback. In a region where good horsemanship has long been highly valued, he fittingly won his kingdom in a great horse race.

THE GODDESS AL-LAT

The cultures of the Arabian Peninsula worshipped a number of deities before the coming of Islam in the 7th century. One of the most important was the goddess Al-Lat, now a shadowy figure, but whose image was once widely seen in West and Central Asia. Her cult was based near Mecca, the place where the Islamic faith was later revealed to the Prophet Muhammad.

THE MYTH

Al-Lat was a popular goddess in many regions of the Arab world before the spread of Islam. Apart from the Arabian Peninsula, she was also widely worshipped in the eastern Mediterranean region and parts of Iran. Essentially a moon goddess, she played a variety of other roles. As a bringer of fertility, she was a goddess of the Earth, and also a deity of love. Moreover, she was connected with the sun, and, although her main symbol was the crescent moon, it was sometimes shown with the disc of the sun resting in it.

THE NAME OF AL-LAT

Al-Lat's cult had a number of followers, especially in the city of Ta-if, near Mecca, Saudi Arabia. It was home to a tribe called the Thaqif, who considered her to be their patron deity. They possessed a stone cube that was held sacred to Al-Lat and two other goddesses, Manat and Al-Uzza – a triad known as the daughters of Allah. Many consider "Al-Lat" to be derived from an ancient Arabic word, *Al-Ilat* (the Goddess). According to another version, the word *lat* referred to the process of mixing or moistening. It was associated with a Jewish man at Ta-if who used to make a mixture of clarified butter and barley meal, which he served to pilgrims

▶ **Goddess Al-Lat**
Depictions of Al-Lat have been found on carved reliefs in many parts of the Arab world. Sometimes she is shown with a spear like the Greek Athena.

at the shrine of the goddess. The word was first attached to the shrine attendant, and after his death, to the rock that marked his burial place. Later, a statue of the goddess was placed on the rock, so "Al-Lat" became identified with the goddess herself. Thus, the goddess was initially linked closely to a specific place before her cult spread to other places in the Arab world. She was a popular figure, and people often named their daughters after her.

THE END OF THE CULT

After the Prophet Muhammad received the revelation of Islam, he gave up worshipping the three goddesses and other gods, claiming they were false deities. The people of the Arabian Peninsula – both the Quraysh, the prophet's own people, and other local tribes – renounced the goddess, and her shrine was destroyed. The cult of Al-Lat remained in other parts of the region for a while, but declined as Islam spread across West Asia. As a result, little is known about the goddess today. Some ancient Greek texts have compared her to Athena (*see pp.36–37*), or to Aphrodite (*see pp.38–39*). They mention that Al-Lat was worshipped alongside a god, probably Dhu Shara, who resembled their wine god Dionysius (*see pp.34–35*).

◀ **Dhu Shara**
The Nabataeans of Petra, in Jordan, worshipped Dhu Shara, a high god and Lord of the Mountains, alongside Al-Lat.

THE DAUGHTERS OF ALLAH

Al-Lat, Al-Uzza, and Manat were often depicted together, and are sometimes confused with one another. Besides the crescent moon, the other symbols of Al-Lat were a sheaf of wheat and a pot of incense. Al-Uzza (the Strong One), a goddess of the morning and evening stars, represented love as well as war. She was similar to Inanna (see pp.154–55), and was often shown with big cats, creatures that were sacred to her. She was an important deity of the Nabataeans (see below), who not only built a temple for her in Petra, but also worshipped her from rooftops and near acacia trees, which were sacred to her. Manat was the goddess of fate and death. People invoked her either to gain her protection, or to ask her to pursue their enemies. Her symbol was a waning moon, and she was often shown as an old woman, holding a cup of death.

Manat   Al-Uzza   Al-Lat

THE NABATAEANS

The ancient people of Jordan, Canaan, and parts of northern Arabia were known as the Nabataeans. Mainly traders, they controlled the oases and roads of the region, and charged merchants to travel across their lands. By the 3rd–1st centuries BCE, they had become so prosperous that they built the magnificent city of Petra, with numerous temples, tombs, and other buildings hewn directly out of cliffs. Although the Nabataeans left little in the way of writing, it is believed that they worshipped early Arabian deities, especially Dhu Shara and Al-Uzza. Their rule ended in 107 CE when the area was conquered by a Roman emperor, Trajan.

◀ **The Monastery at Petra, Jordan**
The Nabataeans imitated the Classical architecture of the Romans, with its columns and ornaments. However, many of the buildings in Petra were created by carving them directly out of the sandstone cliffs.

DEITIES OF THE SKY

In ancient times, the peoples of West and Central Asia looked to the skies for their most prominent deities. Their lives were ruled by the heat of the sun and by the infrequent rains, both of which were necessary to grow crops and ensure survival. They became skilled at predicting the weather and seasonal patterns, attributing both to the activities of the gods. Apart from the triple goddesses, the other sky deities worshipped by the ancient Semitic cultures were Samsu, a sun goddess, Warihu, a god of the moon, and Hadad, or Haddu, a god of storms.

◀ **Rising sun**
As in many other cultures, the ancient people of West Asia regarded sunrise as the return of a deity who had been absent during the night, and the event inspired celebration or worship.

PRE-ISLAMIC IDOLS

With the advent of Islam, most pre-Islamic cultures of the Arab world transformed rapidly – adopting a single god and giving up the practice of idol worship, as the new religion prohibited the veneration of statues. However, the *Kitab al-Asnam* (The Book of Idols), by the Iraqi historian Ibn al-Kalbi (born c.800), is a vital source of information about the early religious beliefs and practices of the region. It describes numerous deities from different cultures, such as Al-Lat, Al-Uzza, and Dhu Shara.

Idols from Syria,
1st century CE

181

SEE ALSO Love deities 38–39, 138–39, 154–55, 244–45, 310–11

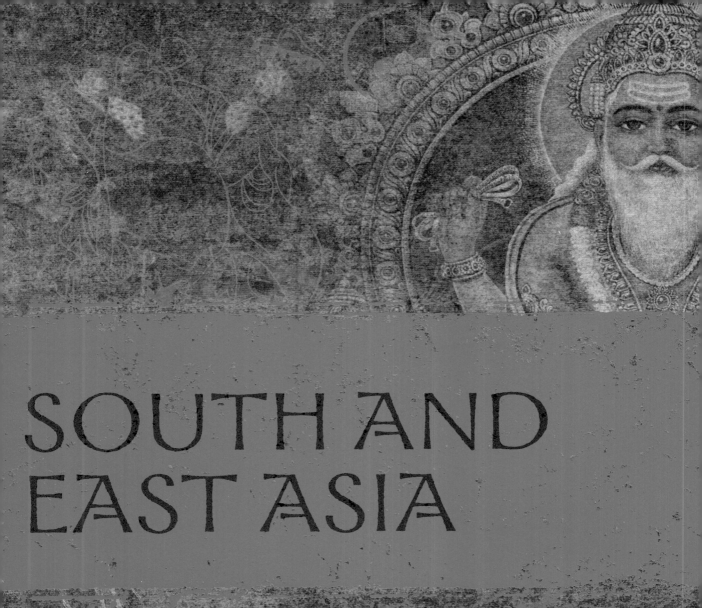

SOUTH AND EAST ASIA

In isolation from other parts of the world for extended periods, India, China, and Japan developed their own distinctive early civilizations. The cultures of these countries were very different, but they did have certain things in common. One of the strongest links was the faith of Buddhism, which emerged from India in the 5th or 6th century BCE, and later spread out to the rest of South and East Asia. In both China and Japan, the influence of Buddhism became even more pervasive than in its country of origin.

The mythologies of India, China, and Japan are very different too, but have one common element – a pantheon containing an almost uncountable number of deities and spirits. There are more gods in South and East Asia than in any other part of the world. The Indian subcontinent alone is the home of four major world religions: Hinduism, Buddhism, Jainism, and Sikhism.

Of the four, it was Hinduism that developed a mythology with many deities, a pantheon of beings who preside over a universe in a constantly turning cycle of history. From little-known local gods to great figures such as Brahma, Vishnu, and Shiva – the trinity who preside over the whole cosmos as creator, preserver, and destroyer, respectively – Hindu deities all have their own stories, personalities, and attributes. They are unified by the concept that, although they are distinct, they all form aspects of one single reality.

China's vast family of gods and goddesses are organized in a very different way. They are seen as an imperial court, headed by a supreme emperor, who is the cosmic equivalent of the human emperor that once ruled China. In theory, each deity has a role analogous to an official or courtier on Earth, but in reality the situation is much less clear. Chinese popular religion, suppressed under Communism but still alive in many Chinese communities, is

IN THE VASTNESS OF MY NATURE I PLACE THE SEED OF THINGS TO COME; AND FROM THIS UNION COMES THE BIRTH OF ALL BEINGS.

Bhagavad Gita, 14:3

highly creative, adding deities to the pantheon and worshipping them as and when devotees need specific help or guidance in their daily lives. Figures from belief systems such as Buddhism and Daoism have been added to the pantheon – and there are even instances of a Chinese version of Jesus being worshipped in the temples of Chinese popular religion. This is an endlessly inventive form of belief, little known outside China and Chinese communities in places such as Singapore.

In Japan, the original indigenous people – the Ainu – have their own religion and mythology, which contains numerous spirits of the natural world. Their stories are told in oral epics in which the spirits take the form of animals such as bears and whales and interact with people.

The notion of a spirit world is central to the more widespread Japanese belief system, Shintoism – "the way of the gods". Shintoism is concerned with maintaining a balance between humankind and the natural world. Its myths – including important stories about the sun deity and the origins of rice cultivation – tackle this subject in many ways. As well as the origins of rice-growing, the origins of such essentially Japanese skills as silkworm breeding are attributed to the work of a culture hero. Even in today's highly advanced – and in many ways Westernized – Japanese society, these stories still feature prominently in the country's culture, hold Japanese people's imaginations, and help shape their fundamental beliefs.

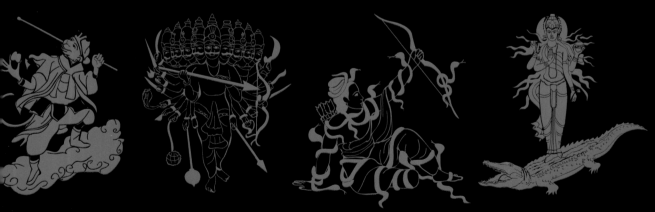

▲ Statue of Vishnu riding on Garuda
The great god Vishnu travels on the back of a giant bird – part eagle and part human
in form – called Garuda. This important animal god is said to mock the wind, so fast
does he fly, and such is his great size that he blocks out the sun.

SOUTH ASIA

The mythology of South Asia is dominated by Hinduism, a religion that has evolved over several millennia. With its thousands of gods and goddesses, Hinduism has one of the largest bodies of mythical narrative in the world.

Hinduism is highly diverse. It has no one sacred text, and no formal statement of belief. Probably the most ancient of the world's major religions, it has evolved steadily, producing countless stories of the cosmos and of the deities. This makes its traditions extremely complex, but at the heart of this complexity lies the belief that all the deities are aspects of a single, overarching reality.

VEDIC DEITIES

The earliest known texts about the gods and goddesses of India are the Vedas, four books whose stories probably date to the 2nd millennium BCE, though they were written down much later, in around 800 BCE. The oldest of them, the *Rig Veda*, comprises just over 1,000 hymns, each addressed to a deity. Many of these early Vedic gods and goddesses relate to specific aspects of the universe or the elements. Among the most prominent are Agni, god of fire, Surya, god of the sun, Vayu, god of the wind, Prithvi, goddess of the Earth, and Indra, chief of all the Vedic gods, who has a highly complex and powerful personality. The texts about these ancient deities still attract many readers, both for their poetry and for what they say about the beliefs of early people in South Asia.

HINDU DEITIES

In the centuries after the Vedas, another group of deities came to prominence. These, the central deities of Hinduism, include the prominent triad of Brahma the Creator, Shiva the Destroyer, and Vishnu the Preserver. Vishnu comes to Earth in a series of manifestations, or avatars, including two – Lord Rama and Krishna – who are worshipped as gods in their own right. Around these figures cluster dozens of other deities – from popular ones such as the elephant-headed Ganesh, Remover of Obstacles, to the various manifestations of the Great Goddess Devi – who play prominent parts in Hindu religion and mythology.

▲ Nandi, the bull
Shiva often travels on a white bull called Nandi, a symbol of strength, fertility, and religious duty. A statue of Nandi as Shiva's gatekeeper faces the main shrine in most temples of Shiva.

EPIC POEMS

The classic texts of Hindu literature are written in the ancient Sanskrit language. They are full of stories about all these deities, covering their various roles in the creation and history of the cosmos, as well as their appearances on Earth and relationships with humanity. Two major sources for these stories are the two great epic poems, the *Ramayana* and the *Mahabharata*, the latter of which is the longest poem in world literature. Although each of these poems has a narrative theme – the *Ramayana* is the story of Lord Rama's life on Earth, the *Mahabharata* the story of a rivalry between two families and of a great battle – they both contain much other material and are rich collections of tales of deities and people. These stories live on as part of a religion with millions of followers in India and elsewhere. They also form a mythology that continues to inspire poets, storytellers, and readers from outside the Hindu tradition, all over the world.

▼ Hindu temple at Bhubaneshwar, India
Large Hindu temples are often decorated with highly elaborate carvings. This stonework depicts episodes in the lives of the gods and goddesses and provides a rich record of the mythology of Hinduism.

THE VEDIC GODS

Some of India's earliest myths are derived from the Aryans, people of Central Asian origin who migrated to the region during the 2nd millennium BCE. Their myths were recorded in sacred texts known as the Vedas, which emphasized belief in gods that controlled the natural world and could influence human wellbeing. Chief among the Vedic deities were figures such as Indra, Agni, and Surya. These early deities were often known as the Adityas, or sons of Aditi, the goddess of space and mother of all creatures and deities.

INDRA

The god of thunder and rain, Indra was the chief of the Vedic gods and known for his strength and virility. He used his powerful *vajra* (thunderbolt) to attack demons who interfered with the process of creation, or threatened life. A popular myth tells how Indra gained his supremacy over the other gods. Once, Vritra (also known as Ahi, the serpent of drought) swallowed the cosmic waters and held back rains. Most gods ran away in fright, but Indra pierced the serpent's body with his *vajra*, allowing the vital waters to flow once again. Indra was worshipped as a provider of cattle and a deity who brought material wealth and wellbeing. The warrior classes especially grew to revere him because of his many successes in battle. His presence was usually signalled by a rainbow in the sky.

▶ Indra on Airawata
Indra is often depicted riding Airawata, a white elephant that emerged from the primal ocean. Here he holds an elephant goad and two thunderbolts (*vajras*).

◀ Giver of Life
Surya is sometimes shown holding lotus flowers in his hands, which represent the deity's life-giving powers. His attendants include two female figures who symbolize the two phases of the dawn.

▼ The sage Agastya
In the *Ramayana* (see pp.200–03), Agastya recites a hymn associated with Surya to Rama before his battle with the demon king, Ravana. It is believed that he introduced Vedic religion into southern India.

SURYA

Also known as *Savitar* (Giver of Life), Surya, the sun god, watched over the world by day, and was said to bring light, knowledge, and life itself to its inhabitants. He travelled across the sky in a chariot with a single wheel, signifying the cycle of the seasons. His charioteer, Aruna, the god of the morning, shielded the world from Surya's extreme heat. A myth tells how Sanjana, a goddess who married Surya, could not bear his brightness, so she turned herself into a mare and hid in the forest. When Surya found her, he changed into a stallion and fathered several children with her. He agreed to reduce his brilliance, and the pair returned to their palace in the heavens.

VAYU

Vayu was the god of the winds. One of the hymns of the *Rig Veda* portrays Vayu as either the breath of *Purusha*, the primal human (*see p.191*), or as being created by *Purusha's* breath. According to a myth about Vayu, the god lost some of his power when he was expelled from Mount Meru, the home of the gods. Vayu attacked the mountain in retaliation, and despite resistance from Garuda, the king of the birds, he tore off the tip of the mountain and threw it into the ocean, where it became the island of Sri Lanka. Later myths have described Vayu as a servant of the god Vishnu and his consort, the goddess Lakshmi (*see pp.196–97*). He was a changeable character, at times stormy, but on other occasions gentle.

◄ **Vayu on his mount**
Vayu is commonly portrayed seated on his mount, an elegant antelope. Sometimes, however, he is depicted riding a lion. Perhaps the differing mounts indicate the changeable character of their rider.

SOMA AND RITUALS

Like many early belief systems, Vedic religion involved the use of psychoactive substances, such as *soma*, a plant that could be identified with the herb ephedra. *Soma* was said to be the drink of the gods, and when mortals drank it, they made a connection with the deities. Accounts of its origin vary – some say Indra discovered *soma*, others that it was first produced from the primal ocean. Its use was quite popular among Vedic priests, who developed a special ritual for preparing the drink: first crushing the herb, and then mixing it with milk and water.

Ephedra

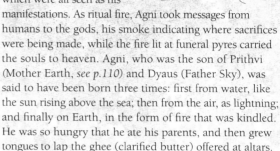

► **God of fire**
Numerous accounts of Agni depict him as a three-headed figure riding a goat or ram, with flames coming out of each of his three heads.

AGNI

The god Agni represented fire in all its aspects, such as lightning, the domestic fire, and fires used in rituals, which were all seen as his manifestations. As ritual fire, Agni took messages from humans to the gods, his smoke indicating where sacrifices were being made, while the fire lit at funeral pyres carried the souls to heaven. Agni, who was the son of Prithvi (Mother Earth, *see p.110*) and Dyaus (Father Sky), was said to have been born three times: first from water, like the sun rising above the sea; then from the air, as lightning; and finally on Earth, in the form of fire that was kindled. He was so hungry that he ate his parents, and then grew tongues to lap the ghee (clarified butter) offered at altars.

VARUNA

The god of the sky, Varuna was the celestial lawgiver. He was the master of the rules that governed sacrifices and of the order that dictated the seasons and the annual round of sowing and harvesting. Some early myths describe him as a creator god, who formed the worlds of heaven, middle air, and Earth by his willpower alone. In another story, he was a ruler of the heavenly ocean, but after a war with the demons, the gods reallocated their powers and Varuna became the ruler of the western sky and of the earthly seas. His rule extended to the tides, and he was said to be the patron god of sailors and fishermen.

◄ **The god of the sky and seas**
Varuna rode a *makara*, a mythical beast that was part-crocodile and part-fish. His mount was seen as a symbol of water and fertility.

SEE ALSO Asian sun deities 160–61, 218–19, 222–23 • Asian sky deities 158–59, 160–61, 162–63

BRAHMA AND THE CREATION

Over their long history, the Vedic religion and Hinduism have produced a number of creation stories. Some involve a primal creator – Prajapati (Lord of Creatures) or the god Brahma – while other myths explain the creation of the various life forms, including humanity. They are told in the context of a cyclical notion of time, in which the universe will one day come to an end and a new era of creation will begin.

THE MYTH

In the beginning, the god Brahma, the Lord of Creation, spread his light around the universe and became the essence of all things. He also embodied time, presiding over a cycle of existence on a truly cosmic timescale. One day and night of his life was said to last 4,320 million human years, and when this period was over, the cycle of creation would come to an end as well.

DARK AND LIGHT

Brahma meditated, contemplating what the universe would be like, and created an image based on this vision. But he realized that since he was ignorant of what the universe would actually become once it came into existence, what he had created was merely an image of this ignorance. He discarded it, and it became Night. Soon Night began to produce dark children of its own, who became the first demons. When these creatures began to multiply, Brahma concentrated and started the process of creation once again.

As he meditated, he gave shape to a succession of beings, such as the sun and the stars, which began to emit light to balance the darkness of Night. According to some accounts, it was at this point that Brahma created the several thousand gods of the Hindu pantheon to balance the many demons that were the offspring of Night.

▶ Brahma
Brahma's four heads symbolize the four Vedas, the four Hindu castes, and, as a reminder of Brahma's omniscience, the four points of the compass.

▲ Lotus flower
Some versions of the creation story describe how Brahma himself was born from a lotus flower that grew in the navel of a primal deity, Prajapati.

AN EVER-CHANGING FORM

One of the beings created by Brahma to bring light into the world was a beautiful creature called Vak (Word). According to some versions of this creation story, Brahma and Vak coupled, and while doing so, they changed their form continuously. As a result, they produced every kind of animal species that populate the Earth. However, other versions say that Vak, considered to be the creator's daughter, was unwilling to mate with him. When he persisted, she turned herself into a deer and fled. Although Brahma pursued and caught up with her, he was unable to impregnate her with his seed, which fell to the ground and became the first man and the first woman.

Since Brahma had changed his shape continuously to create different life forms, he was said to be present in all living beings. But despite his omnipresence, Brahma also had a home, the great citadel-palace of the gods on top of the sacred mountain, Meru. Mount Meru was at the very centre of the Hindu cosmos; from its slopes, the sacred River Ganges flowed down in four streams, each of which ran towards one of the four cardinal points.

CREATORS

Different accounts of the creation story have often used the name Prajapati (Lord of Creatures) for the primal being. Some myths associate the deity Vishnu (*see pp.196–97*) with Prajapati, and Brahma is said to have been born from the navel of Vishnu. The title "Prajapati" is also used for Brahma and his ten "mind-born" sons, who play a key role in creation by giving form to gods, humans, and animals. The Hindu pantheon includes other figures, such as Vishwakarma, who embodies creative power and wisdom, and is considered the architect of the cosmos.

► Prajapati
The primal deity wept at the emptiness about him; some of his tears became land masses in the primal sea, others became the stars and planets in the sky.

▲ Vishwakarma
The god Vishwakarma is usually shown surrounded by the tools that he used to create the universe. He is also considered to be an aspect of Brahma.

THE GOD OF CREATION, BRAHMA [WAS] BORN OF THE GODHEAD THROUGH MEDITATION BEFORE THE WATERS OF LIFE WERE CREATED.

Katha Upanishad

CREATION AND NATURE

The Hindus believe that the material or natural world is made up of five elements: earth, water, air, fire, and space or ether. These are personified by deities such as Prithvi (*see p.110*), the Earth goddess, who is seen as the mother of all creatures. Water is vital in creation, and there are countless sacred lakes in India, as well as seven holy rivers, including the Ganges (*see pp.208–09*). The sea is also considered important; in some myths, the gods churned the primal sea in order to retrieve beneficial items from it, such as Kamadhenu (the Cow of Plenty).

▲ Origin of the moon
Some myths say that the moon emerged from the primal sea; others say it was created from the mind of Purusha (*see right*).

◄ The fire of Agni
Fire is personified by Agni (*see p.189*). In Hindu myths, the smoke and flames of ritual fires helped carry messages to the gods.

THE PRIMAL HUMAN

An early creation myth mentions Purusha, the primal human, who split himself into a male and a female half that mated and gave birth to various life forms. In another version, told in the *Rig Veda*, Purusha created the Hindu castes from different parts of his body, with the Brahmins (priests) emerging from his head, the Kshatriyas (warriors) from his arms, the Vaishyas (farmers, artisans, and traders) from his thighs, and the Shudras (workers) from his feet. In yet another myth, the first human, called Manu, created a wife from one of his ribs and introduced a new era of creation.

▲ Page from the Rig Veda
The *Rig Veda*, said to have been composed orally in the 2nd millenium BCE, is the first Hindu text to mention the divine creation of the different castes.

MOUNT MERU

Mount Meru is accorded special reverence in Hinduism as the home of the gods. Known as the golden mountain, it is said to be in the Himalayas, and the Ganges flows from its top on its way to the Earth. The peak rests on a series of seven lower worlds, which some say are supported by a cosmic serpent, Sheshnag. Others believe the worlds rest on four elephants.

The snow-capped Himalayas

191

SEE ALSO Asian creation stories 150–51, 162–63, 168–69, 212–13, 222–23

The four-headed creator god
Brahma once created a beautiful woman and sprouted four extra heads so that she could never avoid his gaze. Shiva later cut off one head, leaving one head for each of the Vedas.

SHIVA

A member of the triad of great Hindu gods, Shiva (meaning "auspicious") represents the coming together of opposites – he is known as the destroyer, but also embodies great creative power. His complexity of character is reflected in his 1,008 titles, ranging from *Mahadeva* (Great God) to *Kaala* (Death). He is renowned for his profound knowledge, awesome strength, and his cosmic dance, which symbolizes both truth and destruction.

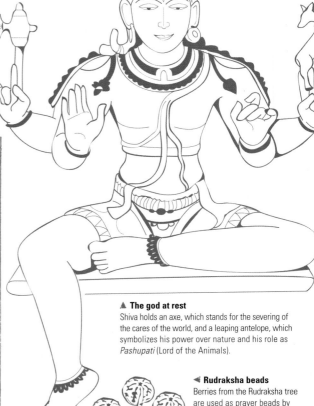

▲ The god at rest
Shiva holds an axe, which stands for the severing of the cares of the world, and a leaping antelope, which symbolizes his power over nature and his role as *Pashupati* (Lord of the Animals).

THE BIRTH OF SHIVA

One day, Brahma and Vishnu were having a discussion about who should be the supreme deity, the most powerful being in the cosmos. As the two gods were talking, a pillar of fire in the form of an enormous phallus appeared in front of them. It was so tall that its tip disappeared into the clouds and its base seemed to be buried deep in the ground. Mystified, Brahma transformed himself into a wild goose and flew up to find the top while Vishnu turned himself into a boar, burrowing deep down into the Underworld in search of its roots. But neither god could find what they were looking for. Just then an opening appeared in the phallus, and Shiva emerged. Immediately, Brahma and Vishnu recognized the power of Shiva, and agreed that the three of them should rule the universe together.

◄ Emergence of Shiva
Shiva appears out of a phallic column, or *linga*, in this carving depicting his birth. One of the god's titles is *Shiva Lingodbhava* (Lord of the Phallus).

◄ Rudraksha beads
Berries from the Rudraksha tree are used as prayer beads by devotees of Shiva, who believe the berries to be Shiva's tears.

► Shivalinga
Shiva is often worshipped as a phallic symbol or *linga*, rather than in his human form. These *lingas* can be found in temples dedicated to Shiva throughout India.

◄ Shiva's drum
Shiva usually carries a small, hourglass-shaped drum. According to the Hindus, its beat recalls the primal sound (*Aum*), with which creation began and with which it will end.

THE DANCE OF DEATH

When Shiva had an argument with Brahma and cut off one of his heads, a bitter feud developed between Shiva and Brahma's son, Daksha. So when Daksha held a betrothal feast in his palace to allow his daughter, Sati, to choose a husband, Shiva was not invited. He came to the feast anyway and claimed Sati's garland when she threw it into the air, and they were married. Later, Daksha held a holy sacrifice where he did not invite Shiva. Furious at this blatant insult, Sati threw herself onto the sacrificial fire and was burned to death. An enraged Shiva picked up Sati's body and began to dance with it, performing the dance of death that threatened to bring an end to all creation. To stop the dance, Vishnu intervened, bringing Sati back to life as the beautiful and benign goddess Parvati.

▲ Shiva's three eyes
The god's two eyes represent the sun and the moon. The third eye, usually closed, symbolizes wisdom. When it is opened, it has the power to destroy everything that is evil.

▶ Lord of the Dance
Sculptures of Shiva as *Nataraja* (Lord of the Dance) show him dancing, surrounded by a ring of fire. The figure crushed under his feet represents ignorance.

▶ Shiva's bow
The bow is one of several weapons associated with Shiva; he once used a single arrow to destroy three castles occupied by a group of demons.

◀ Trident
Shiva's trident is a weapon of great power. Its three prongs reflect the three *gunas*, or principles of the cosmos: purity, energy, and inertia. It is also believed to destroy ignorance.

SHIVA DEFEATS THE DEMONS

A group of demons persuaded Brahma to give them three castles that were so strong they could be destroyed only by a god – and the god had to attack them with a single arrow. Once installed in the castles, the demons began to launch attacks on heaven, and the gods realized that none of them had the strength to defeat these demons. So Shiva suggested that the other gods should combine their strength and lend him half of it. This, coupled with Shiva's already formidable strength – and the ability to control his power – was enough for him to defeat the demons with a single, all-powerful arrow. But when he had achieved his victory, Shiva refused to give back the strength he had borrowed from the other gods. And so Shiva remained the strongest deity of all.

SHIVA'S MOUNT

Shiva rides a white, humped bull called Nandi. As well as being a symbol of fertility, Nandi represents Shiva's strength and power, and is a formidable mount when the deity rides into battle. In Shiva's temples, the statue of Nandi always faces the shrine, symbolizing the soul's yearning for union with the divine. Nandi is also said to represent religious duty, or *dharma*, and has a role independent of Shiva as Nandikeshvara, when he is shown as a human figure with a bull's head and is a master of music and dance.

Nandi the bull

▶ Shiva and Nandi
Shiva and his consort Parvati ride the snow-white bull Nandi, who is garlanded and wears rich trappings of gold.

SEE ALSO Demons 170–71, 176–77, 188–205, 222–23 • Bulls 50–51, 116–17, 156–57

THE TEN AVATARS OF VISHNU

Of the three great Hindu gods – Brahma, Vishnu, and Shiva – Vishnu has a special role as the preserver and sustainer of the world. He intervenes in human affairs by coming down to Earth in different forms known as avatars, meaning "descents". Vishnu appears at times of crisis: when demon kings rule the world or threaten to take it over, when natural disasters such as the great flood occur, or when the structure of society is out of balance. Devotees of Vishnu believe he has visited Earth innumerable times, but there are ten avatars that are especially important. So far, he has adopted nine of these forms, with a tenth still to come. Sometimes he takes heroic human shape, as he did when coming to Earth as Rama and Krishna, and sometimes he adopts the appearance of an animal.

Narasimha, the man-lion

Krishna and his lover, Radha

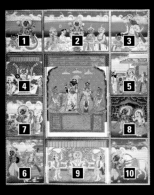

1. Matsya
Vishnu first came to Earth as the fish Matsya, when a great flood covered the Earth. A demon snatched the sacred texts out of Brahma's hands, and Matsya helped Manu, the first man, get them back.

2. Kurma
Vishnu's second avatar was the tortoise Kurma, who supported Mount Meru on his back when the gods used it to churn the ocean and bring back precious objects and divine beings of benefit to humankind.

3. Varaha
As the boar Varaha, Vishnu rescued the Earth goddess Bhumidevi from the great flood. In many versions of the tale he lifted the Earth above the waves with his tusks.

4. Narasimha
Hiranyakashipu, an arrogant demon king, banned the worship of Vishnu, but his son disobeyed. When the king mockingly asked if Vishnu was in a pillar of their palace, Vishnu sprang out of the pillar as the man-lion Narasimha and killed him.

5. Vamana
Vishnu appeared as the dwarf Vamana to defeat the demon king Bali. Vamana asked Bali for as much land as he could cover in three strides. To Bali's horror he then grew into a giant and bestrode the whole Earth.

6. Parashurama
When the warrior, or Kshatriya, caste began to dominate the world, Vishnu was born into the Brahmin, or scholarly, caste as Parashurama, his sixth avatar, to slay the warriors with his axe.

7. Rama
Lord Rama, the seventh avatar of Vishnu, is worshipped as a deity in his own right. The adventures of this brave and virtuous character, who came to Earth to defeat the demon king Ravana, are described in the *Ramayana* (*see pp. 200–03*).

8. Krishna
Vishnu appeared as Krishna to defeat evil King Kamsa. As told in the *Mahabharata* (*see pp. 206–07*), Krishna was also pivotal in the war between the Pandavas and the Kauravas, encouraging the great archer Arjuna to fight with the words of the *Bhagavad Gita*. Krishna is also shown with his lover Radha in the central image.

9. The Buddha
A historical figure, the Buddha is seen in Hindu tradition as the ninth avatar of Vishnu. As such he defeated demons by encouraging them to turn away from the gods and the sacred texts.

10. Kalki
Vishnu's final avatar, Kalki, is predicted to come when the current era of the world ends. He will arrive riding a white horse, destroy the wicked, and renew the world.

SEE ALSO Flood stories 30–31, 212–13, 214–15, 288–89, 314–15, 328–29 • Demons 170–71, 176–77, 222–23

DURGA

The Hindu goddess known as Durga (the Unattainable) usually takes the form of a warrior. She can embody all the martial energy in the cosmos and concentrate it to become an invincible foe of those who threaten her fellow deities. She is renowned as an opponent of demons who threaten the cosmic order. Like her consort Shiva, (*see pp.194–95*), Durga has a complex personality. Although essentially created to be a destroyer, in some forms she can also be a nurturing deity.

THE MYTH

Once, a buffalo-demon called Mahisha (or Mahishasura) acquired great power by practising severe austerities. He asked Brahma (*see pp.190–91*) for the gift of immortality, but when he was refused, he arrogantly demanded that his death should be only at the hands of a woman. Secure in the knowledge that he was almost invincible, Mahisha went on a rampage and attacked the gods. Realizing that none of the gods could vanquish Mahisha, who was protected by Brahma's boon, the all-powerful trinity of Shiva, Brahma, and Vishnu (*see pp.196–97*) concentrated their combined divine energy, which became manifest in the form of the goddess Durga, the epitome of feminine power.

FACING UP TO THE DEMONS

The gods gave the ten-armed Durga special weapons and, mounted on a lion, she rode out to confront Mahisha and his army of demons. The goddess looked fearless and her face radiated awesome power. When the demons saw Durga, they swarmed towards her, but she cut them down in swathes. She dispatched some with her mace, slew others with her trident and sword, and some she lassoed in her noose. Then she took the fearsome form of Kali, with a necklace of skulls and a skirt of severed arms, to fight the enemy.

Durga battling Raktabij
Another demon who threatened the gods was Raktabij (Blood Seed), whose drops of blood created new warriors as soon as they touched the ground. Durga turned into Kali, who drank up all the blood and killed him.

▷ **Durga**
The goddess Durga is usually depicted with eight or ten arms, holding a formidable arsenal of divine weapons.

Hundreds of demons were killed in the battle, but their leader, Mahisha, remained unbeaten and defiant.

THE BATTLE WITH MAHISHA

Fearlessly, Mahisha went for Durga's mount, her roaring lion. Durga got her noose around her opponent's neck but he used his shape-changing power and transformed himself into a man. Durga then stabbed him with her trident, so he swiftly turned into a charging elephant. Durga sliced off his trunk, but this time he changed back into a buffalo and moved out of range. Next, he started to uproot mountains and throw them at the goddess. She deflected them easily and, advancing fearlessly, held the buffalo-demon down with her foot as she stabbed him with her trident and beheaded him. The demon slowly emerged in his original form, dying and repentant. Brahma's gift had been given: Mahisha had finally been vanquished by a woman.

DEMONS

Hindu mythology abounds in beings known as *asuras*, or demons, such as Mahisha. Along with the deities, these demons were children of the creator Prajapati (*see pp.190–91*), but they became the antagonists of the deities and were seen as being the polar opposite of the gods. Some accounts say that both the gods and demons inherited true and untrue speech, but whereas the gods rejected the false, the demons rejected truth. Often the gods were forced to create a being to quell a particular demon's power, as in the case of Durga.

▲ **Malign being**
Apart from Mahisha, there were many other demons who dared to challenge the supremacy of the gods from time to time, and these were all slain by Durga.

▲ **Mahisha battling Durga**
The shape-changing demon Mahisha was the embodiment of evil. Durga's victory in this battle symbolized the eventual triumph of righteousness.

DURGA'S STRENGTH

Like Shiva, Durga has great destructive power, but this very destruction has a positive side as it maintains balance by annihilating threats to the natural order. Durga's appearance has this dual aspect too – her body radiates light but, befitting her role as the personification of destructive force, she is also heavily armed. Her weapons (below) show how she embodies the power of many of the gods. They include Indra's thunderbolt, Vishnu's discus, and Shiva's trident. Varuna's conch shell symbolizes the victory of righteousness. Even her choice of a lion (a tiger in some versions) as her mount indicates her power.

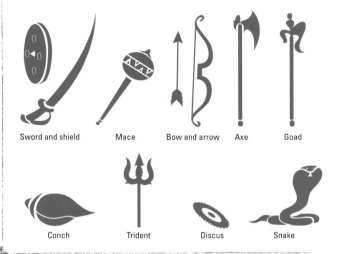

Sword and shield   Mace   Bow and arrow   Axe   Goad

Conch   Trident   Discus   Snake

THE GREAT GODDESS

Durga manifests herself in several forms, all of which are aspects of Mahadevi, the great goddess, who is the personification of *shakti*, the feminine divine energy that is the very heart of creation. Several goddesses are worshipped as forms of Durga. They include the fierce goddess Kali, who emerged from Durga's brow as the embodiment of destruction during the battle with Mahisha; and Sati, the wife of Shiva, who was worshipped to ensure marital longevity. Durga also takes caring, gentle forms, such as Parvati, the mother goddess; Lakshmi, the goddess of wealth; and Saraswati, the goddess of wisdom.

◀ **Lakshmi**
Often worshipped as a daughter of Durga, Lakshmi is depicted with gold coins cascading from her hand, symbolizing wealth and prosperity.

▶ **Saraswati**
Revered especially by students, Saraswati, the goddess of the arts and learning, was said to have invented Sanskrit.

▶ **Parvati**
Parvati was essentially a benign goddess, but she performed a rigorous penance, giving up food and water, to persuade Shiva to marry her.

▲ **Sati**
The daughter of Daksha and wife of Shiva, an enraged Sati threw herself into the sacrificial fire because her father had insulted Shiva (*see p.195*).

▶ **Kali**
After the battle with Mahisha, Kali was unstoppable as she danced the dance of destruction. So Shiva lay down at her feet to stop the carnage.

DURGA

199

SEE ALSO Female warriors 116–17, 132–33 • War deities 36–37, 38–39, 40–41, 142–43, 174–75, 244–45

THE RAMAYANA

The *Ramayana* is one of the two great Indian epics written in the ancient Sanskrit language, and a seminal text in Hindu mythology. It tells the story of Rama, the Prince of Ayodhya and an incarnation of Vishnu (*see pp.196–97*), from his upbringing, through his exile, to the rescue of his wife, Sita, from the demon king Ravana's clutches. Through its depiction of the main characters, the epic extols the virtues of loyalty, kinship, devotion, and duty.

THE MYTH

Dasharatha, the King of Ayodhya, had three wives who bore him four sons: Rama, Lakshmana, Shatrughna, and Bharata. Rama was the eldest and the probable heir to the throne of Ayodhya. As a young man, he learned archery from the sage Vishwamitra. When Rama and Lakshmana were older, they were taken by Vishwamitra to the city of Mithila, where King Janaka had organized a competition to select a husband for his daughter, Sita. The competitors were required to string a great bow that had once belonged to Shiva (*see pp.194–95*). Rama, who had fallen in love with Sita, was the only one who was able to string the bow – he not only strung it, but broke it too. Rama won the contest and returned home with his wife.

RAMA'S EXILE

The time came when Dasharatha had to select an heir from among his sons. He wanted to choose his eldest son, Rama, who was an ideal prince in every way. But one of Rama's stepmothers, Kaikeyi, reminded Dasharatha of a boon he had

▶ **Prince Rama**
Rama was famous as a skilful archer – his prowess with the bow enabled him to win the hand of Sita and, while in exile, to defeat the demons that upset the peace of the forest.

once promised her and demanded that he make her son, Bharata, the heir instead, and send Rama into exile so that he would not pose a threat to Bharata. Bound by his vow, the sad king banished his eldest son to the forest for 14 years. Rama obeyed his father unquestioningly. Sita and Lakshmana insisted on accompanying him.

Dasharatha died of grief soon after Rama's departure. Bharata, who had been absent from the palace during this time, was recalled to ascend to the throne of Ayodhya. Horrified by his mother's greed, he insisted that Rama was the rightful king, and travelled to the forest to bring Rama back. However, Rama refused to disobey his father's last wish, and Bharata had no option but to return home to be crowned as the next king. He devised an honourable compromise so that he could obey their father and show respect to Rama at the same time. Bharata took a pair of Rama's sandals back to Ayodhya and ritually enthroned them, to symbolize his rule as regent on behalf of his exiled stepbrother till the day that Rama returned.

Meanwhile, the exiles settled down, adapting to the hard life of the forest. Rama and Lakshmana frequently fought off demons who attacked the ascetics living in the woods and threatened their lives, or interrupted their prayers, rituals, and meditation. The ascetics were grateful to Rama and Lakshmana for their selfless deeds. Some of them realized that Rama was in fact a divine being.

▲ **Exiled in the forest**
When Rama, Sita, and Lakshmana arrived in the forest, they met the hermits who lived there, and had to adapt to their simple way of living, which was very different from the life of luxury that the royals knew.

»

RAMA AND SITA

In the epic, Rama and Sita are portrayed as the ideal couple. Rama wins his wife in a contest of strength, and fights fearlessly to rescue her when she is abducted. Similarly, Sita is considered the perfect devoted wife. However, Rama has been seen by some as a flawed hero who failed to appreciate Sita's goodness by doubting her chastity twice (*see p.202*). Some accounts interpret Rama's actions as befitting a just ruler who has to place ideals of kingship above all personal bonds.

▶ Rama's marriage
Rama and Sita show their mutual devotion through their actions – she, by following him to his forest exile, and he, by rescuing her from the demon king, Ravana.

◀ Plough
Sita's name means "furrow". Her father found her in a furrow in the the soil while ploughing his fields.

THE IDEAL OF BROTHERHOOD

Brotherhood is thematically integral to the *Ramayana*. The ideal brother is Lakshmana – he accompanies Rama and Sita into exile, guards them, and aids Rama in his battles with the demons and in his rescue of Sita. Bharata, too, shows his love for Rama by overriding his kingly aspirations and placing Rama's sandals on the throne. Shatrughna is similarly devoted to Rama, and outraged at the injustice done to him.

Rama's slippers

▶ Lakshmana
When Ravana's sister tried to take revenge on Rama for spurning her advances (*see p.202*), Lakshmana cut off her nose.

FROM THY FEET CAST FORTH THOSE SANDALS, THEY SHALL DECORATE THE THRONE.

Valmiki, *Ramayana*

THE EPIC

The *Ramayana*, one of the great works of world literature, is said to have been written by a sage, Valmiki, who plays a role in the epic, but may also have been a real person. Varying accounts place its date of compilation between 500 BCE and 200 CE. Valmiki probably did not write the entire poem; several passages were added after the work was originally composed. The epic primarily deals with the life of Rama, who belonged to the *Surya Vansha* (lineage of the sun god) or *Raghu Vansha* (lineage of his great-grandfather, Raghu, a great emperor).

The sun god

▶ Sage Valmiki
In the epic, Valmiki is a sage who lives in the forest, and is often visited by Rama and Sita during their exile. When the pair are estranged, Valmiki lets Sita stay in his hermitage.

THE RAMAYANA IN SOUTHEAST ASIA

Besides its popularity in India, the *Ramayana* is well known in Southeast Asia. The epic reached Indonesia during the early centuries of the Common Era. In Java, Malaya, and Thailand, local writers translated the Sanskrit text, and theatre companies adapted it. In Thai literature, the epic is called *Ramakien*. Episodes from it are presented in Thai *khon* (mask) plays and in such art forms as the Indonesian puppet and shadow theatre.

Mask used in Thai *khon* plays

SURPANAKHA

One day, a female demon named Surpanakha lusted after Rama and Lakshmana, and made advances towards them. When the brothers rejected her, she tried to attack Sita, and Lakshmana retaliated by cutting off her nose. Surpanakha was infuriated at the way Rama and Lakshmana had treated her, so she went to her brother Ravana, the ten-headed demon ruler of Lanka, and incited him to abduct Sita in revenge. Ravana sent a demon disguised as a golden deer to distract Rama and Sita. When Sita wished to have the creature as a pet, Rama went off in pursuit of the deer. Ravana then tricked Lakshmana into following Rama and, having approached Sita disguised as a hermit, carried her off to Lanka.

RAMA AND HANUMAN

Rama and Lakshmana began their search for Sita. On their journey through the forest, they came across the monkey god Hanuman, who served Sugreeva, the monkey king. Sugreeva, like Rama, was also in exile. His brother Vali had taken his place as king. Hanuman asked for Rama's help in removing the usurper. Sugreeva challenged Vali to a duel, during which Rama killed Vali. His kingdom restored, Sugreeva agreed to aid Rama.

Hanuman decided to help in rescuing Sita. Parties of monkeys were sent out to search for her. After many adventures,

▲ The final battle
During the battle, whenever Rama cut off a head or arm of Ravana, a new one grew in its place. Finally, Rama used a celestial weapon gifted by Brahma.

◄ The death of Jatayu
When Ravana abducted Sita, an old vulture called Jatayu tried to save her. Jatayu attacked the demon king and destroyed his chariot, but Ravana cut off his wing, so killing him.

Hanuman found Sita imprisoned on the island fortress of Lanka. Its location made Lanka difficult to attack, as did the fact that Ravana had an entire army of demons. Hanuman and his monkeys built a bridge over the sea so that they could attack Lanka. In a series of battles, Rama, Lakshmana, Hanuman, and the other monkeys killed the most fearsome demons. Finally, Rama slew Ravana and rescued Sita. Then Rama, Sita, and Lakshmana returned home.

Rama was unsure about accepting Sita as she had been a captive of Ravana. Hurt and distressed, Sita offered to walk through fire to prove her chastity. She emerged unscathed, but back in Ayodhya, a chance remark by a washerman prompted Rama to doubt Sita again. She sought refuge in the hermitage of the sage Valmiki, where she gave birth to twin boys. Years later, Rama recognized them as his sons and invited his wife to return after another trial by fire. Tired of constantly having to prove her chastity, Sita appealed to Mother Earth to take her back. On hearing her cry, the ground opened up and Sita disappeared into it.

ALLIES

Rama's greatest allies in the rescue of Sita were Sugreeva, Hanuman, and their army of monkeys. Hanuman's great strength and powers of shape-changing and flight proved invaluable. He made two journeys to Lanka, the first to locate Sita, and the second to help Rama defeat Ravana and rescue his wife. Having found Sita on the first journey, he was discovered by Ravana's guards who set his long tail on fire, but he survived, setting Lanka ablaze as he escaped. During the final battle in Lanka, many of Rama's warriors, including Lakshmana, were killed. Hanuman fetched a magic herb from the Himalayas to revive them. He was rewarded with everlasting youth for his devotion to Rama.

▲ Sugreeva fighting Vali
Since Sugreeva and Vali looked alike, Rama told Sugreeva to wear a garland so that Rama could identify him.

▲ Hanuman carrying the mountain
Hanuman was unsure which magic herb would revive Lakshmana, so returned to Rama with the entire mountain of herbs.

ADVERSARIES

In the *Ramayana*, Rama's enemies are referred to as *rakshasas*, or demons. Traditionally, they were malign beings who attacked women and children or possessed people at night, driving them insane. Prominent among the demons helping Ravana were his brother, Kumbhakarna, a giant who spent most of his life sleeping, and Ravana's son, Meghnath, who had defeated Indra (*see p.188*) and was said to be unbeatable in battle. These demons posed such a great threat that Vishnu had to come to Earth as his avatar, Rama, in order to defeat them for good.

▶ Meghnath
Meghnath's magical serpent arrows vanquished many of the enemy warriors, including Lakshmana.

▲ Kumbhakarna
The giant Kumbhakarna had been given a boon whereby he could sleep for six months at a stretch. When he finally awoke to fight for Ravana, he devastated Rama's army before being killed by the prince himself.

RAVANA

The king of the *rakshasas*, Ravana was a fearsome figure with 10 heads and 20 arms. He was a scholar and an authority on the Vedas. He pleased Brahma with his rigorous austerities and arrogantly sought invulnerability against gods and demons, believing no human could harm him. He also appeased Shiva, who gifted him a sword. He is seen as either a wicked counterpart to the virtuous Rama, or as a tragic figure who had potential for good but was destined to become evil.

▶ Ravana's sword
Ravana attacked Rama with the *Chandrahas* (moon blade), which he had been given by Shiva.

▲ Ravana moving Kailash
Once Ravana angered Shiva by moving his abode at Mount Kailash, and was punished.

FOR THIS DEED OF INSULT, RAVANA, IN THY HEEDLESS FOLLY DONE, DEATH OF ALL THY RACE AND KINDRED THOU SHALT REAP FROM RAGHU'S SON!

Valmiki, *Ramayana*

HINDU FESTIVALS

There are some popular Hindu festivals associated with Rama. He is believed to have worshipped the goddess Durga before setting off to fight Ravana. So during the nine nights of the festival of *Navaratri*, episodes from the epic are enacted, with a climax on the tenth day, *Dussehra*, when Rama slew Ravana. On this day, effigies of Ravana, his brother, Kumbhakarna, and his son, Meghnath, are ritually burned to symbolize the victory of good over evil. Rama also has a role in the festival of Diwali. On Diwali, people light lamps to commemorate the return of Rama to Ayodhya after his long exile.

Diwali, the festival of lights

SEE ALSO Demons 170–71, 176–77, 188–205, 222–23 • Jealousy 24–25, 38–39, 200–03

A scene from the *Ramayana*
This detail from a 17th-century wall painting shows Rama, Lakshmana, and the monkey-king agreeing to join forces to rescue Rama's wife from the clutches of the demon-king, Ravana.

THE MAHABHARATA

One of the longest poems in the world, the *Mahabharata* is the second of the two great ancient Indian epics. Traditionally attributed to the scribe Vyasa, who also compiled the Vedas (*see p.188*), the poem was probably composed by several writers between the 8th century BCE and the 4th century CE. The epic centres on a war between two rival families, but it also contains the *Bhagavad Gita*, a sacred text outlining the key tenets of Hinduism.

THE MYTH

The kingdom of Hastinapura was ruled by Pandu of the Bharata dynasty. Pandu died early, so his blind brother, Dhritarashtra, became the king. He brought up Pandu's five sons, known collectively as the Pandavas, along with his own 100 sons, called the Kauravas.

The Pandavas incurred the jealousy of their cousins due to their military prowess, virtuous conduct, and popularity among the common people. When Yudhishthira, Pandu's first-born, was declared heir-apparent, the Kauravas, led by their eldest brother, Duryodhana, conspired to kill the Pandavas. However, their intended victims got wind of the plan and escaped. To settle the quarrel, Dhritarashtra divided his kingdom between Duryodhana and Yudhishthira. But the Kauravas resented this. They invited Yudhishthira to play a game of dice (gambling being one of Yudhishthira's few weaknesses), and kept increasing the stakes. Eventually, Yudhishthira had gambled away his wealth, kingdom, and even his brothers and wife. The Pandavas were banished for 12 years.

▲ **The great war**
One of the greatest conflicts in Indian mythology, 18 military divisions took part in this colossal war. The epic describes the complex battle formations used by the forces, and the war diplomacy and strategies employed by both sides.

THE ROLE OF KRISHNA

On their return, Duryodhana refused to give back their kingdom, and the rivals prepared for war. Arjuna, Yudhishthira's brother, went to seek the support of his friend Krishna, the eighth avatar of Vishnu (*see pp.196–97*). He found Duryodhana already there for the same reason. Since both were his kinsmen, Krishna gave them a choice – one side could have his army, another could have him. Duryodhana chose the army, whereas Arjuna preferred to have Krishna, who then offered to be his charioteer.

THE BATTLE AND ITS AFTERMATH

The great battle took place at Kurukshetra. The Kauravas were led by Bhishma, the great-uncle of both the Pandavas and Kauravas. Duryodhana fought with Karna (*see p.56–57*) by his side. A great warrior and a dear friend of Duryodhana, he posed a serious threat to the Pandavas. After a prolonged battle, the Pandavas emerged victorious with Krishna's help, and Yudhishthira became the king. Afterwards, the Pandavas, anguished by the carnage of the battle, went on a pilgrimage with Draupadi (*see opposite*) to the Himalayas, leaving Arjuna's grandson, Parikshit, as the ruler of Hastinapura. The journey was long and arduous, and one by one they died, until only Yudhishthira was left. Finally, he too died, and went to heaven, where he was reunited with his family.

◄ **Lord Krishna**
Krishna took part in the war between the Pandavas and the Kauravas on the condition that he would not wield a weapon himself – hence his role as Arjuna's charioteer.

KEY CHARACTERS

The *Mahabharata* has a vast array of characters. Many are warriors, such as Arjuna, the great archer, and his son, Abhimanyu; Bhishma, the leader of the Kaurava army; and Drona, a master archer who taught both the Pandavas and the Kauravas. Some are renowned for their strength, like Bhima, Yudhishthira's second brother, and Duryodhana. Yudhishthira himself is famed for his wisdom and love for truthfulness. Foremost among the female characters is Draupadi, the spirited daughter of King Drupada, who was won by Arjuna, but became the wife of all the five Pandavas. She is rightfully outraged at being used as a pawn in the dice game. After winning her, Duryodhana makes his brother disrobe her publicly. Draupadi's humiliation in this manner is partly responsible for the war.

▲ **Arjuna**
Arjuna was a skilled archer. He won Draupadi in a contest held by her father, by shooting a fish hung from a revolving wheel just by seeing its reflection.

▲ **The game of dice**
Yudhishthira was challenged to a game of dice by Duryodhana, but lost everything at stake, including his wife, because his opponent cheated.

◀ **Draupadi's disrobing**
After winning Draupadi, Duryodhana ordered her disrobing. She appealed to Krishna, who miraculously increased the length of her sari indefinitely.

THE BHAGAVAD GITA

When Arjuna saw his kinsmen arrayed on the opposing side before the war began, he was horrified at the idea of fighting them. He told Krishna he would not participate in the war. In the ensuing conversation that came to be known as the *Bhagavad Gita*, Krishna explained the concept of *dharma*, the correct moral path set down for each individual, helping Arjuna understand that as a warrior, he had to perform his duty without regard to reward or consequences. Krishna's explanation of *dharma* has become a classic text of Hindu philosophy.

Verses from the *Bhagavad Gita*

▲ **Abhimanyu trapped in battle**
Arjuna's son, Abhimanyu, knew how to break into a spiral battle formation used by the Kauravas, but did not know the way out. He bravely led the way in and fought single-handed, but was finally outnumbered and killed.

THE BATTLE OF KURUKSHETRA

A vast plain near modern-day Delhi, Kurukshetra is believed to be the site of the epic conflict of the *Mahabharata*. The battle lasted for 18 days, and the poem narrates how huge armies came from places far and near to ally with either side. The epic describes the great war in detail: complex strategies were employed, and while common soldiers fought en masse, renowned warriors on either side sought to challenge each other in single combat, using weapons ranging from bows and maces to spears and swords. Veterans like Bhishma and Drona were forced to confront their own pupils, the Pandavas, because they were duty-bound to fight for the Kaurava side, although their sympathy lay with the wronged Pandavas. Countless warriors from both sides were killed.

SEE ALSO Wars 18–19, 60–61, 98–99, 104–05, 116–17, 118–19, 126–27, 170–71, 176–77

THE ORIGIN OF THE GANGES

The Ganges (Ganga) is sacred in Hinduism both as a river and as the goddess Ganga, who personifies its waters. According to a popular myth, the Ganges originally flowed in heaven, before being allowed by the gods to descend to Earth and flow through the region that became India. Devout Hindus believe that the river has the property of washing away all sins.

Ganga on her mount
The mount of the goddess is the Makara, which has the body of a crocodile and is sometimes shown with the tail of a fish.

THE MYTH

The kingdom of Ayodhya was once ruled by a king named Sagara who had 60,000 sons. One day, the king decided to perform the *Ashwamedha yagna* (horse sacrifice ceremony), to symbolize his supremacy over other rulers. The ritual involved sending his best stallion around the Earth. Anyone who wished to challenge the king's authority could stop the horse and fight the king. When the god Indra (*see p.188*) saw Sagara's stallion roaming around unchallenged, he hid it in the hermitage of the sage Kapila.

THE LOSS OF SAGARA'S SONS

Anxious to retrieve his stallion, the king told all his sons to look for the missing horse. They found it in Kapila's hermitage. Thinking him to be the thief, the young and arrogant princes began to insult him. Infuriated, the sage turned them to ashes with a single glance. Sagara pleaded with Kapila to liberate the souls of his sons, but the sage replied that they could be liberated only if the Ganges, a sacred river that flowed in heaven, came down to Earth and flowed over their ashes.

Many years later, King Bhagiratha, a descendant of Sagara, was granted a favour by the gods Brahma (*see pp.190–91*) and Shiva (*see pp.194–95*). He asked for the Ganges to be allowed to descend to Earth for the salvation of his ancestors. The gods readily agreed, but they

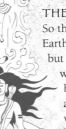

told him that the river was extremely strong and flowed very swiftly, unlike any earthly river. It would cause terrible destruction if it were allowed to flow freely. The waters of the Ganges had to be contained in some way. Finally, Shiva agreed to allow the sacred river to flow through his matted hair. He told Bhagiratha that after breaking the fall of the mighty river, he would ensure that it followed whichever course Bhagiratha took.

THE WATERS OF THE GANGES

So the raging waters of the river cascaded down to Earth, bringing life to the lands over which it flowed, but without causing any destructive floods. The place where the Ganges first touched the Earth came to be known as Gangotri. The river flowed over the ashes of Sagara's many sons, liberating their souls, which then rose to heaven. Ever since, devotees have believed that the waters of the Ganges wash away past sins, and dying people are given a sip of the holy water so that their souls achieve salvation.

◄ Taming the Ganges
Passage through Shiva's hair tamed the life-giving but dangerous waters of the Ganges by slowing its flow and splitting the river into separate channels.

KEY CHARACTERS

The main characters in the story of the origin of the Ganges, besides Sagara, are Kapila and Bhagiratha; both were wise and devoted to *dharma* (moral duty). Kapila's power came from his reverence for Vishnu (*see pp.196–97*) and his knowledge of yogic philosophy. Bhagiratha's kingdom was beset by natural disasters, so he went to the Himalayas and did penance to absolve the sins of his predecessors.

▲ Bhagiratha
Since Bhagiratha was responsible for bringing the River Ganges to Earth by his austere penance, the sacred river was also popularly known as the Bhagirathi.

◄ Kapila's fury
After the sage burned Sagara's sons to ashes, he told the king that their souls would be denied salvation until the River Ganges cleansed them.

THE GODDESS GANGA

The River Ganges is worshipped as the goddess Ganga, a daughter of Himavat (meaning "snow-clad"), the personification of the Himalayas. According to a myth, the goddess agreed to marry King Shantanu provided he did not question any of her actions. They had seven children, but she drowned each of them in her waters as soon as they were born. When the distraught king asked her the reason, she said she was destined to give birth to divine beings called *vasus*, who were doomed to be born as humans. By casting them into her waters, she had released them from this curse.

Ganga, the river goddess

▲ The Himalayas
The Ganges originates from the Gangotri glacier in the Himalayas. These mountains are also the source of the rivers Brahmaputra and Yamuna.

THE SACRED RIVER

All rivers are sacred in Hinduism, and ritual purification by river water has a long history in southern Asia. But the waters of the Ganges are especially sacred and are believed to be a powerful curative. Bathing in the Ganges washes away all the past sins of a person. And if a dead person's ashes are immersed in the Ganges, their soul is freed from the unending cycle of death and rebirth. Many Hindus aim to bathe in the Ganges at least once in their lifetime and hope that after they die and are cremated, their relatives will be able to scatter their ashes in the holy river. Charity is considered another sacred duty of Hindus, so pilgrims give alms to the sages and poor people living on the banks of the river.

◄ Prayer ceremony
Every day at sundown, devotees pay homage to the River Ganges with flowers, lighted lamps, and the chanting of mantras.

WORSHIPPING THE GODDESS

Pilgrims visit the Ganges in thousands, especially in the holy cities such as Rishikesh, Haridwar, Allahabad, and Varanasi, which stand on its banks. Devotees throng these places during major festivals such as the Kumbh Mela, when some of the world's largest gatherings of people are seen. Ritual sacrifices are made to the Ganges and offerings to the river goddess include flowers, fruits, and money.

Devotees on the banks of the Ganges

SEE ALSO River deities 84–87, 244–45, 300–01, 308–09 • Holy places 150–51, 342–43

EAST ASIA

Both China and Japan have complex mythologies involving many thousands of gods, goddesses, and spirits. For centuries these beings have played a central role in the lives of the people and their rulers.

China has been a melting pot of religion and mythology for thousands of years. The great richness and variety of its belief systems comes from several sources. First, the country developed many traditional deities over the thousands of years during which its great civilization was formed. Later, in the 6th and 5th centuries BCE, three major belief systems further shaped Chinese thought and mythology: Confucianism, a philosophy that emphasizes ritual, social order, and duty; Daoism, which stresses harmony with nature; and Buddhism, which embraces ways of avoiding the suffering of the world through following the teachings of the Buddha himself to attain inner peace.

PANTHEON OF IMMORTALS
Of the three traditional Chinese belief systems, Confucianism did not involve the worship of gods and spirits, although Confucius himself was revered as an immortal and became a figure about whom various myths were told. Daoism, on the other hand, involved a belief in thousands of "immortals": deified heroes, scholars, emperors, priests, and sages, who had lived a good life and joined the gods in heaven after their time on Earth. Buddhism was not in its original form a religion of gods and goddesses, but in the form in which it reached China it developed a vast pantheon of Buddhas and Bodhisattvas, saintly beings who had reached the threshold of enlightenment but held themselves back in order to help others attain the same goal. The Bodhisattvas of Buddhism, the Daoist immortals, and a host of traditional deities and

▲ **The goddess Luo Shen**
Me Fei, daughter of the legendary Chinese emperor Fu Xi, drowned in the River Luo and emerged as the beautiful goddess Luo Shen.

spirits surviving from earlier religions, were amalgamated in Chinese mythology into one vast pantheon of immortals. Many of them are the subjects of elaborate stories about how they became deified or what their powers in heaven encompassed. They are said to assist those who pray to them or make offerings at their temples.

JAPANESE MYTHOLOGY
In Japan, mythology developed differently, although there, as in China, the influence of the various deities and Bodhisattvas of Buddhism was also strong. More central to Japanese mythology, though, are the thousands of spirits, or kami, who are said to inhabit the land. Virtually everything, whether animate or inanimate – every place, rock, lake, tree, creature – has its kami, a kind of spirit that has influence over human life and that must be respected and not offended in any way.

In addition, Japan has a number of prominent gods and goddesses whose lives form a national mythology, from the creation of the world onwards. Foremost among these deities are the sun goddess, Amaterasu, and her descendants. Amaterasu's family was said to have been responsible for uniting Japan, and the imperial family that ruled the country until the middle of the 20th century was said to be descended from her. Although Japan's imperial family no longer claims to be descended from the gods, the people of Japan still accord these ancient deities deep respect.

◄ **Wood painting of Confucius**
The great Chinese scholar and teacher Confucius, who lived from 551–479 BCE, had a huge influence on Chinese thought, teaching respect for authority, social harmony, and regard for one's parents. After he died, many people believed that he had become one of the immortals, and some people worshipped him as a god.

► **Stone altar at Qingxiling**
At altars inside and outside Chinese temples, devotees make offerings to the deities – and burn incense – to petition their assistance.

PAN GU CREATES THE UNIVERSE

The Chinese creation myths describe how the primal god Pan Gu beat chaos into order to make the world. After this, a gentler, more nurturing creator deity appeared, the goddess Nü Wa, who formed the first people out of clay. The origin of the many other gods and goddesses is told elsewhere in Chinese myth.

THE MYTH

In the beginning there was only chaos, and amid this disorder slept the lone creator deity Pan Gu. He was in a state of deep slumber, building up his strength for the monumental task of creation. After an immeasurable period of time, Pan Gu awoke. Looking around he saw only disorder and was angered by the sight. He brought his arms crashing through the chaos, his hands hitting the swirling elements with a great echoing bang.

THE CREATION OF THE ELEMENTS

The impact of Pan Gu's blows caused the elements of chaos to move off in different directions. He struck the chaos once again, and the elements started to become more ordered, until the heavier ones began to sink and the lighter ones floated upwards. This process created the Earth and the sky, both of which then began to expand as the elements continued to separate. Pan Gu stood between the two domains, his feet pressed down on the Earth and his hands holding up the sky,

◄ Nü Wa
The name Nü Wa means "Snail Maiden", and the goddess is often portrayed with the body of a snake or a snail and the head of a woman.

► Pan Gu
The creator god is usually depicted wearing a skirt of leaves. He holds in his hands the sky that emerged after the separation of the elements of chaos.

to prevent them from coming together. He grew progressively taller as the two moved further apart. Once the two were permanently separated, the creator lay down to sleep.

As he slept, Pan Gu himself began to transform. His eyes became the sun and the moon. The strands of hair in his beard broke into pieces that became the stars. Some parts of his body turned into the mountains and the rest of his flesh turned into the soil. Soon, the hair on his head became the plants and trees that took root in the Earth. They were nourished by his blood, which formed the lakes and rivers.

THE FIRST PEOPLE

A goddess called Nü Wa appeared when Pan Gu had finished creating the world. She looked at the cosmos that had grown out of Pan Gu's body and considered it beautiful. But after a while she felt lonely, and decided to create human beings who could live on this landscape. She took some clay and moulded it into the first people, and kept making more when she saw that they were happy together. However, she also noticed that after some time they began to age and die. Weary at the prospect of moulding people out of clay indefinitely, Nü Wa gave her creations the ability to procreate; now there would always be people to populate the Earth. Nü Wa stood back, and was pleased with what she had made.

THE DARK LADY

Certain versions of the myth say that the goddess Jiu Tian Xuannü (the Dark Lady) created the human race once again, after the first people were wiped out in a great flood. Some accounts consider her to be the sister and wife of Fu Xi (*see p.214*), although others say he was married to Nü Wa. Fu Xi and the Dark Lady married in order to have children and revive humanity. Some say that she also brought the flood to an end by mending a hole in the heavens. Jiu Tian Xuannü was also thought to be a teacher, who taught many tenets of Daoism, an ancient Chinese philosophy, to Huangdi (the Yellow Emperor), an ancestor of the mortal rulers of China.

◀ Jiu Tian Xuannü
Early accounts of the Dark Lady depicted her with a serpent's body, confusing her with Nü Wa. Later, she was shown as a beautiful woman (shown seated on the right).

▲ The Yellow Emperor
Huangdi, the Yellow Emperor, was a legendary ruler who taught the arts of civilization to the people of China. He was later deified for his achievements.

▶ Lantern festival
Celebrating the New Year, this festival marks the Full Moon on the 15th day of the first lunar month. Deities worshipped include the three primeval emperors.

▼ The three emperors
These primordial rulers were revered in ancient China as deities who brought happiness and had the power to forgive sins and heal.

Tian Guan   Di Guan   Shui Guan

THE PRIMORDIAL EMPERORS

After the human race was created and the first people began to multiply, the Jade Emperor (*see pp.216–17*) sent three great primordial emperors to rule them. The first, Tian Guan (the ruler of heaven), was the bringer of happiness, freedom, and wealth. Extremely powerful, he was second only to the Jade Emperor himself. The second, Di Guan (the ruler of Earth), was known as a great judge of humans and their actions. The third, Shui Guan (ruler of water), controlled the floods and took away disease and sickness. This trio of rulers was worshipped all over China.

GODS OR MORTALS

Two of the true founders of Chinese culture and philosophy were Laoze (born 604 BCE) and Kong zi, or Confucius (551–479 BCE), who helped people make sense of the natural world and their everyday existence. They were hugely influential and attracted many followers. These men became so popular that myths about them began to spread, and they came to be accepted as gods. Laoze was believed to be an immortal, who was born as a human to teach his followers and write the philosophical masterpiece, the *Daode jing*, which later formed the basis of Daoism. Confucius, although a real person too, came to be seen as a semi-mythical figure and was worshipped as a deity in temples.

▶ Laoze
According to Laoze's philosophy, human beings should try to achieve a state of equilibrium within themselves. Since they are a part of nature, they should live in harmony with nature, not violate the natural world.

◀ Yin and Yang symbol
Chinese philosophy states that a fundamental duality exists in the universe between the feminine principle, Yin, and the masculine principle, Yang.

◀ Confucius
The philosophy of Confucius was summed up in his belief in the eight virtues: filial piety, brotherly love, loyalty, honesty, righteousness, politeness, integrity, and chastity.

213

SEE ALSO Asian creation stories 150–51, 162–63, 168–69, 190–91, 222–23

LEGENDS OF THE CHINESE HEROES

Chinese myths often feature culture heroes who teach the skills of survival and civilization to the people. Such heroes are portrayed as emperors – either mortal rulers, or deities who came from heaven to rule China. The origin of the Chinese script, and the art of making silk and weaving it into cloth – key features of China's culture – are explained in these myths. The stories also stress the need for wise and just rulers, showing that a good government is sometimes even more important than the reputation of the imperial family.

THE FOUNDER OF CHINA

Fu Xi was married to the goddess Nü Wa (*see p.212*). He was said to have come to Earth in prehistoric times to become the first emperor of China. Some believed that he had four faces, each overseeing one of the four points of the compass. More importantly, he was one of the foremost culture heroes of China. The invention of clan and family names, and the establishment of social order were attributed to Fu Xi. Some said he also taught the people of China how to domesticate animals, catch fish with nets, and make music with instruments. In addition, Fu Xi showed the Chinese how to make silk thread and weave it into cloth, how to measure time, and how to use a calendar made from a length of knotted cord.

▶ I Ching
Fu Xi is believed to have invented the Chinese script and the trigrams of the *I Ching*, a series of symbols used to predict the future.

▲ Fu Xi
The first of the great Chinese sages, Fu Xi developed skills that were crucial to Chinese life and thus he is often called the Founder of China.

THE LAND OF CHINA

Yangtz'e River

China is a huge country with major variations in climate, and landscapes ranging from high mountain ranges to vast plains. Large areas of the country are dominated by great rivers such as the Yellow River and the Yangtz'e, which link the different regions of China and unify the country. Important as arteries for transportation and sources of fish for food, these rivers can be dangerous during floods – although the silt from the floods helps farmers by making the land on the banks more fertile. So powerful are the rivers that the ancient Chinese writers often depicted them as mythical beings – generally dragons – and only the most powerful deities or rulers could tame their floods.

TWO SAGE RULERS

A mythical emperor renowned both for his wisdom and skill in arms, Yao ruled over vast territories and brought peace to southern China. He had nine sons, but considered none of them capable of ruling. With the help of the gods, he found a simple farmer called Shun, who was more skilled and intelligent than Yao's sons, and bequeathed his throne to him. Shun became the second sage ruler. Governing astutely, he visited every region of his kingdom to ensure that the people obeyed him and had what they needed. He quelled rebellions south of the Yangtz'e River and lived to be 100 years old.

◄ **Shun**
Legend has it that Shun served Yao for 28 years as a farmer before becoming emperor himself.

▶ **Yao**
Known as the Lord of the Golden Age, Yao was an ideal ruler who enjoyed a reign of 98 years.

◄ **Weiqi**
An ancient board game, in which two armies engage in battle, Weiqi, or Go, was said to be invented by Yao, who saw the game in a dream.

THE QUELLING OF THE FLOOD

Shun was gravely troubled by a great flood of China's rivers. The emperor of heaven had sent the flood because he was angry with the sinful ways of humanity. Gun, the grandson of the emperor, took pity on humans and went down to the Earth to build canals and drainage ditches. When the emperor of heaven found out what Gun had done without his permission, he killed his grandson. But as Gun lay dead, a dragon called Yu emerged from his body, saw the terrible damage inflicted by the raging waters, and flew to heaven to intercede on behalf of the people of China. Upon hearing Yu's story, the emperor of heaven relented, and allowed Yu to raise mountains, reroute rivers, and build drainage channels so that the floods could be controlled at last.

▲ **Controlling the flood**
China's long history of trying to control the floods of its major rivers is reflected in its myths. Using large labour forces the Chinese have raised banks and created dams to stem the floods.

THE INVENTOR OF FARMING

Another culture hero, Shen Nong, invented the art of farming. A fertility god who helped plants grow, Shen Nong taught the Chinese how to grow staple foods such as rice and wheat. Some say that he invented the plough and devised ways of growing crops in rotation to preserve the fertility of the fields. Shen Nong is also attributed with revealing the many healing properties of herbs, and is thus revered as the inventor of Chinese traditional medicine. Originally a mortal, Shen Nong was a herbalist who poisoned himself while experimenting with herbs, but was granted immortality by the gods for his bravery and dedication.

▶ **Shen Nong**
The great Shen Nong was both an inventor of farming implements and a pioneer herbalist who was very much in tune with the environment.

▼ **Ancient Chinese plough**
Some myths say that Shen Nong invented the plough, which has been used in China for thousands of years, with iron ploughs being introduced in the 4th century BCE.

SEE ALSO Flood stories 30–31, 196–97, 212–13, 288–89, 314–15, 328–29 • Sages 200–03, 208–09, 220–21

THE COURT OF THE JADE EMPEROR

According to Daoist myths, the vast and complex court of the Chinese emperor was mirrored in a celestial court of immortals who served his heavenly counterpart, the Jade Emperor. Even the deities of other religions such as Buddhism were seen as a part of this huge organization of gods and goddesses. By making offerings, believers sought the blessings and help of these deities.

THE MYTH

The emperor of heaven was popularly known as Yühuang (the Jade Emperor) but was also often referred to as Shang Di (Lord of Heaven). He was a supreme deity but, like Confucius (*see p.213*), he was originally a mortal. Yühuang was the child of a king, Ching Teh, and his queen, Pao Yüeh. For many years, the royal couple could not have children. Pao Yüeh asked the priests to pray for her to have a child and the next night she dreamed that Laoze, the deified father of Daoism, visited her carrying a baby. Soon after, she became pregnant. She gave birth to a son who grew up to be a kind and wise ruler, but after ensuring prosperity for his subjects, he left his throne to follow a life of prayer and meditation. When his perfect life was over, he was deified as the Jade Emperor and became the ruler of the immortals.

THE CELESTIAL BUREAUCRACY

The Jade Emperor lived in a celestial palace and ruled heaven with the help of a huge retinue of other deities, each of whom controlled a particular department of the heavenly civil service. This was a vast bureaucracy that resembled in size and complexity the organization of the civil service that worked for the Chinese emperor on Earth.

▶ **The immortals**
Many ministers and judges assisted the Jade Emperor in the day-to-day running of the heavenly court. Devotees of Chinese popular religion placed statues of these immortals in temples and made offerings to them.

▶ **Yühuang**
The Jade Emperor is usually portrayed as a bearded man wearing the regalia of a mortal emperor, and clasping to his chest a tablet of jade.

At the emperor's side sat Xi Wangmu (Queen Mother of the West), the empress of heaven. A powerful goddess, she had her own palace, built of gold and surrounded by a garden with trees that bore the magical Peaches of Immortality. The fruit took a thousand years to ripen, but when they were ready to eat, they gave eternal life to the eater (*see pp.220–21*).

PROTECTORS OF CHINA

The Jade Emperor's court included many gods who looked after different aspects of life on Earth, helping people in their daily lives. Longwang, known as the dragon king, took care of the waters, especially the seas and rivers, and was also considered to be the god of rain. Yue Lao took the form of an old man who lived on the moon, and cared for couples when they got married. However, the most important to humans was Zao Jun, known as the Kitchen God. People kept his image above the stove in their kitchen. Every year they would put up a new picture of the god and burn the old one. As the smoke rose heavenwards, it took a message to the Jade Emperor, reporting how the members of the household had behaved during the year.

BUDDHIST IMMORTALS

For many Buddhists, the spiritual leader of their faith, the Buddha, is seen as a great human teacher, not as a god. But, in some forms of Buddhism, a multitude of figures (including the Buddha himself, and other Buddhas and Bodhisattvas) attract devotion and worship. In Chinese popular religion, these figures join the ranks of the Daoist immortals and are worshipped in temples. Among the most popular are: Omitofu, Buddha of the Western Paradise; Da Shi Zhi, the Lord of Strength and Success; Mile Fu, the Buddha of the Future; Pilu, the god of wisdom and embodiment of Buddhist law; and Guan Yin, the goddess of mercy.

▲ The Buddha
A prince who renounced the world to achieve ultimate wisdom, the Buddha is revered by the Chinese as one of the greatest of all spiritual teachers.

➤ Guan Yin
The goddess Guan Yin is known as the one who watches and listens. She responds whenever her devotees call upon her for help.

THE QUEEN OF HEAVEN

Known as the Golden Mother or the Queen Mother of the West, Xi Wangmu was one of the most powerful immortals. She heard the reports of the other immortals after they returned from visits to Earth. She ruled the mortal world too, and was able to bring death, or to grant eternal life to a person by allowing them to eat one of the Peaches of Immortality from her garden. Devotees prayed to her for a long life, and women called on her for good fortune when they were about to be married.

➤ Xi Wangmu
As the controller of life and death, the mother goddess Xi Wangmu is often shown holding one of the Peaches of Immortality.

THE EIGHT IMMORTALS

The Ba Xian, or Eight Immortals, were Daoist scholars and heroes who achieved immortality due to their devotion to Daoism. They figure in numerous myths along with the Jade Emperor, flying across clouds, fighting dragon kings, or defeating evildoers, and also in comic adventures, such as getting drunk, or setting fire to the sea. Some, like Han Hsiang Tzun, whose flute was said to give life, were patrons to musicians; some helped the sick, like Ho Hsien Ku, a female immortal who carried objects associated with immortality in her ladle. Chung Li Chuan's fan could revive the dead, and Chang Kuo's castanets prolonged life.

Chung Li Chuan

Chang Kuo

Ho Hsien Ku

Han Hsiang Tzun

THE IMPERIAL COURT

China had one of the largest and most complex systems of government in the ancient world. Hundreds of officials, each with a clearly defined job, worked for the emperor, and these people were chosen by a competitive examination system. There was a rigorous hierarchy, with only key advisers allowed direct access to the emperor, who would meet them, as well as foreign officials, in one of the audience halls in his palace. In Chinese mythology, a similar government existed in heaven.

Audience hall in the Forbidden City, Beijing

217

SEE ALSO Immortality 68–69, 132–33, 156–57, 218–19

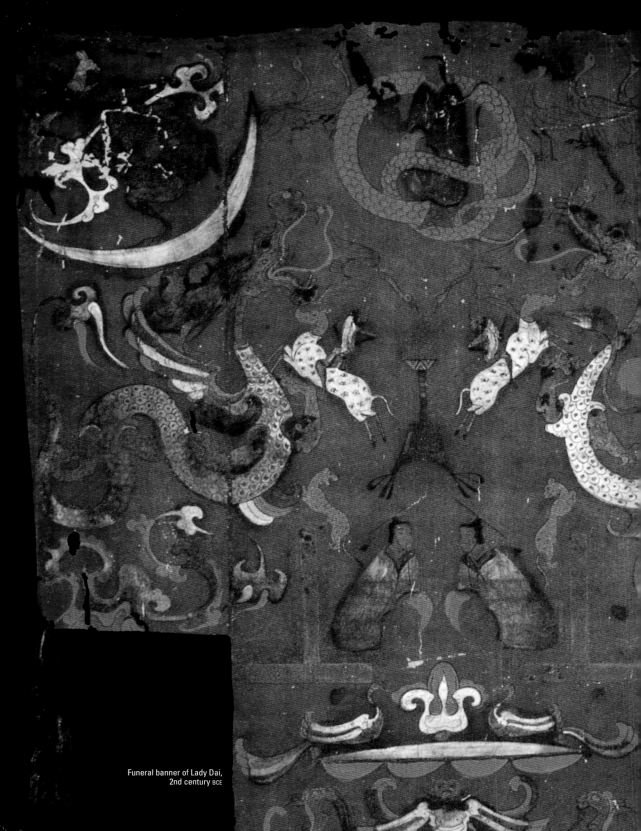

Funeral banner of Lady Dai,
2nd century BCE

THE TEN SUNS OF HEAVEN

A popular Chinese myth tells how there were once ten suns, the offspring of Di Jun, Emperor of the Eastern Heaven, and his wife, Xi He, goddess of the sun. Each morning, one of the suns would take his turn to shine in the sky, but one day all ten mischievously decided to shine at the same time, baking the Earth and killing all the trees and other plants. They would not listen when Di Jun told them to desist, so the emperor sent his archer, Yi, to threaten them with his arrows. But Yi, seeing the terrible drought and the widespread hunger caused by the ten suns, was so angry that he shot nine of them down. When he saw what had happened, the emperor banished Yi and his wife, Chang E, from heaven, so depriving them of their immortality. This famous story is illustrated here on a silk banner from the tomb of a noblewoman, Lady Dai, who lived in the 2nd century BCE.

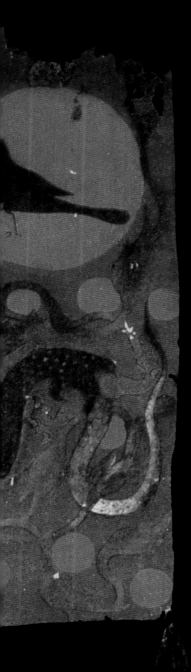

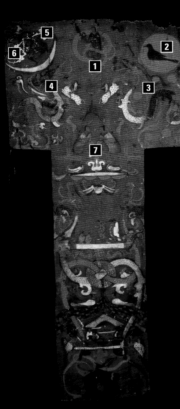

1. Presiding goddess
Flanked by cranes, which in Chinese tradition symbolize long life, and by the moon and the sun, the great goddess Nü Wa – who moulded the first people from clay (see p.212) – presides over the whole of heaven, represented by the top part of the banner.

2. Golden crows
Each of the ten suns contained a crow, a kind of spirit of the sun, whose wings enabled the great golden orb to fly across the sky. When Yi shot down the nine suns, their crows fell too, and people were amazed to see they each had three legs and were golden in colour, like the sun itself. Here, though, the artist took a more realistic approach and painted a real, two-legged, black crow.

3. Small suns
When Yi shot down the nine suns, his arrows pierced the crows they contained, so that they were unable to fly across the sky ever again. The shot-down suns shown here are smaller than the one surviving sun, and without their crow spirits.

4. Auspicious dragons
Dragons have various roles in Chinese mythology. Because they are very wise, and symbolize the goodness of heaven, they are auspicious creatures that bring good fortune. They also represent fertility, and there are dragon kings that bring rain and preside over lakes and streams. Here, with the death of the nine suns, dragons reappear to bring life-giving rain to the Earth once more.

5. Toad in the moon
When he was banished from heaven, Yi knew that he and his wife would soon die, so he got hold of a potion that gave the drinker immortality. He intended to share this potion with Chang E so that they could both become immortal, but she took it all for herself and ascended to the moon, where she lived forever. But to her horror, when she arrived in the moon she found that she had been transformed into a toad as punishment for her selfishness.

6. Hare in the moon
In Chinese tradition the moon is home to a hare, which sits under a tree mixing and grinding together various herbs to make an elixir of immortality. A big-eyed, largely nocturnal animal, the hare is associated with the moon in many other cultures, too.

7. Heaven's gate
A pair of soldiers guard the gate of heaven, through which souls must pass to enter the realm of the immortals. Above them is a bell, rung to announce the arrival of a soul. Below them, about halfway down the banner, ascends the soul of Lady Dai.

SEE ALSO Dragons 106–07, 108–09, 170–71, 216–17, 260–61 • Immortality 68–69, 132–33, 156–57, 216–17

THE ADVENTURES OF MONKEY

One of the best-loved of all Chinese myths is the story of a mischievous character named Monkey. It tells how Monkey runs amok, upsetting all the gods, and causes still more mischief when he is punished. Finally, he is made to join a Buddhist pilgrim on an expedition and reforms himself. Involving Daoist, Buddhist, and ancient Chinese deities, the story appeals to all with its lively plot and likeable, albeit roguish, central figure.

THE MYTH

Monkey was the most intelligent of all his species. When he was young he went to study with a Daoist master, but unable to resist playing pranks on other students, he was sent to the forest. There the other monkeys revered him for his wisdom and skill and made him their king. A feast was held for him, and Monkey, having drunk too much, fell asleep, whereupon the King of the Underworld kidnapped him and took him to hell. There Monkey was confined to keep him out of mischief.

FROM HELL TO HEAVEN

In hell, Monkey broke free and went to look at the register of judgements, which contained the destiny of every living being. When he read that he would die when he was 342 years old, he crossed out his name so that he could live for ever. When the Jade Emperor (*see pp.216–17*) was told about Monkey's impudent behaviour, he decided to summon the irrepressible creature to heaven. He tried to keep him in check by giving him the vital

◄ In the Buddha's palm
After Monkey discovered that he had merely traversed the breadth of the Buddha's palm, he realized that his powers were, after all, limited.

► The monkey king
Monkey's desire for immortality at all costs is comic, but also a reflection of a common human trait.

responsibility of looking after the heavenly peach garden, where the Peaches of Immortality grew. Monkey was very happy in heaven until the gods threw a party for Xi Wangmu (*see pp.216–17*). They forgot to invite Monkey, and in revenge, he stole and ate all the Peaches of Immortality, reaffirming that he was now actually one of the immortals.

MONKEY AND THE BUDDHA

After he had stolen the peaches, Monkey ate some pills belonging to the sage Laoze (*see pp.212–13*) that were made from the Peaches of Immortality. Assured for a third time of eternal life, he began to plan to take over heaven. The baffled emperor appealed to the Buddha, the greatest sage of all. When the Buddha asked Monkey why he wanted to rule heaven, he replied that he deserved to be king as he was the most powerful creature in the universe, and could leap thousands of miles in one jump. Holding Monkey in his hand, the Buddha asked him to demonstrate his power. But when Monkey obliged, the Buddha showed him that he had only jumped across the sage's enormous palm – the mountains where he had landed were the Buddha's fingers. The astounded Monkey was imprisoned inside a magic mountain, and was released when he had truly repented. He was ordered to accompany the monk Xuanzang, who was going on a westward journey to India to find Buddhist scriptures and bring them back to China.

MONKEY'S JOURNEY

The most popular aspects of Monkey's story deal with episodes of his mischief-making, and his meeting with the Buddha. But the tale concludes with his journey to India with Xuanzang and his disciples, Zhu Wuneng (also known as Pigsy) and Sha Wujing. They travel through an imaginary landscape populated by dragons, demons, volcanoes, and other dangers, and Xuanzang's companions do their best to protect him so that he can fulfil his quest for the scriptures. In the end they return to China, and Monkey and Xuanzang are rewarded by being bestowed with the status of Buddhas.

▶ Xuanzang
The Buddha told Monkey to accompany Xuanzang because the monk was too gentle to defend himself.

◀ The Jade Emperor
The emperor of heaven found Monkey hard to deal with, and happily complied with the Buddha's solution to send him with Xuanzang.

▼ Sha Wujing
Sha was a powerful heavenly general who was exiled to Earth because he broke a goblet in the peach garden.

◀ Zhu Wuneng
A heavenly marshal, Zhu was banished to Earth in the form of a pig because he got drunk and flirted with the moon goddess.

THE HEAVENLY PEACH GARDEN

The heavenly garden, where the Peaches of Immortality grew, belonged to Xi Wangmu (Queen Mother of the West). It was a place of great beauty but also power, because eating the fruit made a person immortal. Monkey abused his position in the garden by eating the peaches, which were not only powerful, but very scarce, because the trees rarely bore fruit. Moreover, Xi Wangmu's banquet was held only once every 3,000 years. Eating the peaches was just one of the three ways in which Monkey made himself immortal – each time he was challenging the power of the deities to confer immortality upon him.

▼ The paradise garden
Chinese painters depicted the heavenly peach garden as an elegant Chinese garden, crossed with streams and featuring pavilions where one could rest.

Peaches

THE NOVEL

The story of Monkey is told in a long novel, known outside China as *The Journey to the West*. Published anonymously in 1590, it was probably written by a scholar called Wu Chengen (1506–82). It has always been a popular tale, even in translation, because readers can appreciate it on several levels – as an adventure story starring the colourful Monkey; as a religious narrative about the Buddha and his scriptures; and as a comedy narrating how a subversive character defies imperial power.

The Journey to the West

221

THE JAPANESE CREATION

Japanese myths about the origin of the universe tell how, after six generations of primal deities, the seventh generation, comprising the brother and sister duo of Izanagi and Izanami, set the process of creation in motion. Their union produced some of the most popular deities of Japan, such as the sun goddess Amaterasu and the storm god Susano-O (*see pp.226–27*). However, because Izanami erred during the first marriage ceremony, she was condemned to give birth to monsters as well as to gods.

THE MYTH

At the beginning of time, there existed three invisible deities. These mysterious gods were known as the Heavenly Centre Lord, the High Generative Force, and the Divine Generative Force. Together, they contained all the potential for life and creation. They were followed by several generations of deities, until the time was ripe for the creation of the universe.

THE CREATORS

Creation was started by the seventh generation of deities: the creator god Izanagi (He Who Invites), and the creator goddess Izanami (She Who Invites). These deities represented the two balancing principles of creation, the masculine and the feminine. They stood on the rainbow bridge of heaven, and churned the chaos beneath them with a spear until an island was formed. The two deities descended to this island and decided to marry. The wedding ceremony required Izanagi and Izanami to circle a ceremonial pillar in opposite directions, with the bridegroom reciting the marriage vows first. However, Izanami spoke first, which was considered improper by the other gods. So their union was flawed and it produced Hiruko, the leech-child, who was sent out to sea.

The ceremony was repeated, and this time, Izanagi spoke first. This union was happy and fruitful, and Izanami gave birth to a whole new generation of deities – the gods of the oceans, rivers, winds, trees, mountains, and lowlands. She also gave birth to all the islands of Japan. But Izanami was

▲ **Izanagi and Izanami**
The first two deities to descend to Earth from heaven, Izanagi and Izanami became the parents of deities such as Amaterasu, the sun goddess, and Tsuki-yomi, the moon god.

destined to perish because her final child was the fire god Kagutsuchi, who consumed her in his flames. The goddess died and left for Yomi, the Japanese Underworld.

THE FLIGHT FROM THE UNDERWORLD

Izanagi mourned the loss of Izanami, and travelled to the Underworld to retrieve her, but Izanami's body had already begun to decay. It seemed that he was too late to save her, and he fled from the Underworld, with Izanami following him. The warriors of the Underworld pursued Izanagi, and so he threw some rocks at them, which magically turned into food, delaying the warriors. Izanagi failed to notice Izanami trailing him on his way to Earth. To prevent the warriors from catching up with him, Izanagi placed a vast stone over the entrance to the Underworld, trapping Izanami inside forever.

◀ **The jewelled spear**
The creation myth tells how Izanagi and Izanami stood on the bridge of heaven and churned the water with the heavenly jewelled spear to stir the first land mass into existence.

▲ Shinto shrine
Followers of the Japanese Shinto religion believe in invoking the blessings of the kami. They are worshipped in shrines or in all buildings and homes where their presence is felt.

THE KAMI

The Japanese believe that thousands of gods, goddesses, spirits, and deified ancestors, known as kami, exist across the cosmos, on Earth or in heaven. They are said to reside in natural phenomena such as rocks, rivers, and lakes. They range from popular deities such as Amaterasu, to local and family deities known to only a small number of people. Mostly comprising Shinto deities, the kami also include Buddhist deities, as well as some derived from Hinduism, such as Benten (*see p.164*), the Japanese version of the Hindu goddess Saraswati (*see p.199*).

➤ Shinto spirit
Spirits in the Shinto religion are variously depicted in either human form or in the shape of animals or birds, such as this winged kami, known as a *tengu*, a monster spirit that resembles a bird of prey.

AMATERASU

One of the most prominent of all Japanese Shinto deities, the sun goddess Amaterasu was the eldest daughter of Izanagi and Izanami. When she was born, she was so bright that her parents sent her up to heaven, from where she shone down on the Earth. Her clothes were studded with jewels and her necklace of light formed the Milky Way. Later, having warmed the Earth with her rays and made conditions suitable for living things to grow, Amaterasu came down to Earth. She taught the people of Japan how to grow rice and wheat, and how to keep silk worms, harvest their thread, and weave cloth. According to a popular myth, Amaterasu was angered when her brother, Susano-O (*see pp.226–27*), damaged her rice crops and tarnished her home. She shut herself in a cave, plunging the world into darkness as a result.

➤ Illuminating the world
The gods tricked Amaterasu into coming out of the cave by showing her a mirror with her own reflection. Having never seen herself, she thought it was a new goddess and stepped out, bringing light back to the world.

▲ Sun symbol
Amaterasu's emergence from the cave is a powerful image of the rising sun, which was featured on the Japanese flag for many years.

YOMI

The Japanese land of the dead, Yomi, or Yomitsukumi, was believed to be a place of darkness, full of demons and sinister deities who attacked or pursued whoever arrived there. The ruler of this dismal place was Emma-O, a judge of the dead, who lived in a subterranean castle made of the metals and jewels that could be mined underground. When evil people died and went to Yomi, they were made to wear plaques around their necks. These carried lists of their sins, according to which they were tormented physically before their flesh rotted away, to become a breeding ground for maggots that would turn into demons.

➤ Demon of Yomi
In Yomi there were 80,000 demons; their job was to carry the dead to their land, present them before Emma-O, and then torture them as ordered by Emma-O.

➤ Emma-O
The ruler of Yomi passed judgement on the deceased who were presented before him. He punished the guilty souls and sent the innocent ones to the upper world to be reborn.

SEE ALSO Asian creation stories 150–51, 162–63, 168–69, 190–91, 212–13 • Asian sun deities 160–61, 188–89, 218–19

Amaterasu emerges from her cave
When the sun goddess Amaterasu hid away, all
the light went from the world, so the other gods
had to tempt her out again, as depicted in this
19th-century woodblock print on three panels.

SUSANO-O AND HIS DESCENDANTS

Many Japanese myths deal with the powerful storm god of summer, Susano-O, who, like his sister Amaterasu (*see p.223*), the goddess of the Sun, and his brother Tsukuyomi, the god of the Moon, was conceived by the creator god Izanagi. Susano-O's early years were tumultuous and led to him being banned from Heaven. He later reformed, however, and settled down with a princess in the Izumo region. His son, Okuninushi – the god of abundance, medicine, sorcery, and happy marriages – became a powerful ruler and the most important Shinto deity after Amaterasu.

THE MYTH

When Izanagi returned from his trip to the Underworld (*see p.222*), he felt dirty and so he washed himself in a river. The goddess Amaterasu and the moon god Tsuki-yomi were created when Izanagi was cleaning his eyes, and Susano-O then appeared when he washed out his nose. Susano-O wanted to see his mother, Izanami, so Izanagi decided to go to the Underworld. He went to bid farewell to Amaterasu, but troubled her so much that she hid in a cave (*see p.223*).

SLAYING A DRAGON

The gods punished Susano-O by cutting off his beard and fingernails, and banishing him from heaven. While wandering the Earth, he came across a dragon that was attacking Kusa-nada-pime, the Princess of the Rice Paddies. Turning the princess into a comb and hiding her in his hair, Susano-O sliced the dragon to pieces with his sword. Then, when all was safe, he turned the princess back into a human, and married her. They settled down in Izumo and had a number of children, known as the Earthly Gods, who later became very powerful rulers.

OKUNINUSHI'S ORDEALS

One of Susano-O's sons, Okuninushi, had set his heart on his half-sister, Suseri-hime, but the storm god wanted to make sure his son was worthy of the match. So he set Okuninushi a series of difficult tasks to prove himself. He asked his son to spend a night in a room full of poisonous snakes. Although it was a dangerous task, Suseri-hime gave Okuninushi a magic scarf, which he used to protect himself. Next, he was sent into a room full of wasps and hornets. Again, the scarf came to his rescue. Then Okuninushi was ordered to go to a field and retrieve an object buried there. When he got towards the middle of the field, the storm god set it on fire. Okuninushi asked a field mouse to show him a way out, and it led him to a tunnel where he hid until the fire subsided.

THE ELOPEMENT

Even after his son had succeeded in getting through the ordeals, Susano-O did not agree to the marriage. So one night, while the storm god was asleep, Okuninushi quietly crept up on him and tied his long hair to the roof beams. Then he picked up his father's weapons and a musical instrument called a *koto*, and ran away with Suseri-hime. When Susano-O awoke he had to tear down the beams before he could give chase. Having finally caught up with them, he surprised the couple by forgiving them and consenting to their marriage.

▼ **Kusa-nagi**
After killing the dragon, Susano-O found a sword called Kusa-nagi (Grass Cutter) hidden in the remains of the beast's tail. He offered it to Amaterasu to make peace with her.

► Okuninushi and the rabbit
The story of Okuninushi and the rabbit illustrates the traditional Japanese belief that even the humblest of living things have spirits and that they may, in fact, be powerful deities in disguise.

OTHER JAPANESE DEITIES

Many of the Japanese deities linked to weather and the cosmos belong to the family of Susano-O and Amaterasu. Tsuki-yomi, the moon god, was Amaterasu's husband, while Wakahiru-me, the sun goddess's sister, was the goddess of the rising sun. Takami-musubi, a deity from an earlier generation of gods, became the messenger of Amaterasu. Two wind deities, Shina-tso-hiko and Shina-to-be, were born from Izanagi's breath. Five mountain gods were created when Izanagi chopped the fire god Kagutsuchi into pieces for burning to death his beloved Izanami (*see pp.222–23*).

▲ Kagutsuchi
The fire god was severed to create the mountain gods. But fire can rekindle itself, and so the god returned, burning atop the volcanoes.

OKUNINUSHI'S BRIDE

Once, Okuninushi and his 80 brothers wanted to marry a beautiful princess called Ya-gami-hime, so they went to woo her. On the way, they met a god in the guise of a rabbit that had been skinned alive by a crocodile and was in severe pain. Okuninushi's wicked brothers wanted the rabbit to suffer further, so they advised it to bathe in salt water to restore its fur. But the kind-hearted Okuninushi told the creature to bathe in fresh water and then roll in the pollen of kama grass. The rabbit did as Okuninushi had suggested and re-grew its fur, and being a deity, granted Okuninushi his wish of marrying the princess. Jealous of Okuninushi's success, the brothers killed him twice, but the gods revived him both times.

▲ Hachiman
Originally a fertility god, Hachiman's martial character turned him into a war god, and he was seen in this role as a protector of Japan.

▲ Inari
A god of smiths and craftsmen, Inari was married to Ukemochi, the goddess of food, and thus also became the god of rice and the bringer of prosperity.

SHRINE IN IZUMO

An important Shinto shrine, located in the Izumo province, is dedicated to Okuninushi, the deity of happy marriages. Some say that all the kami (*see p.223*) congregate here in October to discuss issues of love and marriage. This month is known in Izumo as *kamiari tsuki* (the month when the kami are present), elsewhere it is called *kanna zuki* (the month when the kami are absent).

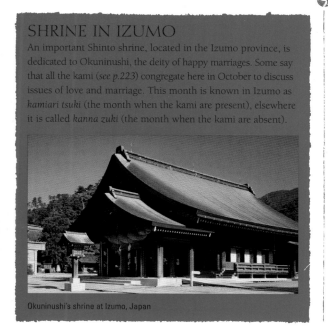

Okuninushi's shrine at Izumo, Japan

CHRONICLES OF THE GODS

Two important texts, the *Nihongi* (Chronicles of Japan) and the *Kojiki* (Records of Ancient Matters), talk about the myths of the kami and describe the early, mythical history of Japan and the role played by the kami in shaping the country. The *Kojiki* also devotes space to a mythical "Age of Men", in which semi-mythical ancestors of the imperial family are described. These books, which date back to the 8th century, have become very important in Japan, giving the country a strong connection to its own mythology and history.

▲ The Kojiki
Containing a mixture of myths and history, the *Kojiki* has played a vital role in the development of the Shinto religion. It is considered to be the oldest surviving book in Japan.

SEE ALSO Weather deities 188–89, 300–01, 308–09, 318–19

KINTARO

One of the most popular stories in Japanese mythology is not about the many great gods of the Shinto hierarchy, but about a superhero called Kintaro (Golden Boy), who possessed superhuman strength even as a child, and grew up to become a heroic samurai. Although Kintaro's career as a samurai may have been based on a real-life figure – the great warrior Sakata no Kintoki – he is essentially a figure of legend. Brought up in the forest, he became both a friend to the animals and a defender of the forest people against monsters when still young. Later on, in his exploits as a samurai, he protected Japan from several even deadlier foes.

◀ **Kintaro's axe**
Kintaro's greatest possession was his axe. It was both a tool for cutting down trees and a weapon that he could use to defeat the monsters of the forest.

KINTARO'S BIRTH

Kintoki was a warrior from Kyoto who fell in love with a beautiful young woman and married her. Soon afterwards, he became involved in a court intrigue and was banished to the forest, because of some malicious gossip that had been spread about him by certain courtiers jealous of his power. He died soon after arriving in the forest, where his wife gave birth to a son. When the boy was born, his mother named him Kintaro. Even as a baby, Kintaro was prodigiously strong; by the time he was eight years old he could cut down trees as easily and as well as the most experienced of woodcutters, and he came to be valued highly by the people of the forest. Once Kintaro became accustomed to the ways of the wild, he protected his mother and the other forest dwellers from many monsters, including terrifying beasts such as the giant earth-spider.

▲ **Killing the giant spider**
The Tsuchigumo (earth-spider) slain by Kintaro features as a monster in several other Japanese legends. The spider generally poisoned its victims to death or trapped them in a vast, net-like web.

▶ **Yama Uba and Kintaro**
In several Japanese legends, Yama Uba is a spirit of the forest who looks like a human and lives in an isolated hut. In some versions of the Kintaro story, she takes the form of a young woman and is the hero's mother.

ANIMALS AS FRIENDS

Growing up without other children for company, Kintaro became friendly with the animals of the forest, especially the bear, deer, monkey, and hare. One day, a sumo wrestling match was organized in the forest, and Kintaro acted as the judge. The monkey wrestled with the hare and lost, but then complained that he had tripped, and so the pair fought again. This time the monkey won. On each occasion, Kintaro awarded a rice cake to the winner, so both were happy. It soon became clear that the bear was strongest of all the animals. But on the way home, Kintaro showed that he was stronger than the bear, when he pulled down a tree with his bare hands to build a bridge over a river for them to cross.

◄ Wrestling the salmon
Kintaro was a skilled wrestler, and was as much at home in the water as on land. Among the creatures he wrestled were giant fish such as carp and salmon.

THE SAMURAI'S FOLLOWER

Kintaro was renowned for his superhuman strength. When he uprooted a tree to make a bridge, he was spotted by a man dressed as a woodcutter, who challenged the boy to an arm-wrestling contest. When Kintaro and the man proved equally matched, the stranger revealed himself to be Sadamitsu, a follower of a powerful lord called Raiko, who invited Kintaro to the capital to become a samurai. With his mother's permission, Kintaro departed, and after a period of service with Raiko, he was promoted to lead an elite quartet of Raiko's followers called the Four Braves. Kintaro led this group against a fearsome man-eating monster that preyed on the city, and used his razor-sharp sword to slice off the creature's head. Thus he became a famous hero throughout Japan.

► The samurai
The samurai were mounted warriors in feudal Japan. They were highly disciplined and skilled swordsmen who protected their patron and helped to enforce law and order.

▲ Judging the contest
Kintaro watched closely as the hare and the monkey wrestled, looking out for signs of cheating or false moves that might be made to beat or push an opponent out of the specified arena.

KINTARO TODAY

Kintaro is a well-known character in Japan and is represented in various ways in modern popular culture. Parents who have a newborn boy place Kintaro dolls in the child's room, in the hope that the baby will become strong. The hero also features in television series and computer games, as well as in Japanese anime series and manga comic books. Other Japanese hero characters in similar publications share some of Kintaro's strength and characteristics, even if they do not share his name. Kintaro is also familiar through his own kind of sweet – a cylinder-shaped candy with his image on every slice.

Kintaro candy

KINTARO

229

SEE ALSO Monsters 46–47, 52–53, 54–55, 64–67, 72–73, 98–99, 106–07, 156–57, 274–75

AFRICA

A frica is an immense landmass that stretches from the Mediterranean Sea, across the equator, to a point far to the south of the tropic of Capricorn. The vast continent's terrain embraces areas as varied as the humid rainforest of the Congo and the dry desert of the Sahara. The history of civilization in Africa has a huge span too, because our very earliest ancestors lived there – the story of humanity in Africa has lasted more than a million years.

As a result, Africa has produced a range of cultures as varied as any on Earth. It has been home to cattle herders like the Masai, hunters like the San, and tribes that spend their lives on the move in search of food. But it has also been the home of empires, from Benin to Egypt, that have settled, taken over large areas of the land, and prospered. Today, the differences between urban and rural, settled and nomadic, and rich and poor still remain,

and are still enormous. All this makes it hard to generalize about African culture and mythology, as each tribe has its own unique traditions and stories, its particular ceremonies and rituals.

Written history came relatively late to Africa. With the exception of Egypt, where a literate civilization developed in c.3000 BCE and lasted for some 3,000 years, much African mythology has been handed down by word of mouth from one generation to the next. This fact renders the mythology of Africa more elusive to outsiders. Writing stories down preserves their content and makes them accessible to readers beyond Africa, but it also takes them away from their important background of oral storytelling. This living context should always be imagined when we read African myths and legends.

Among these diverse mythologies there are a few common themes. One that stands out is the belief in a supreme god. Nearly all tribes, whatever additional deities or spirits form part of their mythology, respect a high god. This

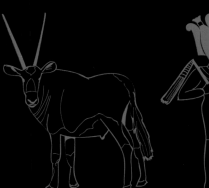

THE COMPLETE COLLECTION OF ALL THE MYTHS OF THE AFRICAN PEOPLES WOULD FILL HUNDREDS OF THOUSANDS OF PAGES, EVEN WITH OUR INCOMPLETE KNOWLEDGE.

Jan Knappert, *African Mythology*, 1990

deity may be regarded in different ways from one place to another – for some he is a creator, for some an ancestor (either a mother or a father), for some a figure like a tribal elder, for some a close companion. The existence of such a supreme deity can explain everything from the sound of thunder to the inevitability of death. For most tribes, his overriding qualities are his power and his omniscience – people speak of his ever-open eye, his knowledge of our every thought, and his surpassing wisdom.

The high god and the gods that accompany him or her communicate with the people by way of ceremonies, and in many African tribes the central figure in such rituals is the shaman or medicine man. Because of his training, the shaman has the ability to communicate with the supernatural world and is thus key to our knowledge of many African myths.

Africa is changing rapidly. Many Africans, faithful to the idea of a supreme God, have embraced Islam or Christianity. Yet traditional myths remain alive on the lips of storytellers and medicine men – and find a still wider audience through the writings of travellers and anthropologists from outside the continent. For Africans and outsiders alike, they are still some of the most enthralling stories ever told.

▲ **Shrine to the Theban Triad**
Some Egyptian temples were vast, state-run edifices, the centres of which only priests or pharaohs could enter. This temple at Luxor (modern-day Thebes) is dedicated to the supreme god Amun, his consort, Mut, and their offspring, Khons. It dates from the reign of Ramesses II (13th century BCE).

ANCIENT EGYPT

Although covering only a small area – the delta and banks of the River Nile –
the civilization of ancient Egypt lasted for some 3,000 years. It produced a
complex mythology that pervaded every aspect of people's lives.

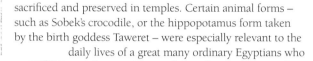

The ancient Egyptians worshipped numerous gods and goddesses who were said to influence the whole of life, from the creation of the universe to the annual flooding of the River Nile, from a person's birth to a person's death. Goddesses such as Hathor watched over women when they gave birth, while the great god of mummification, Anubis, looked on when a body was ritually prepared for the afterlife. There were also more local deities: Horus, the god of the sky, was the great god of Lower Egypt, while Set, the god of chaos, was the ruling deity of Upper Egypt.

ANIMAL GODS

Many of the gods and goddesses of ancient Egypt took animal form. Hathor took the form of a cow; Bastet, goddess of sexuality, had the body of a cat; Sobek, who embodied the power of the Egyptian pharaohs, was a crocodile; and Thoth, the god of wisdom, had the head of an ibis. These animal forms gave the deities a strong sense of identity. Priests at their temples raised real animals, then sacrificed and mummified them in honour of the temple deity. So a pilgrim to a temple of Bastet, for example, could pay to have a cat mummified so that the animal would speak up for humanity in the next world. Over the years, archaeologists have found the mummified remains of thousands of cats, crocodiles, and other creatures that were ritually

▲ **Decorative scarab beetle brooch**
Tutankhamun (14th century BCE) was identified closely with Ra, whom he expected to join in the sky when he died. Many items in his tomb, like this one, were adorned with symbols of Ra.

◄ **Symbols of Ra**
This bronze from around 590 BCE shows two of the symbols of the ancient Egyptian sun god Ra: the head and beak of the falcon Horus, and the solar disc that he carried across the sky.

sacrificed and preserved in temples. Certain animal forms – such as Sobek's crocodile, or the hippopotamus form taken by the birth goddess Taweret – were especially relevant to the daily lives of a great many ordinary Egyptians who frequently came face to face with these often extremely dangerous animals when working on the banks of the Nile, especially when the river was in flood.

CHANGING DEITIES

The animal forms taken by the gods and goddesses of ancient Egypt were not constant, however. Ancient Egyptian deities existed in a state of flux, and some of them could take many different forms at different times. Anubis, for example, was often portrayed as a jackal, but he could also take the form of a snake or a falcon.

The deities themselves could also take the form of multiple gods. The sun god Ra, for instance, took several forms, each with the identity of a separate deity: he could be the beetle Khepri, rolling the sun across the sky as a scarab beetle rolls its ball of dung across the ground; he could be Ra-Harakhty, the hawk that soars across the sky; or he could be Amun-Ra, the king of the gods. In this last form he was identified closely with Egypt's pharaohs, whom he supposedly protected when they led their armies on the field of battle.

THE AFTERLIFE

One area in which ancient Egyptian deities were especially important was that of death and the afterlife. The ancient Egyptians saw life on Earth as preparation for the life to come, so they evolved a whole system of mummification and entombment rituals. Accompanying these were many myths involving Osiris, the god of the Underworld, and the deities who presided over the rituals and assessed the worthiness of the dead person's soul to enter the next world.

THE BEGINNING OF THE WORLD

The creation stories of Egyptian mythology describe how order and life emerged out of the primal chaos. Ra, the sun god (*see pp.238–39*), is featured as the main creator deity in many of these myths. He is aided in the task of creation by deities such as his children, Shu and Tefnut, and grandchildren, Geb and Nut. Ra and his creation exist in the light; the darkness that remains is personified by a serpent, Apep, who constantly threatens to swallow the light.

THE MYTH

The creator deity Ra rose out of Nun, the primal ocean of non-being. When Ra sneezed, Shu, the god of dry air, emerged from his nostrils. Then he spat and Tefnut, the goddess of moist air, appeared from his mouth. Ra sent the two gods on a journey across the ocean. Then, using his powers of creation and perception, he called the primal elements into being, speaking their names and watching them appear. At this time, he also created Ma'at, the goddess of universal harmony, who was tasked with bringing order to his creation.

◄ **Nut, Geb, and Shu**
Shu held up in his hands the sky goddess Nut, whose body curved high above the Earth to make the arch of the heavens. Geb, the earth god, lay below Shu's feet.

goddess Hathor (*see p.244*), to look for Shu and Tefnut. After returning with the two deities, Hathor saw that another eye had replaced her on Ra's face. She wept at being supplanted in this way, and the first people were born from her tears. Ra returned Hathor to his brow, but this time she took the form of a cobra, staying there to help Ra rule over the world he had created.

THE CREATURES OF THE EARTH

Ra needed a dry place to stand on while carrying out his task, so he made Nun recede, which revealed a rocky island or mound, known as the Benben stone. The god stood on the stone and envisioned everything he was about to create. From the primal ocean, he summoned forth the plants, animals, and birds of the Earth; he spoke their names and they appeared before him. Next, Ra told his eye, the

THE GREAT GODS

Shu and Tefnut had two children, Geb, the Earth, and Nut, the sky, who lay together and gave birth to the stars. Jealous of the pair, Shu separated them and forbade Nut from giving birth on any day of the month. But Nut won five extra days while gambling with the god Thoth (*see p.241*). On these days, she gave birth to Osiris, Set, Nephthys, and Isis, Egypt's greatest deities.

► **Ma'at**
Ma'at represented truth, and gave order to Ra's creation. She also judged the dead in the Underworld, where souls were weighed against one of her feathers.

PTAH

In an alternative creation story, the central creator is the god Ptah, a craftsman deity. This myth describes how Ptah began the task of creation by imagining and then naming the different gods, bringing them into being. He then used his skills as a sculptor to produce the other beings of the cosmos. He carved and chiselled some of them from stone, and made the others out of metal, having invented the technology of metalworking for this purpose. Ptah founded several cities, as well as shrines where he could be worshipped, creating each one by thinking about it and then pronouncing its name. Ptah's cult was especially important at Memphis, ancient Egypt's administrative capital.

◀ **Heart-shaped amulet**
In the myths of Ptah, the heart is very important, because the gods and other beings are said to have been created in his heart. The Egyptians believed that the intellect resided in the heart.

▶ **The sculptor god**
Although sometimes portrayed as a craftsman, Ptah was often depicted as a kingly figure in more formal temple art.

KARNAK

At Karnak, near the River Nile, stands a huge complex of ancient Egyptian temples, the most important of which is dedicated to the god Amun. He was originally one of the forces of chaos (some accounts portray the god as a primal snake living in the water), but his name and character became linked to that of Ra to form Amun-Ra, who was known as one of the greatest creator deities and was attributed with all the creative powers of the sun god. The temple of Amun stands in a large precinct, and contains massive columns that are topped with carvings resembling lotus blossoms. The walls of the temple enclose many smaller temples and a sacred lake.

◀ **Temple of Amun**
Stone statues and columns carved with religious inscriptions in hieroglyphic script form the principal remains of this temple's structure.

▶ **Amenhotep I**
A ruler of Egypt in the 16th century BCE, Amenhotep I was also known as "beloved of Amun", and was believed to have joined the sun god after his death.

▼ **Pyramids**
The pyramids of Giza, constructed during the Fourth dynasty (c.2575–c.2465 BCE) were the largest structures of the ancient world, and paramount symbols of the power of the pharaohs.

THE PHARAOHS

Ancient Egypt's rulers were seen as not just kings but gods. During a pharaoh's lifetime, he was supremely powerful, and it was believed that after death, he would spend eternity with the gods. The pyramid-shaped tombs of the early pharaohs were originally designed to resemble stairways, up which the souls of the deceased kings could climb to join the sun god in the sky. The shape also resembled the Benben stone, the primal mound on which the sun god stood when he began to create the world. The sight of the pyramids silhouetted against the sky was a permanent reminder to the people of the link between their kings and the mighty sun god.

THE BENU BIRD

A heron-like creature present at the beginning of creation, the Benu bird was thought to be a form of the sun god. Some versions of the myth said that the bird flew over the ocean to find the Benben stone. On landing on it the bird began calling out loudly, breaking the eternal silence and signalling the birth of sound, light, and life. The priests at Karnak would release a duck to fly across the sacred lake each morning to commemorate this flight.

The Benu bird

237

SEE ALSO African creation stories 250–51, 252–53, 262–63, 272–73 • Birds 140–41, 172–73, 258–59, 286–87, 298–99, 306–07

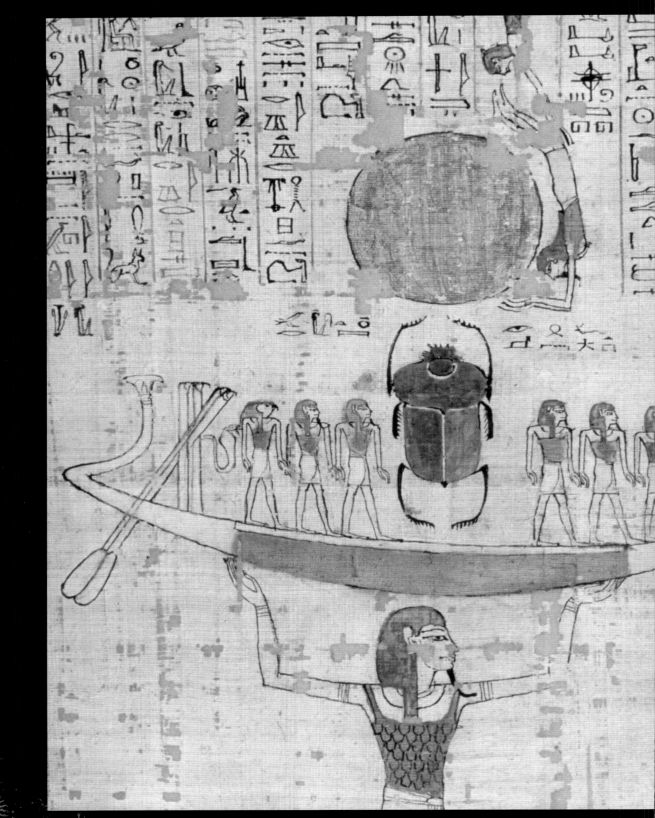

BOOK OF THE DEAD

This painting on the Papyrus of Anhai is part of the Egyptian *Book of the Dead* written in the 13th century BCE for Anhai, a priestess of Ra, the sun god. It shows several different aspects of Ra as he travels across the sky in his solar boat. Ra was one of the most important Egyptian deities – he was depicted and worshipped in several forms, including Amun-Ra, king of the gods. As the rising sun he took the form of Khepri, the scarab beetle; at midday he was seen as a glowing disc moving across the sky; and as the setting sun he was Atum, who took on the identity of an old man. As king of the gods, Ra was also linked to the kings of Egypt. The pharaohs were seen as earthly embodiments of the sun god – the sons of Ra – and they built temples in his honour.

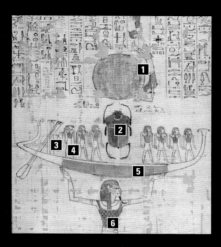

1. Solar disc
This disc is one of the most familiar images of the sun god. In this depiction, the sky goddess Nut is shown raising her son, Osiris, king of the Underworld, towards the disc, ready for the sun god to begin his journey into the night, when Osiris and the sun will become one.

2. Scarab beetle
Just as a scarab beetle rolls a ball of dung along the ground, so the sun god in the form of the beetle, Khepri, rolls the sun disc across the sky. This repeated daily movement made the scarab beetle an icon of self-generation and renewal for the Egyptians.

3. The menace of Uraeus
Uraeus, the cobra, is another symbol of the sun god Ra. It is also the emblem of the pharaoh, and in paintings, the creature's menacing hood often appears on the forehead of the pharaoh. It is believed that the cobra was given to the pharaohs as a symbol of kingship by Geb, the god of the Earth. When the pharaoh became associated with the sun god, he wore a headdress in the form of a cobra, which was said to spit deadly fire at his enemies.

4. The power of Horus
Horus, one of the most powerful Egyptian gods, was the son of Isis and Osiris. Here, he is shown with a falcon's head, emphasizing his role as a god of the sky. His right eye was the sun and his left eye the moon. In the fluid mythology of ancient Egypt, he merges with Ra to become another incarnation of the sun god, known as Ra-Harakhty. As well as being a sky god, Horus is also the god of war.

5. Boat of the sun
The vessel in which the sun god travels across the sky, carried by Nun, is shaped like an Egyptian Nile boat with a large steering oar at the stern. Ra is accompanied on his journey by seven other gods, with Horus at the helm.

6. Nothing but Nun
According to Egyptian myth, in the beginning, before creation began, there was nothing but the endless ocean of Nun. He was also the god of the primal floods. Both he and Ra were vital to the Egyptians' survival, because Ra, as the sun god, ripened their food crops, and the floods brought by Nun deposited rich layers of silt on the Nile's banks, making the fields fertile. So in this myth the two gods move together in harmony. Nun is depicted here holding up the solar boat of Ra.

Papyrus of Anhai, c.1250 BCE

SEE ALSO Sun deities 28–29, 114–15, 160–61, 188–89, 218–19, 222–23, 290–91, 314–15, 318–19

BOOK OF THE DEAD

239

A KING'S MURDER

A popular myth from ancient Egypt narrates the story of a tragic rivalry for the throne of Egypt between two divine brothers, the virtuous Osiris and the wicked Set, and the subsequent dispute between Set and Horus, the son of Osiris. The myth was well known because it dealt with the rule of Egypt, and also because the story of the death and revival of Osiris gave people hope of an afterlife.

▲ **Horus fights Set**
This stone relief from the Temple of Horus at Edfu, Egypt, depicts a scene from the battle Horus fought against Set, with the goddess Isis at the helm of the boat.

THE MYTH

The first king of Egypt was the god Osiris; like some rulers of Egypt after him, he took his sister, Isis, as his wife. He was a good king, much liked by his people, and Isis was a popular queen. But Osiris had a wicked and violent brother, Set, who was jealous of Osiris's power and lusted after Isis. To get rid of Osiris, Set tricked the king into climbing into a wooden chest, which he then sealed and threw into the Nile. Osiris was dead by the time Isis found the box, but she retrieved the king's body. Set discovered what Isis had done so he hacked Osiris's body into many pieces. Although it was supposedly impossible to destroy the body of a god, Set had all but done so.

REVIVING OSIRIS

Isis decided to salvage Osiris's body. With the help of her sister, Nephthys, who was the wife of Set, she gathered the fragments of Osiris's body, joined them together, and bound them tightly to make the first mummy. Then, transforming herself into a bird of prey – a kite – she hovered over the body, beating her wings to infuse it with the breath of life. Osiris breathed for long enough to impregnate Isis. Later, Osiris departed for the Underworld. Isis then fled from Set, taking with her a guard of seven scorpions.

While she was fleeing, Isis was treated inhospitably by a rich woman, and one of the scorpions bit the woman's child. Isis took pity on the child and used her magic

▲ **Hippopotamus**
The hippopotamus was a much-feared creature of the Nile, capable of overturning a craft sailing on the river, as Set did when he took the form of the beast to capsize Horus's boat.

to cure the infant. But later, when she gave birth to her own son, Horus, he, in turn, was bitten by a scorpion and Isis, who had used up her power, could not cure him. Fortunately, Ra, the sun god, saw Isis in distress, took pity on her, and sent the moon god Thoth to cure Horus.

HORUS AND SET

Meanwhile, Set had usurped the kingship of Egypt. When Horus grew up, he challenged his uncle for the throne, and the two fought many times. On one occasion, Set blinded a sleeping Horus. When Isis found her son blinded, she nursed him and restored his sight. Then Set tried to rape Horus, and told the other gods that the young man was unworthy to be king because he had slept with Set. But the gods found out that Set was lying.

Finally, Set challenged Horus to a boat race, insisting that the vessels used in the race should be made of stone. Horus tricked his uncle by using a wooden boat he had plastered to look like stone. Set's boat sank, and in his anger, he turned himself into a hippopotamus and capsized Horus's vessel. But the gods at last saw that Horus was truly worthy and made him king, while Set was exiled.

KEY CHARACTERS

The characters in the tragic story of the murder of Osiris have a number of roles in other aspects of Egyptian mythology. After being killed by Set, Osiris became the ruler of the Underworld, a very important position in the Egyptian cosmos, which meant that he was widely worshipped. Isis was a very prominent deity too, worshipped as the goddess of magic and guardian of the dead. She won great devotion as a mother goddess, on account of the way she cared for both Osiris and Horus. Horus became a sky god who took the form of a falcon, and his eyes were said to be the sun and moon. The eye of Horus, or the Wadjet Eye, became the most popular of all Egyptian amulets. Set, on the other hand, was a sinister figure, a god of chaos and the desert.

▲ Osiris
Wearing a crown of ostrich feathers, Osiris is depicted as a mummy with the king's symbols, the crook and flail.

▲ Set
Set is seen as a mythical beast with a long, curved muzzle, a two-tufted head, and a straight tail.

▲ Isis
Isis wears a throne-shaped crown, which indicates that she originally personified the throne of the pharaohs.

▲ Horus
Horus is often depicted as a falcon or a humanoid figure with a falcon's head, or as a child in human form.

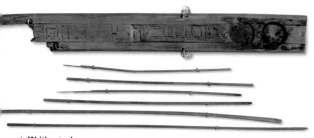

▲ Writing tools
The Egyptians used reed pens to write with, dipping them into ink and making marks on papyrus, a material also made from reeds. The shape of the reed pen was associated with Thoth's narrow beak.

THOTH

The ibis-headed Thoth was the god of time, knowledge, writing, and the moon. His curving beak resembled the crescent moon, and his black and white feathers denoted the moon's waxing and waning. Certain accounts of his origin say that he was the son of Ra, the sun god (*see pp.238–39*), and that he either inherited his wisdom from his father or found it in books belonging to the sun god. Thoth was said to have invented a range of intellectual pursuits, including astronomy, law, music, and – most relevant in the myth of Osiris and Horus – medicine. He was also the inventor of the Egyptian hieroglyphic writing system, and since he was also a god of magic, hieroglyphs were said to have magical powers.

Thoth

THE CULT OF OSIRIS

Osiris was revered by the Egyptians because his myth gave hope of a life after death. He presided over the Underworld, and along with other deities, such as Anubis and Serket, he oversaw a series of rituals through which the souls of the dead passed into the afterlife. His cult originated at Abydos, an important city in ancient Egypt, where a festival was often held, re-enacting the story of the god's murder. The temple at Abydos also held secret rituals that were not disclosed to those outside Osiris's priesthood. By the 1st millennium BCE, other temples began to celebrate the god's death and rebirth, linking them with winter and the spring.

Serket

▲ Temple of Osiris
The sanctuary of Osiris at the temple at Abydos is decorated with inscriptions and murals illustrating various scenes from the life story of this ancient Egyptian god.

241

SEE ALSO Sibling rivalry 158–59 • Death deities 42–43, 158–59, 190–91, 246–47, 298–99, 300–01, 310–11, 340–41

Embalming plaque from an Egyptian tomb
This hand-sized gold plaque – with the Eye of
Horus to ward off evil spirits – was sewn into
the bandaging over the evisceration incision in
the torso of King Psusennes I (1039–991 BCE).

GODDESSES OF THE NILE

Egypt's crowded pantheon included several goddesses who performed a variety of divine functions, ranging from Neith, the creator deity, to the many goddesses who presided over fertility, love, and childbirth. Although most of them were worshipped in temples by their own dedicated staff of priests, these goddesses – who were all, in a way, aspects of a single great goddess figure – were also held in great respect and affection by the common people. Pilgrims made offerings to them, praying for prosperity, protection, and healthy offspring.

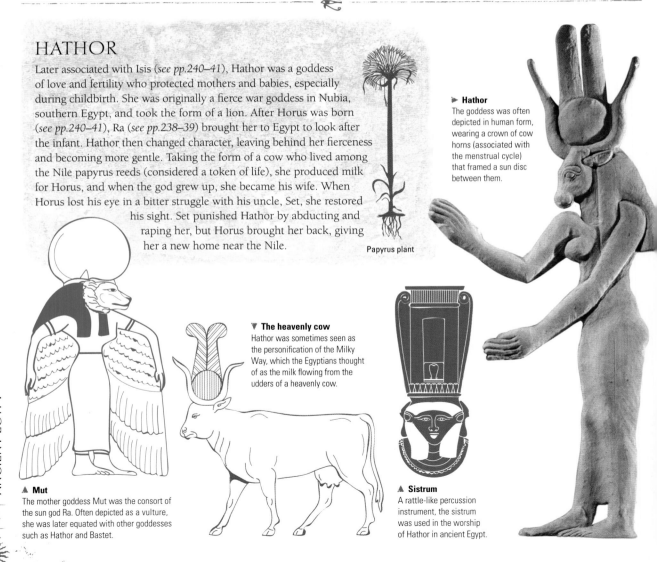

HATHOR

Later associated with Isis (*see pp.240–41*), Hathor was a goddess of love and fertility who protected mothers and babies, especially during childbirth. She was originally a fierce war goddess in Nubia, southern Egypt, and took the form of a lion. After Horus was born (*see pp.240–41*), Ra (*see pp.238–39*) brought her to Egypt to look after the infant. Hathor then changed character, leaving behind her fierceness and becoming more gentle. Taking the form of a cow who lived among the Nile papyrus reeds (considered a token of life), she produced milk for Horus, and when the god grew up, she became his wife. When Horus lost his eye in a bitter struggle with his uncle, Set, she restored his sight. Set punished Hathor by abducting and raping her, but Horus brought her back, giving her a new home near the Nile.

Papyrus plant

▶ **Hathor**
The goddess was often depicted in human form, wearing a crown of cow horns (associated with the menstrual cycle) that framed a sun disc between them.

▼ **The heavenly cow**
Hathor was sometimes seen as the personification of the Milky Way, which the Egyptians thought of as the milk flowing from the udders of a heavenly cow.

▲ **Mut**
The mother goddess Mut was the consort of the sun god Ra. Often depicted as a vulture, she was later equated with other goddesses such as Hathor and Bastet.

▲ **Sistrum**
A rattle-like percussion instrument, the sistrum was used in the worship of Hathor in ancient Egypt.

TAWERET

The goddess Taweret was the consort of Set, although she left him for Horus when the two gods had their dispute about the dominion over Egypt (*see pp.240–41*). Taweret took a bizarre hybrid form that gave her a monstrous appearance: she had the head of a hippopotamus, the limbs of a lion, human breasts, and, in some depictions, a crocodile's tail. Despite her frightening looks, Taweret actually played a protective role, presiding over childbirth and chasing away evil spirits. Depictions of Taweret show her holding an amulet in the shape of the character *sa*, which symbolized protection. This quality made her very popular with Egyptians, who bought her images in large numbers. There were also Taweret-shaped vessels, made with a small hole at one breast, so that milk, made powerful and protective by the goddess, could be poured out as a spell was recited.

NEITH

Known in the Nile Delta region as a creator goddess, Neith was also a huntress and warrior, similar to the Greek Athena (*see pp.36–37*). She was born from the ocean and created both gods and mortals, besides inventing childbirth. She was also a culture heroine who taught the art of weaving to the Egyptians. She had great authority, and when Set and Horus fought, the gods asked her which of the two should win. She said that both the antagonists should survive, but Set must be given two goddesses in return for surrendering his claim to the throne of Egypt. Some myths state that the goddess was the mother of the sinister primal serpent Apep (*see p.247*).

◄ **Neith's shield**
The warrior-goddess Neith's symbol was a shield bearing an image of crossed arrows or crossed bows.

▲ **The weaver goddess**
Neith's emblem, sometimes interpreted as representing a weaving shuttle, was also worn as a crown.

BASTET

The cat-headed Bastet was the Egyptian goddess of sexuality and fertility. She was the daughter of Ra, the sun god, whose temper she expressed in her roar, and was originally depicted as a lion. She was also associated with a myth in which a cat belonging to Ra bit off the head of the primal serpent Apep. As a solar goddess, she was sometimes shown with a scarab beetle (a symbol of the sun) engraved between her ears. In later myths, she was more firmly identified with the cat and became benign in character, helping people by destroying vermin and by bringing fertility. Bastet was regarded as the defender of the pharaoh, and worshipped at festivals where large amounts of alcohol were consumed and participants performed lascivious dances. Her main centre of worship was her temple at Bubastis, but she was a popular deity who also had a large following in other parts of Egypt.

Scarab beetle

◄ **Mummified cat**
The ancient Egyptians revered cats greatly, and often paid for cats to be mummified in honour of the goddess Bastet. Entire cemeteries of these cats have been found at Bubastis.

► **The figure of Bastet**
Bastet took a human form but was said to have the head of a cat. She carried the ceremonial sistrum and a basket. Sometimes she also bore a shield with a lioness's head.

GODDESSES OF THE NILE

245

SEE ALSO Fertility deities 40–41, 84–85, 114–15, 158–59, 214–15, 308–09, 310–11

JOURNEY TO THE LAND OF THE DEAD

Death was considered by the ancient Egyptians to be the potential beginning of a new life. After a person died, the body was carefully preserved as a mummy because it was believed that the deceased began a journey through the Underworld to the next life, where their souls would need to take up residence in their bodies once again. This belief in the migration of the soul to the Underworld was widespread and the journey was described in great detail in a complex myth.

▲ Osiris
Osiris presided over the process in which the deceased travelled from this life to the afterlife.

THE MYTH

The Egyptians believed that many spiritual aspects of a person's being survived death and, if they were correctly cared for, could re-inhabit the person's body in the afterlife. Foremost of these was the *ka*, the person's life force, and the *ba*, the soul. If all went well after death, the *ka* and *ba* would unite to form a spirit that would live again inside the body. To achieve this, the dead body had to be preserved appropriately through mummification, which was a re-enactment of what happened to the god Osiris's body after he died (*see p.240*). The process involved a series of 75 rituals, in which parts of the body would be touched with special instruments to be reanimated – as a result, the body would become a fitting vehicle for the person's *ka*. This process also identified the deceased with the god Osiris, ensuring that they would set out on the journey to everlasting life.

JOURNEY THROUGH DUAT

The deceased then began their journey through a realm known as Duat or the Underworld, which was full of many horrors and perils. Here, they had to contend with dangers such as fiery lakes and venomous snakes. There were many special spells that could be recited to protect the voyagers on the way. These spells were written down in a *Book of the Dead*, a compilation of important texts that was often buried with the mummies so that the deceased had access to the right spells on their journey through the dark realm.

JUDGING THE SOULS

The souls of the deceased were judged at a place near the end of the journey, the Hall of the Two Truths. The souls were put through a test and if they passed, the deceased would declare their innocence and then be judged by Osiris and 42 assessor gods. Osiris was assisted in his task by judges who included Ra, Shu, Tefnut, Geb, Nut, Isis, Nephthys, Horus, and Hathor. Each god judged a particular aspect of the soul. Three possible fates awaited the soul after the assessment. The truly wicked characters were condemned to a second and final death devoid of mummification and with no chance of passing unharmed through Duat. The ordinary souls were sent to serve Osiris eternally, and the virtuous souls were allowed to move on to a happy and free eternal life.

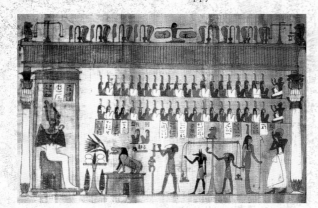
▲ Assessor gods
The assessor gods had names such as Bone-breaker and Blood-drinker, and looked on eagerly when the souls protested their innocence. They drank the blood of the deceased if there was any proof of guilt.

PREPARING FOR DUAT

The preparatory rituals for the afterlife were complex. First, the embalmers took the deceased person's body to their workshop (known as the Beautiful House), where they removed the liver, lungs, intestines, and stomach, placing each organ in canopic jars. Then the body was covered completely with a chemical mixture of salts called natron, packed with dry material such as sawdust, and wrapped in linen bandages, with labels and amulets attached to identify and protect the body. The mummy was then placed in a coffin for secure storage.

An Egyptian mummy

◄ Canopic jar
Jars capped with the heads of Underworld gods, such as Anubis or Osiris, were used to preserve the organs of the deceased person.

▲ Anubis
The ancient Egyptians believed that the jackal-god Anubis had invented the art of mummification.

THE HALL OF THE TWO TRUTHS

Souls were judged in the Hall of the Two Truths, which contained a balance in which the heart – the only vital organ not removed from the mummified body – was weighed. The feather of Ma'at, goddess of truth and justice, was placed against the heart on the scales. If the heart outweighed the feather, it would be deemed full of sin, and Ammut, the Devourer of the Dead, would feast on it. If the heart was lighter, the soul moved on to the next stage of judgement.

➤ Thoth
The god of wisdom and scribe to the gods, Thoth (*see p.241*) was tasked with waiting in the hall to record the judgement passed on the souls of the deceased.

▼ Weighing the heart
The god Amun (*see p.237*) presided over the weighing of every heart, an organ believed to contain a record of a person's former deeds.

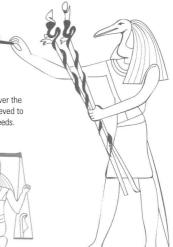

DEITIES OF THE UNDERWORLD

Besides Osiris, Anubis, and the ferocious assessor gods, several other deities were associated with the Egyptian Underworld. Some of these were sinister, shadowy beings with the heads of rams, tortoises, or hippopotamuses. Others included the serpent-god Apep, or Apophis, who constantly waged war on Ra, the sun god. Among the less intimidating deities was the goddess Nephthys, sister of Isis, who led the pharaohs through the Underworld and also cared for the stored organs of the deceased.

Ma'at

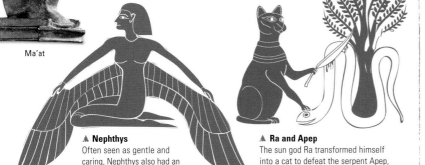

▲ Nephthys
Often seen as gentle and caring, Nephthys also had an affair with Osiris, which led to the birth of the deity Anubis.

▲ Ra and Apep
The sun god Ra transformed himself into a cat to defeat the serpent Apep, one of the most feared and vilest creatures in the Underworld.

BODY AND SOUL

The *ba*, or soul, was imagined to be a winged being with the head of the deceased and the body and wings of a hawk that flew free of the body at the time of death. Each night, it had to be reunited with the dead person's body; this could only happen if the corpse had been mummified correctly. A person's shadow and name were also thought to have an independent existence that could be perpetuated by mummification.

Winged *ba*

247

SEE ALSO Death deities 42–43, 158–59, 190–91, 240–41, 298–99, 300–01, 310–11, 340–41

▲ **Benin palace relief panel**
The people of Benin produced stunning bronze relief panels showing their Obas, or rulers, and these decorated the royal palace. This one shows an Oba magnificently armed and attended by his followers. Many stories were told of the Obas' lives and lineage.

WEST AFRICA

The sophisticated cultures of West Africa produced mythologies in which a variety of different deities are responsible for the entire range of natural phenomena, from the creation of the universe to the weather.

West Africa – stretching southwards from the southern edge of the Sahara to the coast of present-day Ghana and its neighbours – has a long history of civilization. From around 500 BCE, empires and large city-states came and went, each developing its own sophisticated arts and crafts – especially metalwork – that allowed them to trade with peoples from far beyond their own borders. The bronzework of Benin and the gold jewellery of the empire of Ashanti, which flourished in the 18th and 19th centuries along the coast between Ghana and Côte d'Ivoire, are particularly well-known examples.

▲ **West African elephant pendant**
West Africa has a tradition of highly skilled metalworking. Crafstmen from Ghana cast this pendant depicting two elephants, creatures familiar in mythology for their great strength.

SURVIVING TRADITIONS
Trade brought with it many contacts from outside the region, from Berber merchants crossing the Sahara to European slave-traders arriving by sea. Despite these foreign influences, and the legacy of European colonization in the 19th and 20th centuries, many local traditions and beliefs have survived, and some in turn have influenced the religion and mythology of the Caribbean (*see pp.304–11*). Traditions that have been particularly well preserved include those of the Fon of Benin and the Yoruba of Benin and Nigeria.

In the mythology of the Fon, the prominent deities are Lisa and his wife, Mawu, who are sometimes combined as a composite deity. They created the world and all the plants, animals, and humans. They also had a number of children, formed from their faeces, including Dan, a snake god whose thousands of coils support the world. Another son, Gu, is the patron of craftsmen and warriors. He is said to use his skills to make the world a better place for people to live in. Weather gods, including various thunder deities, also abound in the Fon pantheon.

The Yoruba have a supreme being known as Olorun or Olodumare. In addition they have numerous Orishas, or spirits, that are manifestations of this high god. Believers appeal to one or more of the Orishas as a way of communicating with the supreme being. There are countless Orishas, but some are particularly popular. Shango, a powerful sky god and god of thunder, and his consort, Oshun, benevolent goddess of love, are among the most important.

ABIDING THEMES
The role of the hero is a prominent theme in West African mythology. Sometimes he is a culture hero who brings the gifts of craft skills and technology. At other times he is a wonder-child, a being of such power that he has the strength and skills of an adult as soon as he is born. West Africa also has some entertaining trickster myths. The best-known trickster is the spider Ananse, who gets the better of everyone from gods and humans to the most powerful of all creatures on Earth, the elephant. Amusing stories of Ananse's tricks have a wide appeal, and are enjoyed by adults and children alike.

▼ **An Oba's ceremonial arm ornament**
The ceremonial jewellery of the Obas, or rulers, of Benin included arm ornaments such as this one depicting a leopard. The creature's attributes – its speed, strength, and prowess as a hunter – were traits that any ruler would wish to be associated with.

AFRICAN ORIGINS

The peoples of Africa have different stories that explain the creation of the Earth, the origin of the sun, moon, and stars, and the ancestry of each tribe. Sometimes humans emerge from a hole in the ground, sometimes they are moulded by a creator deity. Most of these stories revolve around the activities of one supreme being, although in the creation myth of Dahomey, this deity is helped by a cosmic serpent in the task of creation.

THE MYTH

The story of creation, as narrated by the Fon people of Dahomey, begins with two primal beings: the eternal male serpent Aido-Hwedo, and the female creator deity Mawu. First, Mawu gave birth to the gods and goddesses. She had many children, too many to name, but they formed various groups according to their powers and dwelling places. They included the Earth deities, ruled by Mawu's first son, Da Zodji; thunder deities, ruled by Mawu's second son, Sogbo; and sea deities, ruled by Mawu's third son, Agbè. Once she had made all the gods and goddesses, Mawu turned her attention to the human race, which she made out of clay.

> **Primal serpent**
> Early African sculpture often depicts the creation myth in the form of a serpent coiled around a human figure.

MAKING THE EARTH

Mawu realized that the human beings needed somewhere to live, so she decided to make the Earth. She rode in the mouth of the cosmic serpent Aido-Hwedo, and as the pair travelled they shaped the Earth like a huge calabash. The world was defined by Aido-Hwedo's turning, serpentine motion; as Aido-Hwedo snaked his way along, his path created winding rivers and valleys with steep sloping land on either side. His sinuous course shaped the Earth's high and low places, the curving hillsides, and the round-bottomed valleys. Because of this meandering, the landscape was not even; everything in it was curved and undulating like the track of the serpent.

▲ **Snake track**
The notion of Aido-Hwedo's sinuous track carving out the landscape is grounded in nature because some snakes create a winding track as they slide across sand.

After each of their creative journeys, Mawu and Aido-Hwedo stopped to rest. When they paused, the serpent's excrement built up, creating the higher mountains. As time went by, this waste material solidified to become hard rock, hiding inside it all the precious metals that Aido-Hwedo expelled from his body. So the primal serpent became the source of all the rich mineral resources that are hidden deep in the ground.

SUPPORTING THE EARTH

The Earth that Mawu and Aido-Hwedo had made together floated on a vast sea contained in an enormous calabash. But its wealth of rocks and resources, together with the weight of all the people and animals Mawu had created, made it too heavy. Mawu saw that it must be supported, otherwise it would sink. She told Aido-Hwedo to coil himself all the way around the Earth, holding it up so that it would not sink into the water. Aido-Hwedo was content to lie in the cool sea water because he did not like the heat of the Earth. Mostly he lay still, but now and then he would shift into a more comfortable position, making the ground shake violently and causing an earthquake.

KEY CHARACTERS

The main characters in the Fon creation story are the snake Aido-Hwedo, who helps in the creation, and the more complex creator goddess Mawu. Mawu is actually half of a composite deity – her other half is the god Lisa, and when encountered together they are referred to as Mawu-Lisa, a deity with two faces. Whereas Mawu is the goddess of the Earth and the moon, Lisa is the god of the sky and the sun.

▲ Aido-Hwedo
The cosmic serpent supports the Earth. In some accounts he also holds up the sky, and is visible as the colourful rainbow.

▲ Mawu
The goddess Mawu is said to live in the sky. Her eyes shine with a pale light and are said to create the light of the moon.

> ## ONE DAY AIDO-HWEDO WILL EAT HIS OWN TAIL, AND THE WORLD WILL FALL INTO THE SEA.

KOM ORIGINS

For the Kom people of northwest Cameroon, the snake is an ancestor figure rather than a creator. Once, their chief was mortally wounded in a war with the neighbouring Fon. He told his people to move to new territory, following the track of a python. Soon after the chief died, a python appeared and the people followed its winding track. Finally the snake stopped and the Kom made their new home at this place.

▼ Brass plaque of python
For the Kom, the python was closely linked to the origins of the tribe and their native homeland.

IMAGES OF THE COSMOS

West African peoples, such as the Dogon tribe of Mali, visualized the world and the sky as an egg. Another conception of the universe was in the form of a calabash. To the Fon, for example, the two halves of the calabash represented the sky (also housing the sun and moon) and the water vessel in which the Earth floated. It was the task of the serpent Aido-Hwedo to hold the two halves of the cosmic calabash apart.

Egg

Calabash

YORUBA CREATION

The Yoruba of Nigeria describe how the sky god Olodumare sent his son, Obatala, down to create the Earth. He gave him a bag of earth and a hen, and lowered a palm tree down with him. Obatala took brown earth from the bag and sprinkled it on the water, where it formed land. Then he put the hen on the Earth and she scratched about, scattering the soil to form the continent of Africa. Later, Obatala created humans out of clay.

➤ Palm tree
The palm tree was a precious gift from Olodumare. Its juice, oil, and nuts became useful resources for the Yoruba tribe.

▲ Obatala
According to some accounts, Obatala (king of the white cloth) was the founder of the first Yoruba city, Ife. He was associated with purity, honesty, and peace.

▲ White Hen
Olodumare sent a white hen with five toes to help Obatala create the Earth. The scratching of the hen created hills and valleys on the ground.

251

SEE ALSO African creation stories 236–37, 252–53, 262–63, 272–73 • Snakes & serpents 28–29, 48–49, 92–93, 98–99, 100–03, 160–61, 238–39

ANANSE

The spider Ananse is a trickster and also a culture hero in West Africa, especially among the Ashanti people of Ghana. Besides his tricks, Ananse is well known for using his intellect to outwit creatures much stronger than himself – stories about these pranks are commonly told both for amusement and to highlight the fact that brains are as important as muscles. In some myths, the trickster acts as an intermediary between human beings and the sky god Nyame. Some even believe that it was Ananse who persuaded Nyame to create the sun and moon so that people on Earth could benefit from having night and day.

MESSENGER TO THE SKY GOD

Nyame, the sky god, was the creator of all things, but he sat aloof from his creations. Down below on the Earth, people worked constantly in the fields – there was no time for them to rest. Ananse heard their complaints, and spun a thread up to Nyame to ask for help. So Nyame created night, when everyone could sleep. But the humans were frightened of the darkness, so Nyame set the moon in the sky to provide light at night. Then the people shivered because it was always cold, so yet again, Ananse went to tell Nyame, and he put the sun in the sky to give warmth. This time, the scorching heat was too much for the mere mortals, and once more, Ananse climbed up his thread to ask for help on behalf of the people. This time, Nyame sent great rains to cool everyone, but his rains were so heavy that they caused floods and people drowned. Nyame made the floods recede and, finally, everybody was content.

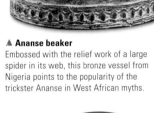

▲ **Ananse beaker**
Embossed with the relief work of a large spider in its web, this bronze vessel from Nigeria points to the popularity of the trickster Ananse in West African myths.

▲ **Ananse weeding grass**
One story talks about how Ananse won the hand of Nyame's daughter by clearing a field full of itchy weeds without scratching himself.

▲ **African sun and moon masks**
Masks representing the sun and the moon are common in West Africa. As the markers of day and night, the sun and the moon are very important, and Ananse was credited with enabling their creation.

MASTER OF STORIES

Nyame owned all the stories in the world. Ananse wanted to buy the stories from him, and as payment, Nyame asked Ananse to bring him some hornets, a python, and a leopard. Ananse tricked the hornets into a calabash. He then went to the python carrying a long staff and declared that he was unclear about which was longer, the snake or the staff. The python lay by the staff, and Ananse quickly tied it to the staff, thus trapping it. Next the spider dug a pit for the leopard and covered it with branches. The unsuspecting leopard fell into it and was caught. Ananse delivered the animals to Nyame and, for fulfilling all the conditions, won the stories of the world.

◀ **Leopard**
Renowned for its speed and hunting prowess, the leopard should have posed an impossible challenge for the spider.

▼ **Python**
The python generally kills its prey by constriction, so Ananse tricked the snake into being tied up so that it could not attack.

TRICKING THE ELEPHANT

One day, an elephant was bored and challenged the other animals to a headbutting competition. Fearing the elephant's strength, none of the animals rose to the challenge, except for Ananse. It was decided that the contest would take place over 14 nights, with the elephant having the first seven butts over the first seven nights. Ananse tricked an antelope into coming to Ananse's house at night to receive some food. Since it was a time of famine, the antelope agreed. That night, the elephant butted the antelope in the dark and killed it. Over the next six days, Ananse tricked more animals in the same way. When it was his turn to butt the elephant, the spider took a hammer and wedge, and aimed with great care at the creature's head. He killed the elephant with a single blow, outsmarting it in this uneven contest.

▶ **Elephant**
In one version of the story, after the first attack with the hammer, the elephant merely complained of a headache, but on the second night, Ananse refined his aim and killed the elephant.

THE ORIGINS OF ARGUMENT

Once, there was a man who argued with everyone, and killed several animals because they disagreed with him. Ananse decided to meet the man. When the man began to tell Ananse fantastic stories, Ananse invited him to his house. On his arrival, the man could not find the spider, but Ananse's children fed him the hottest of chillies, which burned his mouth. He asked for water, but Ananse's children explained that the water at the top of a pot belonged to their father and they were afraid of mixing it with the water below when pouring from the pot. The man argued with this preposterous story, and when Ananse returned, the spider declared that the man must die since he continued to argue. So the spiders killed the man, tore his body to pieces, and threw the bits everywhere. In this way, argument spread around the world.

▼ **Popular folklore ingredient**
Although American in origin, chillies became such a popular ingredient for flavouring in West African food that they found their way into the region's folklore, such as the myth about Ananse and the man.

▶ **African cooking pot**
Metal cooking pots are widely used to boil food over an open fire. Such a vessel can also be used to store water, as in this story of Ananse.

SEE ALSO Spiders 36–37, 228–29 • Tricksters 60–61, 96–97, 100–03, 272–73, 286–87, 288–89, 310–11, 340–41

MYTHICAL HEROES

World mythology is full of heroes, men who often have one mortal and one divine parent. Their parentage gives them such outstanding qualities as superhuman strength, bravery, intelligence, or the ability to travel to dangerous places like the Underworld. They lead their peoples, found nations or empires, play decisive roles in battles, kill monsters, and right wrongs. Their bravery can also lead them to a heroic death.

◀ **Ninigi**
Grandson of Amaterasu, the Japanese sun goddess (*see p.223*), Ninigi was a kind ruler of the Earth who introduced rice growing, and bequeathed royal regalia to the emperors.

▲ **Arjuna**
Arjuna was a great archer in the *Mahabharata*, the Hindu epic (*see pp.206–07*). When unwilling to fight, Krishna persuaded him his destiny was to be a warrior.

▲ **Nezha**
A hero and brave warrior of Chinese legend, Nezha was born from a ball of flesh, had superhuman strength even as a child, and also had the power to grow extra limbs.

◀ **Hayk**
Hayk is a legendary hero of folklore from Armenia in West Asia. A skilled archer, he slew a wicked giant called Bel before going on to found the Armenian nation.

▲ **Moshanyana**
A mythical warrior hero and chief of the Basuto people of Southern Africa, Moshanyana was born fully armed and killed a monster (*see p.275*).

▲ **Aswatthama**
A warrior of the *Mahabharata* (*see pp.206–07*), Aswatthama was the son of Drona, teacher of the Pandavas and Kauravas. He was one of the few survivors of the Kaurava army after the great war.

Gawain
One of the bravest of Arthur's knights (*see pp.126–27*), Sir Gawain accepted a challenge to behead a green giant and then risk having his own head chopped off.

Glooscap
A shapeshifting trickster-hero of many Native American forest peoples, Glooscap bound the wings of a mountain-top eagle whose flapping caused terrible storms.

Neoptolemus
The son of Achilles and Princess Deidamia, Neoptolemus was a Greek hero who fought bravely in the Trojan War (*see pp.60–61*), but was said by some ancient sources to be a bloodthirsty killer.

Hector
King Priam's son Hector (*left*) led the army of Troy in the Trojan War (*see pp.60–61*). None defeated him until he faced Achilles (*right*), who chased him three times around the walls of Troy before killing him.

Wolfdietrich
A hero of Germanic legend – and often identified with the hero Dietrich (*see p.104*) – Wolfdietrich was abandoned by his father, the emperor, but after a long exile returned to fight for and claim his throne.

Orestes
The Greek hero Orestes was Agamemnon's son. When his mother, Clytemnestra, and her lover, Aegisthus, murdered his father on his return from the Trojan War (*see p.69*), Orestes killed them.

Kintu
In the mythology of the Buganda people of Uganda in East Africa, Kintu was the first man on Earth. At first he lived alone with his cow, before marrying the creator's daughter, Nambi.

▲ **The face of a culture hero**
Intricately decorated with cowrie shells and handcarved red, white, and blue beads, this mask from the Democratic Republic of Congo was made by the Kuba Bushongo people and represents their founder and culture hero, Woot.

CENTRAL AFRICA

Central Africa is dominated by the vast and densely rainforested basin of the River Congo, one of the world's longest rivers. Many of the myths originating in the region reflect this rich and vibrant tropical landscape.

Much of Central Africa is home to people who, like many of the inhabitants of southern Africa, speak languages from the Bantu group. The myths of Central African Bantu-speakers share some of the features of those myths found among Bantu-speakers further south, including tales of heroes. These heroes frequently encounter and defeat monsters and evil beings and are often rewarded with power and kingship – Mwindo, the epic hero of the Nyanga people, is a famous example. Other peoples in the region have mythologies with many deities who embrace specific functions in the cosmos.

CREATION STORIES

One indication of the diversity of the myths in Central Africa is the great variety of creation stories. Among the Bushongo people of the Democratic Republic of Congo, for example, the supreme god brings the cosmos into being simply by vomiting it up. In turn he vomits up the sun, the moon, and the stars, then he vomits up all the animals and, finally, the first human beings. For the Fang people, who live in Gabon, the Democratic Republic of Congo, and the Central African Republic, creation takes places in two stages, not one. First, a primal creator deity makes a world egg by mixing his underarm hair with a pebble and part of his brain. He then anoints this egg with his seed, following which three gods hatch out of the egg, including a secondary creator who goes on to make both the land and the people. Other peoples, such as the Efe and Mbuti of the Democratic Republic of Congo, tell a story about how the creator deity, with the help of the moon, makes the human race from clay, adding a skin, and pouring blood into the skin to give people life.

▶ Protector of the home
Statuettes called *bitegues* – like this one from the Bateke people of the Democratic Republic of Congo – are designed to be placed by the head of the family in a corner of the home facing the entrance, to protect the whole household from evil.

▶ Protecting the dead
The Kota people of Central Africa traditionally attach protective metalwork figures called *mbulu-ngulus* to containers of bones and other important relics of their ancestors.

MYTH AND REALITY

In the vast and dense tropical rainforest that makes up much of Central Africa, the close relevance of myths to everyday life is often clear. The Pygmy people, for example, see their supreme deity not only as their creator but also as the god of the hunt. In their mythology he lowered the first human beings from the sky and communicates with his creations through certain animals: often an elephant – known as the Thunderer – or a chameleon. As the god of hunters, he created all the animals as food for the human race, and gives the sustaining light of the sun new life every day by gathering light from the stars to add to its brilliance in the morning.

HEROES AND TRICKSTERS

Whereas the Pygmies' supreme deity is also a helper of humanity, in many Central African cultures there are also culture heroes who bring with them specific skills. The Fjort people of the Democratic Republic of Congo, for example, have a mythical blacksmith called Funzi who receives the gift of fire from a deity and teaches the people how to work copper and iron. Sometimes the task of culture hero is combined with that of trickster, as in Ture, the trickster of the Zande people of the Democratic Republic of Congo, who brings the people fire. Characters like these ensure that the myths of Central Africa have remained vividly relevant to the lives of the native people for many thousands of years.

LONKUNDO

The founder and culture hero of the Mongo-Nkundo people of the Congo basin was called Lonkundo. He is primarily known for teaching his people how to hunt, but there are also myths about other aspects of his life, particularly his relationship with his wives.

They tell of how Lonkundo set up house in the forest, and how he caught his favourite wife, Ilankaka, in one of his animal traps. These myths, which continue with tales of Lonkundo's descendants, reflect the dangerous and unpredictable world of the forest hunter.

THE FIRST HUNTER

The first people did not know how to hunt, and having little in the way of survival skills, they wondered how they would survive. One night, the spirit of Lonkundo's father came to him in a dream. Lonkundo's father told his son to look for animal paw prints in the soil, and to follow the tracks to find the creature's regular habitat. He should then construct a trap for it using raffia fibres and twigs. When he awoke, Lonkundo followed his father's instructions and set a trap in the path of one of the creatures he had tracked. The trap was successful, and Lonkundo then travelled widely, tracking beasts and setting traps, and providing food for his people. He also taught them how to set their own traps for animals, and they were never short of food again.

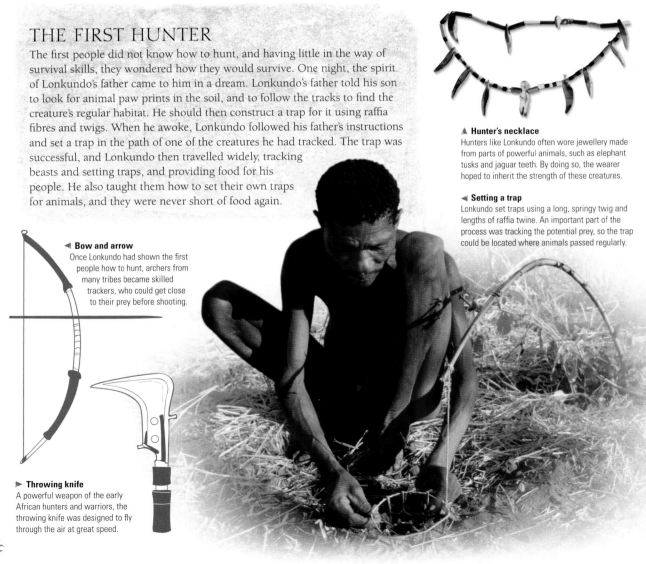

Hunter's necklace
Hunters like Lonkundo often wore jewellery made from parts of powerful animals, such as elephant tusks and jaguar teeth. By doing so, the wearer hoped to inherit the strength of these creatures.

Setting a trap
Lonkundo set traps using a long, springy twig and lengths of raffia twine. An important part of the process was tracking the potential prey, so the trap could be located where animals passed regularly.

Bow and arrow
Once Lonkundo had shown the first people how to hunt, archers from many tribes became skilled trackers, who could get close to their prey before shooting.

Throwing knife
A powerful weapon of the early African hunters and warriors, the throwing knife was designed to fly through the air at great speed.

CATCHING A WIFE

One night, Lonkundo dreamed that he had caught the sun in one of his animal traps. When he awoke, he went to inspect his traps as usual and was amazed to see a bright light coming from one of the traps he had set. He went over and found a beautiful woman, called Ilankaka, caught by the raffia noose of the trap. When he released her, Lonkundo, entranced by her beauty, asked her to become his wife. She accepted on one condition: he must never boast that he had caught her in a trap. He agreed and the two settled down. Later, Lonkundo took other wives, and the extended family became prosperous. When other families became jealous of their success, Lonkundo and his wives decided to move to the forest to start a new life.

➤ Trapping Ilankaka
The myth of the catching of Ilankaka tells how she was caught in the twine of one of Lonkundo's animal traps. Without a knife, she had little chance of freeing herself until the hunter arrived on the scene.

◀ Parrot
The parrot's bright plumage and ability to mimic sounds and voices meant the bird was thought to be able to foretell the future or bring good omens.

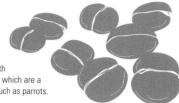

➤ Palm nuts
The oil palm is valued both for its oil and for its nuts, which are a source of food for birds such as parrots.

LOSING A WIFE

In the forest, Lonkundo and his wives travelled to find a new home. After a while they heard the screeching cry of parrots, which was considered a good omen, so they stopped where they were to make their home. They cut down trees to build huts and, as was the custom at that time, made a human sacrifice. But one of Lonkundo's wives, Nsombe, quarrelled with her husband about her hut, which she thought was too small, and she left the village with her son, Yonjwa. Lonkundo's wife Ilankaka was pleased, believing that Lonkundo loved her the best. Ilankaka planted palm trees and harvested the nuts, but when Lonkundo demanded more nuts from the trees, the couple argued. Lonkundo, forgetting he had promised not to boast of catching his wife, exclaimed, "Remember, I caught you in my trap", and Ilankaka disappeared.

ITONDE AND LIANJA

The most famous of Lonkundo's descendants was his grandson Itonde. He was the son of Yonjwa and the grandson of Nsombe, the wife who had left Lonkundo after a quarrel. Itonde was a notable explorer who travelled through the forest and the lands around them, naming all the beasts he found. One day he met a woman called Mbombe among the trees, and the pair were married. When Mbombe became pregnant she had a craving for a strange nut dropped by a bird. Itonde went to search for more of these nuts, but was attacked by rivals and killed. Mbombe, however, went on to give birth to several children, who became the ancestors of the Mongo-speaking tribes of Central Africa. One of these sons, Lianja, became a hero, who avenged the death of his father.

▲ Mongo brass knife
A beautifully made knife was a prized possession among the hunters of the Mongo, and was a sign of great status.

▼ Naming the animals
As the person who named the animals, Itonde was seen to have an intimate knowledge of the animal world and the power to influence its creatures.

SEE ALSO Hunters 266–67, 272–73, 334–35 • Culture heroes 26–27, 214–15, 262–63

MWINDO

The story of Mwindo is a traditional epic of the Nyanga people of the Democratic Republic of the Congo that has been passed down through oral performance. Mwindo's miraculous powers include both invincible strength and the ability to see into the future.

His adventures involve a long rivalry with his own father, and during the course of the epic, Mwindo travels to the Underworld, where he displays his strength, and also to the sky, where he learns new wisdom.

MWINDO'S BIRTH

Mwindo was the son of Shemwindo, the chief of Tubondo, and his favourite wife. From birth, he possessed powers of prophecy, the ability to destroy evil, and the means to move with equal ease whether on land, underwater, in the air, or underground. But Shemwindo did not want a son, especially such a powerful one, as he feared that a younger man would challenge his authority. He planned to kill Mwindo, but was unsuccessful thanks to his son's miraculous powers. Shemwindo therefore told his councillors to seal Mwindo inside a drum and to throw the drum into the river to dispose of his rival. The councillors did so, but the drum found its way to Shemwindo's sister, who rescued Mwindo.

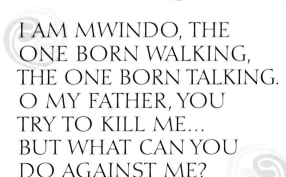

➤ Mwindo
A typical mythical "wonder child" born with the ability to walk and talk, Mwindo had such superhuman strength that not even the greatest fighter could defeat or kill him.

◄ Mwindo's flyswatter
Mwindo carried a flyswatter with magical powers. When someone threw a spear at him, he could deflect the weapon by waving the flyswatter in the air.

▼ Sealed inside a log
In some versions of the myth, Shemwindo's accomplices sealed the young Mwindo inside a hollow log and floated him down the river to what they thought would be certain death.

I AM MWINDO, THE ONE BORN WALKING, THE ONE BORN TALKING. O MY FATHER, YOU TRY TO KILL ME... BUT WHAT CAN YOU DO AGAINST ME?

Aaron Shepard, *The Magic Flyswatter: A Superhero Tale of Africa*, 2008

Cowrie shell belt
Muisa, the ruler of the Underworld, had a magic belt that crushed everyone it hit. Muisa ordered it to strike Mwindo, smashing him to the ground, but Mwindo waved his flyswatter and the belt could do him no harm.

Ntumba the aardvark
While chasing his father, Mwindo came across an aardvark spirit called Ntumba. He saw that Shemwindo was hiding behind Ntumba, whom he punched for concealing his father.

IN THE UNDERWORLD

After Mwindo escaped from the drum in which Shemwindo had trapped him, he vowed to return home and fight his father. His maternal uncles gave him iron armour, and together they destroyed Shemwindo's home, killing many people, but Shemwindo escaped to the Underworld. Mwindo chased him and, upon reaching the Underworld, had to fight its ruler, Muisa, before he could approach his father. Finally, Shemwindo surrendered, and apologized for trying to kill Mwindo. The pair agreed that the kingdom would be split in two, one half ruled by Shemwindo and the other by Mwindo. They returned to Earth and Mwindo restored to life all the people who had been killed in the fighting.

The Lightning Master
The spirit called Nkuba or Lightning Master took the form of a hedgehog. He helped Mwindo with bolts of lightning when he was attacking Shemwindo's village.

IN THE SKY

One day, Mwindo and some of his followers were out hunting when a dragon came and ate some of his companions. Mwindo killed the dragon and rescued his men from its belly, but the spirit Lightning Master, a friend of both Mwindo and the dragon, was upset at the death of the beast. So Lightning Master took Mwindo into the sky to teach him a lesson. In the sky Mwindo had to endure many ordeals, after which Lightning Master reminded him that no human, not even a superhero, should treat any animal with contempt, as they were all considered sacred to the gods. Then Mwindo was allowed to return to Earth, where he explained to his people that all creatures were sacred and should be respected. After this he ruled his people wisely and peacefully for many years.

TELLING THE EPIC

The Mwindo epic has been recorded in writing, but it is essentially a performance piece, and takes the form of a long narrative punctuated with songs, riddles, proverbs, prayers, and other asides, accompanied with the music of drum and flute. The storytellers who perform the epic pass it down from one generation to the next and prize the narrative not merely as entertainment but as an embodiment of the history, values, and beliefs of their people. People believe that the act of performing the epic protects the storyteller from disease and death.

Congo Drum   Congo Flute

Congo dancer
Dancing is central to African culture and storytelling. A complete performance of the Mwindo epic, typically presented in traditional costume, could take several days of dancing, singing, and reciting.

SEE ALSO Battle for kingdom 158–59, 200–03, 206–07

THE WISE KING

A myth of the Bushongo people of the southeastern Congo region describes the achievements of their greatest ruler, Shamba Bolongongo, who is seen both as a king and a culture hero. Shamba, who was wise and just, is said to have been a real king who reigned in the 17th century, a time when many tribes united to create large and powerful political factions. He was revered not only for his great wisdom, but also because he avoided violence and war, preferring to use his intelligence to forge alliances or resolve disputes.

THE MYTH

Shamba Bolongongo, a prince of the Bushongo people, was very inquisitive and loved learning. As heir to the throne, he realized that he would be able to rule over his subjects more efficiently if he knew more about them, their way of living, and their needs. So when he was still young, Shamba set out to journey far and wide. On his many travels, he found out all that he could about the different peoples who lived in his kingdom and in the lands beyond his own. The prince learned many things that he believed would eventually help his own people to prosper and to live peacefully and happily.

THE CULTURE HERO

When Shamba returned from his long journey and became the king of his people, he taught them many new skills that have been used ever since among the Bushongo. The king showed them the technique of making textiles out of raffia fibres, and how to turn these textiles into clothes. He taught them how to prepare the nourishing cassava root properly, ensuring that it was cooked well enough to remove the poison that could be left behind in the plant. Shamba also planted palm trees and used them for making oil. And he introduced the Bushongo to tobacco smoking.

◀ **Shamba Bolongongo**
This carved wooden sceptre depicts the king sitting on his throne, chewing on a medicinal root. His crossed legs and ritual nudity are typical of the Bushongo people.

THE MAN OF PEACE

The Bushongo were a warlike people, skilled in the use of weapons. But Shamba hated violence and killing, and wanted to introduce his people to the ways of peace. Soon after ascending the throne, he issued an order banning the use of bows and arrows, as well as the shongo, a type of throwing knife, in battle. At first the people thought that criminals would thrive under a king who did not allow the use of weapons, but they were proved wrong. Shamba tried harder than any king before him to hunt down criminals and punish them harshly. But he was not very keen on handing out the death penalty, and would only do so as a last resort in the case of the most hardened of offenders.

The people saw that Shamba respected all his subjects. He was especially mindful of women and children, and severely punished anyone who tried to harm them. Whenever people approached him with a problem or a dispute, he would give good advice or offer a fair judgement. Ever since that time, Shamba has been held up as the ideal ruler, an example that every Bushongo king has attempted to follow – even though not all of them have been as successful or as wise. His period of rule is often said to have been a golden age by the Bushongo people.

◀ **Wooden dagger**
Shamba's symbol of office was a dagger, though this was merely a ceremonial weapon, as the king disliked violence so intensely he would have used it only in extreme situations.

Raffia fabric
The fibrous leaves and branches of the raffia palm are useful for making ropes, roof coverings, and other items, but are most commonly seen in boldly patterned fabric.

Cassava
Once introduced, this plant quickly spread across Africa, becoming a staple food. The right way of cooking the plant, by detoxifying it, was said to be one of Shamba's gifts.

THE CULTURE HERO'S GIFTS

Shamba was credited with introducing a number of skills into the lives of his people that later proved beneficial. It is uncertain if these innovations were introduced by the actual 17th-century king on whom the story is based. Items like cassava and tobacco came from the Americas in the 16th century, so the story could well be based on fact. Raffia, however, is native to Africa, and the historical Shamba may have pioneered its use in making textiles.

Tobacco plant
European merchants shipped tobacco from America to West Africa in the 1560s, after which it may have been promoted by local rulers such as Shamba.

KILL NEITHER MAN, WOMAN, NOR CHILD. ARE THEY NOT THE CHILDREN OF CHEMBE [GOD], AND HAVE THEY NOT THE RIGHT TO LIVE?
Shamba Bolongongo

PEACE AND JUSTICE

In traditional West African societies, arguments or disputes between two people or families were resolved by the head of the village. Similarly, disputes on a larger scale would be resolved by the king. People looked up to these leaders because of the authority that their status gave them, an authority that was often enhanced by the belief that the leaders were linked to ancestors and gods. Subjects used to obey their rulers because the ruler had the power to enforce his will, but when a king had a personal reputation for wisdom, his judgements were respected all the more.

Shongo
Banning the shongo, or throwing knife, a traditional Bushongo weapon, was crucial in ushering in an era of peace among the peoples of the region.

THE BUSHONGO

The Bushongo, dominant among the Kuba people of Central Africa, have existed as a federation of tribes since the 16th century. They have a rich mythology, centred on many spirits of nature and past kings. Their creation myth narrates how Bumba, the supreme deity, vomited up the sun, moon, and stars, followed by animals and the first human, Woot. He then handed over the world to the human race. During ritual ceremonies, every king wears a Moshambwooy mask, representing Woot, the primary ancestor.

Moshambwooy mask

THE PEOPLE'S GAME

Another innovation popularized by Shamba was a game called Lele or Mancala. Shamba devised it because he found out that his people were addicted to gambling. Wishing to encourage them to take up a safer amusement, he introduced Lele. Claimed by some to be the world's oldest board game, Lele, in fact, originated in the Arab world and made its way across Africa. It is played using a board with small depressions (about 32 in number), in which the players put small counters, nuts, or stones, which need to be accumulated during the game.

Playing Lele
The game of lele is played by two people. Different boards have different numbers of depressions, but the objective remains constant – to win more counters than an opponent.

SEE ALSO Culture heroes 26–27, 214–15, 258–59 • Journeys 34–35, 44–45, 64–67, 78–79, 120–21, 220–21

▲ Kikuyu ceremonial shield
Shields like this one have been used for centuries by the Kikuyu people, who
live in Kenya. This example was made for use in dances following circumcision
ceremonies that mark a boy's passage from childhood to the world of the adult.

EAST AFRICA

Supreme deities who bring the necessities of life, from rain to cattle, dominate the mythology of East Africa. Side by side with these gods exist thousands of spirits who often have a direct and personal influence on people's lives.

This region covers the eastern parts of Africa from Ethiopia in the north, south through Kenya and Tanzania to the northern areas of Zambia and Malawi. Humans have lived in this part of the world for longer than in any other. The earliest human remains, together with the remains of hominids who are related to our species – some of which date back to four million years ago – have been found at sites such as Koobi Fora in Kenya and the Olduvai Gorge in Tanzania. This long history of human habitation produced cultures well adapted to the varied local conditions, which are generally quite cool and dry in the many uplands, and more hot and humid towards the coasts. Among the many cultures of the region, a number, such as the Masai of Kenya and Tanzania and the Tumbuka of Malawi, have outstanding mythologies.

▲ Masai men dancing
Ceremonially armed with spears, Masai men perform a ritual dance in Tanzania. Such dances traditionally accompany preparations for war, rites of passage, and welcoming guests.

CATTLE MYTHS OF THE MASAI HERDERS
The Masai traditionally live by herding cattle, and their most important deity is Enkai, a creator god who in some of their myths gave them the first cattle. These tales also explain the role of other peoples who live by hunting and gathering or by crop farming. The rich Masai pantheon also includes Enkai's consort, Olapa, goddess of the

◄ Lucky charm
Amulets or lucky charms made from materials such as bone and worn around the neck, wrist, or leg – or simply carried on one's person – are believed to have special power in many cultures around the world. This lucky charm from Ethiopia is said to ensure that cattle breed successfully.

moon. The role of cattle as sustainers of life is also seen in the Masai myths of death and the next world. Each person has a guardian spirit, who looks after them from the day they are born. When the time comes for the person to die, the guardian spirit also acts as judge of the deceased. The spirits of people who led good lives on Earth are taken to a land where there are abundant cattle; the spirits of those who are less worthy go to a place where there is neither water nor cattle.

SPIRITS AND ANIMALS
In addition to a supreme deity, many cultures have a host of other spirits. Sometimes these spirits take the form of animals about whom amusing or moral stories are traditionally told – stories that in some cases have become familiar and well-loved around the world. For example, the Tumbuka, a people of Malawi, have a supreme god called Chiuta. Chiuta is the Tumbuka creator, an almighty being who, as well as creating the universe, is a fertility god and a bringer of life-giving rain. But in addition to myths about Chiuta, the Tumbuka tell stories about three animals: the wise tortoise, the trickster hare, and the wicked hyena. In these it takes the wisdom of the tortoise to defeat the devious tricks of the hare or the villainous behaviour of the hyena.

RITES OF PASSAGE
As well as this body of myths and moral tales, East Africa, like the rest of Africa, has a rich heritage of ceremony and ritual. Special music and dances accompany the rites of passage that mark the key stages of a person's life, especially the initiation rites for when a young person comes of age. These ceremonies survive intact to this day – in spite of a long period of contact with cultures from outside Africa, both during the colonial period and more recently – so keeping traditional beliefs and stories alive.

THE FIRST CATTLE

The Masai, a cattle-herding people who live in Kenya, have several myths about how they came to own cattle. Other herding tribes in Africa have similar stories, which are testimony to the important role of cattle in their prosperity. In one myth, a Masai tribesman is contrasted with a man from one of the hunter-gatherer tribes of Kenya and Tanzania, who are widely referred to by the herding people as the Dorobo (the ones without cattle).

THE MYTH

Long ago there lived a Dorobo man who shared his land with an elephant and a snake. One day, the elephant had a calf. When the Dorobo approached the mother elephant, she attacked him to protect her young, and the man killed her in self-defence. The snake was lurking nearby and he slew that too. The alarmed elephant calf ran away, fearing for its life, and the Dorobo was left alone.

A MESSAGE FROM THE GODS

The baby elephant ran until it met a Masai tribesman called Le-eyo and told him what had happened to its mother and the snake. Intrigued by the tale, Le-eyo travelled to the place where the Dorobo lived, and peered through the bush to see what was going on. He was amazed to see Naiteru-kop, the messenger of the gods, talking to the Dorobo. Naiteru-kop told the Dorobo to meet him the next morning at a clearing in the forest, where he would be given a great gift. Le-eyo decided that he would get to the meeting place early, before the Dorobo arrived. When the next day dawned, Le-eyo hurried off to the meeting place while the Dorobo was still fast asleep. When Le-eyo reached the clearing, Naiteru-kop spoke to him, thinking he was the

▲ Masai house
Le-eyo hid in his hut while the sky god lowered the cattle to Earth. The walls of traditional Masai houses are plastered with cow dung, which dries hard in the sun.

Dorobo. The messenger told him to go home and build a fence around his hut, then kill and skin a wild animal, and put the meat inside the skin. After doing this he was to stay inside his hut and wait. Naiteru-kop insisted that he must stay indoors, even if he heard a great thundering sound outside, and Le-eyo said that he would be sure to obey.

THE COMING OF THE CATTLE

So Le-eyo went home, and did everything as instructed. Soon there was a thundering sound outside. At first, Le-eyo stayed inside, as the sound was so great that he trembled with fear. But eventually he went out to investigate. To his astonishment, he saw that Enkai, the sky god, had lowered a strip of hide from the sky and a huge herd of cattle had come down on it. As he watched, the strip of hide disappeared into the sky. Le-eyo now had plenty of cattle, but the sky god told him that he would have had even more if only he had done as he was told. From then on the Masai became the owners of all the world's cattle while the Dorobo were forced to carry on with their former way of life as hunters.

▲ Making fire
The Masai use friction generated by rotating a fire stick to make fire. Some accounts say the cattle of the Masai came down to Earth on a fire stick.

CATTLE AND THE MASAI

The Masai believed they had been entrusted with the responsibility of safeguarding all the world's cattle. In a traditional Masai settlement, everyone took part in caring for the cattle, the men herding and the women milking. The meat and milk of the cow was the staple diet of the people, its hide was used to make clothes, and its horns and bones were made into utensils. People even drew blood from a cow if there was nothing else to drink. So the number of cows kept by a family was an indication of their wealth and their status in society. Even today, cattle may be used as currency when Masai people are buying and selling other goods.

▲ Masai bride
When a Masai man marries, his family traditionally has to pay a bride-price to the woman's family, and this payment is usually made in cattle.

▲ Status symbol
Masai families own around 15 head of cattle each, sufficient for a regular supply of milk and meat, with enough left over to breed and to exchange in transactions.

ORIGINS OF POLYGAMY

The Kikuyu farming people of Kenya have a history of intermarriage with the Masai. Kikuyu clans carry women's names and yet the men are allowed to take more than one wife. Their mythology says that the opposite arrangement once prevailed, with each woman taking several husbands. The men rebelled, changing the custom when all the women were pregnant and powerless to defend their rights. So the men gained the power to have several wives, but the women insisted that the clan names stay with the female line, threatening to kill their boy children if the men tried to impose male clan names.

▶ Kikuyu man with his wife
This Kikuyu couple are wearing their traditional tribal dress. The shield and spear are generally used today in ceremonial dances.

ENKAI THE CREATOR

In many Masai myths, the creator god Enkai is a central character. Enkai is the sky god who represents both the sun and the rains, and lives in the sky with his wife, Olapa, the moon. Once, Enkai told the people to leave their *kraals* (enclosures) open at night, but not everyone obeyed. Those who did discovered in the morning that Enkai had given them cows, sheep, and goats. These people became the Masai. The Dorobo became hunters and the Kikuyu took up farming for their livelihood.

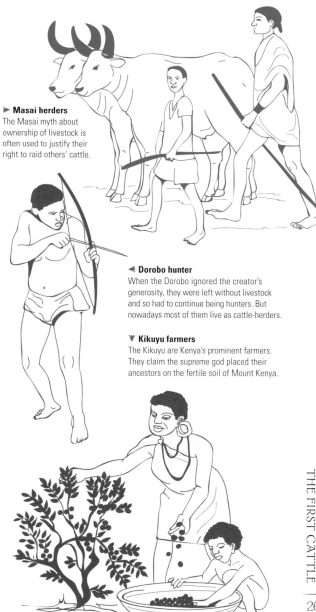

▶ Masai herders
The Masai myth about ownership of livestock is often used to justify their right to raid others' cattle.

◀ Dorobo hunter
When the Dorobo ignored the creator's generosity, they were left without livestock and so had to continue being hunters. But nowadays most of them live as cattle-herders.

▼ Kikuyu farmers
The Kikuyu are Kenya's prominent farmers. They claim the supreme god placed their ancestors on the fertile soil of Mount Kenya.

SEE ALSO Cows 90–91, 172–73, 224–25 • African sky deities 236–39, 252–53

SHAMANS

Acting as both ritual leaders and healers, shamans – also known as medicine men or women – are pivotal in many traditional societies. Most train deeply in the lore and religion of their people, but also gain their power from mystical contact with the spirits. Spirit contact enables them both to defuse the harm caused by malignant spirits, thereby curing illnesses, and to see into the future.

CONTACTING THE SPIRITS

In order to achieve a healing or to consult an oracle, shamans make contact with the world of the spirits. They do this by entering a trance, something that frequently they induce by using the hypnotic rhythm of music and dance, often in conjunction with the use of psychoactive substances. Very often they use the rhythm of a drum, and shaman's drums are sacred objects in their own right. Shamans sometimes see their contact with the spirit world as a journey to that world, and having been in a trance, they refer to visiting the spirits or even flying to the spirit world.

▼ Benin medicine man
Benin in West Africa is one place where medicine men have long been valued – historically they have even become chiefs.

▲ Haida shaman's rattle
Haida shamans in northwestern North America traditionally shook special rattles to help them go into a trance.

➤ African shaman's drum
The typical African shaman's drum is tall and thin. In skilled hands it makes such complex, expressive music that people talk about the spirits actually speaking through the drum.

▼ Siberian shaman
The word "shaman" comes from the language of the Tungus people of Siberia, where the work of shamans in medicine and exorcisms has long been part of the traditional culture.

▲ Lapp shaman's drum
Shamans of northern peoples such as the Lapps and Siberians have traditionally used shallow drums of reindeer hide decorated with magic symbols.

CEREMONIAL MASKS AND DEATH MASKS

Often an important element of a shaman's equipment is a mask bearing the face of a spirit. This does not just disguise the shaman in the same way an actor's mask does, but enables either the shaman to "become" the spirit depicted by the mask, or the spirit to speak through the medium of the shaman. Like all other shamanic equipment, masks are made and treated with great reverence. In some cultures, a deceased shaman is also given a mask, to help in the transition from life to death.

▽ **Powerful mask**
This Mongolian shaman's mask bears the crescent moon and stars, ancient symbols of power.

⌃ **Shaman's death mask**
This mask was placed on a dead Aleutian Islands shaman to stop his spirit reanimating his corpse.

⌃ **Rice spirit mask**
A shaman from Sarawak, Indonesia, wore this mask depicting a rice spirit when performing a ritual in the paddy fields to ensure a good crop.

⌃ **Iroquois mask**
Among the Iroquois people of North America, masks like this were once worn by shamans of the False Face Society to help appease spirits and perform healing.

HEALING AND CHARMS

Since much of a shaman's work is to do with healing, most shamans are highly skilled in the use of medicinal herbal remedies. Also, because many cultures have historically believed that illnesses are caused by the presence of evil spirits, exorcising these spirits has also traditionally been part of a shaman's duties. Many shamans carry charms to keep such spirits at bay.

◁ **Indonesian shaman's doll**
Indonesian shamans have long owned dolls like this one to ward off evil spirits and bring good luck. Scrapings from the dolls can also be used in potions.

⌃ **Medicine bundle**
A vision of an eagle led a Native American shaman to wrap up an eagle to channel the power of friendly spirits.

⌃ **Haida soul catcher**
A traditional Haida belief is that the soul can escape the body, so causing illness. A shaman must then trap the soul in a special device and return it to the body.

◁ **Haida shaman's neck ring**
Haida shamans traditionally wore neck rings festooned with powerful healing charms formed from pieces of bone.

POWERFUL WOMEN

Although most shamans are men, from Korea to South Africa and the west coast of North America there are tribes in which women can also become shamans. Generally they perform the same functions as male shamans, but it is sometimes claimed that female shamans have even greater powers, as they and they alone are able to cure particularly serious illnesses.

⌃ **A female Mongolian shaman**
Mongolia is one country where there are female as well as male shamans. All shamans study hard, learning from tradition, from their forebears, and from the spirits.

▲ **Southern African ceremonial masks**
Masks are used in ceremonies in many parts of Southern Africa. Masks such as these
ones in a museum in Angola completely disguise the wearer, allowing him to assume the
identity of the spirit depicted by the face of the mask for the duration of the ceremony.

SOUTHERN AFRICA

The myths of Southern Africa – an area that has traditionally been home to both hunters and farmers – form two distinct traditions of gods, heroes, and spirits that are still important to the cultural identities of people there today.

Southern Africa encompasses Angola, Zambia, and the countries to their south, and is a culturally diverse region. The area was originally inhabited by peoples commonly known outside Africa as "bushmen": peoples such as the Khoikhoi, San, and !Kung – the exclamation mark expresses one of the clicks in their language – who lived by hunting wild game and gathering wild plant produce. But at some point in the past, groups of farming peoples began to move into the area. These farmers, who spoke languages of the Bantu group, such as Xhosa and Zulu, slowly but surely colonized the land, gradually displacing the various hunter-gatherers to its more remote regions.

▲ San hunting aids
The San have traditional divination ceremonies to establish where best to hunt. Finely carved antelope bones and antlers help provide the answer.

beings. The Khoikhoi of South Africa, for example, call their supreme deity Gamab or Gauna. He is a sky god, but also the god of death, and is said to end people's lives by shooting his arrows into them from the heavens. Other important Khoikhoi deities include Gunab, the god of evil, and Tsui, a rain god and patron of sorcerers who had the power to bring himself back to life after death. The range of malign creatures in the Khoikhoi mythological canon includes the man-eating Aigamuxa, who is human in form but has his eyes in his feet, not his head, and Ga-gorib, a spotted creature resembling a leopard who silently and patiently lies in wait for his unfortunate victims in the bottom of a pit.

THE MYTHS OF THE HUNTER-GATHERERS

The cultural heritage of Southern Africa therefore became a mixture of two diverse sets of peoples. The hunter-gatherers, or "bushmen", of Southern Africa have complex mythologies involving deities, heroes, and a host of monster-like malign

▲ Cave paintings of the "bushmen"
African artists have been drawing on rocks for millennia. Hunter-gatherer artists depicted scenes of hunting – like this one on the walls of caves in the Matobo Hills of Zimbabwe from 2,000 years or so ago – giving us an insight into their ancient belief systems.

THE MYTHS OF THE BANTU-SPEAKERS

Among the Bantu-speakers, Xhosa mythology has a similar mix of deities, ancestral figures, and other spirits. At the head of the deities is the supreme god uThixo. People traditionally communicate with uThixo through ancestor spirits, and special reverence is given to the primal ancestor, Tashawe, from whom all Xhosa believe they are descended. It is the job of the *imbongi*, or praise singer, to accompany the chief on important occasions and to sing songs praising both him and the ancestors, and as a result cement the link between the ruler and the illustrious heroes who have gone before him.

Southern African mythology also features familiar spirits who cause mischief, disease, or even death. A noted example is the *tokoloshe*, a dwarf-like spirit of the Xhosa and Zulu peoples. He is said to strangle people in their beds, so it is traditional to raise one's bed up on bricks, out of his reach.

Despite a history of European colonization, traditional myths survive widely in Southern Africa. Their popularity, connection with important ceremonies, links to essential aspects of life, and long history, sustain the indigenous peoples' cultures and their sense of belonging to the land.

MYTHS OF THE SAN

Part of a group often known as "bushmen", the San are a hunting people who live mainly in Botswana, Namibia, and South Africa. Their mythology includes stories about how the first people of their tribes were created, as well as accounts of events important to them, such as the beginning of hunting. Some key characters in their stories are the bee, which, as the maker of honey, is a symbol of ingenuity and wisdom; the mantis, a primal spirit involved in the creation of humanity; and the eland, a type of antelope and a popular quarry for hunters.

THE FIRST HUMANS

At the beginning of time, a honey bee carried a praying mantis over the dark waters of a river. But the waters stretched far and wide, and as the bee looked for a solid patch of ground on which he could land, he became tired of flying with the weight of the mantis on his back. The mantis seemed to grow heavier and heavier, and the bee flew lower and lower until, quite exhausted, he began skimming on the surface of the water. As he floated, he saw a large white flower that was half open, waiting for morning to come so that the sun's rays could help it bloom. The bee set the mantis down on the flower, planting within the mantis the seed of the first human before dying. When the sun rose, the flower opened wide. As the air warmed, the mantis awoke and the seed germinated to create the first San.

▲ **South African landscape**
The San live in the Kalahari Desert of Southern Africa, a region where water is scarce, unlike at the time of the creation. Water is hence a precious commodity that is, for them, a symbol of life.

▲ **San rock art**
The San are outstanding painters, creating images using natural pigments on the rock of cliffs and caves. The subjects of San artists include the hunt and the animals of the Kalahari Desert, both part of their mythology.

THE FIRST HUNT

The mantis made an eland, the first of its kind, and nurtured it on honey. One day, a young man saw it at a water hole and went to tell his father, the ancestor Kwammang-a, who took his bow and shot the eland dead. The mantis had gone to gather food, and when he returned, he saw the creature dead and Kwammang-a's followers dividing up the meat. He was enraged, and tried to shoot the hunters, but all his shots missed. Then he took the creature's gall bladder and split it open, so that all the world was flooded with darkness as the gall flowed out. Later, he threw the bladder into the sky, where it became the moon. Since then, it has given people light as they hunt by night.

▲ **Eland**
Although San hunters pursue wildebeest or smaller creatures, the eland is a popular subject in their mythology, because it is a symbol of strength.

HLAKANYANA

A trickster figure belonging to myths of the Xhosa and Zulu peoples of South Africa, Hlakanyana was a "wonder-child" who could talk even before he emerged from his mother's womb, and who clamoured to be let out. He could walk as soon as he was born, and immediately headed for the cattle enclosure, intent on satisfying his hunger – not with his mother's milk, but with some roasted meat. When Hlakanyana grew up, he had a series of adventures, most of which involved tricking people or animals out of food.

HLAKANYANA'S POT

One night, Hlakanyana crept out, took a number of birds caught in traps set by some other boys in the village, and gave the birds to his mother to cook. She left them in the pot to cook overnight. The following morning, Hlakanyana got up very early and ate all the meat except for the birds' heads. Then he filled the pot with cattle dung, put the heads on top, and went back to bed, pretending to be asleep. When his mother awoke, Hlakanyana got up from his bed as if he too had just woken up. He complained that she was late and had probably let the food spoil. He told her that the meat would have turned to cattle dung because she had not taken the birds out of the pot soon enough. His mother scorned the idea, but when she went to check on the food, she found the pot full of cattle dung, just as her son had predicted. He then ate the birds' heads, saying she did not deserve any.

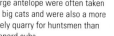

▶ **Cooking pot**
Food is an integral part of many myths associated with Hlakanyana. In yet another myth, he is himself caught and put into a cooking pot by an old woman, but manages to trick his way out.

◀ **Leopard cub**
The leopard is one of the most efficient hunting mammals of Africa, and Hlakanyana needed to use his wits in order to deceive the leopardess and eat her offspring.

HLAKANYANA AND THE LEOPARD CUBS

Hlakanyana once came across four leopard cubs without their mother. When the leopardess returned, she made to attack Hlakanyana. The trickster talked his way out, offering to guard the cubs while she went hunting, and saying he would build a hut for the family too. After she left, Hlakanyana built a hut with a narrow entrance, and then ate one of the cubs. When the mother returned, he brought out the remaining cubs to be suckled one at a time, and tricked her into thinking all four were safe. Over the next two days he played the same trick, and on the fourth day, he brought the single remaining cub out four times to fool her. When she grew suspicious, he escaped from the back door while the leopardess tried to squeeze her way in.

▶ **Antelope**
Large antelope were often taken by big cats and were also a more likely quarry for huntsmen than leopard cubs.

SEE ALSO African creation stories 236–37, 250–51, 252–53, 262–63 • Hunters 258–59, 266–67, 334–35

SOUTHERN AFRICAN FOLK TALES

Storytelling forms an important part of the culture of the peoples of Southern Africa. Legends and folk tales encompass a variety of topics, but abiding themes are the unusual birth and adventures of miraculous "wonder-children" and mythical encounters with animals. Many of these stories combine unusual or unexplained happenings with a firm grounding in the realities of the natural world and everyday life, such as drought and famine.

THE TORTOISE AND THE HARE

There was once a severe shortage of water in the jungle, so all the animals (except for the hare, who could not be bothered) tried to make the water come back. Finally, only the tortoise succeeded, by stamping on the dry riverbed until a pool of water appeared. The animals feared that the lazy and cunning hare would try to steal the water, so they took turns to stand guard over the pool each night. First the hyena stood guard, then the lion, but the hare tricked both of them, and took away a few calabashes of water. Then the tortoise offered to stand guard: he covered his shell with sticky bird lime and hid at the bottom of the pool. When the hare came, he assumed that the water was unguarded. He drank his fill, and then jumped in for a bath. His feet stuck to the tortoise's shell and he remained trapped there until the morning, when all the other animals came to see what had happened, and tied him up as punishment.

▶ **Opposite characters**
The tortoise and the hare feature in many tales as contrasting characters, the hare being fast but impetuous and easily bored, while the tortoise is slow but wise.

BANTU PEOPLES

There are some 400 ethnic groups known as Bantu, who speak related languages. They originated in Central and East Africa, but many had migrated southwards by the 11th century. The Southern African groups include the Xhosa and the Zulu, who traditionally made their living by farming and raising cattle. These peoples have a rich tradition of arts and crafts, and a deep store of myths, from creation stories to tales explaining the origin of death.

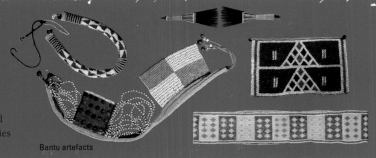
Bantu artefacts

THE EGG CHILD

One day, a girl who was out plucking leaves with her friends found an egg that belonged to a hyena and took it home, but her mother threw it on the fire. Then the hyena came looking for its egg and was angry when the girl's mother explained what she had done. The hyena threatened her, and made her promise to hand over her next child. After that, the hyena waylaid the woman every day, threatening to eat her if she did not give him a child. Then one day the woman noticed a swelling on her shin. This boil grew until it burst and a boy emerged, fully armed and able to walk and talk. He told her he was Kachirambe, the child of the shin bone. When the hyena came to claim him, the wonder child was too swift and clever to be caught. He rounded on the hyena, and killed it.

◀ **Hyena**
The hyena's odd appearance links it in Southern African myth with strange events, hence the tale of it laying an egg.

▶ **Cooking for the family**
The girl's mother had no use for the hyena's egg, so she threw it into the fire used to cook the family's food.

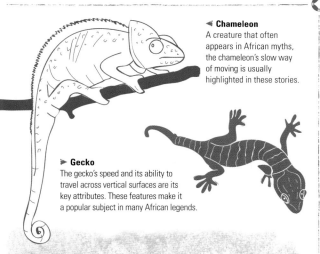

◀ **Chameleon**
A creature that often appears in African myths, the chameleon's slow way of moving is usually highlighted in these stories.

▶ **Gecko**
The gecko's speed and its ability to travel across vertical surfaces are its key attributes. These features make it a popular subject in many African legends.

THE ARRIVAL OF DEATH

When he created humans, the supreme god decided that they should live forever. He looked for a messenger to deliver this good news to them, and his eye chanced upon the chameleon. But chameleons travel slowly, and the creature was distracted, stopping often on the way for food or to take a nap. After a while the supreme god changed his mind, thinking that it was better for his creations to have a limited life. This time, he chose a different messenger to deliver the news – the fast-moving gecko. There is no overturning a divine command once it has been delivered, so whether people would die or live forever depended on which messenger arrived first. Unfortunately for mankind, the gecko soon overtook the chameleon and gave the people the message that they would not live forever.

THE BOY WARRIOR

Once, a terrible monster rampaged through a Basuto village. It ate all the animals and people except for one pregnant woman who had hidden in an animal pen. Then, swollen with food, the monster got stuck in a mountain pass and could not move. The same day the woman gave birth – not to a baby, but to a fully grown young man. She named her son Moshanyana, meaning "little boy" – Ditaolane, in some versions – and told him what had happened. Immediately he killed the beast, and when he cut open its belly, all the people it had swallowed came out alive.

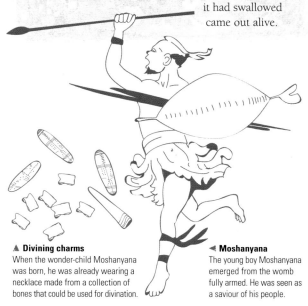

▲ **Divining charms**
When the wonder-child Moshanyana was born, he was already wearing a necklace made from a collection of bones that could be used for divination.

▶ **Moshanyana**
The young boy Moshanyana emerged from the womb fully armed. He was seen as a saviour of his people.

SOUTHERN AFRICAN FOLK TALES

275

SEE ALSO Tortoises 162–63, 196–97 • Monsters 46–47, 52–53, 54–55, 64–67, 72–73, 98–99, 106–07, 156–57, 228–29

THE AMERICAS

It is thought that people first came to the Americas over a narrow land bridge that connected Siberia with Alaska before sea levels rose to create the Bering Strait. No one knows for certain when people first made this journey – experts' estimates vary from as long ago as 60,000 BCE to as recently as 10,000 BCE. Whenever it occurred, it must have been a life-changing adventure for those who actually made it. However, it was merely the beginning of a series of even longer journeys that took people southward, some fanning out across North America, others going still further until a few finally reached Tierra del Fuego, at the southernmost tip of South America.

This series of expeditions, no doubt taking place over thousands of years, separated people into myriad tribes who adapted themselves to local conditions all over both continents. In North America alone there were probably at least 2,000 different tribes – but not all have survived. Wars between one tribe and another and, most devastatingly, subjugation by the European settlers who came to North America from the 17th century onwards, have left a mere 300 or so Native North American "nations".

The old lives of Native North American tribes varied greatly. Many lived in small and scattered communities, but some, such as the Pueblo in the south of the continent, gathered in large urban settlements. Many of these people now live on reservations, where small areas of land have been set aside for them, and where they now guard their ancestral cultural heritages with great care. The surviving nations are custodians of a rich hoard of myths, covering a variety of origin stories, a multitude of animal spirits and deities, and numerous nature gods, tricksters, and culture heroes. According to local conditions and development, traditions linked to hunting, agriculture, and warfare all have special prominence in these mythologies.

WE WILL BE KNOWN FOREVER BY THE TRACKS THAT WE LEAVE. Dakota proverb

Further south, in the area known historically as Mesoamerica, myths of warfare and sacrifice are especially dominant. Amerindian peoples such as the Maya, Toltecs, and Aztecs each developed impressive cities, monumental buildings, and hierarchical social structures. But they made their most lasting impression through the violence that underpinned their religion, which involved making gruesome human sacrifices – sometimes on a vast scale – to appease their bloodthirsty gods.

Unlike the enduring traditions of North America, these practices have thankfully long vanished, but they have left fascinating remains, from tales of the gods to the stone temples where they were worshipped. Likewise, the Incas and other civilizations of South America have left architectural remains that show their devotion to their gods, especially the sun god Inti, whose image is found both in stone carvings and on stunning gold artefacts.

Travellers from South America also settled on the islands of the Caribbean, and they too had a god who represented, or lived in, the sun. But the Caribbean, perhaps even more than the rest of the Americas, became a melting pot of races and cultures after European contact began in the 15th century. From the point of view of mythology, the greatest impact came from the arrival of Christianity – especially in the form of the Roman Catholic Church – and the influx of slaves from Africa. Among the slaves were many who followed the religions of West Africa. These traditions, mixed with local beliefs and Catholic ideas, symbols, and saints, produced religions such as Voodoo. These beliefs still survive – another of the living traditions of the Americas.

▲ **Buffalo hide painting of the Sun Dance**
The Sun Dance was an annual ceremony performed by various Native American peoples of the Great Plains to confirm their beliefs and ensure their continued wellbeing. The presence of Europeans on this 19th-century occasion is indicated by a Christian cross.

NORTH AMERICA

The varied myths of the native peoples of North America are a vital part
of their national and cultural identity to this day. Many of the stories told
are at the very heart of their diverse belief systems and ceremonies.

After the first people arrived in
North America, they spread out
far and wide across the continent,
settling in scattered communities
and adapting to the wide range of local
conditions. As a result, the Native
Americans formed a multitude of separate
peoples or nations, and the cultures of
these different groups vary a great deal.
Their rich mythologies, which still play an
integral role in their lives, are equally diverse.

▲ Shaman's mask
A shaman's spirit can make a
voyage while his body remains
in a trance. The symbols on this
mask represent such a journey.

VARIED CULTURES

Although the lives and myths of Native Americans
are highly varied, there are some similarities from
one group to another, and these often reflect
region and environment. People in the northwest,
for example, traditionally lived in settled villages of wooden
houses. Families told stories of their clan founders, the people
who originally created these settlements and who took the
form of mythical animals, represented on intricately carved
totem poles. There were similar settlements in the southwest
– though here the architecture was more likely to be in
mud-brick, not wood – and large pueblos housing many
families were commonplace. The myths of the southwest
describe the origins of the people of the area, with an
emphasis on "emergence" stories and the beginnings of
agriculture. Rituals in which people put on elaborate masks
and imitate or "become" spirits are also important in the area.

The central Great Plains form another quite distinctive area,
traditionally being home to nomadic peoples who hunted
buffalo and used every part of the animal, from meat to hide,
in their daily lives. Animal myths abound here, as do deities
who control the elements. Important ceremonies include
those involving smoking a sacred pipe. In the eastern United
States, meanwhile, spirits of woods, lakes, and rivers are
prevalent, reflecting the local geography. Further north, there
are yet more distinctive cultures, such as those of the Arctic,
where the myths involve many stories of
animals, such as seals or fish, who are the
hunter-fisher's quarry, but are respected as
being creatures with souls, like people.

MYTH AND LIFE

For Native Americans, myth has always been
closely related to daily life. The ancestors who
gave the tribes of the northwest their identity,
the weather gods of the Great Plains, the animals
of the Arctic – all have long been seen as having
a real impact on real people. Often, such myths
explained thunder and other mysterious natural
phenomena, which could affect the farmer's crop
or the hunter's quarry, thereby influencing the
people's very survival. Many myths were closely
tied to special occasions; these were only to be
told as part of a ceremony, often one performed at a set time
by a priest or shaman. All were stories of power, told for
generations, and of crucial worth to their people. They retain
their power for Native Americans still.

▲ Alaskan clan house decoration
The traditional wooden clan houses of Alaska were decorated with colourful symbols
and figures to indicate the owner's lineage. Both human figures and those representing
animal ancestor figures, such as the Raven visible here, are typical features.

NAVAJO EMERGENCE

The myths of the Navajo people of southwest North America focus on the Emergence, a myth also recorded in the legends of other southwestern tribes such as the Pueblo. It tells how the first people travel upwards through a series of different worlds before arriving in this world, which is widely described as the fourth world. Other related myths talk about Changing Woman, the Earth goddess; her children, the warrior twins; and various other figures who are injured or lost and approach the gods to be healed.

◄ Coyote
An important figure in the Navajo stories of the First People, Coyote is considered to be the bringer of death.

THE MYTH

In the beginning, the First World, or the Black World, existed. It was black and had four corners; standing over each corner was a column of coloured cloud – black, white, blue, and yellow. The black and white clouds came together at the northeast corner to form First Man. At the southwest corner, the blue and yellow clouds merged to create First Woman. A white wind, blowing over two ears of corn, entered First Man and First Woman, breathing life into them. The descendants of First Man and First Woman were the Air People, and had no clear shape or form initially. They began to quarrel among themselves and, becoming dissatisfied with their world, climbed upwards, until they reached the Second World.

WORLDS OF DISCONTENT

When these First People reached the Second World, or the Blue World, they were as unhappy as they had been before. Everyone quarrelled and there was widespread discontent. First Man decided that they should leave this world too, and move on to the next. He took an abalone, a white shell, turquoise, and jet, and made a wand that carried the people up to the Third World, or the Yellow World. This too was an unhappy place. The people lived sinfully and their unnatural ways brought them misery. Then a great flood came to destroy the world. First Man realized that the people needed high ground to escape the flood, and built a tall mountain. Then he planted a cedar tree, a pine tree, and a male reed, but none of these were tall enough to reach up into the next world. So he planted a female reed, and this was sufficient for the people to climb into the Fourth, or Glittering, World.

THE FOURTH WORLD

When the First People arrived in the Fourth World, they performed a Blessingway ceremony (see opposite), and built the first sweat lodge for meditation and healing. They brought up soil from the Third World and built sacred mountains. First Man contructed houses for his people, and put the sun and the moon high up in the sky to create day and night. He was helped by Black God and Coyote (see p.289), deities from the First World. Black God tried to carefully arrange the stars in the sky, but Coyote became impatient with his slowness and scattered them hastily across the sky. Finally, the people could live happily and prosper.

◄ Sacred mountains
The Navajo Indian reservation areas in the US have many mountains that are considered sacred by the Navajo. Some mountains are believed to be female, and some male; together, they symbolize the balance of nature.

CHANGING WOMAN

One of the most important female deities of the Navajo is Changing Woman, who represents the Earth and the stability of the cosmos. Some accounts say that she was created by First Man, and that she later produced the Navajo ancestors from her body. However, others mention her to be either the daughter of the sky and the Earth, or the offspring of First Boy (denoting thought) and First Girl (speech). Changing Woman got her name because she could change from one stage of life to the next (baby, girl, woman, and old woman) rapidly and endlessly. When she reached puberty in four days, people performed a puberty ceremony. This later became a necessity for all Navajo girls on the verge of womanhood.

◄ Cycle of change
Changing Woman represented the cyclical changing of the seasons. She would put on a dress of a different colour for each season to signal its arrival.

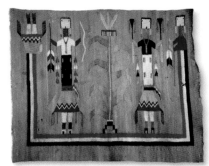

◄ People and corn
This blanket, bearing a design based on a Navajo sand painting, shows First Man and First Woman standing on either side of a corn plant. It underlines the importance of corn for the Navajo people.

FIRST PEOPLE

The First People are central to the origin myths of the Navajo. They directed the journey of the Navajo ancestors through the first three worlds to the final one. First Man and First Woman were the ones who planned for the birth of Changing Woman. The accounts of the First People, the Emergence, and Changing Woman, form the core of the important Navajo ceremony known in English as "Blessingway". Changing Woman passed on the knowledge of this rite to the Navajo; the ceremony is a ritualistic blessing of a person to ensure general health and wellbeing. Blessingway rituals are performed on many occasions, such as births, weddings, and puberty ceremonies for girls. So the First People are remembered at key events in Navajo life.

THE WARRIOR TWINS

Changing Woman had two sons. One of her sons, fathered by the sun, was called Killer of Enemies. The other boy, called Child of Water, was the offspring of water. Although their fathers were different, the boys were born together and were therefore always considered to be twins. Eventually, even the sun accepted Child of Water as his own son. The boys grew up as rapidly as their mother, and one day decided to visit the sun to ask for his help in defeating the evil spirits and monsters that roamed the land. When they reached the sun's house, he gave them powerful arrows and the knowledge to slay the evil spirits. Together, the warrior twins rid their land of evil by defeating a number of creatures, including a man-eating antelope called Teelget, gigantic and fearsome birds of prey called the Tsenhale, and a scaly monster known as Yeitso.

◄ Spider Woman
The warrior twins were said to have a wise grandmother called Spider Woman. She gave them advice that helped them on their missions to outwit and destroy evil.

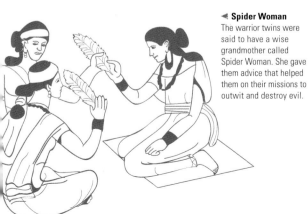

SAND PAINTINGS

A number of Native American peoples – the Navajo, Apache, Cheyenne, and Pueblo – make sand paintings, in which dry materials such as sand, corn pollen, and crushed flower petals are used to create patterns on the ground or floor. These paintings are created as part of ceremonial healing rituals and depict scenes from the various myths. There are, in fact, hundreds of different ceremonies, each associated with its own specific painting design. The images are made during the ritual and swept away afterwards.

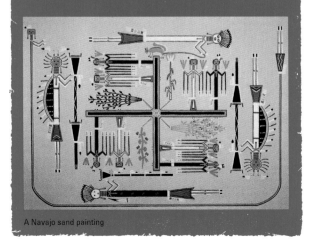

A Navajo sand painting

SEE ALSO American creation stories 286–87, 306–07, 314–15, 330–31

ANCESTORS

Almost all peoples of the world respect and even love their ancestors, both ancient and recent. Many mythologies include stories of the first people, and some cultures include ancestors in their religious devotion. They revere their ancestors in a variety of ways – by depicting them in their religious artworks, by trying to communicate with their departed spirits, or by honouring them with special offerings or other ceremonies. Some cultures go even further, elevating their ancestors' spirits to the status of deities.

REVERENCE FOR THE ANCESTORS

Devotion to ancestors is common worldwide, but among some peoples it is at the heart of their religion. This is the case in East Asian religions such as Shintoism in Japan, among certain Native American groups, and in Australia, where the role of the ancestors is crucial to Aboriginal beliefs. These myriad belief systems see ancestors in very different ways, but all revere the forebears who established their people in their first homes on Earth.

▶ **Day of the Dead**
In Mexico and other countries, the Day of the Dead venerates ancestors. Wearing colourful skull masks, people believe they can contact the souls of the dead, and encourage them to visit the living.

▶ **Ritual wine vessel**
Ceremonial containers like this one were used in ancient China in rituals honouring the people's ancestors, many of whom were deified.

▲ **Shinto shrine**
Devotees of Shintoism regularly visit graves to honour their ancestors and keep the gravestones in good condition, as well as placing amulets on the shrines of the kami, or spirits.

◀ **Totem pole**
For northwest coast Native Americans, totem poles depict animals and mythical beings linked to a family and its past, summing up their history, relationships, and beliefs.

One purpose of myths is to explain where we came from, so nearly every mythology has a tale involving the first humans – often a man and woman made from earth or wood by a god. Frequently the first people are at a loss as to how to live, so a deity or a culture hero has to show them, teaching them such skills as fire-making. Other ancestor myths involve notable beings – culture heroes, or people made famous by great achievements – who are revered as ancestors for helping both their contemporaries and their descendants.

In mythologies all around the world, beings often change shape, and a common transformation is a spirit that takes the form of an animal before turning into a primal human being. Myths of the Australian Dreamtime are full of such ancestors. In other cultures, animal ancestors symbolize a union between two different clans. That animal ancestors figure so widely shows a close relationship between people and nature.

◀ Yu the Great
Yu (*see p.215*) is a Chinese ancestor hero who is said to have built a system of canals and a tunnel through the Wu Shan mountains.

▶ Dazhbog
An ancient Slavic sun god who crossed the sky in his chariot, Dazhbog is also said in some traditions to be the ancestor of the Russian people.

◀ Ask and Embla
Ask ("ash") and Embla ("elm") were the first humans in Norse mythology, carved by the gods Odin, Vili, and Ve (*see p.91*).

▲ The bear
For peoples in Northern Europe, northern Asia, and North America, bears have often been seen as clan ancestors.

▲ The kangaroo
Some Aboriginal Australian groups refer to the kangaroo as a direct ancestor, while others say that the animal was sung into being by a separate ancestral figure.

◀ The snake
Common symbols of life, snakes of various kinds appear in the ancestor stories of many peoples worldwide, from certain Aboriginal Australians to ancient Indo-Europeans.

GHOSTS

The idea of ghosts – the spirits of dead people who appear to the living – is a common one in most cultures. Ghosts are often seen as discontented – they revisit this world because they are not settled in the next, sometimes because their funeral was not conducted properly, or because of some lingering resentment. Such ghosts can be frightening to the living. In some countries, demons couple with ghosts to produce malign spirits, such as the Indian *bhuts*. In others, like Japan, ghosts are seen as a natural part of the afterlife.

▲ Japanese ghosts
In Japanese mythology, in which there are 36 possible stages to pass through between death and rebirth, ghosts are called *gaki*, some of which possess the living on Earth.

▶ Haunted houses
Belief in haunted houses, in which resident ghosts terrorize the human occupants, is common among people of European origin.

▲ Santa Compaña
In Galicia in Spain a *Santa Compaña* (Holy Company) of lost souls led by a cursed living person is said to visit homes at night where death is due.

RAVEN STEALS THE LIGHT

One of the most popular figures in North American mythology is Raven, a trickster and culture hero of the people of the northwest coast. He is credited with bringing light into the world because he placed the sun, moon, and stars in the sky, using his trickery and his powers of shape-changing. In certain cultures, he is also said to be the bringer of fire, and the creator or discoverer of the first human beings.

THE MYTH

In the beginning, the world was shrouded in complete darkness. This was because all the light in the world was hoarded by the sky chief, who guarded it carefully and kept it concealed within a series of boxes piled in a corner of the house. The old chief was very selfish and did not wish to let the light out. Because of this, the other people in the world could not hunt or fish properly in the dark, and had to grope around for their food. They soon became accustomed to finding their way about using their sense of touch, reaching out for familiar trees as they walked by, and following the ruts left in the ground by those who had passed by earlier. They managed to go about their daily activities well enough, but one particular creature, Raven, was upset with the perpetual darkness. He wanted to be able to find food easily, and was tired of blundering about in the dark, looking for things.

Raven
This wooden rattle was made in the shape of Raven by a Tlingit craftsman; the Tlingit consider Raven a friend of humanity.

RAVEN'S TRICK

When Raven learned that the light was hidden in the sky chief's house, he hatched a plan to gain access to the house. He decided to be reborn into the chief's family. He knew that the chief's beautiful daughter walked regularly to a spring to fetch water. One day, when Raven heard her approaching the spring, he transformed himself into a pine needle and then let the breeze blow him towards the young woman. He floated into the pail of water she had filled and was carrying home. Halfway home she stopped to rest and took a sip of the water. Raven, in the form of the pine needle, slipped down her throat inconspicuously.

▲ **Sun mask**
The act of bringing the sun and its warmth to cold northern regions such as Alaska made Raven a popular figure in local myth and folklore.

RAVEN REBORN

With Raven inside her body, the sky chief's daughter became pregnant. When Raven was born as a human child, he had thick black hair and a beak-like nose, and cried harshly like a bird. Soon the infant began to crawl around. The sky chief enjoyed playing with his grandson all day, indulgently giving in to all of his demands. Raven discovered in the course of his explorations that the chief guarded a pile of boxes in the corner carefully. One day, he tried to play with the boxes, and cried insistently when they were taken away. The chief caved in to his demands and gave him the smallest one. When Raven saw the stars inside the box, he took them out and began playing with them happily. Then, before the old man could stop him, he threw them out through the smoke hole of the house, and the stars lodged in the sky.

Afterwards, Raven began crying yet again, and so the chief gave him the second box to calm him down. This box contained the moon, and Raven gleefully bounced it about like a ball for a while, until it too flew out through the smoke hole and into the sky. Finally, still unaware of the real identity of Raven, the chief gave the wailing child the largest box in the set, which contained the sun. This time, Raven transformed back into a bird, took the sun in his beak, and flew up into the sky. The world finally became flooded with bright daylight, but the sky chief and his daughter never saw the child again.

THE CHILDHOOD OF RAVEN

All versions of the myth feature Raven as a demanding child, with an indulgent grandfather who lets him play with his secret sources of light. Some accounts narrate how Raven waited impatiently to resume his true form, and when he saw the family busy feasting, he grabbed his chance. Transforming back into a bird, he snatched the ball of light and flew away. In another variation, the stars were hidden in a bag. Raven, who still had his sharp beak, pecked through the bag, letting the stars out to light up the sky.

◄ **Sky chief**
Raven's grandfather, the old sky chief, was an ambiguous figure. He guarded the sources of light jealously, but let his grandson play with them.

► **Kelp**
After giving light to the world, Raven descended to the ocean floor on a ladder made of kelp. He found the sea creatures to be similar to those on land.

◄ **Fishing net floats**
Raven taught the first people how to hunt and fish. Later, they learned to use net floats like these for fishing.

► **The first people**
In one Haida myth, Raven saw the first humans cowering in a giant clam. With his smooth talking, he cajoled them to emerge.

RAVEN AND CREATION

For many tribes of North America such as the Haida, Raven is a creator entity. One story describes how Raven flew over the ocean carrying pebbles in his beak. With these pebbles he made the stars and planets. Then he beat his wings to make a great wind that blew river beds and valleys into existence, building mountains at the same time. The ground was fertilized by his droppings. Finally, Raven either created the first humans or watched them emerge into the world.

> **TRICKSTER RAVEN COAXED THE CREATURES TO COME OUT. THESE LITTLE DWELLERS WERE THE ORIGINAL HAIDA.**

SEEKERS OF FIRE

A story from the Queen Charlotte Islands, on the Canadian coast, tells how Raven was once white. He befriended the daughter of Chief Grey Eagle – the guardian of the sun, moon, and fire – and stole his precious hoard. He flew around the sky, putting the sun and moon in place, while carrying a brand of fire in his beak. The smoke blackened his feathers, and when the fire grew too hot, Raven dropped it on some rocks. This is why fire appears when two rocks are struck together.

◄ **Robin**
The North American robin was yet another bird associated with the bringing of fire, carrying evidence of the bright flames on its red breast.

► **Mole**
The mole was one of the creatures who failed to find or steal fire in some North American myths.

THE GIVER OF LIFE

Like Raven, different animals and birds play a role in human destiny. They are linked with life and death, which are represented by objects that float or sink when dropped into water. In a version told by the Tlingit people, the fox, who is an ancestor figure, drops some sticks of rhubarb into the sea. The rhubarb floats, and the fox takes this as a sign that humanity will live.

◄ **Buzzard**
A North American myth tells of a buzzard who threw a rock in the sea; it washed ashore after sinking, making life possible.

► **Fox**
Being well-disposed towards humans, the fox hoped that the sticks of rhubarb would float, signifying that humanity would live.

SEE ALSO Tricksters 60–61, 96–97, 100–03, 252–53, 272–73, 288–89, 310–11, 340–41

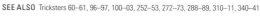

JOURNEY TO THE SKY

The native cultures of North America have long been fascinated with the sky, using the movements of heavenly bodies to time key rituals and predict the changing seasons. Some of the most popular myths deal with the sun, moon, and stars, and some – like the Blackfoot sun dance tale – also narrate the journeys of ancestors to the sky. Besides explaining the role and movement of these heavenly bodies, these stories account for the apparently random arrangement of the stars, said to be the result of someone scattering them across the sky.

THE SUN DANCE

A popular Blackfoot myth tells of Morning Star, the young son of the moon and the sun, who fell in love with a girl called White Feather. She returned his love, and the couple travelled to the sky on a spider's thread. They lived there happily with Morning Star's parents, and had a boy named Star Boy. One day, White Feather was told to harvest the root crop, but to leave one large turnip alone. She became curious and pulled up the turnip, revealing a hole in the sky. As punishment for having disobeyed orders, White Feather was told to return to the Earth with her son. After her death, Star Boy visited his grandparents by ascending to the sky on one of the shafts of light that appeared at sunset. Star Boy learned the sun dance from the sun, who said that he would heal all the sick if the Blackfoot performed a festival in the sun's honour. This is how the sun dance ritual originated.

White Feather
Morning Star's parting gift to White Feather when she returned to the Earth was an elk-skin robe, which he said could only be worn by a pure woman.

Sun dance headdress
This headdress was worn during the sun dance by a sacred woman who had pledged allegiance to the sun. The components of the headdress represent aspects of the myth.

Sun dance
Elements common to the sun dance ritual performed by the different native cultures included singing, dancing, and self-torture.

STAR POWER

The Pawnee performed the sun dance too, to show their gratitude to the sun, and to ask him for protection, fertility, and the renewal of the seasons. However, according to their mythology, the dance originated when it came to a young man in a vision. Keen observers of the sky, the Pawnee aligned their lodges to the four points of the compass, and built them with smoke holes to give views of certain groups of stars. Their ceremonies, such as those heralding the beginning of spring and those performed before hunting, were timed by observing the movements of the stars. The Pawnee believed that if they carried out their rituals according to the stars, the universe would continue to function and the people would thrive.

▲ Star charts
The Pawnee recorded their observations on star charts, maps of the night sky that were often painted on buckskin and wrapped in sacred bundles, indicating their importance.

◄ The Pawnee
The knowledge of the stars and their movement across the night sky helped the Pawnee find their way while travelling across the plains.

➤ Kotcimanyako
The story of Kotcimanyako follows a very common mythological theme. It is that of a person entrusted with something that must not be examined, but the individual cannot resist taking a look.

SPILLED STARS

The Cóchiti Pueblo people tell a story of how there was once a great flood, and the people moved north to escape the waters. When the land began to dry, Iatiku, the mother of the people, told them that it was safe for them to travel southwards to their homeland. She gave a girl called Kotcimanyako (Blue Feather) a bag to carry and forbade her from opening it. But Kotcimanyako was a very curious girl and could not resist opening the bag. As soon as she untied the bag, thousands of stars spilled out, flying around in all directions until they finally settled in the sky. The girl quickly tied the bag up again but only a few stars were left inside. When the Cóchiti Pueblo reached their homeland, Kotcimanyako showed Iatiku what she had done, and they carefully put the remaining stars in their rightful places in the sky. These were the stars whose names are known to the people.

THE ORIGIN OF THE MILKY WAY

A number of Native American myths describe the origin of the Milky Way, such as the Navajo creation story featuring Black God and Coyote (see pp.282–83). Once, Black God, the deity considered to be the creator of fire, was carefully arranging the stars in the sky. This was a slow process as the stars had to be set in the correct patterns, and Black God took great care to get it right. He was observed by the trickster Coyote who was annoyed with Black God's slow progress. After watching for a while, Coyote grabbed the bag with the remaining stars and threw them all into the sky at once, creating the Milky Way.

➤ Milky Way
For many Native American peoples, the Milky Way was a pathway across the sky, and also the route along which the souls of the dead travelled.

◄ Coyote
Coyote appears in a number of Native American myths as a trickster or culture hero, and as a very impatient character in the Navajo story of the Milky Way.

JOURNEY TO THE SKY

289

SEE ALSO Flood stories 30–31, 196–97, 212–13, 214–15, 314–15, 328–29 • Stars 318–19, 334–35, 340–41

MYTHS OF THE FAR NORTH

The people of the northernmost region of North America traditionally lived by hunting and fishing in the cold Arctic seas. Their myths, therefore, feature stories of the sea and its deities, including tales explaining the origins of sea animals and the fluctuations in the availability of creatures such as fish, seals, walruses, and whales. Many spirits figure in these myths; among peoples such as the Inuit, shamans (*see pp.268–69*) were said to be able to communicate with them, often with the help of Inua, spirit helpers who took animal form.

THE SEA GODDESS

Sedna, also known as the Sea Woman, was the goddess of the sea. She whipped up storms, and influenced the migration of birds and animals. Sedna was originally a beautiful girl with long flowing hair. She married a young man, who promised to give her fur blankets and good food every day. But on reaching his home, she found out that he was a bird-man in disguise. He mistreated her, and when Sedna's father found out, he killed her husband and took her away in his kayak. But the spirit of the bird-man raised a great storm, and in order to appease the angry spirit, Sedna's father threw her overboard. He stopped her from climbing back into the kayak by cutting off her fingers, which then became the first sea creatures. Sedna sank to the ocean floor and became a sea goddess.

◄ **Sedna**
A walrus-like creature, Sedna had no fingers, so she was pleased when shamans dived down to the ocean floor to comb out her tangled hair.

◄ **Seal-shaped artefact**
One of Sedna's gifts to the Inuit, the seal supplied meat, skins, and blubber. Inuit craftsmen carved artefacts shaped like seals, such as this one in the shape of a seal rising to the surface.

► **Harpoon**
Shamans summoned Sedna's spirit and struck it with an enchanted harpoon in a ritual to ensure a good catch.

▼ **Sedna overboard**
As Sedna's father chopped off her fingers, each of them turned into different sea creatures, such as the seals, whales, and fish that now inhabit the oceans.

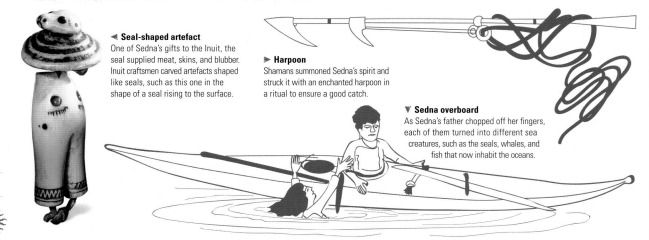

THE SUN PERSON

The spirit of the sun began life as a young woman who was abused by her brother. In deep distress, she mutilated herself and then went to live as far away from her cruel brother as she could. She took up residence high in the sky, where she became known as the Sun Person. There she appeared every morning, often taking on an orange colour, with streaks that represented her dreadful wounds. Undeterred, her brother turned into the moon and chased her across the sky, trying in vain to capture her, thereby causing the alternate appearance of the sun and moon in the heavens. People were sorry for the way the Sun Person had been treated, but mothers also saw her as a valuable source of energy in their cold homeland, and would expose their infants to her warm rays.

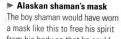
Alaskan shaman's mask
The boy shaman would have worn a mask like this to free his spirit from his body so that he could commune with other spirits.

THE BOY SHAMAN

The myths of the Gwich'in of Alaska tell of a poor boy who had the powers of a shaman. For some time, he used his powers to bring his tribe plentiful food. He also ensured that they were always well supplied with caribou, which provided them with meat to eat and skins to make clothes and tents. But one day the boy shaman made a momentous announcement. He told his mother that he was travelling to the sky. He said to her that she should look for him on the moon, and that she would be able to tell merely by looking at him what the prospects were for the food supply on Earth. If she saw him upright or bending backwards, there would be food aplenty for the people. Then they should share their food with the old and helpless. But if he was bent forwards, they should expect that caribou would not be very plentiful, so they should build up their stores.

Wounded sun
The orange sun, which often creates a blotchy colour in the Arctic sky, reminded people of the wounds of the Sun Person. The Inuit believed that the sun's warmth would infuse strength into their children's limbs, making them swift runners and nimble hunters.

ALIGNAQ

The guilty brother of the Sun Person (*see above*) was called Alignaq. After turning into the moon, he continued his lustful pursuit of his sister, giving up eating, and hence growing thinner and thinner. Then he disappeared for three days to eat his fill, before returning to chase his sister again. This is why the moon waxes and wanes. As the moon god, Alignaq also ruled the weather and the tides. He lived in a large igloo on the moon, along with the souls of game animals such as the caribou. The souls of the land animals lived inside his igloo, while those of the sea creatures, such as seals and walruses, swam in a vast tub of water that he kept outside his door. Most of the time Alignaq wandered the sky on his celestial hunting expeditions, keeping a close eye on human behaviour. If people did evil, he withheld game from them until they mended their ways.

Caribou
The Inuit believed that even animals had souls, so they needed to be appeased after being killed. The souls of dead game animals resided with Alignaq.

Moon spirit
This finger mask, made of wood and polar bear hair, was worn by Alaskan women during dances. It represented Alignaq, the spirit of the moon.

SEE ALSO Sea deities 30–31, 158–59, 160–61, 294–97, 338–39

 **Relief carving, Yaxchilan**
A series of carvings from the Mayan city of Yaxchilan in the state of Chiapas, Mexico depict rituals that took place when a ruler called Shield Jaguar took the throne in 681. His name is recorded in the glyphs at the top of the stone relief.

MESOAMERICA

The civilizations of Mesoamerica worshipped a varied and vivid group of gods
at their imposing pyramid-shaped temples. Rituals of blood sacrifice played
a key part in both the mythology and worship of these deities.

Mesoamerica is the name now given to an area made up of Mexico and parts of the neighbouring countries – mainly Belize, Guatemala, and Honduras – where there developed a highly sophisticated urban civilization before the arrival of the European conquerors in the 16th century. Several cultures built this civilization. The first, the Olmecs (c.1500–400 BCE), lived in southern Mexico, at sites such as La Venta. The Zapotecs (c.300–600 CE) built cities at Mitla and Monte Alban, also in southern Mexico. The Maya (c.300–900) were based in the Yucatan Peninsula, at sites such as Uxmal and Tikal. The Toltecs (c.900–1180) had their home city at Tula, north of Lake Texcoco. Finally the Aztecs (c.1300–1521), the last of the great Mesoamerican cultures, built their base at Tenochtitlan, the site of present-day Mexico City.

COMMON ACHIEVEMENTS

The Zapotecs, Maya, Toltecs, and Aztecs had several things in common. All developed a system of writing using picture symbols called glyphs. All were skilled astronomers who used two parallel calendars: a solar one similar to the modern calendar, and a religious one based on a 260-day ritual year. And all had complex mythologies with numerous deities, many of whom governed areas such as the weather and farming, which Mesoamericans depended on for survival. Some of these deities had several identities, partly because they were handed down from one culture to the next and partly because of their varied roles. The Aztec deity Tezcatlipoca was Yaotl when he was god of war and Yoalli Ehecatl when he was god of the wind. Another Aztec high god, the plumed serpent Quetzalcoatl, also took on the role of wind god, as Ehecatl.

The temples in which these deities were worshipped were also broadly similar. Set on tall, stepped pyramids, often in large plazas, they dominated the early Mesoamerican cities.

◀ A page from the Codex Fejervary-Mayer
Details of the Aztecs' rulers, deities, and sophisticated calendars are recorded in the glyphic writing of a number of books called codices. Not all of these texts have been fully deciphered, puzzling experts to this day.

Many still stand, impressive testimonies both to the skill of their builders and to the great resources the Mesoamericans poured into their religious worship.

BLOOD SACRIFICE

Another aspect common to most Mesoamerican cultures was the practice of blood sacrifice. The Aztecs and their predecessors believed that the deities needed to be nurtured with human blood, partly because they had spent their own blood in creating humanity, who therefore owed the gods a debt. The Toltecs and Aztecs, especially, sacrificed people – often prisoners of war. Much Mesoamerican ritual art, including carvings of skulls, images of priests wearing victims' flayed skins, and statues holding dishes for victims' hearts, reflects this religious practice.

▼ A statue from Chichen Itza, Mexico
Toltec and Aztec temples feature reclining statues, called Chacmools, each one holding a plate. Priests placed the still-warm hearts of their sacrificial victims on the plates as offerings to the deities.

POPOL VUH

The creation story and other myths of the Quiché Maya, a native people belonging to the highlands of Guatemala, are told in a book called the *Popol Vuh* (Council Book). This text was written down in the mid-16th century, after the Spanish conquest of the area, and was copied from an earlier version in Maya glyphic writing. It records myths dating back many centuries; one important section of the narrative concerns the adventures of a pair of Hero Twins, who travel to the Mayan Underworld, Xibalba.

THE MYTH

In the beginning, the sea god Gucumatz and the sky god Heart of Sky decided to create a human race to populate the Earth and do honour to the gods. But their first creations were a failure: they could not say the names of the gods and were only able to howl and chatter, so they became the first animals. The creators took some clay and tried to make another race, but these turned out limp and twisted; they were unable to speak, and dissolved in water. Frustrated by these failures, the two gods went to see the diviners Xpiyacoc and Xmucane, wise beings who were even older than the gods. The diviners told the creators to make men from wood and women from reeds. But these creatures did not please the gods either, as they refused to worship them, so Heart of Sky sent a flood to overwhelm them. It became clear that other events had to take place before humans could be successfully created.

THE UNDERWORLD

The diviners had two sons, the twins Hun Hunahpu and Vucub Hunahpu. They spent all their time gambling and playing ball. While playing, they made a terrible noise that annoyed the lords of Xibalba (the Underworld), who sent messengers to challenge them to a ball game. When the brothers went down to Xibalba, the lords of the Underworld began to play cruel tricks on them. First they told the brothers to sit down on a bench, but it

▲ Hun Hunahpu and Xquic
When the maiden Xquic reached out to pick a tempting fruit from the gourd tree the head of Hun Hunahpu in the tree spat at her, making her pregnant.

> **World tree**
> The Mayan world tree is a symbol of their conception of the cosmos. Its roots are in Xibalba, the Underworld, its topmost branches the heavens.

was so hot that they jumped up at once. Then the twins were sent to stay in a section of the Underworld called the Dark House for the night, with only a torch and two cigars for light. In the morning, the lords of Xibalba came back to claim their torch and cigars and, on finding they were burned up, proclaimed that the brothers would be punished with death. So the two brothers were killed at the sacrificial ball court, and the head of Hun Hunahpu was sliced off and displayed on a tree. The tree's fruit took the form of the first gourds.

THE BIRTH OF THE HERO TWINS

A girl from Xibalba called Xquic went to look at the gourd tree. When she tried to pick a fruit, Hun Hunahpu spat at her. This made Xquic pregnant, and her angry father ordered her to be put to death. She escaped and went to live with Hun Hunahpu's mother. Later, she gave birth to the Hero Twins, Hunahpu and Xbalanque.

Like Hun Hunahpu and Vucub Hunahpu, the Hero Twins loved to play ball. When they learned that their father and uncle had been killed by the lords of Xibalba, they decided to avenge their death. One day, they began playing ball, making a lot of noise. The lords of Xibalba challenged them to a game, and they accepted. »

PRIMAL DEITIES

Mayan deities were often known by alternative names, and certain gods became important at different points in their history. Itzamna was a high god of the early Maya, although by the time of the Quiché Maya, he was more of an abstract force. For the Quiché Maya, the gods occupied two separate realms, the sea and the sky, each of which had a ruler – the gods Gucumatz and Heart of Sky respectively. There were also malign deities like Vucub Caquix (Seven Macaw), the Underworld god who falsely claimed to be the sun. He was attacked by the Hero Twins, who eventually tricked and defeated him.

▼ Hunahpu shooting Vucub Caquix
Vucub Caquix was an arrogant bird-god who ruled the world after the primeval flood. Although one of the Hero Twins, Hunahpu, shot at him with his blowpipe, he escaped.

◄ Itzamna
An early sky-dwelling creator god, Itzamna was also said to be the god of medicine and inventor of writing. He is sometimes portrayed as a human, occasionally as a lizard.

◄ Gucumatz
One of the creators of humanity, Gucumatz was a feathered serpent, and the Quiché Maya equivalent of the supreme Aztec deity Quetzalcoatl (see pp.298–99).

HEART OF SKY ONLY SAYS THE WORD, "EARTH" AND THE EARTH RISES LIKE A MIST FROM THE SEA.

Popol Vuh

THE HERO TWINS

Like many cultures around the world, the Maya saw twins as magical beings with a special role in their history, and they sometimes claimed that the Hero Twins, Hunahpu and Xbalanque, were the ancestors of their rulers. The twins used ingenuity and courage to outwit and defeat the lords of Xibalba, as well as to fight their jealous half-brothers – the Howler-Monkey Gods – and the tyrannical Vucub Caquix. At the end of the story they reigned supreme in the sky as sun and moon deities. They were also often pictured with the Mayan Maize God (see p.296), who, in some accounts, is seen as a resurrected form of their father, Hun Hunahpu.

▲ Rabbit scribe
A rabbit helped the Hero Twins during the ball game (see p.296), and sometimes is depicted on Mayan vases as a scribe.

▲ Hunahpu and Xbalanque
The heroic exploits of the twins cleared the universe of evil and made way for the successful creation of the human race.

FIRST CREATURES

The jaguar, deer, and serpent were among the first creatures created by Gucumatz and Heart of Sky. All were powerfully symbolic, the jaguar as a hunter, the deer as a sacred creature eaten at feasts honouring the gods, and the serpent as a symbol of the sky because of the similarity between the words for "snake" and "sky" in the Mayan language.

Deer

Serpent

Jaguar

SURVIVING IN XIBALBA

When the Hero Twins reached Xibalba, they were subjected to a series of deadly tests. They were made to stay each night in a different house fraught with peril. They survived the Dark House, the Razor House, the Cold House, the Jaguar House, the Fire House, and the House of Bats. They spent a night in each one of these houses and on each of the following days, they played the ball game against the lords of Xibalba. Every night they survived by using their wits – in the Dark House they avoided the trap their father and uncle had fallen into, by using fireflies to stop their cigars from going out. Then on the final night they hid inside their blowpipes to avoid the vicious bats, but Hunahpu put his head out and a bat bit it off and rolled it to the ball court.

When Hunahpu lost his head, Xbalanque carved a new one for his brother and the pair went to the ball court once more. At first they used Hunahpu's head as the ball. Xbalanque hit it right out of the court and a rabbit brought it quietly back to him. While the lords of Xibalba searched for it, Xbalanque stuck his brother's head

► Maize God
The first humans were finally made from maize, so the Maya worshipped the Maize God, depicted here with a headdress resembling maize fibres.

back on, and the game resumed with another ball. The Hero Twins won the game easily.

CONQUERING DEATH

The lords of Xibalba were angry at their defeat. They caught the twins, burned them in their oven, ground down their bones, and sprinkled the dust in the river. But after six days the twins reappeared, saying that they had put themselves together again, and claiming that they had discovered how to bring the dead back to life. The lords were sceptical, so they challenged the twins to prove what they said. Xbalanque held down Hunahpu, cut out his heart, and then commanded his brother to get up. Hunahpu did so, and the lords of Xibalba were beside themselves with amazement. They were so impressed that some of them insisted the Hero Twins do the same thing to them, so that they could experience what it was like to come back to life. So the Hero Twins held them down in turn and cut out their hearts. But the crafty brothers did not bring the lords back to life again. In this way the Hero Twins conquered death – reducing its power and, consequently, the power of the kingdom of Xibalba. Hunahpu and Xbalanque then returned to the Earth and from there ascended to the sky to become the sun and the moon. Having completed their work of overcoming the all-pervasive power of death, they had ensured that the universe was now ready for the proper creation of human beings to inhabit the Earth.

◄ A ball player
As shown on this pot, the Hero Twins found the padded clothing worn by their father and uncle, and used it in their ball game. It included a wooden or leather yoke around the waist with which to hit the ball.

THE BALL GAME

The Mesoamerican ball game was played between two teams, each comprising two to eleven players. The object of the game was to get a small solid rubber ball across the opponent's goal line, or to succeed in lobbing it through a narrow ring, placed high up on the side wall of the court. The players could use only their knees, elbows, and hips to hit the ball – use of the hands or feet was forbidden. Seen by the Maya as a re-enactment of the struggle between the Hero Twins and the lords of Xibalba, the game also had a religious purpose, and sometimes ended in the ritual sacrifice of the losers.

◄ Ball court
This clay model shows the typical shape of a Mayan ball court. The spectators sat on the sides and enjoyed the sight of players fighting for the ball.

THE MAYAN UNDERWORLD

Known as Xibalba (Place of Fear), the Mayan Underworld was the place where everyone – whether they had lived a good and virtuous life or not – went after death. It had nine levels, and was a grim place, ruled by gods who were the bringers of drought, hurricanes, and war. On arrival, the deceased had to cross rivers of blood, and undergo a series of trials with the fearsome lords who lived in Xibalba. If they passed these tests they were allowed to live with the Hero Twins in the sky. The Mayan people hoped that they would be as successful in passing the tests as the Hero Twins, who survived all the ordeals.

◀ Funerary vessel
Among the Maya, funerary customs varied; some high-ranking people were cremated, and their ashes placed in ornate vessels.

THE FIRST PEOPLE

The creators finally succeeded in creating the first four men out of maize dough, and four women were created for them. Heart of Sky blew mist into their eyes, so that they could only see what was close by, and not aspire to be gods. These people flourished, but they longed for light. They asked the gods for fire, and the gods agreed, provided the people made sacrifices in thanks.

▶ Blood-letting rite
To honour the gods, blood-letting rites were conducted, in which a priest ceremonially cut a worshipper's tongue on a rope of thorns.

◀ Mayan people
The Maya referred to themselves as the "true people", and believed they were mediators between their world and that of the gods.

HERE IS THE NEW CREATION, MADE OF MUD AND EARTH. IT DOESN'T LOOK GOOD.

Popol Vuh

MAYAN RELIGION

The Maya worshipped a pantheon of nature gods, and the priests who presided over their religion were well versed in history (especially the genealogies of the Mayan rulers, which confirmed their power), rituals, and the calculation of the calendar. Their rituals honoured groups such as fishermen, hunters, and beekeepers, and the most important ritual is believed to be the festival that marked the Mayan new year.

▶ An inscription from Palenque
Temple inscriptions at sites like Palenque used the Mayan pictorial glyphic writing to record the history of the rulers, including their conquests and alliances.

▼ Mayan temple
The typical Mayan temple, like this one at Chichen Itza, was set on top of a pyramid with nine levels, mirroring the levels of the Mayan Underworld.

THE MAYAN CALENDAR

The Maya had a number of different ways of counting the days, months, and years, and these calendars were used in their religion to calculate feast days and other important dates. The oldest of the Mayan calendars, dating from at least the 6th century BCE and attributed to the god Itzamna, was a 260-day calendar incorporating cycles of 13 days. This system was usually chosen for working out when to hold religious rituals and feasts. The Maya also had a 365-day calendar that incorporated cycles of 20 days. The two calendars were sometimes combined to form longer cycles.

Mayan calendar stone

SEE ALSO Twins 78–79, 282–83 • Revenge 18–19, 38–39, 46–47, 70–71, 100–03, 150–51

MYTHS OF THE PLUMED SERPENT

The great Aztec god Quetzalcoatl – called the Plumed Serpent, because he was half *quetzal*, or bird, and half *coatl*, or snake – had many important roles. He was both a creator god, showing people how to cultivate maize, and a culture hero, who taught people how to measure time. In the guise of Ehecatl, Quetzalcoatl was also the god of the wind, blowing the sun across the sky and sweeping across the heavens with his great gusts. One story tells how as Ehecatl he once descended to the Underworld, which was ruled by his father, Mictlantecuhtli, the god of death, and tried to steal the bones of the dead in order to create a new human race. But he dropped the bones as he fled, and before he could pick them up again a quail pecked at them. As a result, the bones were deformed, and when Ehecatl tried to bring them back to life by sprinkling them with his own blood, they grew into people of different sizes who were condemned to die once more.

1. Mictlantecuhtli
The god of death takes the form of a skeleton wearing a necklace from which eyeballs dangle. Spattered all over his bones are red dots representing spots of his victims' blood. The Aztecs thought that the gods had used their own blood to create the human race, and so regularly made human sacrifices to them to repay the debt.

2. Ritual staff
Mictlantecuhtli holds in his hand a ritual staff, or *chicahuaztli*, made from bone and adorned with bells. Like the death god's own bones, it is dotted all over with spots of blood from his victims.

3. Ehecatl
In his guise of the god of the wind, Quetzalcoatl wears a red mask with the beak of a duck, and on his breast is a conch shell ornament known as the "jewel of the wind". Aztec priests wore similar ornaments, often with the shell cut in curves like the eddies of the wind.

4. Plumed hat
Quetzalcoatl wears an elaborate hat with several symbolic features. The broad brim has a stepped black, red, and white pattern, which may symbolize the gusting of the wind. At the back, the plume with red feathers and a pair of eyes recalls the feathers of the quetzal. The conical crown of red, black, and green was mirrored in the conical roofs of some of Quetzalcoatl's temples. The object projecting from the front of the hat is a knife similar to those used by Aztec priests to make human sacrifices.

5. Grinning skull
Mictlantecuhtli and Quetzalcoatl stand on a human skull, which is painted in a stylized form and is upside-down. The skull has long rows of hideously grinning teeth and gums, and between its large staring eyes is a circular glyph, or picture writing symbol, that indicates a sacrificial victim. Like the bones of the god of death, the skull is spattered with dots of "blood".

6. Aztec calendar
On either side of the two gods, columns of glyphs make up a calendar, with each symbol representing one of the 20 periods of 13 days each – sometimes referred to as "ritual months" – that made up the 260-day "ritual year" of the Aztecs. One night in every 260 days, Aztec priests sacrificed a man representing the god of death. Some scholars believe the priests then ritually ate their victim.

7. Day discs
The two rows of red discs at the top and bottom of the image represent the days of the "ritual months" of the Aztec calendar. There are 12 discs in each row, rather than 13, because in each case one of the glyphs in the columns on either side stands for the first day of each "ritual month".

Ehecatl and Mictlantecuhtli,
from the Aztec *Codex Borgia*, 15th century

SEE ALSO Snakes & serpents 28–29, 48–49, 92–93, 98–99, 100–03, 160–61, 238–39

AZTEC NATURE GODS

Many Aztec gods controlled the natural forces on which the people depended for their survival. Some of these deities were dreaded beings, ruthless in their dealings wth the Earth and its inhabitants; their actions reflected the harsh climate and conditions of Aztec lands, in the region now known as Mexico. Their stories are frequently associated with the custom of human sacrifice – one deity, for example, demanded an offering of human blood before allowing the crops to ripen.

XIPE TOTEC

The name of the god Xipe Totec means "flayed lord", and this gives a clue to his story. He was the god of spring, and whenever there was a famine on Earth, it was said that he skinned himself to show the seed heads how to burst out of their buds. The rituals dedicated to Xipe Totec involved the devotees taking the flayed skins of sacrificial victims and putting these on themselves – the skin would fall off just as Xipe Totec's skin had done, revealing the devotee beneath, symbolically encouraging the plants to sprout in spring. In another sacrificial ritual dedicated to Xipe Totec, victims were tied up and shot with arrows. Their blood was made to drip onto a round stone that represented the Earth; this symbolized the fertilization of the ground.

▲ **Flayed lord**
The god of spring, maize, and fertility, Xipe Totec was usually portrayed as a young man, as if to symbolize the young crops about to mature.

▶ **Aztec farmer**
Maize was a key crop of Mesoamerica, and many pictures and statuettes from the region depict this staple crop being harvested by the people.

▲ **Foaming waters**
Whirlpools, waterfalls, and other manifestations of rapidly moving water were especially sacred to Chalchiuhtlicue, who was often shown seated in front of flowing water. Her titles included the "Foaming One".

▶ **Goddess of beauty**
Chalchiuhtlicue was often depicted as a beautiful woman dressed in blue and green and wearing elaborate jewellery; sometimes she also wore a reed headdress.

CHALCHIUHTLICUE

Chalchiuhtlicue (She of the Jade Skirt) was the Aztec goddess of beauty and the sister of the rain god Tlaloc (*see opposite*). She was seen as the embodiment of the patterns of light shining on moving water. As a water goddess, she was close to her brother, and for a while the two became man and wife. But the presence of two water-related deities in heaven caused many floods and storms on the Earth. So the pair had to part, and the god Quetzalcoatl (*see pp.298–99*) took Chalchiuhtlicue to the Earth, where she became the presiding goddess of rivers, streams, lakes, and other bodies of water.

◄ Dark deity
Tezcatlipoca was often said to be black in colour and to represent the "black sun" as it travelled across the sky in the hours of darkness.

▼ Tlaltechutli
In one version of the Aztec creation myth, Tezcatlipoca defeated the primordial monster, Tlaltechutli, and created the Earth upon its back.

TEZCATLIPOCA

Originally a sun god, Tezcatlipoca (Smoking Mirror) was deposed from his position and ended up as the Aztec god of the Underworld. One of his physical forms was a great wind that blew at night; on other occasions, he took the shape of a black jaguar (*see below*). The deity also sat in the sky as the Great Bear constellation. He was believed to roam the Earth at night in the form of a skeleton, with his heart visible behind his ribs. It was said that the only way to defeat him was to tear his heart out. Tezcatlipoca carried a mirror to see into people's minds, and allowed those who had the skill to see its images to have a glimpse of the future.

TLALOC

The Aztec rain god Tlaloc had four palaces, each one atop a mountain, and in every palace he kept a vast tub of water. One of these brought about the morning rain, one the midday showers, one the evening drizzle, and one fierce storms. The deity kept cloud servants, the Tlaloques, who carried the rain to Earth, where it served a dual purpose; the rain fertilized the ground, and also acted as the manifestation of Tlaloc's anger during a severe storm. Tlaloc also had a beautiful garden that was filled with flourishing plants and lush orchards. It was an idyllic place where the souls of the people who had died from illness went after death; victims of Tlaloc's own power (those who were killed by lightning strikes or by drowning) were also allowed to enter the god's paradise.

➤ Rain god vessel
Vessels made in the shape of Tlaloc's head are thought to have been used to collect rainwater during sacred rituals performed to honour the god. Many such vessels have been found at the Aztec site of Tenochtitlan, in Mexico City.

◄ Quetzalcoatl
The feathered serpent god Quetzalcoatl came to be identified with Ehecatl, the Aztec god of wind. He became linked with Tlaloc, as the Aztecs believed that winds heralded the coming of the rain.

➤ Tlaloc's weapon
Tlaloc's thunder was sometimes compared to the sound of a vast tomahawk or axe striking the sky. Consequently, this weapon became closely associated with the deity.

THE JAGUAR

In Aztec religion, the jaguar represented the deity Tezcatlipoca, Quetzalcoatl's rival. After being removed from his position as the sun god by Quetzalcoatl, Tezcatlipoca took the form of a jaguar, and came to be known as Tepeyollotl (Heart of the Mountains). As the Aztec deity of the night, he would roar loudly, a sound people associated with the noise of falling rocks and erupting volcanoes. Tezcatlipoca's destructive power was enormous, and in one myth, after losing his status as the sun god, he destroyed the world in revenge. The jaguar became a symbol of power to the Aztecs, and one group of elite Aztec warriors was even known by the name of the creature.

Tezcatlipoca as the Jaguar

SEE ALSO Weather deities 188–89, 194–95, 308–09, 318–19

▲ **Museum display of voodoo spirits**
This selection of diverse objects from a display in a museum dedicated to the
voodoo religion includes a human skull and crossbones and several colourful
and elaborately carved wooden representations of various gods or spirits.

THE CARIBBEAN

The indigenous people of the Caribbean region, the Taíno, had a rich mythology of gods and spirits that not only endured, but influenced the beliefs of those who arrived later from Europe and Africa.

The Taíno came to the Caribbean from South America around 5000 BCE. They brought with them beliefs about high gods who presided over a series of creations, as well as beliefs about countless spirits who permeated the world and had the power of shape-changing – a highly relevant concept in a region often drastically altered by hurricanes and storms.

The Taíno believed there were two classes of spirits: *goeiza*, spirits of the living, and *hupia*, spirits of the dead. *Hupia* were said to look like bats and to seduce or kidnap women at night. There were also gods called *cemís*, chief among whom were Yúcahu, "spirit of cassava", and god of the sea, and Atabey, goddess of fertility and fresh water. Some accounts also name Yukiyú, who helped farmers and loved peace, and Juracán, god of storms and hurricanes. The term *cemís* was also used for figures that were imbued with great spiritual power, being inhabited by the gods they represented.

NEW ARRIVALS

The end of the 15th century was the beginning of European influence in the Caribbean, with the arrival of Christopher Columbus in the Bahamas. Later, Europeans brought African slaves to the area, further adding to the cultural mix. Caribbean mythology's best-known myths developed as an amalgam of local

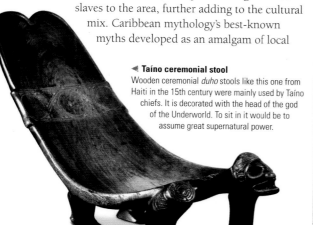

◄ Taíno ceremonial stool
Wooden ceremonial *duho* stools like this one from Haiti in the 15th century were mainly used by Taíno chiefs. It is decorated with the head of the god of the Underworld. To sit in it would be to assume great supernatural power.

► Imported thunder god
Shango, the thunder and lightning god of the Yoruba people of Nigeria, became an important figure in many parts of the Caribbean. He is often represented as he is here by an *oshe*, or double-headed axe.

Taíno, European, and African elements. The most famous example of this mix of cultures is undoubtedly the Haitian belief system called voodoo, also known as Vodou.

Voodoo combines folkloric elements from the indigenous Taíno peoples, African beliefs based on the mythology of peoples such as the Yoruba, Kongo, and Dahomey, and rituals strongly influenced by the Roman Catholicism of the French colonists who first came to the Caribbean in the 17th century. It also features a large number of gods or spirits, known as *loa*, who govern all areas of existence from fertility to death and from elephants to fish. Rituals of the religion are presided over by priestesses as well as priests. The less well-known Santería religion of Cuba displays a similarly rich and complex combination of local and imported beliefs and practices.

A HOST OF SPIRITS

Other parts of the Caribbean developed different blends of these multiple cultures. In Guyana, for example, as well as in many of the island communities of the area, people spoke of a host of malevolent spirits called *jumbees*, spirits that embraced all kinds of beings, including spirits that lived in rivers, malevolent animals, and the spirits of women who died in childbirth. There were also *jumbees* who resembled European creatures like werewolves and vampires. For many people in the region, such spirits were vividly and universally present, exerting a huge influence over their daily lives.

THE FIVE ERAS

The creation story of the Taíno people of the Caribbean island of Hispaniola is unusual in that it describes not only the creation of men and women, but also outlines a series of five historical eras, narrating in brief the history of the people up to the arrival of the European settlers in the 15th century. In addition, there are other myths that describe the activities of the primal humans, as well as how the ocean, fish, moon, trees, and birds came into being.

▲ **Rock drawings**
Taíno petroglyphs (rock carvings), with their strong, graphic outlines, often depict the deities that inhabit the Taíno mythological universe. This image of the Earth goddess Atabey (see p.309) shows her sitting in the position sometimes adopted during childbirth.

THE MYTH

The creation of the universe and the people who live in it spanned five eras. At the beginning of the first era, the son of the supreme god Yaya rebelled against his father, and Yaya killed him. The great god placed his son's bones in a huge gourd that he hung up in his house. A few days later, Yaya looked in the gourd and found that the bones had turned into fish swimming in water. Yaya's wife took some of the fish and cooked them, and the pair relished the meal. One day, the gourd broke open – some say it was done by visitors to Yaya's house – and the water poured over the Earth, forming the ocean that surrounds the Caribbean islands.

THE EMERGENCE OF HUMANITY

The second era began when the first people, the Taíno, appeared on Earth. They emerged from one of two caves in Caonao on the island of Hispaniola, and learned to survive by fishing in the sea. But some of those who came out were caught by the sun and transformed into trees because they returned home at dawn. Another man, who was supposed to stand guard at the cave while the others were fishing, was turned into stone by the sun for neglecting his duties. Seeing this, one of the men awoke before dawn, hoping to catch fish before the sun rose, but he was captured by the sun and made into a bird that sings at first light. As time went by, the remaining Taíno left to explore the other islands, and began to cultivate the fertile soil they found there.

A NEW WAY OF LIFE

In the third era, women were created as partners for the men, so that the population could grow, and the people

▲ **Taíno symbol**
The outer and inner circles in this seal of one of the Taíno tribes depict the sun and moon respectively.

became civilized and learned the art of survival. The fourth era saw them spreading across the islands of the Caribbean, founding settlements, and learning how to cultivate cassava, their staple crop. They built villages and developed their eloquent language, living in harmony. For many years all was well, but things changed when the first Europeans arrived in the Caribbean.

The fifth and final era of the Taíno began with the arrival of Christopher Columbus, the European navigator, in 1492. The Taíno saw this event as a disaster, because it led to the destruction of their traditional way of life. The European settlers treated the Taíno cruelly and brought with them new diseases, which led to the extinction of many tribes.

YAYA AND THE SONS OF ITIBA

Some versions of the story about the creation of the ocean tell how Yaya left the gourd containing the fish unattended one day. It happened that the four sons of Itiba Cahubaba, an Earth mother figure who had died in childbirth, arrived at Yaya's house. When they saw the gourd, they took it down to investigate and ate some of the fish. Suddenly, they heard Yaya returning, and they hurriedly tried to replace the gourd, but it fell to the ground and was smashed, spilling its contents. The four brothers then fled to the home of their grandfather.

THE FIRST CREATURES

The Taíno creation story tells how the sun turned various people that came out of a mythical cave into birds, trees, or stone. Birds feature in many Taíno myths; one of the Taíno people is turned into a bird that sings at dawn, and the woodpecker helps make the first women (*see below*). Another myth tells how the hummingbird got its iridescent feathers: a man was once punished for committing incest by being turned into the moon, with its stained face; the hummingbird carried the son of the moon in its beak to show him to his father, so the moon rewarded the bird with its brilliant plumage. Taíno myths also narrate tales of Guayahona, part culture hero and part shaman (*see pp.268–69*), who travelled to distant lands in search of the alloy guanin, revered by the Taíno for its golden sheen.

Hummingbird with jewel-like feathers

▲ **Cave of origin**
The first Taíno emerged from a cave called Ceibajagua. The other Caribbean peoples came out of another cave, and followed different customs.

THE WATER FROM THE GOURD GUSHED OUT. THIS THEY SAY IS THE ORIGIN OF THE OCEAN.

▲ **Fish of the ocean**
The fish contained in Yaya's gourd spilled out when it broke. This bounty of the sea became the source of the Taíno's livelihood.

▶ **Taíno gourd**
The gourd is both a storage container and a symbol of temptation. Some myths say that the broken gourd became a canoe in which Itiba's sons rowed away.

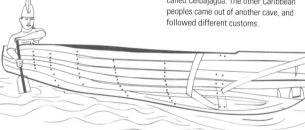

▲ **Guayahona the explorer**
The mythical hero Guayahona travelled on many journeys of exploration; on one occasion he persuaded all the women on his island to come away with him.

◀ **Caribbean fisherman**
Taíno myths often refer to fishing expeditions, since fishing was one of the main occupations of the Taíno, who were also excellent boat builders.

THE CREATION OF WOMEN

The Taíno creation myth explains that the first humans were only men. When returning from fishing one rainy day, the men saw curious creatures falling from the trees. They looked like women but were asexual. Instinctively, the men knew that these creatures were the women they needed, and, having captured them, fastened woodpeckers to their bodies. Thinking them to be trees, the woodpeckers bored openings in them, thus carving out female sexual organs. And so the first women were created.

◀ **Woodpecker**
The *inriri* or woodpecker, referred to in the myth as the "one who makes holes in the trees", was greatly revered by the Taíno for its role in creating women.

SEE ALSO American creation stories 282–83, 286–87, 314–15

GODS AND SPIRITS

The Taíno lived in the Greater Antilles and the Bahamas in the centuries before the arrival of the European settlers in the Caribbean. These people were the rivals of the Caribs, who lived mainly in the Lesser Antilles. Although the occupations of the Taíno included hunting and fishing, they also developed agriculture and grew both corn and the cassava plant. Their religion involved the worship of spirits, gods, and ancestors. Especially prominent were the deities who presided over the fertility of the soil and the growth of crops. Many of their myths were perpetuated through ceremonial dances and oral retellings.

YÚCAHU

The staple food in the Caribbean was the cassava plant, the starchy root of which was widely eaten. Of all the gods of the indigenous people, the most powerful were those who helped cassava to flourish. Among these deities, Yúcahu was the most important. Known as the Fruitful, Yúcahu was a god of the sea, as well as a fertility god who looked after the crops and made them grow. In addition, he was also a guardian deity, who watched over people and protected them. Yúcahu was seen as having a triangular form with his face in the centre, and on some images of the god there were patterns resembling the stems and foliage of plants. People made carvings of the deity that they buried in the fields, pouring offerings of water on the soil where the image was interred. This action of pouring the water "fertilized" the image, which in turn spread Yúcahu's growth-bringing powers to the fields.

◀ **Three-pointed stone**
Images of Yúcahu in the form of three-pointed stones have been found in the Caribbean. These were often buried as offerings. Sometimes the top of the deity's head was shaped like a nipple.

◀ **Cassava**
The cassava plant is known in the Caribbean as yuca. It can be boiled, or made into bread. The three-pointed image of Yúcahu is often thought to represent the triangular shape of the cassava tuber.

▶ **Taíno people**
The Taíno lived in villages of circular thatched houses. They grew their crops on large mounds of soil called *conucos*, which were said to be an invention of Yúcahu.

ATABEY

The goddess Atabey was the mother of the great god Yúcahu, and like her son, she was a fertility deity. Atabey was the goddess of the Earth, the mother goddess, and the deity who presided over the lakes and rivers. As a bringer of rain, she was sometimes attended by her messenger, Guatauva, and the goddess of the floods, Coatrischie. She was often portrayed in a squatting pose. In this position, her legs were bent double like those of a frog, a creature with which she was frequently associated. Frogs call loudly during their mating season, which coincides with the start of the tropical rainy season, the part of the year when the new cassava crop has just been planted. All these factors established a natural link between the frog and the goddess, who was said to preside over both the fertility of the soil and the fresh waters.

ZEMI IMAGES

The images used in Taino worship were known as the *zemi*; they were seen not just as statuettes but as embodiments of the gods. These images represented the whole range of deities, from high gods such as Yúcahu, who were worshipped by everyone, to family ancestors known only to their descendants. Often arranged in a hierarchy, the *zemi* were used in many different ways – in public ceremonies at sacred sites such as caves, and in private worship at home, where they would be set on altars. Devotees made offerings to the *zemi* in the form of libations, sang songs in their honour, and spoke to them in prayer or supplication.

▲ Wooden statuette
It was sometimes said that the spirit of a tree would "ask" devotees to give it physical form by carving its wood into a ritual statuette or *zemi*.

▲ Face of a spirit
Many of the *zemi* depict unknown spirits. They probably represented ancestors who formed an important focus of worship for their families.

GUABANCEX

The Taino saw the Caribbean weather patterns as evidence of the ascendancy of different deities. The rains were brought by the god Boinayel (Son of the Grey Serpent), who was heralded by the dark rain clouds across the sky. But he was balanced by his brother Márohu, the god of the clear skies, who ensured fair weather. Occasionally, this climatic harmony was broken by the mighty anger of Guabancex, the goddess of storms and bringer of hurricanes. She shattered the calm and, when the deities Guatauva and Coatrischie joined her, she was unstoppable.

◄ **The goddess of hurricanes**
Images of the goddess Guabancex show her limbs curving in opposite directions. This pattern is seen as representing the snaking path that a hurricane can take across the landscape.

▲ The angry goddess
The devastating winds caused by hurricanes were a regular part of life in the Caribbean. Life for the islanders was put on hold until the anger of Guabancex, the Lady of the Winds, blew itself out.

SEE ALSO Fertility deities 40–41, 84–85, 114–15, 158–59, 214–15, 244–45, 310–11

GHEDE

Ghede was an ancient Haitian god of love, sex, and fertility. In Haitian voodoo, Ghede is the god of death, as well as the name for a group of spirits who represent both death and fertility. The concept of the "loa" is essential to voodoo culture. The loa are important ancestral spirits who symbolize and influence specific aspects of the natural world. They include the spirit known as Baron, who, according to different voodoo traditions, is either the leader of the spirits or an aspect of Ghede. All these spirits are the focus of a number of Haitian beliefs and rituals concerning the opposite – but linked – themes of death and sexuality.

GHEDE AND SEXUALITY

As a spirit of sexuality, Ghede regards sex as something inevitable, not a matter of good or evil. He has a rapacious sexual appetite, which is mirrored by a healthy craving for food and alcohol, aspects of his character that serve to emphasize the earthy and high-living side of this spirit. Ghede likes to engage in explicit sexual conversation, and holds up for ridicule or embarrassment those people who try to suppress their sexual feelings, or who generally tend to adopt a repressed attitude to sex. He frequently makes erotic jokes and flaunts his sexuality without any inhibition. He is also an embodiment of resurrection and life energy, hence he has potent healing powers, which are believed to be especially effective on children. The sophisticated and stylish Ghede is closely linked to his bumbling, peasant-like younger brother, Azacca, the spirit of agriculture and the patron of farmers, whose ceremonies he often attends.

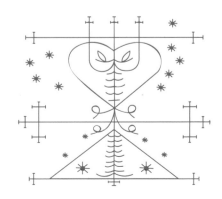

▲ **Followers of Ghede**
Ghede is believed to enjoy dancing, and his dance is fast and expressive. During festivals held in Ghede's honour, such as the Day of the Dead, his followers dance in abandon, often swept up into an ecstatic trance.

◀ **Black rooster, symbol of Ghede's consort**
Ghede is a spirit of death and fertility, and offerings to the god include black roosters, candles, miniature coffins, and sequined bottles containing rum. The black rooster is also one of the symbols of Maman Brigitte, who is Ghede's consort.

▶ **Maman Brigitte's sign**
Like Ghede, Maman Brigitte has a strong sexual appetite. In voodoo rituals, designs known as *vevers* are drawn on the earth to invoke the gods. Maman Brigitte's *vever* incorporates a heart and crosses.

BARON SAMEDI

Baron Samedi is the most familiar aspect of the ancestral spirit, or loa, known as Baron, other incarnations being Baron La Croix and Baron Cimetière. Baron is seen by different traditions as the chief of the Ghede spirits, or as their father, or as the personification of the spirit known as Ghede. He is often portrayed as an elegant figure with a white or skull-like face, black clothes, a white top hat, and dark glasses. He smokes a cigarette in a long holder and carries a cane. Baron Samedi is a "psychopomp", a being who is able to communicate between the worlds of both humans and spirits. He leads the souls of the dead to the Underworld (*see p.43*). He is also said to control the zombies – the soulless bodies of the dead – and possesses the power to bring them back to life by restoring their souls.

▲ Baron Samedi
Baron Samedi is portrayed in various ways. Sometimes he wears a large, elaborate hat with the image of a human skull on the front.

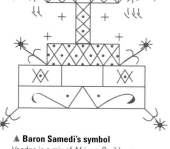

▲ Baron Samedi's symbol
Voodoo is a mix of African, Caribbean, and Roman Catholic beliefs, and the cross is prominent in Baron Samedi's *vever*, since he is associated with death.

▼ Tarot cards
Originating in medieval Italy, the tarot pack is used for divination and probably came to the Caribbean with the early European settlers. Ghede often dispensed advice through tarot cards.

GHEDE AND DIVINATION

The traditional haunt of Ghede is the crossroads, symbolic of the place where the worlds of the living and dead, of people and spirits, come together. As the spirit who presides over this meeting place, Ghede is believed to have special powers of prophecy and the gift of second sight. People therefore come to the spirit seeking answers to pressing questions, especially those concerning fertility. They make an offering to the spirit and request a priest to ask Ghede questions. The answer comes back in the form of a pattern of drops of rum trickled onto the ground, or in the form of cryptic messages from rolls of a dice or the turning of particular tarot cards. The advice that the spirit gives may often be unpalatable to the supplicants; nevertheless, they believe it to be sound, and give it great respect.

GHEDE SPIRITS

Ghede is also the name for a group of spirits who perform different functions as psychopomp and mediator between the worlds of the living and the dead. They are easily accessible to devotees, and ready with their advice. These spirits have distinct characters and roles. For example, Ghede Nibo takes the form of a young man who died early, perhaps as a result of violence; he is considered to be a guardian of tombs and a protector of people who die young. Ghede Ti Malis is a trickster spirit, whose pranks include tricking people out of food.

► Voodoo flag
Among the objects that are considered essential for voodoo rituals is a sequined flag depicting symbols of Ghede. The unfurling of this flag signals the formal start of the ceremony.

SEE ALSO Fertility deities 40–41, 84–85, 114–15, 158–59, 214–15, 244–45, 308–09

▲ **Inca gold plate**
The Incas valued gold as being the sweat of their sun god Inti, but the Spanish
conquerors in the 16th century valued it simply as a precious metal and melted
down most Incan gold artefacts. This gold plate depicts Inti in all his glory.

SOUTH AMERICA

Although South America produced a number of cultures with different deities and myths, the most enduring civilization was that of the Incas, who were based on the west coast of the continent and in the high Andes.

South America has been home to a succession of highly sophisticated civilizations during the last three millennia. Most of the more advanced cultures were based in the Andes, in the areas now forming parts of Peru, Chile, Bolivia, and Ecuador. Beginning with the Chavin culture (c.850–200 BCE) in northern Peru, there were a number of other empires based in and near Peru, including the Paracas Empire, the Moche culture, and the civilizations of Huari and Tiahuanaco, all between around 600 BCE and about 900 CE.

MYTHICAL THEMES

Although they left substantial physical remains – such as buildings, carvings, pottery, gold jewellery, and textiles – none of these cultures developed a writing system, so little is known in detail about their myths. However, scholars interpret many of the figures in their art as deities, and they are usually described today by their salient features: the Staff God, the Fanged God, the Jaguar God, and so on. Study of later indigenous peoples shows their reverence for ancestor spirits, for deities associated with the local landscape, and for fertility gods.

Local spirits, creator deities, and culture heroes – figures who bring important skills such as farming to the people – are typical of the belief systems of the various peoples of the rest of South America. A further theme that stands out clearly in some of these early cultures is their devotion to the sun. The great gateway at the major archaeological site of Tiahuanaco has a figure that resembles a sun god, and one important Moche temple is believed by experts to be a place where people worshipped the sun.

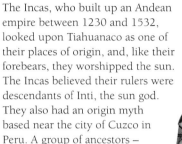

➤ Silver cob of maize
Skilled Inca metalworkers made this silver model of cobs of corn, which shows how important cultivated maize was to the Incas as a staple food. At a large ceremony during the annual maize harvest in May, young Inca nobles processed through the streets of Cuzco, chanting hymns.

ARRIVAL OF THE INCAS

The Incas, who built up an Andean empire between 1230 and 1532, looked upon Tiahuanaco as one of their places of origin, and, like their forebears, they worshipped the sun. The Incas believed their rulers were descendants of Inti, the sun god. They also had an origin myth based near the city of Cuzco in Peru. A group of ancestors – three brothers and three sisters – emerged from caves near Cuzco and set various precedents for the real Inca rulers, such as wearing gold jewellery, marrying their sisters, and setting up mountaintop shrines.

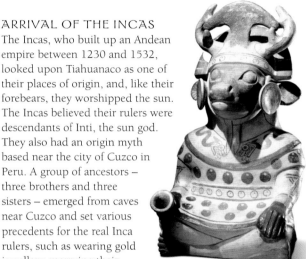

▲ Deer-headed figure
Animal spirits, as represented by this deer-headed Moche pottery figure, played an important role in traditional South American mythology and religion.

EMPIRE AND GODS

The Incas had a huge empire, stretching all along the western edge of South America from Ecuador to central Chile. Their capital was at Cuzco, but they had other urban centres, such as Machu Picchu. The empire was held together by an advanced bureaucracy and a good road network. Their state religion centered on worship of Inti at a large temple in Cuzco, but the Incas had many other deities, including a creator, Viracocha, a fertility god, Ilyap'a, and a moon goddess, Mama Kilya. Skilled metalworkers, they also gave gold great religious significance. An enduring myth of El Dorado ("the golden man"), well known to the Incas, originated in Colombia, where the initiation ceremony for a new king involved him being covered in gold dust, after which he was taken to the centre of a lake and offered more gold to its waters. Such stories gripped the imagination of Spanish conquerors who arrived in the 16th century in search of great riches – and still fascinate people to this day.

INCA BEGINNINGS

In the centuries preceding the Spanish conquest of Peru in the 16th century, the Incas built a vast empire in the Andes mountains of western South America. They had a sophisticated oral culture, and their mythology tells many different tales of their origin, all of which feature an ancestor called Manco Capac who, together with a number of followers, emerges into the world from a cave.

THE MYTH

The Incan creator god, called Con Tiki Viracocha, or simply Viracocha, was one of the most important deities in Incan mythology. In most versions of the creation story, he emerged from the waters of Lake Titicaca to create a race of giants. But he was dissatisfied with these creatures, and so he brought about a great flood called *Unu Pachacuti* that drowned them. Subsequently, he created the first humans out of pebbles that he found beside the lake. He gave these people a variety of languages, costumes, and foods, and then spread them around the world; though some say that Viracocha sent the first humans to a cave to await the appropriate time for emergence. It was believed by some that the cave was at a place called Pacaritambo (Tavern of the Dawn), which is about 25km (16 miles) southwest of modern-day Cuzco. Others believed that the real name of the place was Tambotocco (Tavern of the Windows), because the people had made three ceremonial entrances to the natural cavern.

> ▶ **Manco Capac**
> Like all Incan rulers, Manco Capac was always associated with the sun. Some said he wore a cape of gold during his arrival ceremony in Cuzco.

A number of people representing the lower classes of peasants and slaves emerged from the other two entrances to the cave. Then the first Incan settlements were established.

THE PEOPLE AND THE SUN GOD

Some chroniclers of the origin myth told a different version of the story. They said that Manco Capac and the other Incas had been set down by the sun god Inti (*see p.318*), on the shores of Lake Titicaca. The deity gave Manco Capac a staff or rod of gold and instructed the people to travel around the region, advising them to plunge the gold rod into the ground whenever they stopped to eat or rest. Inti told them that after travelling for a while, they would arrive at a place where the staff would vanish completely into the ground on being plunged. This would indicate that the soil at that location was deep and fertile, and Inti told Manco Capac to build a grand city at that site. The people followed the sun god's commands and after having wandered for some time, they reached a place where the rod disappeared from view into the ground. The Incas built their capital city of Cuzco not far from this spot, and Manco Capac became the first ruler of the Incan kingdom. Thus began the Incan dynasty.

THE EMERGENCE

Chief among the Andeans was a man called Manco Capac, who dwelt in the cave with his three brothers and three sisters. One of his sisters, Mama Ocllo, was also his wife. Together, they constituted the Incan royal family and became the ancestors of the Incan rulers who followed them. Eventually, a small group of people representing Incan nobility came out of the cave through one of its entrances.

▲ **Cuzco**
The Peruvian city of Cuzco was the Incan capital. Second only to Lake Titicaca, Cuzco and its neighbourhood was the most important area in Incan religion, with a number of shrines and sacred sites.

VIRACOCHA

The Incas believed that after creating humans, Viracocha stayed back to watch over them. The deity disguised himself as a beggar and wandered among the Incas to work miracles, and to teach his people how to live. But most humans did not listen to what the god had told them, and he returned from his trip to Earth in tears. He thought that one day his tears would cause another flood that would destroy all of humanity. This is why masks depicting Viracocha often show tears descending from the god's eyes.

Viracocha gold mask

▼ Quipu
The Incas used a device called a quipu, made of lengths of knotted string or leather, to keep records and accounts.

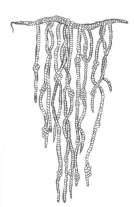

▲ Machu Picchu
This mountaintop city is an impressive Incan site. It has a temple with three windows, perhaps recalling the Incan emergence from a three-mouthed cave.

➤ Incan pot
Anthropomorphic pots, brightly glazed and sometimes depicting the heads of deities, were common in Incan pottery.

THE INCAS

Although they did not develop the wheel or a conventional system of writing, the Incas had a sophisticated civilization. Their craftsmen excelled in textiles and pottery, and the Incas were master builders too, constructing stone buildings with walls that fitted together without mortar. The long network of roads built across their Andean territories ensured that the Incas could develop a system of communication to hold the empire together. Their myths acknowledge both their humble beginnings at Lake Titicaca and their aspiration to create a vast empire beneath the rays of the sun god Inti.

PACA MAMA IS MOTHER EARTH, TO WHOM WE ALL MUST RETURN SOME DAY.

DEITIES OF THE SEA AND THE EARTH

In Incan mythology, the sea and the Earth were actually two goddesses. The sea was Mama Cocha (Sea Mother), who was the patron of fishermen and sailors. The Earth was Paca Mama (Earth Mother), who was a very important Incan deity; she was the consort of the sun god Inti, and the people sacrificed llamas in her honour. Some stories in later Incan mythology describe how Paca Mama was married to Pachacamac, the god of fire and rain, and together they created the stars, the sun, the moon, and the world.

◀ Paca Mama
The Earth goddess was seen as a fertility figure and portrayed as a naked woman. A ritualistic sacrifice of her creature, the llama, was made before the Incas first entered Cuzco.

GARCILASO DE LA VEGA

The son of a Spanish conquistador and an Incan princess, Garcilaso de la Vega (1539–1616) spent most of his adult life in Spain, but staunchly defended the culture of his mother's people. In 1609, he published the *Royal Commentaries*, in which he described the Incan culture and way of life; a second volume eight years later told the story of the Spanish conquest of the Incas. His portrayal of Incan life is invaluable because it comes from first-hand knowledge, though his account of the Incan religious beliefs and practices seems to have been distorted by his Christian outlook.

Garcilaso de la Vega

315

SEE ALSO American creation stories 282–83, 286–87, 306–07

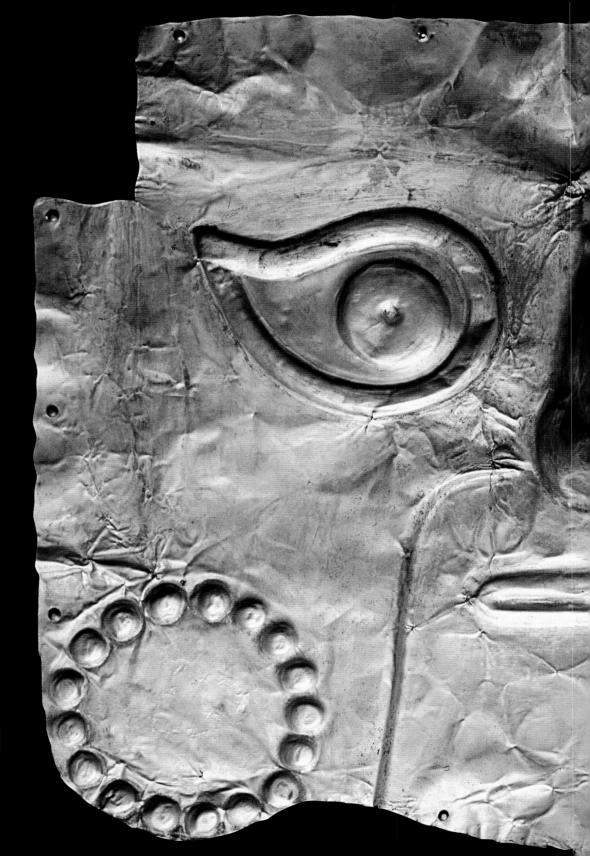

SKY GODS OF THE ANDES

The Incas were known as the people of the sun. Their emperors traced their descent from the sun god Inti, and the deity had pride of place in important temples. But the people also revered a host of other deities of the sky, beings who usually protected the Incas, and ensured that there was enough water for their crops. Occasionally, they also reminded the people of their godly power, with dramatic phenomena such as lightning bolts or eclipses.

INTI

The Incan sun god was called Inti, and was also known as "the leader of the daytime". For the Incas, he was the most important among all their deities. A friendly god, he did not simply look down on the Earth and warm it with his rays, but also actively helped the inhabitants. In one such myth, the Incan ancestors – Manco Capac and Mama Ocllo (*see p.314*) – were Inti's son and daughter, whom he taught the skills of life and sent to Earth to show the Incas how to live. They then became the ancestors of the Incan dynasty. The Incan rulers built many lavish temples to Inti in Cuzco, the Incan capital, one of which was known as the House of Gold because of its rich decoration. Its main chapel was oriented in a such a way that the image of Inti's face caught the light of the rising sun each day. Inti was often depicted as a golden disc with rays of light emanating from it.

▶ **Priestess figure**
Ceremonies in honour of the sun god were performed by specially trained priestesses called *mamaconas* (chosen women), who also acted as concubines of the Incan emperor.

▲ **Inti motif**
This cotton textile from the early Nazca culture of Peru has a design featuring radiating elements and warm colours that represent the sun god Inti.

▶ **Intihuantana post**
This structure at Machu Picchu, known as Intihuantana (hitching post of the sun), is thought to have been used for rituals or calendar calculations.

▲ **Incan farming**
Incan farmers, who grew a wide range of crops, from potatoes to squashes, were especially attached to the thunder god Illapu, and made sacrifices at his altars in the hope of rain.

ILLAPU

The Incan thunder god Illapu was a warlike deity whose weapon was the slingshot. One myth describes how he crossed the sky with giant strides, casting a great shadow, which became the Milky Way. He aimed his sling at a pot of water carried by his sister. As he fired, the leather of his sling made a booming noise that was the thunder, and the stone flashed with lightning as it flew through the air. When it hit the pot, rain poured down from the sky. As a bringer of rain, Illapu was widely revered by the Incas. They built temples to the god – usually on mountains to get closer to the sky where Illapu lived – and went there to pray for rain. If the people needed rain desperately, they sometimes made human sacrifices to appease Illapu.

MAMA KILYA

The moon goddess Mama Kilya was the consort and, some say, the sister of Inti. As the sun god's female counterpart, she was seen as the maternal ancestor of the Incan rulers, and presided over the night. During a lunar eclipse, the Incas thought that a monster was taking a bite out of Mama Kilya, and considered this omen to portend disaster – they waved weapons at the sky and made loud noises to frighten the monster away. Mama Kilya was also the goddess of women, guarding them during their monthly cycle, protecting female fertility, and enforcing marriage vows.

MAMA KILYA (placeholder)

▲ Moon goddess
The Incas believed that the goddess Mama Kilya watched over them at night, and her large face and big eyes could be seen clearly on the night of a full moon.

▲ Silver artefact
Gold was Inti's metal, and silver was Mama Kilya's. Silver objects were made in her honour, and her shrine at Cuzco's main temple was richly decorated with silver.

▼ The heavenly bridge
The many shimmering colours of the rainbow, together with its apparent ability to connect the realms of the humans and the gods, gave Chuichu a special place in the pantheon of Inca deities.

CHUICHU

The Incas believed that the rainbow was a two-headed dragon-like deity called Chuichu. They realized there was a connection between the rainbow and the sun, though they did not quite understand how its multicoloured effect was produced. They considered the rainbow to be a gift or message from the sun god Inti, indicating the presence of the benevolent deity Chuichu. Because he linked the world of the gods in the sky with the Earth, Chuichu was thought of as a kind of heavenly messenger or courier, who helped the deities of both the sun and the rain in bringing their life-giving gifts to the Earth. Some people regarded the rainbow god as an even more magical presence that linked the three fundamental parts of the Incan cosmos – the sky, the Earth's surface, and the underground realm.

STAR DEITIES

The Incas considered the stars to be benevolent deities, looking down on them at night just as Mama Kilya did. Unlike some cultures in other parts of the world, who saw the stars as rather randomly scattered across the sky, the Incas identified different star groups or constellations, just as astronomers and astrologers do today. But their groupings of stars had specifically Incan names and identities: they thought of Lyra as the Llama, Scorpio as the Cat, and the Pleiades as the Little Mothers or the Storehouse. Some of these constellations were revered by specific sections of Incan society. For example, the Storehouse was widely worshipped by farmers and growers, because it was said to protect and nurture stocks of seed.

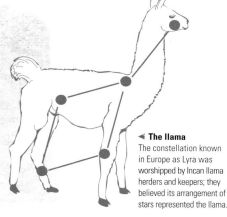

◄ The llama
The constellation known in Europe as Lyra was worshipped by Incan llama herders and keepers; they believed its arrangement of stars represented the llama.

319

SEE ALSO Weather deities 188–89, 194–95, 300–01, 308–09 • Stars 288–89, 334–35, 340–41

SPIRITS OF PLACE

Early peoples saw the whole Earth as being full of spirits (or sprites), many of whom inhabited and guarded a particular place. Sites that seemed to possess special supernatural significance were especially likely to house spirits – mountains, lakes, rivers, woods, and large rocks all stood out from the landscape in this way, and local people and travellers alike would make offerings to their spirits.

SPIRITS OF WATER

Rivers, lakes, and springs all have their deities or spirits, which reflect the double nature of water – something that is vital for life, but which can also bring danger. Some of these entities are benevolent, like the Hindu spirit Ganga, but many have two sides to their character, bringing fertility or life but also the risk of death by drowning.

◄ Ganga
The personification of the Ganges, Ganga (*see pp.208–09*) is the most sacred of India's river goddesses, purifying all who bathe in her.

► The Lady of the Lake
A spirit of Arthurian and Celtic myth, the "Lady of the Lake" (*see pp.126–27*) gave Arthur his famous sword, Excalibur, and was the protector of the king and his knights.

◄ Sobek
Crocodile-headed Sobek was the Egyptian god of rivers and lakes. Though a protector of the pharaoh, he was sometimes linked with the god Set, an enemy of the pharaoh.

▼ Nereid
The Nereids of Greek mythology were the 50 daughters of the Titan Nereus, the Old Man of the Sea. They always helped sailors in peril.

► River spirit
When pleased, this Central European water spirit guided fish into nets. When angry, he caused dangerous currents and storms.

◄ Rusalka
Slavic myths tell of Rusalkas (*see p.136*), female water spirits who lured unwary men into their lakes with seductive songs. But at times they also danced in meadows to make the soil fertile.

▲ Undine
In Germanic and other European legends, Undines were water nymphs born without a soul. They could only gain a soul by marrying a mortal and having his child.

SPIRITS OF PLACE

SPIRITS OF THE LAND

People have long believed that outstanding features such as high mountains and unusual outcrops have their own presiding spirits or deities. Usually these were local entities who only received offerings from people living nearby and passing travellers, but the deities of particularly spectacular sites such as great mountains could attract pilgrims from far and wide.

▲ Mount Fuji
The Shinto religion of Japan recognizes countless spirits, or kami, many of whom are associated with notable features of the landscape, such as the sacred, snow-capped, volcanic peak of Mount Fuji.

► Genius loci
The Romans called the guardian spirit of a particular place its *genius loci*. Such a spirit could look like a child with wings — or like a snake.

▼ Tipua
In Maori mythology, demon spirits called Tipua inhabit such features of the landscape as trees and rocks — places where travellers would be sure to make them offerings.

SPIRITS OF THE WOODS AND FORESTS

The great age and height of many trees, and the dark, mysterious atmosphere of woods and forests, led many peoples to imagine that certain individual trees, woods, and forests were home to guardian spirits. These were unpredictable entities, but their main interest was protecting their domain and the creatures living in it, and sometimes also local foresters. Travellers about to pass through an unfamiliar wood or forest might make an offering to its guardian spirit or spirits in the hope that they would then be protected from accident, robbery, or some other mishap for the duration of their journey.

► Dryad
The dryads of Greek mythology were nymphs who were especially associated with oak trees. They were usually portrayed as very beautiful and shy young girls.

▼ Tane
The Maori god of trees and forests is the spirit Tane. One myth describes how he created the first woman out of sand to be his wife (*see pp.340–41*).

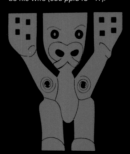

◄ Silvanus
The Roman spirit Silvanus was protector of trees, forests, and fields. He also guarded boundaries, to make sure no one stole land from their neighbour.

◄ Leshii
In eastern Slavic folklore, Leshii were spirits who guarded the trees and animals in woods. They usually looked like men, but could change their form to that of any animal.

OCEANIA

Oceania is made up of Australia and the islands to its north and east. Spread over an enormous geographical area, these lands have produced four distinct cultural zones: Australia itself; Melanesia, which consists of the island of New Guinea and a string of smaller islands and volcanic archipelagos such as the Solomon Islands and the New Hebrides; Micronesia, which consists of the island groups north of New Guinea; and the vast and thinly scattered islands of Polynesia, which occupy the triangle bounded by New Zealand, Hawaii, and Easter Island.

Australia is home to many Aboriginal tribes with distinct languages and cultures. Despite the variety of their traditions and beliefs, there is a common pattern of a remote sky god and a number of other deities who act as ancestor spirits or culture heroes – beings who long ago travelled over the land, creating its features, making the first humans, and teaching people how to live. The travels of these ancestral beings make the land sacred and therefore central to Aboriginal beliefs, and are remembered and relived in rituals and art.

The scattered islands of Oceania are home to many different myths. In Melanesia, for example, the Earth has traditionally been seen as always existing. Supernatural spirits – who altered the form of the world to give it its present shape – and ancestor spirits alike have historically been worshipped and held in awe for their possession of a mystical power known as *mana*. *Mana* explains everything that seems outside the control of humankind or the normal natural processes of the world. Natural and supernatural power are, moreover, often interdependent. In the Caroline Islands, spirits known as *ani* combine the roles of ancestors and gods and have traditionally been seen as dwelling in the bodies of specific beings – such as birds, fish, animals, and trees.

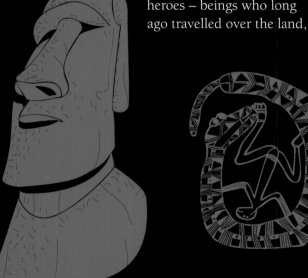

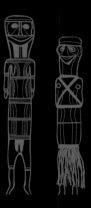

> ## THE PACIFIC'S SPIRITUAL WORLD IS AS MULTICOLOURED AS ITS CORAL REEFS OR THE FLORA OF ITS COASTS, WHERE OVER A THOUSAND DIFFERENT LANGUAGES ARE SPOKEN.
>
> Jan Knappert, *Pacific Mythology*, 1992

The mythology of the many diverse islands of Polynesia is complex, but remarkably unified, reflecting what were probably relatively recent migrations from one island or group of islands to another. The islands have large pantheons and complex stories. The creation story of New Zealand, for example, features a god, Rangi, who has to be separated from his partner – Papa, the Earth mother – and forced into the sky. Their offspring are then free to have children, and so the large pantheon grows, followed by the creation of humankind and a familiar story of female sin and transgression. The peoples of Polynesia – maritime peoples whose ancestors must have voyaged far across unknown waters – also tell myths involving fantastic journeys across the cosmos. Their Underworld is often seen as a pit where the souls of the dead are sent after death – unless they are the souls of heroes, in which case they are admitted to a paradise in the sky, which they share with the gods. For these island peoples, the gods are everywhere – below the Earth, above it, and across the boundless sea.

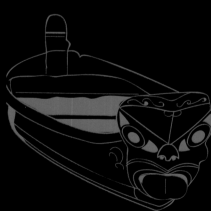

▲ **Aboriginal cave art**
Rock painting has a long history in Australia. Aborigines paint pictures of their
ancestors and early families directly onto rock to form a close link between them
and the land. This example is in Kakadu National Park in the Northern Territory.

AUSTRALIA

The myths of the indigenous people of Australia are diverse and yet share many similarities. They explain and reinforce the bond between the people and the land, which is said to have been brought into being at the very beginning of time.

When the Europeans arrived in Australia at the end of the 18th century, they found a continent inhabited by around 400 different Aboriginal tribes. Each of these tribal groups was small – sometimes just a handful of families, sometimes as many as 50 – and each had found a niche in which Australia's sometimes extremely harsh landscape could sustain life. The Aborigines lived by hunting and gathering, and had done so for millennia – no one is sure when people originally came to Australia, though they may have arrived from Indonesia around 50,000 years ago. Although the incoming Europeans saw the indigenous people as "primitive" because they had not developed skills such as metalworking or pottery production, they were in fact very well adapted to living on their land.

▲ **Kangaroo spirit**
This Aboriginal artwork shows a number of ancestor figures, including a prominent kangaroo spirit. Such images reflect the key position of stories of origins and their importance for the identity of the people.

MYTHS OF ORIGIN

Each of Australia's Aboriginal tribes has its own language and its own myths, and for them these stories explain the origins and the very existence of the Aboriginal people. For the Aborigines, the historical, European account of their arrival on the continent many thousands of years ago is largely irrelevant. Instead, their existence in Australia is accounted for by their myths, which describe each tribe's intimate association with the land where it lives and their ancestors' roles in giving form to the land. Unfortunately, because not all of Australia's tribes have survived, some of these myths have been lost. But those that are still known remain central to Aboriginal beliefs, and are constantly retold.

ANCESTRAL JOURNEYS

Although these sets of Aboriginal myths are all different, they share many similarities. They focus on ancestral beings – often animal spirits – who in the beginning made journeys across the country, bringing the land and all its geographical features into being, bringing to life all the plants, animals, and other living things that inhabit it, and giving life to all the spirits of the place: even to the spirits of people and beings who will be born in the future.

This ancient process of bringing all aspects of the world to life is known as the Dreaming, or Dreamtime, a name that reflects the idea that the ancestor spirits awoke from a long sleep in order to carry out this process of animation, and then subsided into an eternal sleep when they had completed their great task.

STORIES OF THE DREAMTIME

The ancient events of the Dreaming or Dreamtime still exist on a level that can be experienced today. By retelling stories of the Dreamtime, and by carrying out the correct rituals, Aborigines can relive the creative process and achieve a kind of communion with the spirits. In this sense, the Dreamtime is always present. Dreamtime stories consist of journeys across the land, which is criss-crossed with ancient pathways that represent the narratives of different tribes and explain the existence of a variety of natural features, from rocks and mountains to creeks and water holes. Many such sites have profound spiritual meaning, as do the many myths themselves, which are dramatically brought to life in tribal rituals and in artistic depictions.

➤ **Bark painting depicting a Wandjina**
In the Kimberley region of Western Australia, the Wandjina are ancestral creator spirits who also bring life-giving rain. Paintings of such beings are said to embody them and are deeply revered.

THE RAINBOW SNAKE

Known by many names, the Rainbow Snake is an almost universal spirit in the Aboriginal mythology of Australia. He has many roles to play, and in some cultures, even plays a part in the creation of humanity. Two themes stand out in the myths about the Rainbow Snake. One is his ability to bring forth water – which gives life, but can turn into an overwhelming flood that is capable of wiping out entire tribes. The other is his function as a bridge, linking the Earth and the sky, and giving humans access to the wisdom of the spirit world.

ESCAPE FROM THE SNAKE'S BELLY

In western Arnhem Land, the wooded area on the coast of the Northern Territory, the Rainbow Snake is called Ngalyod, and is sometimes portrayed with a pair of slender horns and the tail of a crocodile. Ngalyod was feared for eating humans and known for his foul temper, and in one particular myth, devoured a child who had annoyed him by crying. A popular tale about Ngalyod links him with the creation of humanity. One day, the snake was hungry and ate three birds, one of which was a pewee. As snakes do, he swallowed his prey whole. Once inside the serpent's belly, the birds tried to escape, beginning to peck a hole through Ngalyod's abdomen. The three finally emerged as the first humans, and soon afterwards, killed the Rainbow Snake to set up home on Earth.

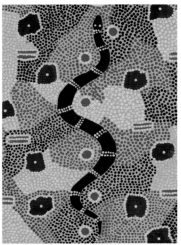

◄ **Ngalyod**
The Rainbow Snake is a favourite subject of the artists of Arnhem Land, where he is revered as the presiding spirit of the rainy season, and is also associated with fertility, abundance, and life-giving powers.

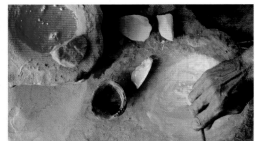

▲ **Ngalyod and Yingarna**
In the creation myth of western Arnhem Land, Ngalyod is the son of the primal Dreaming mother, Yingarna, and helps her look after her other children.

◄ **Aboriginal bark painting**
The Aborigines painted images of their myths with natural pigments on bark. Depictions of an individual's spirit land were often painted on the coffin when the person died.

THE INUNDATION

The Djauan people of Arnhem Land tell how a fisherman found the black bones of a fish that other men had eaten. He recognized the bones as those of a rare fish that he had been looking for, and became both angry and sad. The fisherman sang a song to Kurrichalpongo – the black rock snake – and it came down from the sky in a great curving bow of many colours (the Rainbow Snake). The snake made a hole in a billabong (a lake), releasing a great flood over the land that swept away all the neighbouring tribes, leaving behind only the Djauan. Then the snake laid some eggs, which, when they hatched, carved out rivers, hills, and other features of the landscape.

▲ **People and the snake**
The Rainbow Snake was a teacher of shamans and the bringer of water, but according to certain myths, he was also the creator of the first man and woman.

▲ **Aboriginal healers**
Shamans were assisted by the spirits that they contacted when they were engaged in shamanic healing rituals. Here, a healer performs a traditional bloodletting ceremony using an ox horn.

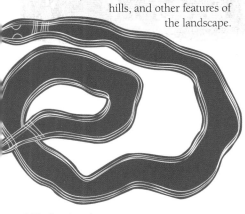

▲ **Black rock snake**
Because of the creature's power to cause floods, the Djauan traditionally ask the black rock snake's permission before taking water from a billabong, or before fishing.

THE END OF THE RAINBOW

The shamans (*see pp.268–69*) of Aboriginal Australia have always been regarded with respect for their power to heal the sick and to see the future. It was believed that the shamans received their knowledge from the spirits, and different myths describe how they gained this knowledge. These stories usually involve the shamans travelling to the heavens, sometimes flying through the sky. One version of the myth describe how the shamans journeyed to the sky by travelling up the body of the Rainbow Snake. The voyage up the rainbow took the shamans from the land of the living to the realm of the spirits and ancestors at the end of the Rainbow Snake's body. Here, they dwelled with the spirits for a period of time, receiving instruction in the arts of healing and divination.

TAIPAN

The snake known as Taipan is often identified with the Rainbow Snake. He had awesome power over life and death, and could even control the rain and the thunder. Taipan had a son whom he loved deeply, but one day, his son fell in love with the daughter of Wala, the blue-tongued lizard, and the pair eloped. Wala was angry that his daughter had taken a husband without asking his permission, and so pursued the couple, killing Taipan's son. Distraught over his son's death, Taipan sent most of his family to live in the dark depths of the Earth, and two of his sisters to heaven, where they took some of their dead nephew's blood and added its colour to the rainbow.

▲ **Blue-tongued lizard**
The myth describes how the blue-tongued lizard Wala carried the heart and blood of Taipan's son to the grieving Taipan, to show the latter what the lizard had done in his fury.

SEE ALSO Snakes & serpents 28–29, 48–49, 92–93, 98–99, 100–03, 160–61

THE PRIMAL SISTERS

A widespread Aboriginal myth from Australia describes a pair of ancestral sisters, often known as the Wawilak or Wagilag Sisters, who travel across Arnhem Land. They have a traumatic encounter with the Rainbow Snake (*see pp.328–29*), seen as a conflict between the male and female entities, which culminates in the snake swallowing the women. The sisters survive, however, and finally escape the snake's stomach to coexist with their arch rival, reinforcing the idea that both male and female forces are needed for creation to be balanced.

THE MYTH

One day, two women walked out of the ocean and stepped onto the shore of Arnhem Land, in Australia's Northern Territory. They were sisters and the elder one was carrying a baby, while the other one was pregnant. The sisters walked inland looking for animals to eat. Both carried spears and were proficient in their use. The sisters were creators, and as they travelled, they gave names and shapes to the landscapes through which they walked – essentially bringing them into existence. They made steady progress until the pregnant sister began to feel apprehensive about her impending delivery. So the sisters set up camp and lit a fire by a water hole at a place called Mirrirmina.

THE RAINBOW SNAKE'S CREATURES

The elder sister went to hunt for food, while the younger sister lay still and eventually gave birth. But something strange happened when the elder sister came back and began to prepare a meal. All the animals that she had caught and killed leapt out of the cooking pot, ran off, and jumped into the water hole. The sisters did not know that the pool was home to the Rainbow Snake. He owned all the animals in the area, and would not let the sisters eat them. After this had happened a few times, the elder sister went to the pool to

The sisters
The Rainbow Snake encircles the two women, along with their children, in the centrepiece of this painting depicting the myth about the primal sisters.

investigate. The Rainbow Snake heard her coming and was at last roused from his sleep. He reared up and attacked the two women who had invaded his land, and he swallowed both the sisters and their children.

THE SISTERS RETURN

The Rainbow Snake made a lot of noise doing this; his commotion roused all the other snakes, who asked him what was going on. At first he lied, saying that he had caught and eaten a kangaroo, but they did not believe him. He finally admitted to eating the sisters. Immediately, a mighty wind blew and a monsoon lashed its way across the landscape. The rain and wind were so powerful that the Rainbow Snake was forced to vomit up the sisters and their children onto an ant hill, where they were returned to life.

◄ Ant hill
When the Rainbow Snake vomited the sisters onto the ant hill, the painful and repeated bites of the ants brought the women and their children quickly back to life.

WAWILAK SISTERS

The story of the two sisters – often known as the Wawilak Sisters – is told in different versions by the many Aboriginal tribes. However, the common theme in every version of the story is the depiction of a confrontation between opponents of opposite sexes. The primal sisters represent female wisdom – they are praised as accomplished hunters and they have the power to give form to the land. When the Rainbow Snake swallows them, he gains some of their wisdom in the process. Since that time, it has always been the male members of the tribe who look after the traditions of tribal wisdom and lore, and hand them down from one generation to the next.

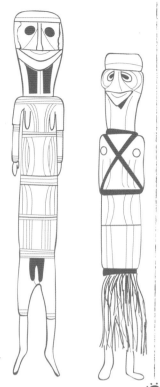

► Tribal representations
The sisters are often depicted in carvings used during rituals. The younger sister (on the right) wears a girdle across her chest to strengthen her breasts since she has just given birth.

KUNAPIPI

Certain versions of the story depict the Earth Mother Kunapipi as the mother of the Wawilak sisters. She is also sometimes considered to be an eternal "Old Woman" figure, and the female counterpart to the male Rainbow Snake. Other myths describe her as the creator of men, women, and the animals of the world. Kunapipi asked her followers to paint themselves to show allegiance to specific families or groups. She is also believed by some to have been an ancient wanderer who travelled with a group of primal heroes and heroines. Her wise and creative character represents the feminine side of spirituality.

▲ Galah parrot
The Galah parrots painted themselves in a ritual as per Kunapipi's instructions.

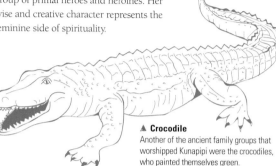

▲ Crocodile
Another of the ancient family groups that worshipped Kunapipi were the crocodiles, who painted themselves green.

ABORIGINAL DEITIES

There are thousands of deities in Aboriginal mythology, and the common feature among them is that they are thought to be closely connected to the land they cross and bring into existence; this is clearly illustrated in the myths of the Wawilak sisters. Many of the deities are shape-changers, who may take the form of an animal (*see p.285*), but can, at the same time, be the ancestors of a human tribe or family. Most are specific to certain regions and rooted in the land, but some, such as the Rainbow Snake, are known all over Australia.

◄ Wandjina
The Wandjina are spirits that control fertility and the natural elements. They are depicted with white stripes on their bodies, representing falling rain.

▼ Sun deities
According to one myth, the sun is a torch carried across the sky each day by the solar goddess Gnowee, who is looking for her lost son.

RITUALS AND CELEBRATIONS

Aboriginal rituals are performed on many occasions, from the celebration of a birth to the burial of the dead. Other ceremonies – attended by the whole tribe – can retell in song and dance the stories of the spirits of Dreamtime (*see p.327*). A few rituals are thought to have been first performed by the primal sisters to keep the Rainbow Snake at bay. The rituals show how all of creation is linked together by the ancestors.

Painting of an Aboriginal ceremony

SEE ALSO Snakes & serpents 28–29, 48–49, 92–93, 98–99, 100–03, 160–61, 328–29

THE KILLING OF LUMALUMA

The Yolngu people, inhabitants of Arnhem Land, northern Australia, tell how a whale called Lumaluma came out of the sea and adopted human form. He then took two wives and travelled across the country imparting sacred rituals. Although they respected his teachings, the Yolngu people began to get frustrated with Lumaluma because of his voracious appetite and the way he abused his sacred status to satisfy it. Whenever he found mouth-watering food, Lumaluma knocked together his clapping sticks and announced that the food was sacred, so that only he was allowed to eat it. This happened many times and the people grew exasperated, so they killed him and his wives. Even as he was dying, Lumaluma continued to teach the sacred rituals, which the people of Arnhem Land have repeated ever since.

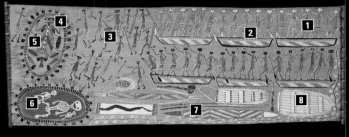

AUSTRALIA

Djorlom Nalorlman, *The Killing of Lumaluma*, 1988

Angry at Lumaluma, who had been taking their food, the men of the Yolngu people set out in pursuit of him. All things in Arnhem Land, including the Yolngu people, were said to belong to one of two moieties (ritual groups), the Dua or the Yiridja. The Dua believed their ancestors had come by sea, while the Yiridja thought their forefathers had come by land. Here, the members of the two moieties can be distinguished by their differently coloured body paint.

2. Canoes

The Yolngu men travelled in canoes, in recognition of the fact that Lumaluma had originally come from the sea. Although he had taken a human form, Lumaluma was still able to transform himself back into a whale whenever he wanted to catch fish.

As they ran after their quarry, the men from the Dua and Yiridja moieties raised their spears and sticks, ready to attack. After putting Lumaluma to death, they propped up his body against a tree, and tied twines tightly around his chest and neck to hold him firmly in place.

4. Shade huts

After securing Lumaluma, the men built shade huts to shelter his body. These structures, made of leaves and branches, were similar to those that the whale had taught them to build. Even though they were angry with him, the Yolngu people still recognized that Lumaluma was an important being. Such huts are still built over sacred ground in the performance of rituals handed down from Lumaluma.

Lumaluma continued to teach sacred ceremonies, even while he was being speared. Here, his body is shown covered in sacred designs – patterns that he has cut into his body just before his death, so that he could teach the people one last time the sacred ritual called *mareiin*. These designs symbolize the stories of the Yolngu peoples' ancestry.

6. Skeletons

The skeletons of Lumaluma's wives lie next to his. The two women, who he had stolen from the Yolngu people, travelled with him everywhere and taught religious ceremonies (especially those used by the women of Arnhem Land). They too were speared and died at their husband's side.

Objects used by Lumaluma in sacred ceremonies were gathered together by the Yolngu and are shown at the bottom of the painting. These include a stone axe with a wooden handle; a *bondok*, or spear thrower; clapping sticks, which were banged together to produce the sound that accompanied the rituals; and a pair of dilly bags.

8. Dilly bags

Made of woven fibre, dilly bags concealed the secret ritual objects. Two kinds of dilly bag are shown here – the one with a handle was used by the Yiridja moiety, while the bag without a handle was used by the Dua. The shape of the dilly bag represents the womb of an ancestral pair of sisters, the Djanggawuls, who are believed to be eternally pregnant.

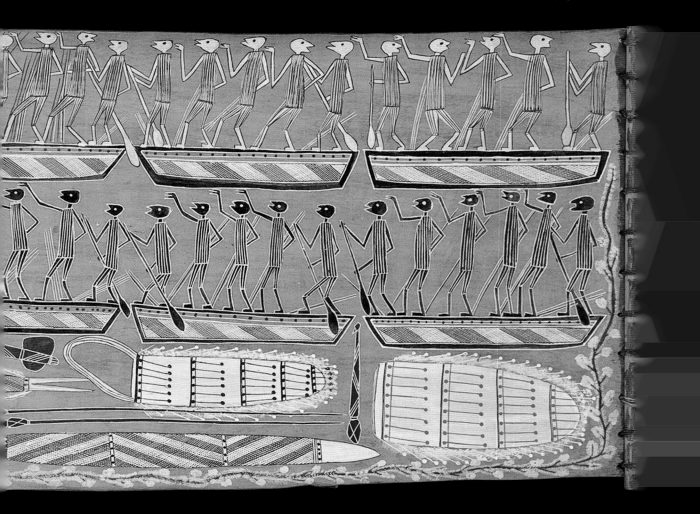

THE BRAM-BRAM-BULT

A number of Aboriginal myths centre around pairs of brothers. One such story describes the adventures of two ancestors, Yuree and Wanjel, who are also known as the Bram-Bram-Bult. Their myth not only explains how the brothers name and bring to life the different features of the Australian landscape, but also narrates their encounters with deadly rivals, including an echidna spirit called Wembulin who the brothers fight and kill to avenge their nephew's death.

THE MYTH

There was once a great spirit called Doan, a powerful hunter who had taken the form of a small gliding possum. One day, he began hunting a mighty kangaroo called Purra. The chase went on for many miles, but the kangaroo continued to elude Doan. The possum had almost caught up with Purra when he entered the territory of an echidna spirit called Wembulin, who was resting with his two daughters. Wembulin attacked Doan, and although at first the possum managed to escape, he was eventually caught and killed. Wembulin and his daughters ate Doan and set off in pursuit of the kangaroo.

THE BROTHERS' REVENGE

Doan's two maternal uncles, Yuree and Wanjel, were brave warriors who had won renown for their many adventures. They were very fond of their nephew, and when Doan went missing they set off to look for him. As they searched they found a colony of ants carrying strands of a possum's hair and bits of its flesh to their nest, and the brothers began to suspect that their nephew had been killed. Soon they came to the place where Wembulin had attacked Doan, where they found the

> ► **Carved figure**
> Australian Aboriginal art is rich in carved figures. According to the Bram-Bram-Bult myth, Yuree carved a figure resembling Wanjel out of wood, bringing his brother back to life.

remains of his body and signs of a tremendous struggle all over the ground. The two brothers started off in pursuit of the echidna to avenge their nephew's death. Being highly accomplished trackers they soon found his trail and followed it tenaciously, finding Wembulin and his family on the third day. The brothers launched a surprise attack and killed the echidna; they then took his two daughters as their wives.

THE WORK OF CREATION

On the journey home Yuree and Wanjel began to regret marrying the echidna sisters. They saw that the pair were angry at their father's death and seemed likely to take revenge. So the brothers killed their wives and set off into the countryside. As they travelled, they brought the world around them into existence, by naming all the plants, rocks, trees, and rivers of the region, gradually transforming a chaotic void into a vibrant landscape.

As time went by, Yuree and Wanjel completed the task of creation and undertook a series of adventures that culminated in Wanjel's death. However, the resourceful Yuree revived him and the two brothers began a long journey from which they never returned. Some accounts say that they live on as Castor and Pollux, the two bright stars of the constellation of Gemini.

▲ **Killing Wembulin**
After tracking Wembulin for three days, the two brothers found the echidna sleeping. They crept up on him silently and killed him.

KEY CHARACTERS

Like most characters in the Aboriginal stories of Dreamtime (*see p.327*), some in the myth of the Bram-Bram-Bult take the form of animals, though they are seen as eternal spirits. Some of these spirits are the ancestors of the people who told the story, and are therefore assigned supernatural roles. Thus, although no ordinary possum can kill a kangaroo, Doan could chase Purra because he is playing out an incident in the lives of the ancestors. However, in spite of the power and energy of Doan and Wembulin, the story's true heroes are Yuree and Wanjel, who are admired for their bravery and resourcefulness.

▲ **Purra**
In the Bram-Bram-Bult, the mighty Purra is the prey of a hunter. However, in many other Australian myths, the kangaroo is a hero and an ancestor spirit.

▲ **Doan**
A creature of remarkable strength for his size, Doan's speed in the hunt is perhaps inspired by a gliding possum's ability to move effortlessly through the air.

THE SOUTHERN CROSS

The night sky plays an important role in Aboriginal myths, including the story of the Bram-Bram-Bult. During one of their exploits, the brothers stopped a ferocious emu called Tchingal from attacking a man named Bunya – they transformed the man into a possum and killed the emu with their spears. The constellation of the Southern Cross, often associated with the brothers, is believed to represent the emu, the possum, and the spears used to kill Tchingal.

➤ **Southern Cross**
The Aboriginal people of the northwest coast saw the four "pointer" stars of the Southern Cross as symbolizing the origin of fire, a very vital resource.

> WE ARE ALL VISITORS TO THIS TIME, THIS PLACE... OUR PURPOSE HERE IS TO OBSERVE, TO LEARN, TO GROW, TO LOVE AND THEN WE RETURN HOME.
>
> Australian Aboriginal proverb

THE DEATH OF WANJEL

At the end of the story of the Bram-Bram-Bult, Wanjel was bitten by a poisonous snake called Gertuk. Yuree tried hard to save him, but the snake's venom killed his brother. So Yuree took a tree trunk and carved it into a figure resembling Wanjel, and then magically gave it life. After reviving Wanjel, Yuree taught him to walk and talk, and the two brothers continued on their travels. They finally reached the end of the country and made their home in a cave. After their death, the Bram-Bram-Bult ascended to the sky, where many believe they continue to live on as a pair of stars.

◄ **Gertuk**
Venomous snakes such as the one that bit Wanjel are found all over Australia. In certain versions of the myth, the snake called Gertuk was actually a mopoke, a small spotted owl of Australia.

SIBLING PAIRS

Pairs of siblings, especially brothers, are quite common in the Aboriginal myths of Australia. These range from close, devoted brothers like Yuree and Wanjel, to contrasting brothers with opposite characters, who are often in conflict with each other. One such myth describes how a flood is unleashed when two brothers fight over the ownership of water. One of the brothers prudently stores all the water he finds in a leather bag, while the other does not. When the second brother is thirsty, he upsets his brother's bag, making the water spill out and causing a great flood.

➤ **Aboriginal bark painting**
Sibling pairs are commonly portrayed on Aboriginal bark paintings. One such pair is the Warti-kutjara (the Iguana Men), who rescue a woman from an attack, and later ascend to the sky.

SEE ALSO Hunters 258–59, 266–67, 272–73 • Stars 288–89, 318–19, 340–41

▲ Iconic Easter Island statues
There are around 600 large stone heads on Easter Island, some of them almost
20m (65ft) high. Many stand on stone burial platforms known as *ahu*. The heads
probably represent ancestors, although their exact significance is not known.

POLYNESIA

Living on a group of islands thinly spread over an enormous area, the peoples of Polynesia have countless gods and myths, many of which eloquently show their awareness of their beautiful but dangerous marine environment.

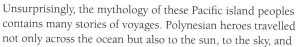

The many small Pacific islands that make up Polynesia are mainly spread around the vast triangle defined by Easter Island, Hawaii, and New Zealand. Many archaeologists also include in the group the Melanesian islands to the east – the band extending roughly from the Caroline Islands in the northwest to Vanuatu in the southeast – because they share many cultural similarities. The most likely reason for these similarities is that groups of settlers from the Philippines and eastern Indonesia passed through Melanesia on their way to the Polynesian islands. These migrations probably took place over hundreds of years some time before 1000 BCE.

EARLY VOYAGES

Amazingly, people originally reached these tiny, remote islands by sailing simple dug-out canoes – and, later, plank-built vessels – that were stabilized with outriggers. Although these early navigators developed efficient paddles and sails, they still had to travel the open ocean without compasses or any other navigational aids. To work out which direction they were going in they must have relied instead mainly on the positions of the stars, on wave patterns, and on the prevailing winds. But little is known for sure about how they navigated or whether, once they had reached an island after a voyage of hundreds of kilometres, they were able to return to their homelands again.

◀ **Supreme Hawaiian deity**
This 19th-century wooden statue represents the supreme Hawaiian creator called Tu or Ku. This powerful god was also a god of war, weather, and plant and animal fertility.

▲ **Clan ancestor figure**
This wooden female ancestor figure is one of a number covering the wall of a Maori clan meeting house built in Manutuke on New Zealand's North Island in 1842.

Unsurprisingly, the mythology of these Pacific island peoples contains many stories of voyages. Polynesian heroes travelled not only across the ocean but also to the sun, to the sky, and to the Underworld, where they found fire and brought it back for the people to use. Other travelling deities include gods of fishing, such as Ndauthina of Fiji. His mother tied burning reeds on his head when he was a child and ever after he travelled across the coral reefs, spreading his light across the sea.

ABANDONED HERO

The culture hero and trickster Maui is widely known across Polynesia, where he is also associated with the sea. He was said to have been abandoned as a baby, when his mother threw him into the ocean. Closely linked to the water for the rest of his life, he went fishing and caught land instead of fish. Maui did this using his magical weapon, which was made from the jawbone of an ancestor goddess. He levered up the land with the point of the bone, but when his brothers saw what he had done they kicked up all the land and threw it around the sea, bringing the islands of Polynesia into existence.

STORIES OF THE FLOOD

Maui was in his element in the water, but Polynesian myths also reveal the great dangers of the sea. Hawaii, for example, has a flood myth in which a goddess rose up from the depths to create a giant tsunami, or tidal wave. The resulting flood caused great destruction, but the hero Nu'u built himself a boat in which to escape. Melanesian islands have a similar story in which a hero called Qat escaped a flood in his boat. As is so often the case, the myths of the Pacific island peoples show both their great respect for the dangers of their environment and their ability to cope with them.

TANGAROA

One of the most prominent deities of the Pacific islands is Tangaroa (also known as Ta'aroa or Tagaroa). He is considered to be a sea god in some places, but in Tahiti and among the other island communities, including Samoa, Tonga, and Tuvalu, Tangaroa is known as the creator of the cosmos and all its inhabitants. Some people believe that he was the son of the primal deities Rangi and Papa, but another version of the myth says that he created the universe after tearing apart the two halves of a great shell when emerging from it.

THE MYTH

Long before the world was made, and before even the gods came to control the universe, nothing existed except an endless void, floating within which was a great shell. This was called Rumia, and was shaped like an egg. There was darkness everywhere and nothing could be seen, not even the solitary floating shell. But inside the shell, something was stirring. It was Tangaroa, the creator. He had no father or mother, and no other gods lived with him in the shell. He had brought himself to life and was biding his time before bringing the world into being.

THE SKY AND THE EARTH

At last, Tangaroa began to move. Pushing against the inside of the shell, he heaved until the walls of the shell broke in two. Upon emerging, Tangaroa shouted, "Is there anyone there?" But there was no reply – all around him was only darkness and silence. Subsequently, Tangaroa set about the task of creation. First he took one half of the broken shell and lifted it up to make the great arch of the sky. Next he took the other half and laid it below, to make the ground. Then he looked

► **The sea god**
Since Tangaroa created the other gods from his own body, he is frequently depicted giving birth to the gods who crawl over his body.

around and saw that nothing else but his body was left to be used for the task of creation. So Tangaroa took his own flesh and made the soil on the ground. The god made use of his backbone to create a mountain range and from his inner organs he made the clouds in the sky. Tangaroa even used the nails of his fingers and toes to give shells and scales to the creatures in the sea.

POPULATING THE EARTH

Then Tangaroa called forth the other gods from within him. They began to emerge, and one in particular – the craftsman god Tu – helped Tangaroa continue the process of creation. The pair worked together to make the trees and animals that populated the Earth. Then they made the first humans, who were called Til and Hina, and persuaded them to approach one another to procreate.

Tangaroa saw that everything he had created had a shell, just as he had had one in the beginning. The sky was the shell that contained the sun, the moon, and the stars. The Earth too was a shell; it was an enormous container for all the rocks, rivers and lakes, and for the plants that grew on its surface and the animals that walked on it. Even human beings had their shells; the wombs of women were the shells from which new life was born.

◄ **The seal deity**
An Easter Island myth relates how the god Tangaroa landed on the island in the form of a seal with a human face and voice.

TANGAROA IN NEW ZEALAND

In New Zealand, Tangaroa is the Maori god of the sea and the son of the primal deities Papa (the goddess of the Earth) and Rangi (the god of the sky). At the beginning of time, Papa and Rangi held each other tight, locking their children within their embrace, but Tangaroa and some of his siblings wrenched them apart to initiate the process of creation. This angered his brother Tawhirimatea, the wind god, who unleashed fierce storms on them. Terrified, some of Tangaroa's descendants hid in the forest. Tangaroa quarrelled with his brother Tane (see pp.340–41), the god of forests, for having given shelter to the runaway creatures. He attacked Tane's land with his tides and swept away all the creatures into his watery realm.

▲ Yam
Certain nights of the lunar month were named after Tangaroa. It was believed that the yams planted on these "Tangaroa nights" would produce the best roots.

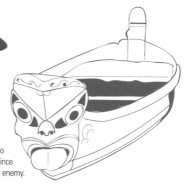

▶ Maori canoe
The people of the forest made offerings to Tangaroa before setting out in their canoes, since they were entering the realm of Tane's mortal enemy.

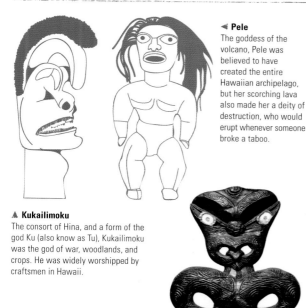

◀ Pele
The goddess of the volcano, Pele was believed to have created the entire Hawaiian archipelago, but her scorching lava also made her a deity of destruction, who would erupt whenever someone broke a taboo.

▲ Kukailimoku
The consort of Hina, and a form of the god Ku (also know as Tu), Kukailimoku was the god of war, woodlands, and crops. He was widely worshipped by craftsmen in Hawaii.

▶ Papatuanuku
Mother Earth, or Papatuanuku, was the female half of the primal couple. When she raised her arm during her long embrace with her husband, Rangi, she gave her children their first glimpse of sunlight.

POLYNESIAN DEITIES

Tangaroa is one of the oldest Polynesian deities, and in some myths, the primary god. Many of the Polynesian deities were worshipped as sky gods, whose forces were unleashed in the form of storms or hurricanes, as in the case of the wind god Tawhirimatea. According to some myths, Tangaroa's son Maui (see p.341) slowed down the sun by lassoing it, and forced it to shine for longer periods in summer. The goddess Hina controlled the tides, and in some versions, was also the goddess of the west wind. There were many powerful Earth deities too, such as the volcano goddess Pele, who was dominant in Hawaii. Other deities included the mother goddess, known variously as Papatuanuku, or Papa, who was present at the beginning of creation.

OTHER POLYNESIAN CREATION MYTHS

Several creation stories told in the Pacific islands feature Maui, who created the islands of Polynesia by fishing them up from the bottom of the sea using a great fish-hook. Some creation myths centre on a primal goddess in the Underworld who plucked the first gods and humans from her own body. Others describe a series of sexual unions, beginning with the coupling of light and dark, which engendered everything in the cosmos. Still other stories describe how the islands were formed from the discarded wood chips of the carpenter son of the sky god Tagaloa. However, most myths regard Tangaroa as the creator deity and patron of sailors.

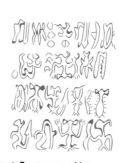

▲ Rongorongo tablets
The mysterious hieroglyphic inscriptions on the wooden tablets discovered at Easter Island may record an as yet unknown creation myth.

▶ The creators
In a Fijian myth, the first humans were a boy and girl, the abandoned children of the hawk Turukawa. The snake god Degei brought them up and they came together to create the human race.

> ## O TANGAROA IN THE IMMENSITY OF SPACE, CLEAR AWAY THE CLOUDS BY DAY.
>
> Dennis Kawaharada, *1992 Voyage: Sail to Rarotonga*, 1992

339

SEE ALSO Sea deities 30–31, 158–59, 160–61, 290–91, 294–97

THE ORIGIN OF DEATH

The Maori story of the origin of death involves their forest god Tane. He is one of the sons of the primal deities Rangi and Papa (*see p.339*), who had only male children. Tane brings death into the world by breaking a taboo, when, after making a wife for himself out of sand and clay, he goes on to marry his own daughter, the beautiful Hine-titama (Dawn Maiden). It is a sad story, because in many ways Tane, a god who plants the first trees, is a friend of humanity, and yet it is he who becomes the bringer of death.

THE MYTH

Tane's story starts at the beginning of time when there were few gods and no people in the world. Tane spent his time tending to his forests. He faced a great deal of difficulty at first due to improper planting of trees, but eventually they began to flourish. When the trees started growing successfully, Tane no longer had enough to do and became lonely. He wanted a wife, but did not know where to look, because all the children of Rangi and Papa, the primal couple, were male. He first turned to his mother but she rejected him; then he took a number of partners, but their offspring turned out to be reptiles, stones, and streams. This did not please Tane at all, and he wondered how he could find a partner who would satisfy him.

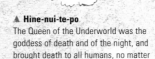

▲ **Hine-nui-te-po**
The Queen of the Underworld was the goddess of death and of the night, and brought death to all humans, no matter how hard they tried to avoid it.

and, while talking to the local people, happened to mention that she did not know the name of her father. They told her that she was, in fact, Tane's daughter. This revelation shocked and ashamed her so much that she fled to the gloomiest place in the universe – the Underworld, which was also known as the kingdom of Po, or darkness. After some time, Tane realized that his young wife was missing, so he began to look for her everywhere and finally heard her singing. It was a very melancholic song, and its words were "Are you Tane, my father?" Tane realized that Hine-titama had come to know the truth. He knew that her voice was coming from the Underworld, but he could not enter the dark realm – he was prevented from doing so by Hine-titama herself.

MAKING A WIFE
Finally, Tane went to a beach, mixed together some mud and sand, and shaped the mixture into a woman. He stood by her and breathed life into her, and gave her a name – Hine-hau-one (Earth-formed Maiden). After the two lay together, Hine-hau-one gave birth to a daughter called Hine-titama (Dawn Maiden). Hine-titama did not know who her father was, and when she grew up, Tane made her his wife as well. One day, she went to a village

THE COMING OF DEATH
Soon Hine-titama called out to Tane. She told him to stay in the world of light above the ground and be a good father to her children, and to let her remain in the Underworld. She said she would reach out and drag her children down to the dark realm when their time came. From that point on, all humans and animals have had to die. So it was that death came into the world, and the Dawn Maiden from then on became Hine-nui-te-po, the Great Goddess of Darkness.

TANE

As the forest god, Tane gave humanity the gifts of wood and plant fibre, enabling people to make many useful things. But when he planted the first trees, things did not go smoothly. Tane saw the trees as human in form, with their branches as "legs" and their roots as "hair". So he planted them upside-down, with their roots waving in the air, and they did not grow. Then he remembered his stance from when he and his brother, Tangaroa, pushed Rangi and Papa apart at the time of creation (*see p.339*), and planted the trees the right way, so that they could take root. Among Tane's other gifts to humanity were light, in the form of the sun and the moon.

▶ Rangi and Papa
The Maori creation story describes how the primal deities, Rangi, the sky, and Papa, the Earth, embraced each other before Tane and his brothers pushed them apart to form the world.

▼ Tane and his brothers
Maori wood carvings often depict Tane and his brothers in the act of separating the Earth and the sky.

MAUI IN THE UNDERWORLD

The trickster Maui was a mortal but he did not want to die, and so he decided to trick Hine-nui-te-po, the goddess of death. Maui's mother had told him that if a person could crawl through the body of the goddess, then that person would not die. Moreover, the goddess would die herself, and death would be banished for good. One day, Maui came across Hine-nui-te-po when she was asleep. Delighted, he climbed inside the goddess's body, and this made all his friends burst out laughing. One creature, the fantail bird, laughed so much that the sound woke Hine-nui-te-po, and the enraged goddess crushed Maui inside her before he could escape through her mouth. As a result, Maui died and the goddess of death continued her reign.

◀ Gateway to the Underworld
The Maori myths describe the process of dying as "creeping into the womb of Sleeping Mother Death", so the gateway to the Underworld is seen as the entrance to Hine-nui-te-po's body, the dark interior of the Earth.

▶ Maui
Maui was a great trickster-hero. One Maori myth tells how he hauled up a massive fish from the ocean floor. The fish later became the North Island of New Zealand, which is roughly fish-shaped.

LET THE WATERS BE SEPARATED, LET THE HEAVENS BE FORMED, LET THE EARTH BE.

Maori creation chant

MYTHS OF THE STARS

The Maori gave names and human attributes to the stars and linked them with their deities. For instance, the alignment of the stars of the Matariki (Tiny Eyes), Tautoru (Orion's belt), and Takurua (Sirius) at the end of the year was such that to the Maori they represented the signpost of the goddess of death, rising from the Underworld. Constellations like the Matariki, also known as the Pleiades, were believed to watch over the Earth, and were always seen as a harbinger of a time of plenty.

◀ The Matariki
Some myths claim that this star cluster comprises Matariki and her six daughters, who assist the sun on its journey southward.

341

SEE ALSO Forests 134–35, 136–37, 258–59 • Stars 288–89, 318–19, 334–35

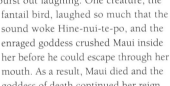

Among the most striking relics of ancient religious beliefs are the often huge stones that people erected or carved in temples or simply in the landscape. Representing powerful myths and deities, they held great magic for their makers. Hundreds or even thousands of years on, they still retain an air of mystery.

STANDING STONES

In many parts of the world, sites with special meaning were marked with large standing stones – either single stones or several stones arranged in circles, long rows, or small groups. Most of these stones were erected thousands of years ago, and in many cases their exact purpose is still uncertain, but some are known to have been tombs, others outdoor temples. Commonly, they were carefully aligned with the sunrise or with prominent patterns of stars, suggesting that myths of the heavens played a part in their meaning.

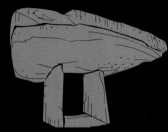

▲ **Japan**
At many sites in Japan, standing stones act as pillars supporting large, flat stones. These impressive structures were once tombs, the flat stones being their roofs.

▲ **Avebury**
This vast stone circle from around 2500 BCE is part of a huge ritual landscape in southern England that incorporates earthworks, an avenue of around 100 standing stones, and other prehistoric monuments.

Carnac
Dating mainly from about 3300 BCE, 11 long rows containing some 1,100 stones still stand at Carnac in France. They run east to west, suggesting an astrological purpose.

Stonehenge
Around 5,000 years old, Stonehenge in England is a temple-like complex centred around a ring of stones. The midsummer sun rises directly above one of the stones.

SACRED ROCK

In Australia's Northern Territory, a natural outcrop that glows in the setting sun has deep meaning for local Aborigines. They call it Uluru, a landmark on the old pathways of the great ancestors of the Dreamtime (*see p.327*). Every feature on the rock has a special meaning: a mark down one side is the blood of the venomous snake people, shed in a battle; a pair of holes are the eyes of an ancestor.

Uluru

CARVED STONES

In most cultures people carve images of their gods, and because it is so enduring, stone is a favourite material for such portrayals. Frequently, people saw the carvings as more than just works of art. They believed that a deity would actually inhabit an image made in the right way and with due reverence. As the eternal dwelling-places of gods, spirits, and ancestors, carved stones held real magic for those who made them.

▶ Mayan stela
The ancient Maya of Mexico and Guatemala erected stelae – flat, carved stones – to honour their rulers' real and legendary ancestors. This one depicts the god Quetzalcoatl as the Morning Star.

▲ Buddha's head
Legend has it that this stone head of the Bud[...] trapped in the roots of a bodhi tree at the W[...] Mahathat temple in Thailand was originally [...] then emerged from the ground as the tree g[...]

◀ Aztec warrior
Warrior columns, some of them standing 5m (16ft) tall, surround the temple of the god Quetzalcoatl at Tula, Mexico. They inspired Aztec soldiers to fight.

▼ The omphalos
The Greek god Zeus (*see pp.24–25*) had two eagles fly from the world's eastern and western edges until they met in the middle, a spot marked with the omphalos or "navel" stone.

▲ Naqsh-i Rustam
The site of Naqsh-i Rustam in Iran has several tombs of early Persian kings. The relief shown here depicts the victory of King Shapur I over two Roman emperors, Valerian and Philip the Arab, in the 3rd century CE.

◀ Olmec head
The Olmec, who thrived in Mexico 800–500 BCE, carved colossal stone heads, perhaps representing ancient leaders, out of single blocks of basalt.

▲ Easter Island heads
Rows of stone heads weighing up to six tonnes eac[...] stare out to sea on Easter Island in the South Pacifi[...] They probably honour the original islanders' ances[...]

INDEX

ACKNOWLEDGMENTS

The publisher would like to thank the following for their kind permission to reproduce their photographs:

(Key: a-above; b-below/bottom; c-centre; f-far; l-left; r-right; t-top)

1 Alamy Images: Deco (c). 7 The Bridgeman Art Library: Musée de l'Homme, Paris, France (tr). 8 DK Images: Judith Miller Image Archive (tl). 10 The Bridgeman Art Library: Museum of Fine Arts, Boston, Massachusetts, USA/ Gift in honour of Edward W. Forbes from his friends (l). 14 The Art Archive: Museo della Civilta Romana Rome / Gianni Dagli Orti. 15 4Corners Images: SIME/ Johanna Huber (t). The Trustees of the British Museum: (b). 17 Alamy Images: INTERFOTO Pressebildagentur (br). Photo Scala, Florence: (l) (tr). 18 akg-images: Erich Lessing (b). 19 The Bridgeman Art Library: Whitworth Art Gallery, The University of Manchester, UK (b). 20 Photo Scala, Florence: BPK, Berlin (b). 21 The Bridgeman Art Library: Kunsthistorisches Museum, Vienna, Austria (t); Musee Massey, Tarbes, France/ Lauros / Giraudon (b). 22-23 The Art Archive: Palazzo del Te Mantua / Alfredo Dagli Orti. 24 Réunion des Musées Nationaux Agence Photographique: Hervé Lewandowski (bl). 25 The Bridgeman Art Library: Kunsthistorisches Museum, Vienna, Austria (b). Photo Scala, Florence: Courtesy of the Ministero Beni e Att. Culturali (t). 26 Ancient Art & Architecture Collection: (b). The Bridgeman Art Library: Prado, Madrid, Spain/ Index (t). 27 The Bridgeman Art Library: Galleria Palatina, Palazzo Pitti, Florence, Italy (t); Greek Museo Capitolino, Rome, Italy (c). 28 akg-images: Erich Lessing (b). iStockphoto.com: Volkan Ersoy (t). 29 The Bridgeman Art Library: Staatliche Museen, Berlin, Germany (b). DK Images: Peter Wilson (t). 31 The Bridgeman Art Library: Musee du Petit Palais, Avignon, France/ Peter Willi (cl). 32 Corbis: Araldo de Luca (br). 33 Alamy Images: ephotocorp (bc). 34 akg-images: Rabatti Domingie (t). The Bridgeman Art Library: Musee des Arts Decoratifs, Saumur, France/ Lauros / Giraudon (b). 35 akg-images: (cr). 36 The Trustees of the British Museum: (br). DK Images: Nick Nicholls / The British Museum (bl). 37 Corbis: Summerfield Press (c). 39 akg-images: Erich Lessing (bl). Corbis: Mimmo Jodice (c). Getty Images: The Bridgeman Art Library (tl). 40 The Bridgeman Art Library: The De Morgan Centre, London. 41 akg-images: (b). The Art Archive: Harper Collins Publishers (tr). 42 The Bridgeman Art Library: Museo Regional de Oaxaca, Mexico/ Giraudon (tr). 43 Alamy Images: The London Art Archive (cl). The Bridgeman Art Library: Private Collection / The Fine Art Society, London, UK (b). 44 The Bridgeman Art Library: Louvre, Paris, France (b). 45 akg-images: (br) (tr). 46 The Trustees of the British Museum: (tr). 47 akg-images: (cr). The Bridgeman Art Library: Musee des Beaux-Arts, Angers, France/ Lauros / Giraudon (br). 48 The Bridgeman Art Library: Lady Lever Art Gallery, National Museums Liverpool. 49 The Bridgeman Art Library: Lady Lever Art Gallery, National Museums Liverpool. 50 akg-images: Erich Lessing (b). The Bridgeman Art Library: The Dayton Art Institute, Dayton, Ohio, USA / Museum purchase with funds provided by the James F. Dicke Family in memory of Timothy M. Webster. 51 The Bridgeman Art Library: Archaeological Museum of Heraklion, Crete, Greece/ Lauros / Giraudon (c). 53 The Bridgeman Art Library: Look and Learn (cl); Tabley House Collection, University of Manchester, UK (tc). Corbis: Gianni Dagli Orti (br). 54 akg-images: Peter Connolly (bc). 55 The Bridgeman Art Library: Museumslandschaft Hessen Kassel/ Ute Brunzel (t). Corbis: Christie's Images (cl). 56 The Art Archive: (tr). 57 akg-images: (tl). The Art Archive: Accademia San Luca Rome / Alfredo Dagli Orti (bl). 58 The Bridgeman Art Library: Prado, Madrid, Spain/ Index (l). 59 The Bridgeman Art Library: Christie's Images (cl). Corbis: Bettmann (tr). 60 Ancient Art & Architecture Collection: (bl). 61 akg-images: Erich Lessing (tc). Ancient Art & Architecture Collection: C M Dixon (br). 62-63 Alamy Images: The London Art Archive (b). 65 The Bridgeman Art Library: Leeds Museums and Galleries (City Art Gallery) UK (cr). 66 The Bridgeman Art Library: Johnny van Haeften Gallery, London, UK (c). 67 The Art Archive: Civiche Racc d'Arte Pavia Italy / Alfredo Dagli Orti (tl); Museo Capitolino Rome / Alfredo Dagli Orti (br). Penguin Books Ltd: (br). 68 akg-images. Photo Scala, Florence: courtesy of the Ministero Beni e Att. Culturali (b). 69 The Art Archive: Musée Archéologique Naples / Gianni Dagli Orti (t). Photo Scala, Florence: Parma, Galleria Nazionale (br). 70 Alamy Images: The London Art Archive (br). The Bridgeman Art Library: Fitzwilliam Museum, University of Cambridge, UK (bl). Photo Scala, Florence: (cr). 71 Mary Evans Picture Library: (tr). 72 Corbis: The Art Archive (bl). 73 The Bridgeman Art Library: Louvre, Paris, France (cb). 74-75 The Bridgeman Art Library: Bradford Art Galleries and Museums, West Yorkshire, UK. 76 The Bridgeman Art Library: Louvre, Paris, France (bc). Corbis: Larry Lee Photography (tr). 77 Réunion des Musées Nationaux Agence Photographique: Jean-Gilles Berizzi (c). 78 The Art Archive: Musée Archéologique Naples / Alfredo Dagli Orti (c). 79 The Bridgeman Art Library: Private Collection/ Johnny Van Haeften Ltd., London (bl). Werner Forman Archive: Museo Capitolino , Rome (br). 80-81 Bildarchiv Preußischer Kulturbesitz, Berlin: Gemäldegalerie, Kaiser Friedrich-Museum-Verein, SMB / Volker-H. Schneider. 82 Alamy Images: INTERFOTO Pressebildagentur (tr). Archivi Alinari: Franco Cosimo Panini Editore (cl). Werner Forman Archive: (cl). 83 Archivi Alinari: Franco Cosimo Panini Editore (tr). 84 Corbis: Alinari Archives (cl). 85 The Bridgeman Art Library: Ferens Art Gallery, Hull City Museums and Art Galleries (br). Corbis: Mimmo Jodice (c). Photolibrary: Vladimir Pcholkin (bl). 86-87 The Bridgeman Art Library: National Gallery, London, UK (l). 87 The Bridgeman Art Library: National Gallery, London, UK (c). 88 The Bridgeman Art Library: Royal Library, Copenhagen, Denmark. 89 Getty Images: Robert Gibb (bl). Werner Forman Archive: Statens Historiska Museum, Stockholm (c). 90 TopFoto.co.uk: (t). 91 DK Images: Alan Hills/The British Museum (b). Werner Forman Archive: Statens Historiska Museet, Stockholm (b). 92 akg-images: (t). The Bridgeman Art Library: Arni Magnusson Institute, Reykjavik, Iceland (b). 93 Werner Forman Archive: Statens Historiska Museum, Stockholm (br). 94 TopFoto.co.uk: The Granger Collection (cr). 95 akg-images: (c). The Bridgeman Art Library: Private Collection / The Stapleton Collection (b). 96 akg-images: (t). Werner Forman Archive: Statens Historiska Museum, Stockholm (b). 97 Alamy Images: The London Art Archive (tl). 99 The Bridgeman Art Library: Museum of Religion and Atheism, St. Petersburg, Russia/ RIA Novosti (bl); Peter Anderson / Courtesy of the Statens Historiska Museum, Stockholm (cl); Peter Anderson / Dorling Kindersley, Courtesy of the Statens Historiska Museum, Stockholm (tc). DK Images: Peter Anderson / Danish National Museum (tl). 100 Alamy Images: Esa Hiltula (c). 102 akg-images: (cl) (tr). 103 akg-images: (tr); Juergen Sorges (t). Getty Images: AFP (b). 105 The Art Archive: British Library (t). The Trustees of the British Museum: (cl). 107 akg-images: British Library (br). The Trustees of the British Museum: DK Images: The British Museum (bc). 108 The Bridgeman Art Library: Private Collection/ The Fine Art Society, London, UK (tr); Viking Ship Museum, Oslo, Norway (bl). 109 TopFoto.co.uk: Ullsteinbild (br). 110 The Bridgeman Art Library: Louvre, Paris, France (cr). Corbis: Gianni Dagli Orti (b). 111 akg-images: Erich Lessing (br). 112 The Bridgeman Art Library: Bradford Art Galleries and Museums, West Yorkshire, UK. 113 akg-images: Erich Lessing (b). TopFoto.co.uk: EE Images / HIP (c). 114 Werner Forman Archive: National Museum, Copenhagen. 115 The Art Archive: Musée des Antiquités St Germain en Laye / Gianni Dagli Orti (cl). Corbis: Weatherstock (bl). TopFoto.co.uk: CM Dixon / HIP (br). 116 Mary Evans Picture Library: (bl). 117 The Stapleton Collection: (cl). 118 Getty Images: Mark Hamblin (bl). 119 The Art Archive: National Gallery Budapest / Alfredo Dagli Orti (t). Devonshire Collection, Chatsworth. Reproduced by permission of Chatsworth Settlement Trustees: (b). 120 akg-images: Christian Darkin (b). 122-123 The Bridgeman Art Library: Whitford & Hughes, London, UK. 124 Alamy Images: Ivy Close Images (br). 125 Alamy Images: The Photolibrary Wales (c). 126 The Bridgeman Art Library: Private Collection / Christopher Wood Gallery, London, UK (bl). 127 akg-images: (bl). The Bridgeman Art Library: Birmingham Museums and Art Gallery (cr). Bradford Art Galleries and Museums, UK (tl). 128 The Bridgeman Art Library: Birmingham Museums and Art Gallery (t). 128-129 The Bridgeman Art Library: Birmingham Museums and Art Gallery. 130 The Bridgeman Art Library: Nationalmuseum, Stockholm, Sweden. 131 Alamy Images: isifa Image Service s.r.o. (c). The Bridgeman Art Library: Private Collection/ Archives Charmet (b). 133 The Art Archive: Bibliothèque des Arts Décoratifs Paris / Gianni Dagli Orti (tr). Corbis: Scheufler Collection (br). 134 The Bridgeman Art Library: Private Collection/ Archives Charmet (l). 135 akg-images: (tr). The Bridgeman Art Library: Bibliotheque des Arts Decoratifs, Paris, France/ Archives Charmet (b). 136 Alamy Images: Chris Fredriksson (bl). Corbis: The Irish Image Collection (tr). 138 The Art Archive: Musée du Louvre Paris / Gianni Dagli Orti (c). Mary Evans Picture Library: (br). 139 The Art Archive: Private Collection / Eileen Tweedy (tr). 140 The Bridgeman Art Library: Bibliotheque des Arts Decoratifs, Paris, France/ Archives Charmet (t). 141 Alamy Images: The London Art Archive (t). Robbie Jack Photography: (c). 143 Alamy Images: Pat Behnke (br). Corbis: KazumasaTakahashi / amanaimages (tl). Getty Images: Tim Rand (bl). 144 Corbis: Araldo de Luca. 148 Ancient Art & Architecture Collection. 149 Corbis: Nik Wheeler (t). DK Images: Alan Hills and Barbara Winter / The British Museum (br). 150 The Art Archive: Musée du Louvre Paris / Gianni Dagli Orti. 151 akg-images: Erich Lessing (tl). Alamy Images: isifa Image Service s.r.o (c). 152-153 The Bridgeman Art Library: The Detroit Institute of Arts, USA/ Founders Society purchase, General Membership Fund. 154 Ancient Art & Architecture Collection: (bc). Réunion des Musées Nationaux Agence Photographique: (r). 155 Alamy Images: Lebrecht Music and Arts Photo Library (tr). 156 Réunion des Musées Nationaux Agence Photographique: René-Gabriel Ojéda (tr). 157 akg-images: (c). Alamy Images: The London Art Archive (bc). Corbis: Nik Wheeler (bl). 158 Ancient Art & Architecture Collection: (bc). Getty Images: Martin Ruegner (t). 159 akg-images: 159Gerard Degeorge (cl). The Bridgeman Art Library: Museum of Latakia, Latakia, Syria/ Peter Willi (b). 160 akg-images: Erich Lessing (bc). Werner Forman Archive: Schimmel Collection, New York (t). 161 akg-images: Erich Lessing (cl); Gerard Degeorge (b). 162 The Bridgeman Art Library: Musee de l'Homme, Paris, France (bl). 163 The Bridgeman Art Library: Private Collection/ Roger Perrin (cr). Corbis: A & J Verkaik (bl). 164 Alamy Images: INTERFOTO Pressebildagentur (l). Ancient Art & Architecture Collection: T. Paramjit (tr). 165 The Bridgeman Art Library: Private Collection/ Paul Freeman (c). 166 The Art Archive: Musée Condé Chantilly / Gianni Dagli Orti. 167 The Art Archive: Musée du Louvre Paris / Gianni Dagli Orti (t). Werner Forman Archive: Museo Nazionale Romano, Rome (b). 168 Werner Forman Archive: Euan Wingfield (cr). 169 akg-images: Erich Lessing (t). Corbis: James Chen (cr); Kazuyoshi Nomachi (bc). 171 The Art Archive: Bodleian Library Oxford (br); British Library (tc); Musée Condé Chantilly / Gianni Dagli Orti (bl). 172 akg-images:

(c). Getty Images: Koichi Kamoshida (br). 173 The Art Archive: Musée des Arts Décoratifs Paris / Alfredo Dagli Orti (bl). Corbis: Michel Setboun/Sygma (c). 174 Ancient Art & Architecture Collection: B. Wilson (cr). Mary Evans Picture Library: (cl). 175 Werner Forman Archive: Musee Royal de L'Afrique Centrale, Tervuren, Belgium (tl). 176 Robert Harding Picture Library: Jochen Schlenker (cl). 177 Alamy Images: Craig Lovell / Eagle Visions Photography (cr) (bl). 178-179 China Tourism Photo Library. 180 Réunion des Musées Nationaux Agence Photographique: Christian Larrieu (tr). 181 Getty Images: Willard Clay (bl). 182 Werner Forman Archive: Nick Saunders (cl). 182 Corbis: Araldo de Luca. 186 The Art Archive: Rijksmuseum voor Volkenkunde Leiden (Leyden) / Dagli Orti. 187 Werner Forman Archive: (b); Theresa McCullough Collection (t). 188 akg-images: Ullstein Bild (c). The Bridgeman Art Library: Victoria & Albert Museum, London, UK (bl). 189 The Bridgeman Art Library: Bibliotheque Nationale, Paris, France/ Archives Charmet (br). DK Images: Derek Hall (bl). 191 Alamy Images: ArkReligion.com (tr). Corbis: Hans Georg Roth (bl). Courtesy of The Schøyen Collection, Oslo and London: (br). 192-193 The Art Archive: Musée Guimet Paris / Gianni Dagli Orti. 194 The Trustees of the British Museum: (bl). Dreamstime.com: Drbouz (bc). 195 DK Images: Courtesy of the National Museum, New Delhi/ Andy Crawford (br). Dreamstime. com: Paul Prescott (c). 196 The Bridgeman Art Library: Victoria & Albert Museum, London, UK. 197 The Bridgeman Art Library: Victoria & Albert Museum, London, UK. 198 Tannishtha Chakraborty: (t). Corbis: Brooklyn Museum (c). 199 Alamy Images: Louise Batalla Duran (bl). Corbis: Christie's (tc). 200 DK Images: Courtesy of the National Museum, New Delhi/ Andy Crawford (bl). 201 Corbis: Luca Tettoni (br). DK Images: Courtesy of the Crafts Museum, New Delhi/Akhil Bakshi (tl). 202 www.dinodia.com: (bc). 203 Alamy Images: INTERFOTO Pressebildagentur (tr). The Bridgeman Art Library: Private Collection / Archives Charmet (cl). Corbis: Ajay Verma/Reuters (br). 204-205 Werner Forman Archive. 206 The Bridgeman Art Library: Oriental Museum, Durham University, UK (cr). 207 The Bridgeman Art Library: The Trustees of the Chester Beatty Library, Dublin (c). 209 4Corners Images: SIME/Pavan Aldo (br). The Bridgeman Art Library: National Museum of India, New Delhi, India (c). DK Images: Ian Cumming (tr). Getty Images: Robert Harding/Gavin Hellier (bl).

210 China Tourism Photo Library. 211 China Tourism Photo Library: (b) (t). 212 Mary Evans Picture Library: (bl). 213 China Tourism Photo Library: (l). 214 Ancient Art & Architecture Collection: Uniphoto (bl). 215 Ancient Art & Architecture Collection: Uniphoto (cr). 216 Ancient Art & Architecture Collection: Uniphoto (tr). 217 China Tourism Photo Library: (br) (tl). 218-219 China Tourism Photo Library. 219 China Tourism Photo Library: (c). 221 Ancient Art & Architecture Collection: Uniphoto (br) (cl) (cr). 222 Corbis: Peter Harholdt (cr). 223 Corbis: Asian Art & Archaeology, Inc (cr); Demetrio Carrasco/JAI (t). 224-225 akg-images: Erich Lessing. 226 The Trustees of the Chester Beatty Library, Dublin: (tr). 227 Alamy Images: Japan Art Collection (br); JTB Photo Communications, Inc (bl). 228 Lebrecht Music and Arts: Rue des Archives/PVDE (cr). 229 The Bridgeman Art Library: Victoria & Albert Museum, London, UK (cl). Getty Images: ULTRA.F (br). 230 Ancient Art & Architecture Collection. 234 Werner Forman Archive. 235 Ancient Art & Architecture Collection: (b). Corbis: Sandro Vannini (t). 236 Mary Evans Picture Library: (c). 237 Getty Images: Richard Nowitz (cr). Werner Forman Archive: Egyptian Museum, Cairo (cl). 238 The Bridgeman Art Library: British Museum. 239 The Bridgeman Art Library: British Museum. 240 Ancient Art & Architecture Collection: P.Syder (tr). Werner Forman Archive: Egyptian Museum, Cairo (b). 241 Ancient Art & Architecture Collection: (cl) (br). 242-243 Ancient Art & Architecture Collection: R. Sheridan. 244 Werner Forman Archive: Egyptian Museum, Cairo (br). 245 Ancient Art & Architecture Collection: (bc). Werner Forman Archive: (tc) (br). Werner Forman Archive: (clb). 246 DK Images: John Hepver / The British Museum (br). 247 Ancient Art & Architecture Collection: (tc) (br). Werner Forman Archive: (clb). 248 Werner Forman Archive: Museum fur Volkerkunde, Berlin. 249 Werner Forman Archive: British Museum, London (b); Private Collection, New York (t). 250 Alamy Images: Suzy Bennett (b). Werner Forman Archive: Entwistle Gallery, London (tr). 251 Werner Forman Archive: (bl). 252 The Art Archive: Antenna Gallery Dakar Senegal / Gianni Dagli Orti (bl). 254 Corbis: Frédéric Soltan (tr). 255 akg-images: British Library (tl). The Art Archive: Royal Palace Caserta Italy / Gianni Dagli Orti (br). 256 DK Images: Judith Miller Image Archive. 257 akg-images: Erich Lessing (b). Werner Forman

Archive: Entwistle Gallery, London (cr). 258 Corbis: Anthony Bannister / Gallo Images (br). Werner Forman Archive: (tr). 260 DK Images: Judith Miller / Jean-Baptiste Bacquart (cl). 261 Corbis: Studio Patellani (br). 262 akg-images: Erich Lessing (c). DK Images: Courtesy of the Pitt Rivers Museum, University of Oxford (bl). 263 Alamy Images: INTERFOTO Pressebildagentur (cl). Corbis: Peter Adams (br). DK Images: David Garner / Exeter City Museums and Art Gallery (bl). Werner Forman Archive: Kasmin Collection (tl). 264 The Bridgeman Art Library: British Museum. 265 Corbis: Michele Burgess (c). DK Images: Courtesy of the Powell-Cotton Museum, Kent (b). 266 Alamy Images: Images of Africa Photobank (b); Robert Estall photo agency (t). 267 Alamy Images: Frantisek Staud (bl); Images of Africa Photobank (br). 268 Getty Images: Yuri Yuriev/Afp (bl). 268 Werner Forman Archive: Private Collection, New York (tr). 269 Getty Images: David Edwards (br). Werner Forman Archive: Private Collection, New York (tr). 270 Getty Images: Volkmar Wentzel (tr). 271 Ancient Art & Architecture Collection: (bl). DK Images: Courtesy of the Pitt Rivers Museum, University of Oxford (c). 272 Werner Forman Archive: Ariadne Van Zandbergen (cr); Timothy O'Keefe (bl). 274 The Bridgeman Art Library: Bonhams, London (cl) (br). 276 Werner Forman Archive: Pigorini Museum of Prehistory and Ethnography, Rome. 280 Werner Forman Archive: Haffenreffer Museum of Anthropology, Brown University, Rhode Island, USA. 281 Getty Images: Melissa Farlow (b). Werner Forman Archive: Sheldon Jackson Museum, Sitka, Alaska (c). 282 Corbis: James Sparshatt (b). 283 Corbis: Geoffrey Clements (b). Werner Forman Archive: Schimmel Collection, New York (br). 284 Alamy Images: World Religions Photo Library (bl). 285 Corbis: Asian Art & Archaeology, Inc (cr). Werner Forman Archive: Denver Art Museum, Colorado, USA (c). 286 DK Images: Lynton Gardiner / Courtesy of The American Museum of Natural History (tr). 287 Alamy Images: Marvin Dembinsky Photo Associates (bl). Corbis: Gunter Marx Photography (tr); Peter Harholdt (cra); Stuart Westmorland (cl). 288 Werner Forman Archive: Glenbow Museum, Calgary, Alberta, USA (c). 289 Science Photo Library: Science Source (b). Werner Forman Archive: Field Museum of Natural History, Chicago (ca). 290 Werner Forman Archive: Museum of Mankind, London (t). 291 Alamy Images: SCPhotos (cl). Werner Forman Archive: Phoebe Apperson Hearst Museum of Anthropology & Regents of Uni of

Cal. (bc); Private Collection, New York (tr). 292 Werner Forman Archive. 293 Photo Scala, Florence. 293 Werner Forman Archive: Liverpool Museum (t). 294 Alamy Images: Mary Evans Picture Library (cb). 295 The Bridgeman Art Library: Museo Arqueologico, Mexico City, Mexico (c). Werner Forman Archive: David Bernstein, New York (cl). 296 The Bridgeman Art Library: Worcester Art Museum, Massachusetts, USA (br). Werner Forman Archive: Dallas Museum of Art (cl). 297 Alamy Images: Deborah Waters (br). Ancient Art & Architecture Collection: Dr S. Coyne (cr). 298-299 The Bridgeman Art Library: Jean-Pierre Courau (t). 299 The Bridgeman Art Library: Jean-Pierre Courau (c). 300 Alamy Images: imagebroker (cr). The Bridgeman Art Library: Musee de l'Homme, Paris, France (bl). 301 Ancient Art & Architecture Collection: (br). Werner Forman Archive: British Museum, London (tl). 302-303 Werner Forman Archive: National Museum of Anthropology, Mexico City. 304 Corbis: Robert Holmes. 305 The Bridgeman Art Library: Musee de l'Homme, Paris, France (b). Werner Forman Archive: (tr). 306 Corbis: Stephanie Maze (cr). 307 Alamy Images: Banana Pancake (bl). Getty Images: Tom Walker (br). 308 Photo Scala, Florence: Metropolitan Museum of Art/Art Resource (t). 309 akg-images: (ca) (cl). Alamy Images: Mike Hill (br). 310 Corbis: Les Stone/ZUMA (cr). 311 Alamy Images: Mary Evans Picture Library (tr). TopFoto.co. uk: Tony Savino/ The Image Works (br). 312 Alamy Images: Deco. 313 Werner Forman Archive: (b) (t). 314 Alamy Images: Mireille Vautier (tr); North Wind Picture Archives (b). 315 Wikipedia, The Free Encyclopedia: (br) (c). DK Images: Sean Hunter (t). 316-317 akg-images. 318 The Art Archive: Alfredo Dagli Orti (bc). Werner Forman Archive: David Bernstein, New York (cl). 319 Ancient Art & Architecture Collection: Corbis: Kazuyoshi Nomachi (tr). 320 V&A Images: (t). 321 The Bridgeman Art Library: The De Morgan Centre, London (t). Photo Scala, Florence: The Newark Museum / Art Resource (tl). 322 The Trustees of the British Museum. 326 Ancient Art & Architecture Collection. 327 Ancient Art & Architecture Collection: (t). Werner Forman Archive: (b). 328 Alamy Images: Penny Tweedie (bc). The Bridgeman Art Library: Corbally Stourton Contemporary Art, Australia (bl). 329 Corbis: Michael & Patricia Fogden (b). Getty Images: Hulton Archive (br). 330 Réunion des Musées Nationaux Agence Photographique: Hervé Lewandowski (t). 331 Alamy Images: Horizon International

Images Limited (bc). Werner Forman Archive: (br). 332 National Gallery Of Victoria, Melbourne: Gift of Penny Blazey, 1989 (t). 332-333 National Gallery Of Victoria, Melbourne: Gift of Penny Blazey, 1989 (b). 334 Corbis: Penny Tweedie (r). 335 Corbis: Takashi Katahira (tr). Werner Forman Archive: (br) (clb). 336 Corbis: Ric Ergenbright. 337 Ancient Art & Architecture Collection: (bl). Werner Forman Archive: (c). 338 The Bridgeman Art Library: British Museum, London, UK/ Peter Willi (tr). 339 Werner Forman Archive: British Museum, London (clb). 341 Werner Forman Archive: Museum fur Volkerkunde, Berlin (br); Otago Museum, Dunedin (tr). 342 britainonview.com: James Osmond (tr). Getty Images: Joe Cornish (c); Navaswan (bl). 343 Getty Images: Daryl Benson (tr). Photo Scala, Florence: (bl)

Jacket images: Front and Back: iStockphoto.com: Bülent Gültek (background). Front: Alamy Images: INTERFOTO Pressebildagentur cr; Christine Osborne Pictures tc; david sanger photography br (behind); Corbis: Randy Faris ftr; Getty Images: Randy Wells tr; Richard Ross fbr; iStockphoto.com: AF-studio (top band); TopFoto.co.uk: 26 Alinari l. Back: Alamy Images: bygonetimes tl; Mary Evans Picture Library tc; david sanger photography tr; iStockphoto.com: AF-studio (top band)

All other images © Dorling Kindersley For further information see: www.dkimages.com

DK would like to thank Sarah Tomley; Camilla Hallinan; Richard Horsford; Elizabeth O'Neil; Alicia Ingty; Chuck Wills; Caroline Hunt for proofreading; and Pamela Ellis for the index.